JAGUAR
E-TYPE SIX-CYLINDER
Originality Guide

Dr. Thomas F. Haddock
Dr. Michael C. Mueller

DALTON WATSON FINE BOOKS

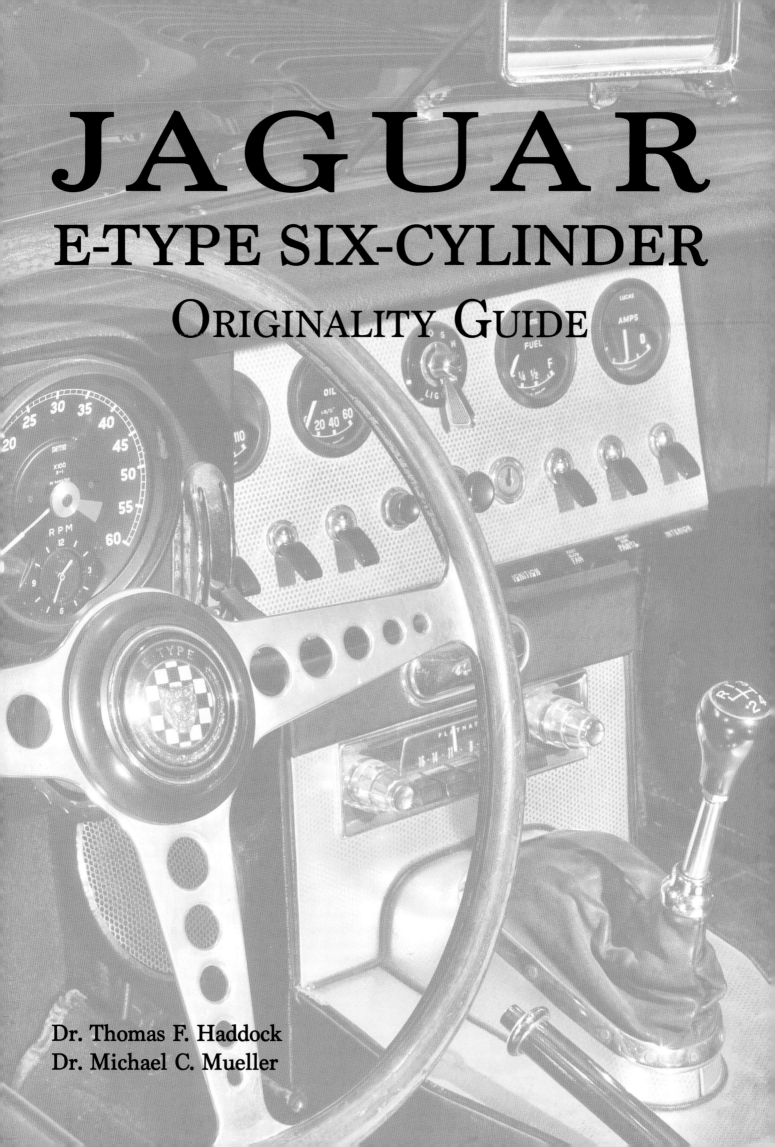

JAGUAR
E-TYPE SIX-CYLINDER
ORIGINALITY GUIDE

Dr. Thomas F. Haddock
Dr. Michael C. Mueller

JAGUAR E-TYPE SIX-CYLINDER ORIGINALITY GUIDE

by Dr. T. F. Haddock and Dr. M. C. Mueller

Published 2017

Regular Edition ISBN: 978-1-85443-284-1

Printed by Interpress Co. Ltd., Hungary
for the publisher

Dalton Watson Fine Books
Glyn and Jean Morris
Deerfield, IL 60015 USA
www.daltonwatson.com

CONTENTS

While I am grateful to many people for many things in this life, I must say that I owe Dr. Thomas F. Haddock, the co-author of this book, an especially large debt of gratitude. The research and photography he did on his earlier iteration of this volume probably saved me several hundred hours of time – and many, many gallons of gasoline. Let me explain.

About 16 years ago, I purchased a 1967 Jaguar E-type Coupe, warm beige in color, with a moss green interior. It was the last of the three carburetor, 4.2-liter cars with the covered headlights. The car had come out of Texas, so it was

Peter Egan (left) and Tom Haddock (right), in Peter's shop where he has restored so many interesting cars and motorcycles.

dry and rust-free, but mechanically tired. It had also been repainted once, and not very well. So I did what I always do with cars like this and took it completely apart, filling my workshop with piles and boxes of Jaguar parts. The next three years were spent sequestered in my garage, restoring this lovely artifact.

E-types, of course, are very complex cars, so when you go to put them back together, many questions present themselves. Does the bolt that holds the brake light switch junction have a washer under it? On both sides, or just one? And does the bolt go through from the front or the back? If I install it the wrong way, will it hit something later? Is the wiring loom in the engine compartment routed above or below the frame rail? And so on.

Many of these questions I had to answer by hopping in my (other) car and driving 30 miles to visit a friend who had an original '66 E-type Coupe in his garage, so I could examine the details – often making a drawing, in my own crude and childish fashion. Then I'd get home and remember I'd forgotten to look at something else. Back again.

Enter Dr. Haddock's *Originality Guide*, with its meticulously researched production history and detailed photographs. Suddenly those trips tapered off drastically. You could almost say I worked with his book in one hand

and a wrench in the other, and the thumbprints of hypoid oil and brake fluid are still on the cover to prove it. The book was an invaluable asset, and Dr. Haddock was my friend on many late nights in the workshop.

And here we have a vastly expanded version of that book, with a wealth of new information and hundreds of extra photographs – nearly all in vivid color, with a crispness of detail made possible by the superior light metering of our digital age. We also have the co-authorship of Dr. Michael C. Mueller, whose personal expertise and large collection of mostly unrestored E-types (50 cars! The mind boggles…) and parts has added another dimension of fine focus in the search for originality and authenticity.

The E-type restorer has never had it so good. Open your toolbox, turn toward your project car and enjoy!

Peter Egan
December 2016

Peter Egan has written about automobiles for decades, both in books and in magazines, including extensive work in Road & Track. *While his work includes monthly columns, feature articles and road tests on all manner of cars, his writing about the E-type has articulated, perhaps better than anyone else, the subtle nature of this car.*

This book is an outgrowth of the prior works of one of the authors, Dr. T. F. Haddock, combined with significant new information derived from the knowledge and collection of the other author, Dr. M. C. Mueller. The individual parts and disassembled cars of the Mueller collection permit access to information that is typically hard to observe or catalog. The large volume of new data, from the Mueller collection as well as other sources, combined with that of the earlier two volumes, permits a deeper level of analysis of production changes in the Jaguar E-type than in either of the two prior works. The format of this book is new, as is the use of color photographs and it brings forth substantial new information beyond what has been published previously.

Four basic model types are recognized for the E-type in this work: the 3.8-liter cars (all Series 1) and the 4.2-liter cars: Series 1, Series 1.5 and Series 2. Three body styles were available: roadster (also called an open two seater, or OTS), a coupe (also called a fixed-head coupe, or FHC), and a 2+2 coupe (a variant of the FHC body style that became available during Series 1 4.2-liter production, also referred to simply as 2+2).

While it is assumed the reader possesses an understanding of the basic specifications of the cars in each of these divisions, a very brief description is given in Chapter One. However, though Chapter One describes the differences between the four basic models and depicts them in photographs, this chapter is not meant to be an exhaustive and detailed comparison of these four models. The subject of this book is the variation of the production specifications within each of these four model runs, not the myriad changes that took place at the transitions between the model divisions. The latter is well-discussed in the literature and it is assumed the reader has a good understanding of this topic. Detailed discussions of the specification changes between the various model types is available from many sources, including Wikipedia and many of the books listed in the Literature section. However, in a few instances where it might be helpful, differences between these basic model groups are discussed.

With the exception of the illustrations in Chapter One, each photograph is meant to illustrate just the specific feature or features discussed in the caption. Other features appearing in the photograph are incidental and may or may not represent any original configuration of the E-type. They generally should be disregarded or referred to with caution. Unlike the illustrations in Chapter One, there are typically no notes in the caption on unoriginal features showing in the associated picture.

The history of the Jaguar E-type has been told many times (see the partial list of publications below) and even

the history of production changes has been covered. The earliest analysis of the history of production changes of which the authors are aware was done in the April 25, 1968 issue of *Autocar* and in the March 21, 1970 issue of *Motor*. The topic has subsequently treated in several books (for example Porter's *Original Jaguar E-Type*, Clausager's *Factory-Original Jaguar E-Type* and the earlier Haddock books and articles). This book continues in this tradition, dealing exclusively with the evolution of production changes within the different model groups of the E-type. Its purpose is not to discuss reasons for production changes; the underlying engineering motivation for any change is beyond the scope of this book. The purpose here is to indicate the configuration of the cars as they left the factory (or, in some cases, the Jaguar dealerships) and not why they were that way, which is a much larger topic. However, occasionally some information on the motivation for a particular change may be given. It is neither the goal of this book to discuss the history of component suppliers (Marston, Lucas, Smiths, Timken, William Mills, West Yorkshire Foundry, S.U., AC, Borg & Beck, Dunlop, Kelsey-Hayes, Triplex and the many others), the racing history of E-types, the Jaguar models preceding or following the six-cylinder E-types, techniques or methods of repair, restoration or performance enhancement, the place of E-types in cultural history, aesthetic discussions, or any other aspects of the E-type. These subjects may be occasionally mentioned anecdotally, but they are not the subject of this work. For this type of information, the reader is referred to the numerous other books on the subject. These include Porter's *Jaguar E-Type: The Definitive History*, *The Iconic E-Type: Celebrating 50 years of the E-Type Jaguar*, *Ultimate E-Type: The Competition Cars*, *Jaguar E type: The Most Famous Car in the World*, Jenkinson's *Jaguar E-Type 3.8 & 4.2 6-cylinder; 5.3 V12*, Skilleter's *The Jaguar E-type: A Collector's Guide*, *Jaguar Sports Cars*, FP Creative Ltd.'s *Jaguar E-Type - Fifty Years of a Design Icon*, Fowler and Morgan's *The Little Book of E-Type Jaguar*, Haynes' *Great Cars - Jaguar E-Type*, Crespin's *Jaguar E-Type: The Essential Buyer's Guide*, Whyte's *Jaguar E-Type 3.8, 4.2 & 5.3-Liter Super Profile*, Wood's *Jaguar E-Type The Complete Story*, Rooke's *E-Type Jaguar DIY Restoration & Maintenance*, Harvey's *E-Type: End of an Era* and numerous others. This list is far from complete.

Chapters Two through Five list the production changes of the Jaguar E-type organized by the area of the car in which they occurred, or by their function. This is in opposition to listing them in the order of the component serial number, or by the chassis number of the car. Changes for which the chassis number, engine number or transmission number transition point is known are listed in the Appendices in serial order, rather than by region of the car or function. Chapter Six covers production changes spanning all six-cylinder E-type production that do not easily fit into the model categories. Chapter Seven discusses factory or dealer options and Chapter Eight discusses labels and markings used on the cars. This latter topic is touched on to some extent in Chapters Two to Five, but Chapter Eight focuses on this subject

exclusively. Chapter Nine briefly discusses factory literature associated with the cars and Chapter Ten gives a review of some NOS (New Old Stock) parts and their packaging (possibly the first time this subject has been addressed in a book on E-Types). Following standard practice, for example, on the title page of Section A of the 3.8-liter *Service Manual*, Publication number E/123/5, "All references… to 'right-hand side' and 'left-hand side' are made assuming the person to be looking from the rear of the car or unit."

This book analyzes production changes in cars carrying chassis numbers lying in the four standard production series and produced by Jaguar's Production Department. About six of the ten very early cars produced by Jaguar's Experimental Department carry chassis numbers in the standard four chassis numbering sequences as well (for example, cars with chassis numbers 850001, 850002, 885002). Because of this and the fact that some Experimental Department cars were produced in a form quite close to the final production configuration, occasional discussions of some of these cars are included in this book. However, due to the many idiosyncrasies of these early standard chassis number cars and the fact that apparently none of them survive in original, unrestored condition, a full and complete description of their unusual features is difficult and their description is not a main component of this book. Much information remains to be chronicled by future historians and these cars could be the sole subject of a future book (they have already been the subject of several articles). In this book the designation "production car" will indicate cars made by Jaguar's Production Department, as opposed to the Experimental Department.

The information presented here comes from period sources (factory literature, commercial publications and photographs), some carefully-vetted current sources (book, articles and on-line information), but principally from observations of hundreds of E-types from over almost fifty years of research. The focus of the research has been on observations of cars that are in the main unrestored and close to their original configuration (irrespective of condition).

It is important to state what is meant by the word "original" in this book. Here "original" indicates the part in question is the exact one that was installed at the factory (or, in some cases, the official Jaguar dealership) on a given car. The designation "original" does not apply to a part (no matter how correct in configuration) selected by a conservator or restorer and later placed on the car. That is, "original" means that the actual physical material (metal, wood, rubber, *etc.*) of the part is that which was with the car when it was sold as new (or perhaps supplied by an official Jaguar dealership). The same criteria apply to the finishes on a part such as chrome or paint. A part supplied with a car as-new, but that has subsequently been re-chromed or re-painted, has diminished originality in that it has been altered (especially in the case of a re-chromed part that may have been ground or polished to a different shape during the re-chroming). Thus a completely original part is the exact physical part with its exact original surface finish (not re-painted, re-chromed or re-polished) that was affixed to the car as it was delivered new. Note that this definition of an original part specifically excludes NOS parts or other period parts that may be apparently otherwise identical to those fitted to the car as new. Such replacement parts (that perhaps may be called "replacements of the original type") might be the best choice for the correction of a missing or significantly defective original part. However, since they were not part of the car when it was new and since they may embody (often unknown or unnoticed) differences from the true original part, they cannot be relied upon for later analysis of the original configuration of the car. They are not "original" parts, but are replacement parts.

While the articles used for research for this book were mainly those written at the time the cars were new (and thus generally show only cars in, or close to, their factory-original condition), in some instances information was gathered from modern magazine articles or pictures. This was done with care. Similarly, some information was gathered from restored cars. This was done sparingly and also with care, taking note of the history of the restoration. On the whole, though, research on currently-existing cars was confined to those principally retaining their original parts. While some of these cars were very well preserved, often they were in extremely poor condition, as is evident from the photographs.

Using unofficial sources, such as books and magazine articles, may seem an odd way to gather information on a subject such as this. It is true many factory records of various types are available, for example the Service Manuals, Spare Parts Catalogs, Driver's Handbook, Service Bulletins and others. One would expect these official records could merely be transcribed to yield a listing of the detail configuration changes of the cars as production progressed. However, through decades of study it has become very apparent that many changes were not reported in the official literature well, if at all. There are many production variations in the cars, such as the change in the shape of the necks of the convertible top hold-down clasps, or the different types of cast iron "Moss" type gearbox housings, that do not appear in any official publications.

Several writers have obtained information on production changes from the factory and the reports of these writers do not entirely agree with each other. The changes reported by these authors were used in this work to supplement the official factory publications in creating a master listing of serial number-related changes. This listing is given in the appendices. At times, when a reported change was suspect or seemed an outlier, this was pointed out. Generally, when a change is reported by only a single reference and not in the official factory literature, this is pointed out as well. Despite using all these sources, it is very likely there are still errors and omissions in the listing here; more research is needed to improve it.

In some discussions, the serial numbers (chassis, engine, *etc.*) of cars used to gather information are cited. In addition, it will often be noted if a car examined for this research was restored, or otherwise clearly disturbed from its original state. This is important because, in the absence of reliable information about how accurate a restoration process was, the data from a reworked or restored car should be regarded with much more skepticism than data from a car believed to be principally unaltered from the state it was in when delivered from the dealership. Since much of the information in this work was gathered from observations of cars (rather than from lists of production-change information citing the chassis, engine, transmission or body serial numbers at which the changes occurred), the exact serial numbers or dates at which the change took place are typically not listed. If known, the chassis numbers of the cars from which the observations were made are cited, as this can help suggest when a change occurred.

In some instances, descriptions in the literature of changes occurring at a given serial number may be somewhat unclear or incomplete. For example, it may be stated, in factory or other literature, that a change occurred in a given component at a specific serial number, without any mention of what the change was. Thus some entries in this work are, in the absence of additional research, of the same nature. Even though six factory-published parts catalogs, numerous previously-published works and hundreds of cars were examined to complete this work, such entries were unavoidable. In addition, while some of the new information presented here is in a somewhat incomplete form, reflecting the authors' current state of knowledge, it was felt better to report poorly-understood observations now, rather than to leave them out of the book until their nature is fully understood (which, of course, may never happen). Thus this work contains some material with little explanation and with statements such as "it seems," "it appears," "apparently," and so forth.

Even though care and skepticism have been applied to the sources of the information presented here, it is unavoidable that errors will be made. It is the authors' goal to identify and correct these in future editions of this work. Since nobody has seen and examined all components of all six-cylinder E-types produced, it will likely remain impossible to compile a complete and definitive guide to the exact state of all of these cars as they left the factory or dealership.

As the authors have continued their research, new production-change information was found that was previously unknown to them. This includes:

▶ Different configurations of the buttresses on the early fabricated sheet steel rear transmission mounts

▶ Extended bosses covering the low-fluid-warning rods on the top of brake fluid reservoir caps

▶ Variations between early and late E-type "Moss" type cast-iron transmission housings, 4.2-liter engine block and head part numbers and configurations

▶ Subtle sheet metal variations in the tub, bonnet and doors (including details of the slight changes in coupe bodywork that took place early in 3.8-liter E-type production)

▶ Obscured markings on instruments

▶ Variations in ignition coils and cooling fan motors

▶ Coupe sun visor evolution

▶ Markings on the OEM tires supplied on E-types from the factory

While it is possible some of this information may have been cited in other sources, it is very likely the majority of it is presented here for the first time. The subject is far from completely treated, here or elsewhere.

The reader should be aware that when references are made to model years, these are unofficial and loosely defined. The cars were not shipped from the factory as 1963 models or 1964 models, but merely as E-types (a possible exception being the 1968 and 1969 U.S. model-year cars, as these cars introduced specific modifications required by new U.S. Federal regulations). However, some production changes coincide well with the production of a given model year and occasional references will be made to model years. In addition, the assignment of dates to particular production changes is not considered of particular significance in this work (unless no serial number transition point is known and the date of the transition is all that is given). Dates of changes will be given when they have been cited in the literature, but in many cases different source cite different dates for the same serial number change points. For example, the end of the first 500 E-types, that took place at chassis numbers 850091/2 860004/5, 875385/6 and 885020/1 is stated to have occurred by different authors at both September and October 1961. The authors take the chassis numbers of the cars as the fundamental means of identifying the individual cars and the flow of production (at least within the four chassis number sequences). When possible, discussions of production changes are best tied to this fundamental parameter (sub-component serial numbers, *e.g.* engine, transmission, body, radiator, however, are

sometimes not is the same order as production date, so are not always in car production order). The chassis number can then later be associated with dates, registration numbers, or other less-significant historical aspects, if so desired.

Similarly, to facilitate the advancement of the understanding of the subject, the authors make an appeal to those discussing and describing E-types in the literature to refrain from using terminology such as "the twenty-third E-type," or the "twenty-third roadster," and so on. Terminology such as this is ambiguous and misleading; is "the twenty-third E-type," left-hand drive roadster 875023, or is it a different chassis number, determined (by engine number, body number, date of production or some other means) to be the twenty third of all E-types produced? Similarly, referring to cars by the somewhat randomly-assigned registration or license number (typically used in discussing U.K. cars) offers little of use to subsequent researchers. At least parenthetically citing chassis number (or, much more useful, chassis, engine, transmission and body numbers, as are conveniently collected on the commission plate and found on Heritage Certificates) unambiguously ties the presented information to useful parameters that can help in future research. While many of these registrations are well-known (77 RW, 9600 HP, 848 CRY, 1600 RW, 9023 DU, as well as many others) and can be helpful in that they are often clearly visible in period photographs (while the chassis numbers generally are not), a mention of the chassis numbers would tie the registration numbers to the fundamental system used by the factory to identify the cars.

Some serial numbers, such as 3.8- and 4.2-liter engine and transmission numbers, and 4.2 chassis and body numbers have an alphanumeric format. In many cases, the factory printed literature, for example the *Spare Parts Catalogues* and Service Manuals, have periods between some of the alphabetic characters and the digits of the serial number. An example is the note "Fitted from Engine No. R.1001 to R.7103." on page 3 of *J.30 Spare Parts Catalogue* (June 1963). In fact, the authors have never observed an engine to be stamped in the format "R.7103," but rather without a period, thus, "R7103" (the suffix for compression ratio, "-9" also appears on the stamping when it is placed on the block or head). In addition, they have also never observed periods used in the four serial number stampings that appear on the aluminum commission plates. Thus, an engine with serial number "RA3074-9" stamped on it would be referred to as "RA.3074-9" in the Jaguar literature. To avoid confusion in this book, the authors will refer to serial numbers as they appear on the parts themselves, using a "no-period" convention. The periods will be used only in the cases when a direct quote is being made from a book, article, *etc.*, and the source has used a period. In these cases, quotes will be used to denote a literal string and the period will appear only if it is there. This will come up mostly in quoting the parts catalogs. In the case of part numbers (as opposed to serial numbers), e.g. block part numbers where sometimes the parts carry periods and sometimes they do not, the exact characters appearing on the part will be cited in the book (with a period only if it is there).

All photographs in this book are by Dr. T.F. Haddock. Some were taken under good conditions when the subject could be well illuminated and framed, but many were taken over a period of many decades, some as quick snapshots only to capture information. When possible, older photographs of lower quality were re-taken during the preparation of this book. However, in a number of cases the subject cars or parts in the pictures were no longer available and older pictures were used. It was felt better to include a picture of a feature, even if lower quality, than to omit the information. In some cases, pictures of detailed features of restored cars were used to illustrate a given feature. Such pictures generally do not represent the basic research material used to determine the validity of the characteristic in question, but are just used to illustrate it. Many of the pictures in this book were taken at the Mueller collection, where a local insect (possibly the *Trypoxylon* wasp) seals holes by secreting a white substance. Consequently, many of the holes in components shown in the illustrations here are filled with this white material. It does not reflect anything about how the cars were painted during assembly, nor any plugs that might have been inserted in these holes at the factory.

Lastly, the authors would like to thank all the other numerous owners whose cars were studied and photographed in the compilation of this work.

CHAPTER 1

OVERVIEW OF MODELS AND SERIAL NUMBERS

During the ten-year production run of the six-cylinder Jaguar E-type, four distinct models were produced. Each of these was available in roadster, coupe and, in some cases, 2+2 body styles. Good detailed discussions of the characteristics of the basic models can be found in numerous books and this information will not be repeated here in great detail. However, a brief overview is given below to serve as a baseline against which to reference the detailed production changes that are the subject of this book.

The following is a short history of the basic models in which the E-types appeared. For information on the motivations for the model changes and the effect they had on the overall character of the car, the reader is referred to the numerous books found in the Introduction and the books in the Reference Literature section.

Since so many of the production changes discussed in this book are referenced to the particular serial numbers at which they occurred, it is important to have a good grasp of the serial number system used for the chassis and large components. This will be included in the following discussions of each model.

THE SERIES 1 3.8-LITER CARS

The 3.8-liter cars represent the E-type in its earliest and crudest form, nearer to a sports car than the GT it evolved into. Introduced in March 1961, the 3.8-liter cars were the first E-types to go into production. Thus, there were more specification changes during their production than in any other E-type model (given that the so-called Series 1.5 is taken to be a separate model). There are several distinct variations, which are discussed at the end of this chapter. Offered in only the roadster and two-seater coupe versions, all with the original short (96-inch) wheelbase, the 3.8-liter cars suffered from many "problems." These included what are often regarded as poor seats (but possibly the most beautiful sports car seats ever made, similar to the seats in World War II fighter airplanes) and an antiquated (but classical and charming) gearbox. In contrast to the more sophisticated 4.2-liter cars that followed them, the 3.8-liter E-types had the features of a traditional British sports car, with a Moss gearbox, generator (instead of a modern alternator), a positive-ground electrical system, and a rather stark interior including crude but effective bucket seats.

A later 3.8-liter coupe, restored chassis number 887868, shows the standard two-seater coupe body style of all 3.8-liter cars, and all 4.2-liter cars except the 2+2.

ABOVE: The interior of the 3.8-liter cars remained relatively stark throughout production. This 1963 coupe, chassis 887868, shows an unusual upholstered lower section of the console, while the front console and center instrument are in the embossed cross pattern version of the aluminum trim. The full provenance of the car is known and this is very likely how it was delivered. The rubber floor mats are an after-market addition.

LEFT: The seats of the 3.8-liter cars were adjustable for reach only; there was no incline adjustment. This seat shows the gently-rounded top typical of 3.8-liter coupes.

Left-hand side of the engine compartment of 3.8-liter coupe 887868. The tires, shocks, coil and radiator are not correct here, and the exhaust manifold finish is more matte than the original shiny porcelain. Otherwise this is a reasonable representative of the mid-production 3.8-liter E-type engine compartment.

This right-hand side view of the 3.8-liter engine from 887868 shows the later version of the complex throttle linkage on the three intake manifolds. The same comments on originality for the left-hand side view apply here.

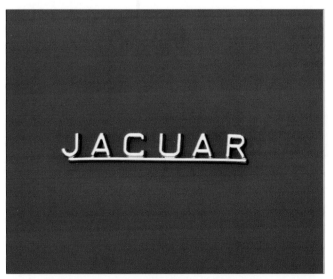

The only readily apparent outside difference between the 3.8-liter and 4.2-liter cars was the badges on the lower part of the rear door (or on the boot lid in the case of roadsters). The 3.8-liter cars showed only a "JAGUAR" badge.

Four independently-running chassis number series were used for the 3.8-liter cars, separate ones for right- and left-hand drive, and for coupes and roadsters. The starting chassis numbers for each of these series was:

Right-hand drive Roadsters:	850001
Right-hand drive Coupes:	860001
Left-hand drive Roadsters:	875001
Left-hand drive Coupes:	885001

It is important to note that the rate of production in each of these categories was not the same and the numbers naturally advanced much faster in the high-production-rate groups. Thus, for example, the ninetieth left-hand drive roadster 875090 (engine R1086-9) may have been produced earlier than the eighteenth left-hand drive coupe 885018 (engine R1447-9). The total production of 3.8-liter E-types was:

Right-hand drive Roadsters:	942
Right-hand drive Coupes:	1,798
Left-hand drive Roadsters:	6,885
Left-hand drive Coupes:	5,871

This amounted to a total of 15,496 3.8-liter E-types. As with all E-type production numbers, there is some uncertainty here.

The engine numbers for the 3.8-liter cars ran from R1001-X, where X was a 7, 8, or 9, that denoted the compression ratio of the engine (7:1, 8:1, or 9:1). Later on during engine production, the "R" prefix was changed to "RA." This denoted a shift in the four-digit engine numbering system, with the new number system starting over at RA1001-9.

The transmission numbers ran from EB101JS and the body numbers ran from R1001 for the roadsters and V1001 for the coupes. The numbers in each of these serial number series ran forward independently of the others. That is, for example, the bodies were labeled R1001, R1002, R1003,… for the roadsters and V1001, V1002, V1003,… for the coupes. This system was used instead of having a single increasing series that was labeled at coupe or roadster as they happened to come along, e.g. something like R1001, R1002, V1003, R1004, V1005,… The same is true of the chassis series. Thus there are at least, for example, four "number eight" E-types: right-hand drive roadster 850008, right-hand drive coupe 860008, left-hand drive roadster 875008 and left-hand drive coupe 885008, giving rise to the ambiguity of referring to cars as the "eighth E-type," as noted in the introduction. This same system of several independently-advancing chassis number series was used throughout E-type production on all the model types.

As mentioned above, the 3.8-liter production run had several identifiable subgroups and several of these are discussed on the following pages.

THE "FIRST 500" CARS

The first, and most interesting, E-type subgroup is the so-called "First 500" cars. These cars were produced up to and including chassis numbers:

Right-hand drive Roadsters:	850091
Right-hand drive Coupes:	860004
Left-hand drive Roadsters:	875385
Left-hand drive Coupes:	885020

This indicates a production of 91 right-hand drive roadsters, 4 right-hand drive coupes, 385 left-hand drive roadsters and 20 left-hand drive coupes, for a total of 500 cars, or a little more than 3.2 percent of 3.8-liter E-type production.

These 500 cars are different in many ways from the cars that followed them in production. It is believed that a production lull occurred after 500 bodies had been delivered to the factory and this opportunity was used to make some improvements. This assumption is based on several mentions found in the literature. In *The Jaguar E-type: A Collector's Guide*, Skilleter stated, "In fact, an almost fortunate hold-up caused by a delay at the bodyworks enabled Jaguar to rectify a number of obvious faults noticeable in the prototype production cars (which the motoring press sampled and whose comments perhaps helped Jaguar in this respect) before many cars had left the factory." *Road & Track* magazine of September 1961 noted that, "While it is unfortunate that a strike at the body plant has delayed production, this lull may prove to be beneficial, in that Jaguar can make the few obvious corrections that are needed before real production commences." The strike is also referred to in Porter's *Jaguar E-Type: The Definitive History*.

This roadster seat shows a small radius of curvature on the top, typical of 3.8-liter roadster seats. While this seat on unrestored chassis number 875026 shows some wear, it is the original material from the factory.

The outside bonnet latches (see inset) used on the first 500 3.8-liter Series 1 cars are seen in this side view of chassis number 875026. The short resonators suggest the exhaust system has likely been replaced.

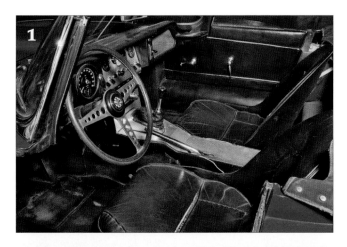

1 The etched circular dot pattern version of the aluminum trim on the console and dash center is typical of the first Series 1 3.8-liter cars, shown here on 875026. The early, flat dash top is evident. The seats of the 3.8-liter cars do not have any adjustment for rake.

2 Left side of the engine compartment of Series 1 3.8-liter 875026. The corrugated aluminum breather pipe, also a feature of the first 500 cars, can be seen coming from the left front of the cylinder head.

3 Right side of the engine compartment of 3.8-liter 875026. Here the multi-piece throttle linkage is evident, as well as the spark plug wire organizer with chrome ring bolted to the front-most lower right cam cover stud, as was generally the case with outside -latch cars. Somewhat later it appears these organizing rings were bolted to the fourth cam cover stud from the rear, on the top side of the intake cam cover.

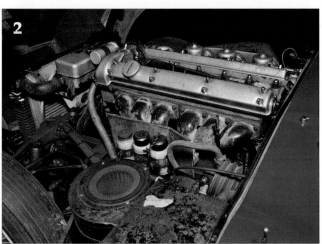

The most pronounced feature of the first 500 cars is the bonnet-latch mechanism, which is operated from outside the bonnet with a T-key. This key is similar to those used on numerous postwar British cars and it goes in keyholes on each of the lower rear corners of the front fenders. The keyholes are covered with teardrop-shaped chrome-plated cast escutcheons, as used on Jaguar Mk V fender skirts and the boot lids of early Triumph TR roadsters. These covers are a very prominent feature and the first 500 cars are often referred to as "outside bonnet latch" cars.

While these exterior bonnet latches are the most pronounced of the differences between the first 500 cars and their successors, there are numerous others. Also, within the group of the first 500 cars there are many changes in specifications. This is discussed in detail in Chapters Two and Three. The same is true for any other group of E-types mentioned here; changes in production and specification occurred frequently.

It is interesting that some possible references to this group of 500 cars are described specifically in the early factory literature, before the standard Parts Catalogue came out. One example is the *3.8 Interim Spares List (April 1961)*. The first page of this document states, "The Notes and Spares List is provided to assist in servicing the car pending issue of an official factory Service Manual and Parts Catalog." On page P.2 of this document 750 cars are mentioned as the point at which the generator (dynamo) changed from part number 22531 (as used on the first 500 cars, to part number 22902 (as used on subsequent cars). From this it appears that the dynamo change (and possibly others) was planned from early on and perhaps the strike, slowing production, caused this change to occur at 500 cars rather than the planned 750 (which would have given us the "first 750" instead of the "first 500" that occurred). (Similarly, on page M.2 there is a note about an exhaust change at 1000 cars).

THE "FLAT FLOOR" CARS
Another well-known subgroup is the so-called "flat floor" cars, distinguished by the relatively flat cockpit flooring in front of the seats. The floors were not truly flat, having support grooves pressed into them, but they were flat compared to the floors of the subsequent cars, which had separate, dished-down troughs. Unlike the numerous coordinated changes between the first 500 outside latch cars and subsequent cars, the flat floor change was a relatively isolated change. These cars were produced up to and including chassis numbers:

Right-hand drive Roadsters: 850357
Right-hand drive Coupes: 860175
Left-hand drive Roadsters: 876581
Left-hand drive Coupes: 885503

This indicates a production of 357 right-hand drive roadsters, 175 right-hand drive coupes, 1,581 left-hand

drive roadsters and 503 left-hand drive coupes, for a total of 2,616 cars, or about 17 percent of 3.8-liter E-type production.

The left-hand drive roadster chassis number 876581 is cited in most references as the final flat floor left-hand drive roadster, but in the *J.30 Spare Parts Catalogue (June 1963)*, chassis number 876381 is cited for the transition. Normally this would be the accepted number and the error would be assumed to lie with the other sources. However, since all sources the authors have reviewed agree with the 876581 number, it is more likely the *Spare Parts Catalogue* is in error, a situation that is not unusual. The end of flat floor car production came in early 1962.

In 1963, after E-type production was well under way, a series of 12 lightweight, aluminum-bodied roadsters was produced for competition purposes. These are extremely interesting cars, possessing such features as aluminum engine blocks and vented aluminum hardtops. On a detail level, however, these special-purpose racers have little relation to the production E-types and fall outside the scope of this book.

In the last year of 3.8-liter E-type production, 1964, the cars incorporated several of the features of the soon-to-be-released 4.2-liter cars. These included an upholstered center dash and console with storage compartment armrest, armrests on the doors, sculpted windscreen L-post trim. This is discussed in more detail in Chapter Two.

EXPERIMENTAL DEPARTMENT CARS

As noted above, Jaguar's Experimental Department produced a number of cars (about ten) during early E-type development. These cars were produced over a period of many years, but mostly were made in the period just before E-type production began in Jaguar's Production Department. Unlike the lightweight cars, whose chassis numbers are set outside the normal production series of chassis numbers by an "S" prefix (the chassis numbers of some early race-prepared cars are sometimes cited with an "S" prefix as well, but it is not clear this was a factory assignment), many of these Experimental Department cars carry standard chassis numbers. Thus, while not truly a production subgroup, they form in interesting set of cars. While some of the standard chassis number sequence Experimental Department cars share features with each other, for example the hand-stamped, thick body number plate and some have a firewall-mounted number plate, generally it does not appear that any two of them were identical. For example, 850002 had what appear to be rubber headlight cover seals and no T-key hole covers on the bonnet and 885002 even had several different configurations, including both left- and right-hand drive. This all apparently occurred while 885002 was still owned by the factory, thus making it a car with multiple "original" configurations. A good overview of these Experimental Department cars, as well as a few very early standard production cars, is given in "The First E-types," *Jaguar Quarterly*, April 1991 (no author cited,

but likely by Paul Skilleter). They are also discussed in Porter's *The Most Famous Car In the World*, as well as in other sources.

While some of the "production" changes that occurred during these few prototype or production-prototype cars are discussed in this book, but the main focus of this work is the changes that took place during manufacturing by the Production Department.

While the tremendous appeal of the 3.8-liter cars tended to overshadow their failings, the improved 4.2-liter version was welcome when it was introduced in 1964. In retrospect, however, it is the 3.8-liter cars that now generally carry the greatest appeal.

THE SERIES 1 4.2-LITER CARS

The new 4.2-liter cars were very different from their predecessors. In addition to numerous changes in the engine, the generator was replaced with a more modem alternator, the electrical system was changed from positive to negative ground, the seats and gearbox were replaced with more up-to-date versions, the brake system was reworked and the interior trimming was redone

BELOW: *This 4.2-liter coupe, number 1E30779, has basically the same exterior appearance as its 3.8-liter predecessors. This car is restored.*

1 Before the end of 3.8-liter production, all the aluminum trim used on the dash and console (both the early etched dot pattern type and the later embossed cross pattern types) had been phased out and the armrests on the doors and center console had been introduced, as seen here on this Series 1 4.2-liter car, chassis 1E30779. The new seats shown here came in with the 4.2-liter and were a big change from the 3.8-liter cars. The interior of this coupe is very original and representative of this group of cars, with the exceptions of the shift-boot material and trimming, the escutcheons on the radio blanking plate and console, which are after-market additions, and the rubber floor mats.

2 The Series 1 4.2-liter seats had a reach and incline adjustment, although the latter was minimal. These later seats were generally considered to be more comfortable, but did not have the same lateral support as the earlier 3.8-liter seats.

3 Left-hand side of the engine compartment of 4.2-liter Series 1 coupe 1E30779. Generally this car represents the basic state of the Series 1 4.2-liter cars. Some details that are not correct include the tires, radiator cap, alternator heat shield, radiator, coil, the matte finish on the exhaust headers and shiny finish on the heat shield.

4 Right-hand side view of the engine compartment of 1E30779, shows several features of the Series 1 4.2-liter cars, including the flat-top of the integrated single piece intake manifold (the throttle
Continued on next page...

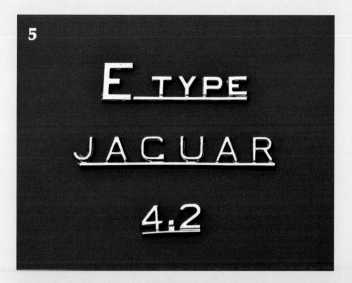

linkage was located below the manifold instead of above, as it had been on the 3.8-liter cars), the three grooves in the top of the triangular fiberglass air intake box and the silver color of the cylindrical sheet steel air cleaner shell assembly (located directly below the air intake box; this unit was typically painted black on 3.8-liter cars). Note the black plastic dampener caps on the carburetor suction chambers, a feature that came in with the late 3.8-liter cars, and ran through to the replacement of S.U. carburetors with Strombergs for the U.S.-market Series 1.5 cars. The tires here are not original specification, and the windscreen-washer cap appears to be of the blue material of the early 3.8-liter E-types. It should be black for later Series 1 and all Series 1.5 cars.

5 In contrast to the single "JAGUAR" badge on the rear of the 3.8-liter cars, the 4.2-liter cars carried the "E-TYPE" and "4.2" badges.

6 This three-quarter rear view shows the location of the badges on the rear of the car. The badges were in this same location on both 3.8-liter and all variants of 4.2-liter cars.

to give the car a more sophisticated look. The exterior appearance was essentially unchanged.

The change in the engine was more than just a boring-out of the cylinders. Numerous changes took place, including relocating the cylinders in the block, changing the intake manifold from a multi-piece construction to a single-piece construction and a change from a Welch plug seal for the water jacket at the back of the block to a bolted-on plate (except for a few very 4.2-liter early cars).

The new fully synchromesh gearbox (also referred to in this book as a transmission) is often cited as the main improvement of the 4.2-liter cars over their 3.8-liter predecessors. It is interesting that *Autocar Magazine* of May 14, 1965 notes that the 4.2-liter E-type with synchromesh gearbox was originally announced as an alternate model to the still-produced 3.8-liter E-type with

the old gearbox. The new 4.2-liter model was listed as going for about £66 more for the roadster and £78 more for the coupe.

In 1966 a third variety of body style was made available with the introduction of the 2+2 coupe. The two-seater roadster and coupe body styles continued in production. This elongated wheelbase version of the coupe had a raised roof line and dropped floor to increase interior room. The two small back seats had a squab that could be moved forward to cover the seat-bottoms if more rear luggage area was needed. While this car was welcomed by some owners, for example larger owners or those with small children, it clearly had less of the sporting character possessed by the two-seater versions. The domesticated nature of the 2+2 was enhanced by the availability of an optional automatic transmission that could not be ordered on the two-seater cars.

Like their predecessor, the 4.2-liter cars initially had four independently-running chassis number series. With the introduction of the 2+2 body style in 1966, two more series were introduced to bring the total to six series. The starting chassis numbers for each of these series was:

Right-hand drive Roadsters: 1E1001
Left-hand drive Roadsters: 1E10001
Right-hand drive Coupes: 1E20001
Left-hand drive Coupes: 1E30001
Right-hand drive 2+2s: 1E50001
Left-hand drive 2+2s: 1E75001

While this is the typical chassis numbering system, it has been estimated that as many as 500 of the early 4.2-liter cars did not have the "1E" prefix in their chassis numbers (see page 439). As in the case of the 3.8-liter cars, the rate of production in each of these categories was not the same. The total production of 4.2-liter Series 1 E-types was:

Right-hand drive Roadsters: 1,182
Left-hand drive Roadsters: 8,366
Right-hand drive Coupes: 1,957
Left-hand drive Coupes: 5,813
Right-hand drive 2+2s: 1,378
Left-hand drive 2+2s: 4,220

This amounted to a total of 22,916 4.2-liter Series 1 E-types.

The engine numbers for the 4.2-liter Series 1 cars had a 7E prefix and an X suffix, where X denoted the compression ratio, as in the case of the 3.8-liter engines. The starting engine numbers for the Series 1 4.2-liter cars were:

Two-seater cars: 7E1001
2+2s: 7E50001

The transmission numbers had an EJ prefix and the body numbers had a 4E prefix.

THE SERIES 1.5 CARS

These cars represent a transition between the classic Series 1 cars, which all had basically the same exterior appearance and the Series 2 cars, which were the final result of the 1968 U.S. automotive safety and pollution

The side-view of this very original Series 1.5 car, chassis number 1E17271, is very close to that of the preceding 3.8- and 4.2-liter Series 1 cars, with the exception of the uncovered headlights and earless knock-off hubcaps. While a few of the last Series 1 4.2-liter cars shared the uncovered lights (these are sometimes referred to as Series 1.25 cars), the great majority of Series 1 cars had covered lights.

ABOVE: *The interior view of Series 1.5 car chassis 1E17271 shows some of the features required by the U.S. Federal regulations that went into effect beginning 1968. Among these are the rocker switches (replacing the toggle switches of the Series 1 and Series 1.25 cars) and the new choke and heater controls that are recessed into the dash (at least when not in the extended positions).*

RIGHT: *View of the driver's seat on Series 1.5 roadster 1E17271.*

The left-hand view of the engine compartment chassis 1E17271. Numerous changes have taken place since the end of Series 1 production, mostly to meet U.S. Federal regulations. These include replacement of the three S.U. HD8 2-inch throat carburetors with direct intake manifolds, with two 1.75-inch Stromberg carburetors and a two-stage manifold that had valving for direct input or input routed through a crossover pipe, over the top of the cam covers, across the top of the rear exhaust manifold (to be heated for better combustion) and back into the induction system. The domed nuts holding on the crossover pipe are somewhat unusual, but likely original. The cooling-system header tank is now mounted on the left side of the firewall. Note also the presence of two cooling fans, each with four blades, injection-molded as a unit. This is in contrast to the previous cars that had a single fan, with a single bar of bent sheet steel for the blade. The gold-colored coil here is not original, nor are the battery or tires.

The right-hand view of the engine compartment of Series 1.5 roadster 1E17271 shows the integration of the crossover pipe into the rear of the intake manifold. The tires and coil are not original.

control regulations. While the Series 1.5 cars could be considered a subgroup of the Series 1 cars, here they are treated as an independent model in their own right.

The topic of Series 1.5 cars is complex, with the transition to the Series 1.5 cars occurring at different times, and in different versions, in different markets. For example, the Series 1.5 cars for the U.S. market had two Stromberg carburetors, while for other markets the three S.U. carburetors were still used. In addition, what is usually taken as the outward form of the Series 1.5 cars, the cessation of the glass covers on the headlights (the "open-headlight" cars), occurred at an earlier point. An excellent treatment of this topic, clarifying many of the misconceptions often encountered, was given by Stew Cleave in his *JCNA Model Year '68 E-Type Judges' Guide*, published by Jaguar Clubs of North America (JCNA) and accepted at the 48th Annual AGM in Seattle, Washington, March 2006. This work gives the date of the implementation of the open-headlight bonnets as January 1967 and describes it as a change occurring within Series 1 production, before and independent of the implementation of the Series 1.5 configuration. Cleave refers to these open-headlight Series 1 cars as "Series 1.25," a useful designation that will be used here. The chassis number transitions for this change, from Cleave, are given in Chapter Four. Following Cleave's work, the chassis numbers of the Series 1.5 cars are:

Cars for the U.S. market:

Left-hand drive Roadsters:	1E15980
Left-hand drive Coupes:	1E34583
Left-hand drive 2+2s:	1E77709

Cars for other markets:

Left-hand drive Roadsters:	1E16010
Left-hand drive Coupes:	1E34752
Left-hand drive 2+2s:	1E77709

Cleave notes that while the chassis numbers listed for the beginning of the left-hand drive 2+2 Series 1.5 production, both for the U.S. market cars and for the outside-U.S. market cars, are the same (1E77709), he states has seen one copy of an interim parts list that has the words "to be determined" instead of listing 1E77709. This is likely an early copy of an interim parts list. Perhaps this suggests chassis number 1E77709 was set aside to begin Series 1.5 production, but it was not yet determined if this car would be shipped to the U.S. market or not. He cites the ending numbers on all cars sold worldwide as:

Left-hand drive Roadsters:	1E18367
Left-hand drive Coupes:	1E35814
Left-hand drive 2+2s:	1E79221

He cites, then, total build units of:

Left-hand drive Roadsters:	2388
Left-hand drive Coupes:	1232
Left-hand drive 2+2s:	1513

This amounts to a total of 5133 left-hand drive 4.2-liter Series 1.5 E-types. Cleave notes that while the starting numbers here are those for the U.S. market, the ending numbers are for cars going to both markets. Cleave's work does not give the right-hand drive chassis numbers; turning to XKEdata.com (www.xkedata.com/catalog/numbers) these chassis numbers are cited for the beginning and ending build of both left-hand drive and right-hand drive Series 1.5 cars:

Right-hand drive Roadsters:	1E1864 – 1E2184
Left-hand drive Roadsters:	1E15889 – 1E18368
Right-hand drive Coupes:	1E21584 – 1E21959
Left-hand drive Coupes:	1E34250 – 1E35815
Right-hand drive 2+2s:	1E50975 – 1E51379
Left-hand drive 2+2s:	1E77645 – 1E79222

Indicating a total production of:

Right-hand drive Roadsters:	320
Left-hand drive Roadsters:	2,479
Right-hand drive Coupes:	375
Left-hand drive Coupes:	1,565
Right-hand drive 2+2s:	404
Left-hand drive 2+2s:	1,577

Further research on the topic of Series 1.5 chassis numbers yields yet other numbers. The above material is not felt to be definitive.

This side view of restored 1970 Series 2 coupe chassis number 1R27925 shows the enlarged side lamps and earless knock-off hubcaps. Note the headlights are uncovered, as in the case of the Series 1.5 cars, but they have been raised further above the bonnet line.

1 The interior of the Series 2 was nominally the same as the Series 1.5, but had several changes over production. This 1970 car has the short armrests.

2 This 1970 Series 2 seat shows the leather with embossed indents and the headrest typical of U.S.-market cars.

3 The right-hand side view of this 1970 Series 2 engine compartment shows the corrugated pipe feeding the fabricated crossover pipe. Also evident here are the two cooling fans that ran throughout Series 1.5 and Series 2 production.

4 The centrally-mounted, black-painted crossover pipe is typical of the XK engine configuration of the later Series 2 cars. Series 2 cars were also produced with no crossover pipe in the period between the rear-mounted cast aluminum crossover pipe and the one shown here.

5 The plastic leaping Jaguar medallion, seen here on model year 1971 Series 2 roadster is a feature of the very late Series 2 cars. Interestingly, it gives these last six-cylinder cars the appearance of the first cars with the outside bonnet latches.

THE SERIES 2 CARS

While the Series 1.5 kept Jaguar in the U.S. market for the 1968 model year, a more integrated response to the new U.S. regulations was being developed for model year 1969. This new model was for a time referred to as the Mk II in *Car* and *Road & Track*, but came to be officially known as Series 2, probably to avoid confusion with the Mk 2 sports sedan. With this new name came the designation of Series 1 and Series 1.5 for the earlier cars that had previously been known simply as E-types (and later, following Cleave, Series 1.25).

The changes in the Series 2 cars were not focused exclusively on meeting the U.S. regulations and included numerous unrelated improvements. For example, the air intake aperture was increased for better cooling and there were changes in the braking system.

With the introduction of the Series 2 cars, the E-type's exterior appearance noticeably changed for the first time. Not only was the enlarged and reshaped air-intake readily apparent, but the rear end bodywork and trim were changed to increase bumper protection and accommodate the larger lights required by the new regulations. While these changes typically improved functionality, it is generally regarded that they diminished the original purity and beauty of the car. The cars were offered in the same three body styles as the late Series 1 and Series 1.5 cars.

With the introduction of the Series 2 came another new chassis numbering system. It followed the same pattern as the preceding systems, with the models broken down as follows:

Right-hand drive Roadsters:	1R1001
Left-hand drive Roadsters:	1R7001
Right-hand drive Coupes:	1R20001
Left-hand drive Coupes:	1R25001
Right-hand drive 2+2s:	1R35001
Left-hand drive 2+2s:	1R40001

To further specify details of an individual car, prefixes and suffixes were used in the numbering system. A prefix P was used to denote that the car was fitted with power steering. A suffix BW for Borg-Warner was used to denote that an automatic transmission was fitted. This was only available on 2+2 cars.

The total production of Series 2 E-types was:

Right-hand drive Roadsters:	775
Left-hand drive Roadsters:	7,852
Right-hand drive Coupes:	1,070
Left-hand drive Coupes:	3,785
Right-hand drive 2+2s:	1,040
Left-hand drive 2+2s:	4,286

This resulted in a total of 18,808 4.2-liter Series 2 E-types.

Engine numbers for the Series 2 cars ran in two separate series, one for the two-seater cars and one for the 2+2s, in the same manner as for earlier 4.2-liter cars:

Two seat chassis:	7R1001-X
2+2 chassis:	7R35001-X

The X denoted the compression ratio, as before. The later cars used letters to denote the compression ratio.

Transmission numbers had a KE prefix (except for those cars fitted with automatic transmissions), and the body numbers had a 4R prefix

This background information on the four basic six-cylinder E-type models sets the stage for examining the detailed production changes that took place within each of these model classifications.

LOCATIONS AND APPEARANCE OF SERIAL NUMBER MARKINGS

Given that so much of the material of this book relates directly to the many serial numbering systems used on E-types, it is appropriate to discuss and illustrate the appearance and locations of these markings before beginning the main analyses of the book. While in later chapters discussions and illustrations of particular details and evolution of some of these marking systems are given in detail, this general overview is best given at the outset of the book.

SERIAL NUMBER MARKINGS 3.8-LITER CARS

Serial numbers for different components are marked on the car in numerous places. Detailed variations of some of these markings is given in Chapter Eight, but an overview will be given here. A number plate, often referred to as the "commission plate", summarizing chassis, body, engine and transmission numbers, is located on the horizontal section of sheet metal on the right rear of the firewall, in the engine compartment. A few very early cars had this summary plate mounted vertically on various places on the firewall, and at least one factory lightweight racer had the plate mounted on the bonnet, on the back of the left front wheel well (seen on page 333 of Porter's *Jaguar E-Type, the Definitive History*).

The chassis number is stamped on the top of the right-hand side of the front frame member, just above the top shock absorber mounting point and on the commission plate. Initially, production cars had this stamping toward the front of the frame member, and later it was moved slightly back toward the rear of the car, so it was close to the center of the frame member. Based on observations of original cars, the numbers appear to be stamped on after painting of the frame.

The engine number on 3.8-liter cars is stamped on the

block above the oil filter, on the back of the cam chain gallery at the front of the head, on the crankshaft, on the edge of the flywheel and on the commission plate.

The transmission number is stamped on the top aluminum transmission cover, on the iron transmission case, and on the commission plate.

The body number is stamped on a pressed plate, affixed to the firewall in the engine compartment on the right-hand side on early cars, on the left-hand side bulkhead in the boot on later cars, and on the commission plate. The following chassis numbers had the body number on the firewall:

- ▸ 875026 (body number R1044)
- ▸ 875038 (body number R1067)
- ▸ 875090 (body number R1138)
- ▸ 875109 (body number R1129)
- ▸ 875186 (body number R1263)
- ▸ 875251 (body number R1362)
- ▸ 875331 (body number R1443)

The main number plate, or commission plate, had chassis, body, engine and transmission numbers stamped on it. It was pop-riveted on the right-hand side of the engine compartment throughout 3.8-liter E-type production (with the exception of a few of the very early cars, likely only a few manufactured by the Experimental Department). Many variations (including errors) associated with these plates are discussed in later chapters.

A plate added by the state of California. J-62 means 1962 Jaguar.

RIGHT: *The aluminum California tag was found in numerous places, but typically near the commission plate. Some were pop-riveted on and some were screwed on. This one is pop-riveted on next to a body number plate on the firewall of an early 3.8-liter left-hand drive roadster.*

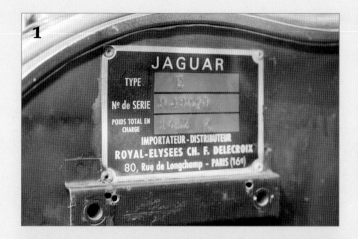

1 An additional chassis number plate mounted on the right-hand side firewall of this French-specification car.

2 The chassis number was stamped on the front section of the front cross member assembly, above the right shock absorber mount on the right-hand side. From many observations of original cars, it appears the stamps were generally made after the painting of the frame member, as the paint around the numbers is chipped off. Note that this is the case here with the very original left-hand drive coupe chassis 885056.

3 This close-up of the "885056" stamping shows the chips in the paint.

4 Another car, the very original left-hand drive roadster chassis 879408, shows the same chipped-paint effect.

5 This close-up of the stamping on the cross member assembly on early left-hand drive roadster 875026 not only shows the chipping in the paint, but also the positioning of the stamping more toward the front of the car, as was typical for early cars.

6 "E-TYPE" and "J" were stamped on the front frame member, next to the chassis number, on this French-specification car. These were probably not factory stampings. This frame member has been re-painted (as many have) and does not show paint chipping around the stampings.

The engine number was stamped on the head, behind the camshaft chain gallery. The number was also stamped on the crankshaft, as illustrated on page 179.

The engine number was stamped in several places. Here is number RA3074-9 stamped on the block on top of the oil filter boss. This location for the engine number remained throughout 3.8-liter XK engine production and well into 4.2-liter production.

1 *The engine number was stamped on the outer edge of the flywheel.*

2 *The transmission number was stamped in two places. Here it is on the transmission cover.*

3 *The transmission number, EB9925JS, is seen in the lower right quadrant of the picture, stamped on the raised boss on the top left-hand side of the cast-iron case.*

On early cars, the body number plate was pop-riveted on the right-hand side of the firewall, above the brake and clutch fluid bracket (used only on right-hand drive cars, so unpopulated on this left-hand drive car).

Later on, the body number plate was pop-riveted on the left-hand side of the boot. The trim has been removed to show this plate. This is a coupe, but the roadster had the plate in the same basic location.

The differential number was stamped on the bottom of its case. The "62" on the left of the number sequence apparently indicates the year, "1962."

The aluminum radiators had a serial number plate on top. It was held in place by four small hemispherical-head screws. Later on in 3.8-liter production, it appears these number tags were replaced by painted numbers.

Some early cars had the body number stamped on the upper right rear of the bonnet.

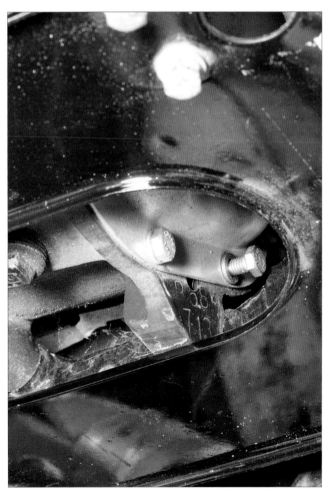

The body number, in this case "1044" denoting body "R1044," was marked in crayon on the inside right fender of the bonnet of some early bonnets. This one also denotes the destination of the car as "USA." These markings have faded over the past four decades, even without being touched, perhaps suggesting the marking material may sublimate with time. This effect has been observed with other similar markings.

Later on, the differential number was moved from the bottom of the front section of the casing, to the lower right rear machined surface of the housing, as seen here. The latest date the authors have observed stamped on the bottom was "63," and the earliest seen on the back was "64," so the transition from bottom to rear stamping occurred in the 1963-1964 time frame. The date seen here appears to be "68," suggesting the unit is from a 4.2-liter car.

RIGHT: The body number marked in crayon on the right-hand side of the firewall of a 1962 left-hand drive roadster. Such markings were found in many places, including the top of the front frame cross member.

These chassis numbers had the body number in the boot:

- ▸ 875340 (body number R1460)
- ▸ 875954 (body number R2210 or R2202)
- ▸ 876052 (body number R2301)
- ▸ 885358 (body number V1526)

In addition to these usual markings, others are sometimes used. For example, chassis number 875109 has its body number 1129 (without the R prefix) stamped on the right rear of its bonnet, as do many early cars. 875026 does not have this stamping, but has its body number, 1044, written in crayon on the inside or the right wing of the bonnet. Other cars have been observed with crayon markings of body numbers in other places, including the firewall, the inside of the coupe rear door and outside license plate area.

The body number and interior color written in crayon inside an early convertible top cover.

ABOVE: The body number and interior color were crayoned on numerous pieces of the interior trim. Here they are found inside the trim panel behind the right-hand side door of a 1962 coupe.

BOTTOM RIGHT: The number "1055," representing body number "R1055" crayoned on the back of a footwell carpet. Note that the number is written twice; this is not unusual.

SERIAL NUMBER MARKINGS 4.2-LITER CARS

There are a few differences between the serial number markings on 3.8- and 4.2-liter cars. The number plate on 4.2-liter cars, summarizing chassis, body, engine and transmission numbers, is located on the horizontal areas in front of the bonnet latches. On earlier 4.2-liter cars, it was on the right side, in the same location as on the 3.8-liter cars, and later it was found on the left side. When an automatic transmission was fitted, the serial number plate denoted this fact. Later in production, the plate changed from the traditional Jaguar plate proportions to a more elongated shape and it was mounted on the left-hand side.

On very late cars, another plate was placed on the left-hand side door panel. The date of manufacture was stamped on the plate.

As in the case of the 3.8-liter cars, those sold in California received an additional plate, with the letter J and the last two digits of the year of the car. This small aluminum plate was usually mounted near the commission plate.

The chassis numbers on post-1967 U.S.-specification cars were also displayed on the left side of the windscreen on a small aluminum plate that could be seen from outside the car.

A right-hand drive Series 1.5 car is shown without a driver's side window chassis number plate in *E-type: End of an Era* and a right-hand drive Series 2 is shown without a window chassis number plate.

The engine number on early 4.2-liter cars is stamped on the block above the oil filter, on the back of the cam chain area of the head, on the crankshaft on the edge of the flywheel, and on the number plate. Later on, the engine numbers stamped on the head and above the oil filter were deleted, but the engine number was stamped on the left-rear of the engine block, on the flange in the rear of the casting that butts against the left front of the bell housing.

The transmission number is stamped on the aluminum cover, and on the iron transmission case.

The body number on early 4.2-liter cars is stamped on a pressed plate affixed to the rear of the body, under the center of the area by the rear license plate.

On Series 2 cars, the body number plate is found in the same region, but mounted off-center to the right.

As in the case of the 3.8-liter cars, the body number was often written in crayon on the body and frame in numerous places.

The differential number is stamped on the bottom of the differential housing case.

The Jaguar E-type: A Collector's Guide a serial number plate is shown on the inner left wheel well of the bonnet of an early right-hand drive 4.2-liter car.

The early 4.2-liter commission plates were pop-riveted on the right-hand side of the engine compartment. This is the same position used for all the 3.8-liter cars.

At engine numbers 7R6305/6 and 7R38105/6, about August 1969, the engine number stamping was moved from the area above the oil filter to the left side bell housing flange, near to the dipstick

Later on, the serial number plate was mounted on the left-hand side of the engine compartment.

When an automatic transmission was fitted, a special serial number plate was used. Note the "AUTOMATIC TRANSMISSION NO." marking in place of the "GEAR BOX NO." marking otherwise found on these plates. The automatic transmission was available on the 2+2 cars only. Note the "BW" suffix on the chassis number, denoting Borg-Warner, the manufacturer of the automatic transmission. As with all commission plates, it was held in place with pop-rivets.

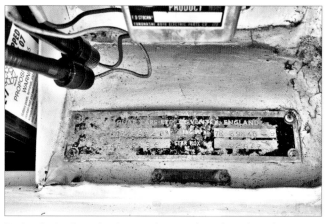

During Series 2 production, an elongated serial number plate was adopted. It was mounted on the left-hand side of the engine compartment.

This additional windscreen frame-mounted chassis number plate was required by U.S. Regulations. This is likely the earliest version. Note the "1R" part of the chassis number is anodized on the plate before stamping, as is a black border around the edge of the tag.

This is probably the last variant of the tag, as this is the configuration of the early Series 3 V-12 cars (e.g. 1S20001).

This tag has no anodizing on it.

Series 2 cars also had this number plate on the left-hand door panel.

A later variant of the door-panel plate.

1 *Likely this was the final variant of the door-panel plate.*

2 *On later cars, the engine number was stamped on the left-hand side edge of the circular flange cast into the block for the bell housing to bolt against.*

3 *Later cylinder heads did not have the engine-number stampings that were found on the earlier cars. The area on the back of the timing chain gallery was blank.*

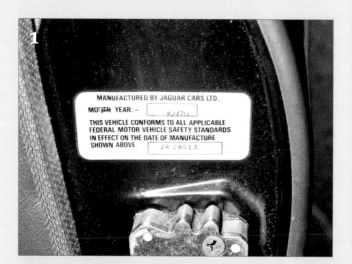

4 As in the case of the "Moss" type transmissions used with the 3.8-liter cars, the transmission number was stamped in two places. This is the cover stamping. Note the "K" is stamped with a larger-size punch set than that used for the other characters. The bolt to the left of the stamping is not original.

5 The transmission number, here KE7112, was also stamped on the side of the case.

6 A body number plate mounted on the right rear of a Series 2 car.

7 An early, centrally-mounted body number plate on the rear of a 4.2-liter car, in the center of the license plate area.

CHAPTER 2

3.8-LITER BODYWORK AND INTERIOR COMPONENT CHANGES

T his chapter analyzes the changes made to bodywork, interior and associated areas during the full production run of 3.8-liter E-types from 1961 to 1964.

EXTERIOR: HEADLIGHTS AND TRIM

The color of the finishing panel in the headlight recess was of the same color as the bodywork on the earlier cars. This later changed to a flat silver or silver-gray color finish.

The screws retaining the headlight cover surround were initially flat-head, running perhaps through all 3.8-liter cars, and were changed to Phillips-head screws at least by the 4.2-liter cars. Unrestored and very original cars 876037, 876163 and 879032 all have flat-head screws.

The headlight trim rings were black on at least one very early car, probably chassis number 850002 assembled by the Experimental Department. Apparently this car is no longer extant. Another example is a coupe with black trim rings, referred to as the "first coupe," (885001?) pictured on page 21 of Skilleter's *The Jaguar E-type: A Collector's Guide.*

The first style of headlight finisher panel in body color. At least some of the surround retaining screws are not original.

A later finishing panel in silver, not matching the body color. Flathead screws were used on the headlight cover retaining ring on this restored car.

The headlight units were shown by factory literature as variants of either PL.700, F.700, depending on country of destination, given in table on the next page.

Although, as seen in the following material, it is possible GE lights were on earlier cars as they were delivered from the Jaguar dealerships. At least one of the Experimental Department cars was equipped with non-PL lights. One example of this is the period picture of 850003 (77 RW) on page 159 of *All About the Jaguar E-Type.*

In *Autocar,* April 26, 1963, it is stated that the "full beam of the lamps is good and penetrating, apparently unhindered by the toughened glass covers to the lamp wells. On early cars these were of transparent plastic material." The authors have never seen plastic covers on an any E-type, nor found any other references to this. This is may be an erroneous statement, but then the very few early cars produced by the Experimental Department differ in many particulars from early production cars, so perhaps some plastic covers were used very early on. For example, Porter in *The Most Famous Car in the World*, states 885002 had a plastic rear window and an aluminum rear hatch door. These features, however, may have been used to enhance performance of this early car used for testing by the press.

About April 1964, sealed-beam headlights were adopted for cars going to Brazil, Canada, Chile, Colombia, Cuba, Dominican Republic, Egypt, El Salvador, Greece, Guatemala, Haiti, Hawaii, Jordan, Lebanon, Madeira, Mexico, Newfoundland, Nicaragua, Panama, Persian Gulf, Peru, Philippines, Puerto Rico, Saudi Arabia, South Vietnam, Syria, the United States, Uruguay and Venezuela, at chassis numbers 880631/2 and 889526/7.

Right-hand drive cars	58662/B-PL.700 (clear 60/36 Watt 416 bulb)
Left-hand drive cars *(except France, Austria, Sweden and USA)*	58663/B-PL.700 (clear 60/36 Watt 417 bulb)
European export *(except France, Austria, Sweden and USA)*	58664/B-F.700 (clear 45/40 Watt 410 bulb)
For export to France	58665/B-F.700 (yellow 45/40 Watt 411 bulb)
For export to Austria	58667/B-F.700 (clear 45/40 Watt 410 bulb)
For export to Sweden	58666/B-F.700 (clear 45/40 Watt 410 bulb)
For export to USA	58439/D-F.700 (sealed beam, no separate bulb)

Headlight types for different markets, as cited in the Spare Parts Catalogue.

A Lucas PL headlight. These lights employed a separate bulb and were fitted to most non-U.S.-market cars. The three support arms hold a chrome reflector in front of the bulb. The enamel-filled letters on the central crest are "LUCAS" and "PL."

1 Note the molded-in "LEFT HAND DRIVE," "700 HEADLAMP" and other markings on this NOS light. The "PL" shield in the center has black enamel around the letters on original PL headlights. Black paint is used on some modern reproductions.

2 Back view of the same NOS PL light showing the wire retainer for the separate bulb.

3 U.S. market cars typically were delivered to customers from the dealerships with these GE sealed-beam headlight bulbs, instead of the PL headlight units which contained a small, separate bulb inside them. It appears the cars were shipped from the factory without headlights and these GE headlight bulbs were fitted in the U.S. before delivery. These are 12-volt units, but they were also supplied in a 6-volt variety. The 6-volt variety was for other cars, and not appropriate for an E-type.

4 Front view of a GE bulb. The GE logo is generally in a large size, as shown in the pictures here. The authors have never seen a smaller size on an E-type.

5 Close-up of the GE logo in the center of the bulb.

6 Back view of the same GE bulb showing the "12-V" marking. As noted, these come in 6-volt variants, inappropriate for E-types.

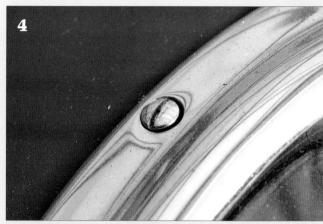

OPPOSITE

1 *Lucas sealed-beam headlights were also fitted to U.S.-specification cars. These units are marked "LUCAS" in a circle the center of the lens, but otherwise have the standard appearance of typical U.S. sealed-beam bulbs of the period. This unit is shown fitted to an unrestored, very-original Series 2 car. Generally, it appears, the Lucas sealed-beam bulbs were fitted later than the GE sealed-beam bulbs. The authors are not sure at what point this transition occurred. There also may have been other variants of headlights fitted to the U.S.-market cars.*

2 *Front view of a Lucas sealed-beam headlight. Note the "LUCAS" lettering in a circle is about the same size as the GE symbol used on the alternate bulbs.*

3 *Close-up of the Lucas symbol in the center of a sealed-beam headlight bulb.*

4 *At least initially, cars were fitted with slot-head headlight cover retaining ring screws, but some later 3.8-liter cars may have had the Phillips type. There are also suggestions the slot-head screws may have been used up to around 1965, into 4.2-liter production. There may have been some overlap.*

5 *The Phillips-type headlight cover retaining ring screws were possibly used on later 3.8-liter cars.*

6 *These headlight retaining ring screws have the small slash marks in between the troughs of the recess for the screwdriver. These appear to be Pozidriv identification marks. The authors have never seen evidence of a Series 1 E-type being delivered from the factory with Pozidriv screws retaining the headlight rings and suspect these are non-factory replacement screws.*

7 *This marking was used on the glass headlight covers. Glass markings are covered in more detail in Chapter Six. This marking appears on some later replacement headlight covers.*

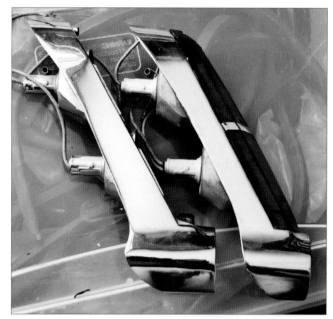

Two stop/tail/flasher lamp assemblies. The one on the left is a roadster light, as seen by the relatively straight trailing edge between the cylindrical reflector section and the opposite end, as well as the longer cylindrical reflector section. It is likely there was only one type of roadster light. The right stop/tail/flasher lamp assembly also has a relatively straight trailing edge, but a short cylindrical reflector section and appears to be from an early coupe or a 2+2; both lights are very similar.

Here an early coupe (or possibly 2+2) stop/tail/flasher lamp is shown on the left, with the relative straight trailing edge and short cylindrical reflection section. In the middle is a later coupe light with a bulge in the center of the trailing section and a short cylindrical section. To the right is a roadster lamp.

PARKING, BRAKE LIGHTS AND TRIM

There were at least two types of patterns on the front sidelights. The early style had horizontal parallel lines throughout the area of the front triangular lens. Later lenses had a section running down the middle of the triangular lens with small vertical features. The early lenses were typically retained by flat-head screws, while later lenses appear to have been retained with Phillips head screws.

The stop/tail/flasher lamp assemblies came in many different shapes to accommodate fitting on the roadster or coupe bodywork and on the various types of coupe bodywork. The very early coupes had a different bodywork shape than the later coupes and this necessitated different stop/tail/flasher lamp assembly shapes. There were different stop/tail/flasher lamp forms to accommodate the various bodywork forms and it is likely this change occurred at chassis numbers 860478/9 and 886013/4.

The rear stop/tail/flasher lamp assemblies were changed. This occurred about June 1962 and the change was to adapt the lights to the altered body panels. This was part of the extensive rework of the coupes that took place at chassis numbers 860478/9 and 886013/4.

The taillight lens colors varied as a function of the country the car was to be delivered to. For cars shipped to the United States, both lenses were red. For most other cars, the stop taillight lens in the rear stop/tail/flasher lamp was red and the flasher lens was amber.

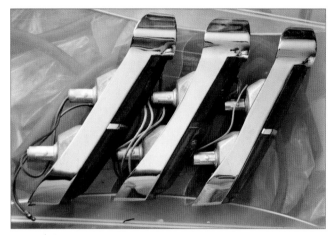

On the left is an early coupe or 2+2 light with a short cylindrical reflector section and a relatively straight trailing edge. A roadster light is in the middle with a long cylindrical reflector region. On the right is a late coupe light with the short reflector section and the curved-in trailing edge for the later coupe bodywork shape.

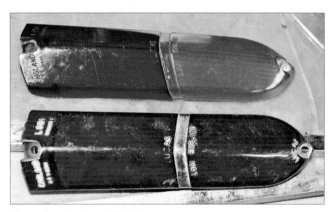

The red and amber taillight lenses.

LICENSE PLATE LIGHTS AND TRIM

Initially the lights were marked "BUTLERS ENGLAND," but later they were marked "LUCAS L.705." From observations of original car as well as NOS stock, the chromed steel shroud on the back of the light does not have markings, while the later types have "ENGLAND" marked on them. This is reasonable, as the Butlers lights have "ENGLAND" on the chrome surround, while the Lucas lights do not state the country of origin.

An early-type license plate light with unmarked shroud and "BUTLERS ENGLAND" on the surround.

This later-type light shows the Lucas L.705 markings and carries an "ENGLAND" marking on the shroud.

A license plate light with no markings, seen on a restored car. It is not known if these were ever originally used on any E-types and the authors have seen no evidence they were. It is likely this is a reproduction light.

There are license plate lights with no characters stamped on any of the components, neither the frame nor the cowl, but the authors have seen theses only on restored cars. It has been suggested that these may have been originally fitted on very early cars.

Observations indicate that chassis numbers 875026, 875109, 875166, 875407, 876052 and 876270 all had two Butler lights, 860084 had one Butler and one Lucas (perhaps the Lucas was a later replacement) and 860005 had two Lucas lights.

Jaguar International Magazine, March 1986, stated that early license plate light covers were black and marked Butler-Made in England, not Lucas. This is the only reference the authors have found to license plate lights being black and they have never seen any black ones. Perhaps a few very early cars left the factory with black license plate-light covers, in the same manner as the black headlight trim rings on the first few prototype cars.

This standard taillight lens reflector shows a pattern that is symmetrical, but different on either side of the vertical center line.

Taillight reflector on a 3.8-liter car with a distinctly different pattern.

This close-up view of the standard taillight reflector lens shows a dividing line down the center where the left and right patterns come together. This lens has been installed somewhat off-axis; the dividing line should be vertical.

This close-up view shows the unusual pattern of the alternate reflectors. Note the central dividing line is lacking here. Contrast this pattern to the standard pattern shown in other figures.

BACKUP LIGHT AND TRIM

There were at least two backup light configurations: mounted beneath the left bumper and mounted under the license plate in the center. The central mounting is the common, with the left mount and no light configurations appearing on only a few of the earliest cars. The change to the conventional centrally-mounted backup light took place very early on, during or just after the Experimental Department to Production Department transition after only a few cars were made. It is possible there were some Experimental Department cars with standard-sequence chassis numbers that had no backup light at all.

A backup light mounted on the left side of the license plate aperture is seen on the Geneva shows car, chassis number 885005, in *The Jaguar E-type: A Collector's Guide* and in *Motor magazine*, March 22, 1961. This car appears to have no backup light in some illustrations, but this may be due to the angle of the pictures.

On page 14 of *Jaguar E-Type 3.8 & 4.2 6-cylinder, 5.3 V12*, by Denis Jenkinson, the backup light is seen mounted in the center on a roadster (with body number 2892 crayoned on the license plate area). In the same source, on page 65, an early right-hand drive E-type, called chassis number 45, (so likely 850045) is shown in a current photograph with a centrally-mounted backup light. Left-hand drive roadster chassis number 875026 has a centrally-mounted backup light.

The lenses of the backup lights were initially marked LUCAS L595 along the top and MADE IN ENGLAND along the bottom. Later lenses, or perhaps just replacement lenses made at a later date, had these same markings along with additional markings: on the left was an "A" in a square box, with a mold ejector circle below and below that the number "7139." On the right was "SAE RP 70" oriented vertically. There may be variations in these later, additional, markings.

1 *A left-mounted backup light on coupe 885005. Only a few of the very early cars built by the Experimental Department had this feature.*

2 *Very early on in production the backup light was moved to a central position directly below the license plate and directly between the two exhaust pipes.*

3 *This close-up view of the early left-mounted backup light on prototype coupe 885004 shows the housing shape to be more truncated than those of the later cars. Only a very few cars were fitted with this light.*

4 *The later central-mounted backup light had a housing that was more tapered to the bodywork. This was the style used on almost all E-types. The screws retaining the chrome frame that holds the lens in place have cylindrical heads. The heads are chromed, and are of the slot-head style. These screws are typical of the backup lights. It appears that on some later and/or reproduction lenses there are more characters than shown on the early-type lenses.*

5 *The original early-type backup light lens.*

6 *A later backup light lens with additional markings. It is not certain if these were fitted to later cars, perhaps during the late 3.8-liter or 4.2-liter production period, or if they were made as replacement lenses after E-type production ceased.*

7 *A chromed cylindrical section slotted screw, with domed head, as used to retain the chrome surround holding the backup light lens in place. This is noted for its unusual character and because other types of screws are sometimes seen on restored cars; the authors are not aware of this part changing during E-type production.*

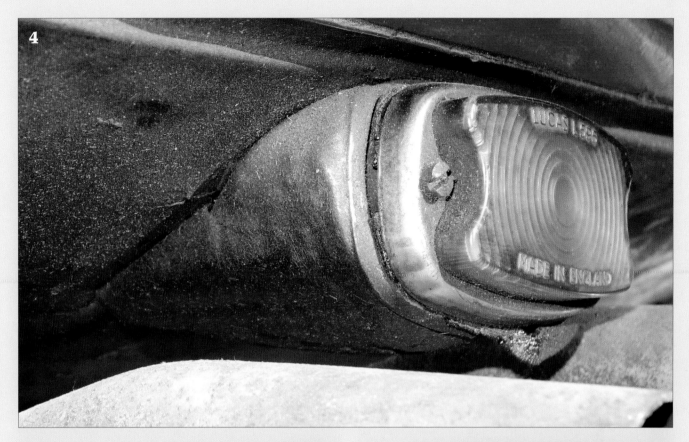

WIPER ARMS, BLADES AND WINDSCREEN SQUIRTER NOZZLES

The wiper arms on early cars came in two types: with two rivets showing on the outside of the lower part of the arm and without rivets.

About November 1963, the wiper arms were changed to carry longer blades at chassis numbers 861274/5, 880165/6 and 889134/5.

The original wiper blades were marked Aermic. A common replacement for these blades are the Rainbow blades.

The authors are not aware of any changes to the squirter nozzles.

Rivets, seen in the upper right-hand side of the picture, on an early wiper arm.

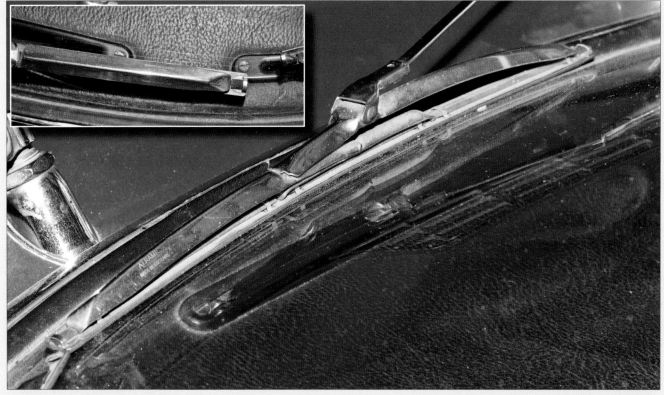

An Aermic wiper blade, as originally fitted to early 3.8-liter cars. INSET: This close-up of the end of an Aermic wiper blade shows some of the stamped-in markings.

BUMPERS

Some of the early cars appear in pictures without bumper overriders. For example, this is seen on coupe 885002 in *Classic and Sportscar*, April 1986 and in *Jaguar E-Type: The Definitive History*, where Porter states that the overriders were removed to enhance top speed. Bumpers without overriders were likely never a production configuration and aside from a few early examples, all production 3.8-liter E-types seem to have had the same bumper overriders.

However, the configuration without overriders may have been considered for the early cars. A rear bumper is illustrated this way in a line drawing in Jaguar handbook numbers E/122/1 and E/122/6.

An unusual front overrider is shown on a coupe, stated to be the "first one" (885001?) on page 21 of *The Jaguar E-type: A Collector's Guide*. A similar unusual large overrider is also shown on the right rear of an early coupe. These strange and asymmetric overriders are likely bumper protection experiments and bear no resemblance to overriders found on production cars.

T-KEY HOLE COVERS

A few early cars produced by the Experimental Department are pictured without T-key hole covers. Other than these few illustrations, it seems there were no production T-key hole cover changes. All evidence indicates the covers were of the pear shape as found on Mk V Jaguar sedan fender skirts and early Triumph TR boot lids.

The pear-shaped covers are marked on the back with "WB Birmingham" in a box, sometimes a heart symbol (a "kite mark") and a number M1121/X, where X represents a variable single digit. M1121 is likely the part number and the suffix is a mold or revision number. The authors have seen this last digit range from 2 to 6. M1121/2 appears on an original-looking cover from a 1950 Mk V sedan. A cover, believed to be an original from chassis number 875026, is marked M1121/4. Two NOS covers acquired in 1975 are marked M1121/6.

One cover from a Mk V Jaguar sedan is marked M1121/4, with the heart in a circle with some small letters, a small 1 and the WB symbol. Another is marked M1121/2, without the heart symbol, with a small 2 and with the WB symbol.

Various reproductions have been made of these covers. Some obtained in 1975 were cast in a brass-like material, instead of the original pot metal. They were chrome plated and looked like the originals, but the greater density of the brass caused the hinges to break. There were no markings inside these covers. In 1988 such reproduction

covers were purchased made of a material with a density similar to that of the original cover. These are marked on the inside with M1121/6, the WB symbol, a small 2 and two recessed holes about half the diameter of the four pushpin ejector holes. There is no heart symbol. Other

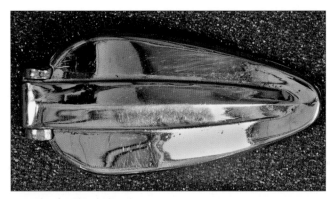

Outside of a T-key hole cover.

Inside of an M1121/4 T-key hole cover. Note the round and square markings and the four round ejector pin marks, typical of an original early "/4" cover. These appear to be the correct covers for E-types.

Inside view of a cover marked M1121/6 T-key hole cover, likely a reproduction. This cover has two additional small ejector-pin marks on either side of the center.

Inside view of another M1121/6 T-key hole cover, also likely a reproduction. Note that the four ejector-pin marks stick out further than on the other two covers shown. Also, the round marking is not present here.

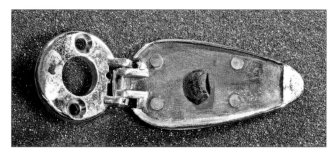

A reproduction cover without any inside markings. This is made of a low-density material similar to that of the originals. The black material is stuck on, possibly to hold the cover closed, since the spring is missing on this particular unit.

reproductions have been seen, cast in a material similar to the original, with no markings on the inside face.

The round-type T-key covers, such as found on XK-120 fender skirts, are sometimes used as replacements for the original pear-shaped covers, but it is unlikely such covers were ever fitted to production E-types at the factory.

The *J.30 Spare Parts Catalogue (June 1963)* reports that about September 1961, the bonnet latch and its escutcheon was discontinued on the transition to the inside bonnet latch design. This is the most obvious change of the many changes that took place at the end of the first 500 production at chassis numbers 850091/2 860004/5, 875385/6 and 885020/1.

VENT TRIM
ON REAR OF BONNET

There appear to be variants in the chrome vent grille at the center rear of the bonnet. Some later cars, perhaps late 3.8-liter cars, but more likely 4.2-liter or late 4.2-liter cars, have a sloped or angled rear face to this vent grille.

On the cover of *Car and Driver*, May 1961, the chrome trim was absent on an early or prototype car, but it is unlikely this reflects how any production cars were made.

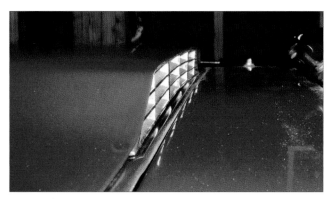

The rear face of both the bonnet center section and the chrome grille are seen here oriented in a vertical plane.

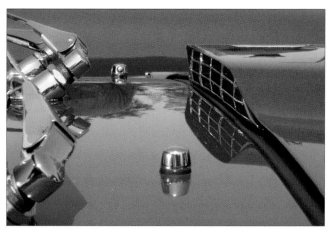

The rear face of this grille on a restored 3.8-liter car is bowed out toward the rear. These are often seen, but the authors have never seen such a grille on a 3.8-liter car known to be original.

The chrome grille on this restored early 3.8-liter car is not planar, with the top two of the three vertical sections canted forward. The authors are not sure if this type of grille was used on any later cars or not, but have never seen such a grille on a 3.8-liter car known to be original. The sloped termination of the center bonnet sheet metal also shows here.

DOOR HANDLES AND LOCKS

Holes are seen instead of door handles on illustrations of a few prototype cars, but this configuration likely does not reflect the state of any production cars. Other than these examples, the authors are not now aware of any door handle variations.

TOP DOOR TRIM
(ROADSTERS ONLY)

About October 1961, the chrome finisher at the top of the doors was changed, at chassis numbers 850087/8 and 875299/300.

The *Spare Parts Catalogue* notes that at chassis number 850506/7 and 877201/2 the chrome finisher at the top of the doors was changed. This occurred about May 1962 and some cars before these chassis numbers may have also been modified.

The chrome door top finisher came in at least two types; with a dip or depression running along the bottom lip and without this dip. Some early cars had no dip, then the parts with the dip were used and finally the finishers did not have a dip.

At chassis numbers 850856/7 and 881249/50, about April 1964, the chrome finishers on the top of the doors were changed. This point of change seems to the authors to be too late in production to represent the cessation of the dip running along the bottom of the finisher. If it is not this, then the exact nature of the chrome finisher reported at these chassis numbers is unclear.

The depression running along the bottom edge of this door top trim strip was a feature of some of the early cars.

A door top trim strip without the depression running along the bottom.

The roadster door trim finishers came in two shapes as well. Here two are contrasted by being set on top of each other with pieces of paper to show the edges. This illustrates the thinner section on top.

CONVERTIBLE TOP TRIM

The chrome trim strip that runs around the rear of the convertible top (where it is tacked to the rear of the cockpit) has a lip running along it on some early cars. The early-type strip was used on chassis number 875109, but by 875954 it was replaced with the later type.

This lip was likely used to help retain the convertible top cover and the four hooks seen on some later cars were introduced as an alternate to the lip when it was removed. These hooks are mentioned in the factory *J.30 Spare Parts Catalogue (June 1963)*, but with no cutoff serial numbers, as if they were on all 3.8-liter E-types.

These hooks were present on chassis number 876577. However, they appear to be absent in all early 3.8-liter roadster photos the authors have reviewed, but are typically found on later cars. This part, referred to as a "hook plate," carries Jaguar part number is BD.20658 and is listed on page 209 of the *J.30 Spare Parts Catalogue (June 1963)* and no changes are indicated there.

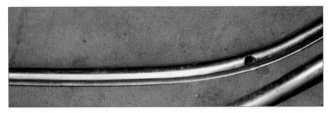

This early convertible top chrome strip shows the lip running along the bottom. This lip presumably played a role in the retention of the convertible top cover, as the four hooks found on later cars to retain the cover were absent on the earlier cars.

Another view of an early convertible top strip, this one in-situ.

A later convertible top chrome strip without a lip. The convertible top cover retaining hooks are typically found fitted under these strips to help retain the top cover when the top was stowed.

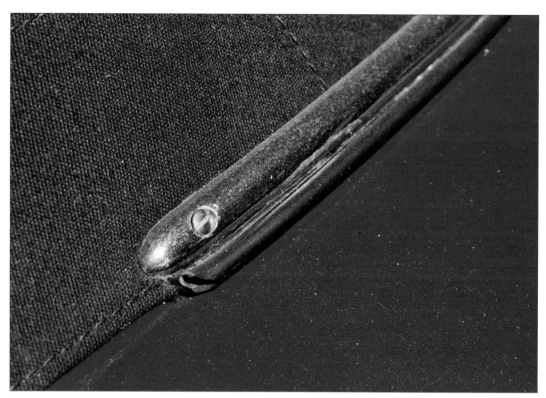

OUTSIDE MARKINGS AND DECORATIVE TRIM

The outside markings on all production 3.8-liter cars were the horizontal grille bar in the front aperture (with the image of the forward-facing Jaguar head but no characters), the chrome "JAGUAR" badge on the boot lid and the recessed "JAGUAR" markings on the four knock-off hubcaps. These comprise the full outside markings of the 3.8-liter cars.

The chrome finishers on the roof gutters were changed. This was part of the extensive rework of the coupes that took place at chassis numbers 860478/9 and 886013/4.

Roadster chassis number 876577 had only a JAGUAR badge on the boot lid, 879325 and 887129 had JAGUAR and E-TYPE badges on their boot lids and 879093 had JAGUAR, E-TYPE and 3.8 badges on its boot lid. These observations were made many years ago and in one instance, 879325, when the car was six years old when the observation was made. Of course, these may be cases of badges added after the cars left the dealership. *Jaguar E-Type: The Definitive History* reports that about June

1963, "various new items" of boot lid trim were added at chassis numbers 861178/9 and 888658/9. It is not clear if this is alluding to the E-TYPE badge and perhaps a 3.8 plate, that may have appeared on some later 3.8-liter cars. The authors have seen no hard evidence that any 3.8-liter cars left the factory with other than just a JAGUAR badge on the boot lid.

Additional pieces of windscreen-pillar outside chrome trim were added at chassis numbers 850734/5, 861218/9, 879680/1 and 888885/6, about August 1963.

About May 1964, the grille bar mounts were changed to incorporate a rubber mount at chassis numbers 850882/3, 861661/2, 881437/8 and 890487/8.

At chassis numbers 850888/9 and 881590/1, about August 1964, the chrome finishers at the sides of the windscreen were changed.

The form of the "JAGUAR" badge on the boot was different on the early verses the late 3.8-liter cars. The

The top surface of this JAGUAR badge from the boot lid of early left-hand drive roadster chassis number 875026 has a relatively flat surface with somewhat sharp corners, as appears to be typical for the labels on early cars.

Partial side view of the same early badge showing the flat top surface and relatively sharp edges.

Top view of a later JAGUAR badge with rounded-top letters. The change to this type came early on in E-type production.

Partial side view of a later JAGUAR badge showing the rounded edges to the letters.

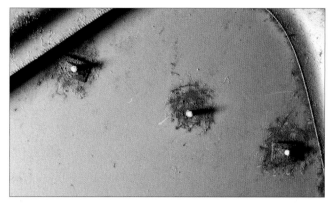

The steel clips used to retain the JAGUAR label to the boot lid. This is an inside view of a roadster boot lid. The central clip is missing.

earlier characters were somewhat sharp-edged and flat on the top, while the later letters were more rounded. This is cited and illustrated, for example, by Howe in a June 21, 2014 posting on the etypeuk.com forum. Incidentally, in his post he cites Joseph Fray of 36 Albion Street, Birmingham, likely as the manufacturer of these boot lid labels.

WINDSCREEN AND PILLARS

On early cars, a hard rubber pad was screwed to the top of the L-post. This is found on cars at least as late as chassis number 875235, but seems to be gone at least by 876577.

On early cars, a chrome strap went over the interface between the chrome trim on the L-post and the early-type wide chrome strip running along the bottom of the windscreen. Later, the strap was omitted, the chrome strip along the bottom of the windscreen was made narrower, and the windscreen pillar trim was given a pointed tip. Roadster chassis numbers 875026 and 875109 had the wide trim and the rectangular chrome strap, 876577 had the narrow trim and no strap.

Jenkinson's book shows a car (with the early multi-piece throttle linkage), with a pointed L-post chrome trim and no strap. This throttle linkage was discontinued at engine numbers R2933/4, so the pointed L-post trim likely came in before this.

The trim strip along the bottom of the windscreen is missing altogether in illustrations of numerous early Experimental Department cars, at least one of which was chassis number 850002.

About September 1961, the chrome finisher on the windscreen glass was changed. It is likely this note is referring to the point at which the removal strap between the windscreen chrome strip and the L-post was removed, and the windscreen chrome strip went to the narrower type. This change is listed to have occurred at chassis numbers 850087/8 and 875309/10.

The L-post trim was changed again late in 3.8-liter production to a type with a bulge along the bottom, in the fashion of 4.2-liter L-post trim. At chassis numbers 850888/9 and 881590/1, about August 1964, the chrome finishers at the sides of the windscreen were changed. This may be referring to the inclusion of the bulge in the L-post trim.

About August 1963, more windscreen-pillar outside chrome trim was added (two more pieces). This is stated to have occurred at chassis numbers 850734/5, 861218/9, 879680/1 and 888885/6.

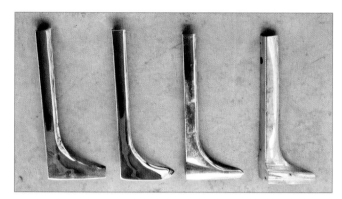

Windscreen pillar trim pieces extending through to the V-12 Series 3 cars. On the left is the trim from a roadster with chassis number earlier than the 850087/8 (Right-hand drive) or 875309/10 (Left-hand drive) transition, showing the truncated end upon which the chrome strap attaches. The second from the left is a later 3.8-liter type trim with pointed end not incorporating a chrome strap. A chrome L-post trim from a Series 1 4.2-liter roadster follows, and on the far right is the trim from a V-12 roadster. These latter two show ever-pronounced indentations along the bottom, with the V-12 cars showing the most pronounced bulge.

The upper strip here is from coupe 885008 and shows the very pointed leading edge. The lower one is from a later car and is rounded. From the author's observations, it appears that the edge continued to become more rounded throughout six-cylinder car production.

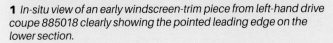

1 In-situ view of an early windscreen-trim piece from left-hand drive coupe 885018 clearly showing the pointed leading edge on the lower section.

2 The upper leading edge of the windscreen pillar trim piece on 885018 also shows a pointed termination. Later this evolved into a rounded termination. The screw retaining the end of the trim piece is not original.

3 Early (left) and later (right) roadster windscreen-pillar chrome trim caps. The early unit on the left has a short section to receive the end of the top windscreen trim piece and a small hole to retain the rubber pad attached to the top of the cap. On the right is a later cap with a continuation of the boss receiving the top trim piece and no hole. These caps did not have rubber pads. Very early roadsters may not have had rubber pads and may have had caps of the early type, but

without the small hole. No changes are listed in the J.30 Spare Parts Catalogue (June 1963) for this part.

4 In-situ view of an early top cap on roadster 875122.

5 The small, rectangular chrome strap characterizes the early three-piece L-post trim. The chrome strip running along the lower front of the windscreen is thicker than on later cars with the two-piece trim. The small screw at the bottom of the strap is not original and was likely put in later to help retain the clip.

6 This is the second type of the two-piece L-post trim. The L-post chrome trim comes to a pointed termination, while on the earlier cars the strap was used to cover a blunt end. The lower windscreen trim strip is now narrower.

SIDE WINDOWS, TRIM, FRAMES, WINDING MECHANISMS AND SEALING RUBBER

Some early Experimental Department roadsters did not have the chrome channel guide at the front of the window aperture to guide the window as it is cranked up. On page 37 of *All About the Jaguar E-Type* cars 875002 and 875003 appear to not have the channel in what look like period photographs, but the pictures are not definitive. On pages 161, 164, 166 of *All About the Jaguar E-Type* 850003 (77 RW) is shown with the channel in a non-period photo of the unrestored car. The period photo on page 168 shows the guide to be present. However, on page 119 of *Jaguar E-Type: The Definitive History* a period picture of 850003 shows a door without a guide. Perhaps the car was updated at some point. These September 1961 issue of *Road & Track* shows a left-hand drive roadster, apparently without the

The late 3.8-liter roadsters had a bulge along the bottom of the L-post trim. This served to integrate it with the chrome trim along the top of the roadster doors. This trim is on a 4.2-liter roadster, but is representative of the late 3.8-liter trim.

Very early cars had a black rubber cap screwed on the top of the windscreen post.

channel guide (this car has a left side backup light as well). On page 176 of *Jaguar E-Type: The Definitive History,* a right-hand drive roadster with U.K. license plate 1600 RW is shown possibly with the guides (on page 38 of *All About the Jaguar E-Type* it states that 1600 RW is chassis number 850004).

Several changes are listed in the literature. In about October 1961, the sealing rubber around the windows was changed at chassis numbers 850091/2 and 875373/4. The frame for the door window was changed and the rubber seal and the seal retainer for the cantrail was changed (part of the extensive rework of the coupes that took place at chassis numbers 860478/9 and 886013/4). The casing assembly below the quarter lights and the quarter lights were changed, about August 1963, at chassis numbers 861098/9 and 888301/2.

At chassis numbers 861098/9 and 888301/2, the shut pillar was changed. In November 1963, the A-post rubber seals were changed: on the roadsters the two-piece seal was replaced by a one-piece seal and on the coupes the separate cantrail seal and A-post seals were replaced by a single seal (the seal retainer on the cantrails on the coupes was no longer required after this change), at chassis numbers 850766/7, 861294/5, 880212/3 and 889235/6. The sealing rubber on the door shut pillar was changed about November 1963 at chassis numbers 850778/9, 861341/2, 880458/9 and 889374/5 and that about April 1964 the rubber seals were improved (not clear which ones) at chassis numbers 850842/3, 861556/7, 881260/1, 890250/1 and a few earlier cars.

WING VENTS
(COUPES ONLY)

The wing vent clasps on the copes came in several types. Early clasps were similar to the sort found on the rear windows of Mk 2 sedans. The later clasps were of the basic design found on subsequent 3.8-liter E-types.

Listed changes to the clasps in the literature are:

▸ About March 1962 the glass and clasps for the rear quarter lights were changed (the mounting for the attachment block for the catch arm to the quarter light frame was changed from brazed to screwed) at chassis numbers 860194/5 and 885584/5;

▸ About May 1962 the glass, hinge and the catch for the quarter light were changed as part of the extensive rework of the coupes that took place at chassis numbers 860478/9 and 886013/4;

▸ The catch operating the quarter lights was changed again at chassis numbers 861098/9 and 888301/2.

Chassis number changes: at 860194/5 and 885584/5, the brazed mount (obviating the need for mounting holes) was changed to screwed on (which needed two holes per side). It is likely that at this point the knob was changed from a conical shape to a flat shape, at 860478/9 and 886013/4. This is part of extensive coupe changes at these numbers. The shapes of both rear sidelights changed, from a smaller window to a larger one (likely taller); and at 861098/9 and 888301/2 this may be the point at which the clasp got longer, permitting the window to open wider.

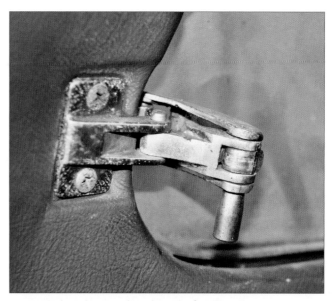

A rear-window clasp used on about the first 500 coupes.

The earliest brazed-on clasp. Note the central hinge pin ends are flush with the edges of the outer shell of the clasp.

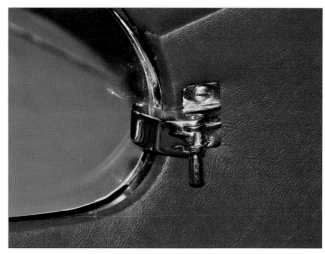

A rear-window clasp of the early type in the closed position. This is restored coupe 885008.

This later-type clasp is affixed to the quarter light by two conical-head slotted screws. The central pivot extends into a knob on one side to facilitate operation of the clasp.

A late-type 3.8-liter rear window clasp. This is the third-type clasp that permitted a wider opening of the rear window. This can be seen by noting the longer extent of the right-most pivot in this picture, in contrast to those in pictures on page 59 of earlier hinges.

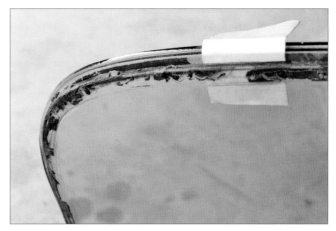

A later-type 3.8-liter coupe rear-window clasp is shown on the top and an early style on the bottom. The longer extent of the later-type clasp is evident. This permits a wider opening of the rear window. Another style of clasp, similar to the top later hinge but shorter, was used in between the two styles shown here.

REAR WINDOW

The rear defroster was available as of April 1962.

About June 1962, the glass in the boot lid (clear or Sundym), and the chrome finisher at the top of the rubber seal for the rear windows were changed at chassis numbers 860478/9 and 886013/4. In *The Jaguar E-type: A Collector's Guide*, Skilleter cites this change with chassis numbers 860475/6 given instead of 860478/9. This is likely part of the extensive rework of the coupes that took place at these chassis numbers.

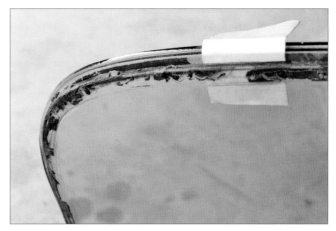

The rear-window glass that changed when the extensive coupe rework occurred. The early glass, with lower shoulders, is in the front, and the later glass is behind. The paper is inserted between the two pieces of glass to show the edge of the front glass.

FRONT LICENSE PLATE MOUNT

On home-market (British) cars, the front number plate was applied directly to the front of the bonnet, while at least two arrangements were used for mounting the front license plate on U.S. market cars. On the early cars, two small chromed-steel straps were screwed to the bottom of the air intake aperture. The tops of these

Front license plate mounts appear to have been an afterthought on the early U.S.-market cars. The tops of these two straps are bent around the lower edge of the air intake aperture and the bottoms are retained by sheet metal screws.

straps were bent over and folded around the lower lip of the aperture. These straps may have been made of stainless steel.

Later these straps were replaced by a mount incorporating a pivoting arrangement with a connecting rod, connected to the front subframe. When the bonnet was raised, this pivoted the license plate upward and kept it from hitting the ground. It is interesting to note that sometime after the introduction of this pivoting mechanism, cars not fitted with a front license plate mount had the same oval connecting rod hole in the sheet metal beneath the air intake aperture.

Close-up of the screw attachment of the strap-type mount. Note the screw is similar in shape to the flat-topped slot-head screws used on the heater box. Note also the round hole in the bonnet under panel as typically seen on early cars.

A view of the underside of the early strap-type mount showing the sheet metal screw mounting system.

From research of surviving cars: Chassis numbers 875026 and 875109 had the strap mounts, 860084 had no straps but an oval connecting rod hole and 876577, 879325 and 889076 had the tilting mount.

About October 1961, a new plastic license plate holder was introduced at chassis numbers 850078/9. It is not clear exactly what this is referring to.

Once the pivoting front license plate mechanism was introduced for the U.S.-market cars, the connecting rod hole in the lower part of the bonnet was apparently standardized for all production, even right-hand drive cars without any front license plate mount.

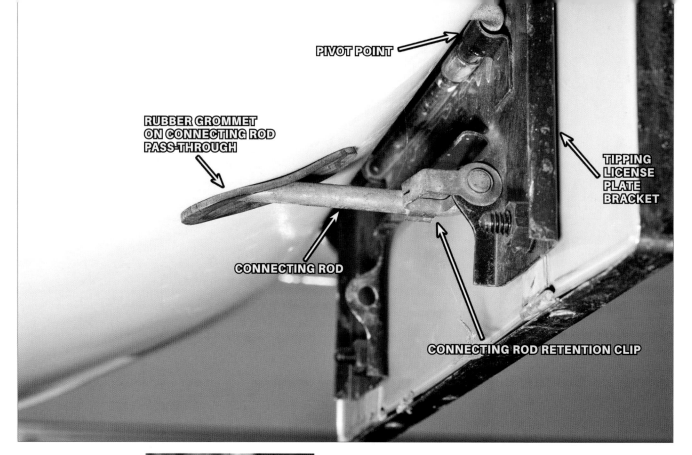

PIVOT POINT

RUBBER GROMMET ON CONNECTING ROD PASS-THROUGH

TIPPING LICENSE PLATE BRACKET

CONNECTING ROD

CONNECTING ROD RETENTION CLIP

YOKE

BOSS

The front bar of the front subframe from left-hand drive roadster 876163 shows the license plate tipping mechanism boss brazed on the top. The yoke is in place in this picture on the boss, held in place with a pin. A small cut-off section of the connecting rod is protruding from the yoke, and the locknut on the connecting rod is evident.

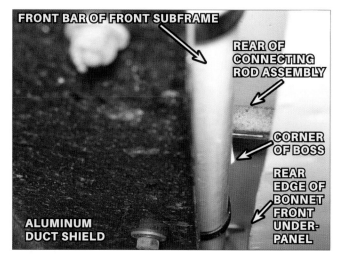

FRONT BAR OF FRONT SUBFRAME

REAR OF CONNECTING ROD ASSEMBLY

CORNER OF BOSS

REAR EDGE OF BONNET FRONT UNDER-PANEL

ALUMINUM DUCT SHIELD

TOP: On later U.S.-market cars, a pivoting front license plate mount was used to prevent fouling of the plate on the ground when the bonnet was opened. The mechanism on left-hand drive roadster chassis number 879032, a very original car, has the rubber grommet around the edge of the connecting rod pass-through hole in the bonnet under panel assembly. The connecting rod can be seen here passing through the hole and attaching to the tipping license plate bracket with the connecting rod retention clip. This clip is similar or identical to the clips securing the S.U. HD8 carburetor control rods to the levers on the slave shaft and carburetor throttle shafts. The license plate bracket pivot point is seen at the top.

ABOVE: The attachment point of the rear of the connecting rod assembly on the front bar of the front subframe. The yoke at the rear end of the connecting rod is seen in the center right of the picture, just behind the rear edge of the bonnet front under-panel and the front bar of the front subframe. The yoke is attached to a boss brazed to the front bar of the front subframe. The black aluminum duct shield is on the left side of the picture, attached by straps to the front bar of the front subframe. The duct shield is painted black here, rather than the body color painting typically seen. This is likely to be the original paint, so may represent a change in color of the shield on later cars from body color to black.

INTERIOR: INSTRUMENTS AND CONTROLS

SPEEDOMETER

The speedometers came in different types to accommodate the different rear axle-ratios available on the E-type. The different versions were marked on the face. Speedometers were supplied calibrated in miles per hour or kilometers per hour, depending upon the market of the car.

See additional information on speedometers in Chapter Six.

A later-type NOS speedometer showing the green bulb filters. Note the covers for the light, drive and reset cable openings still installed for protection during shipping and storage.

The speedometers carried numbers "SN 6322/XX" where "XX" was two digits, 00, 01, 02, etc., denoting the calibration of the speedometer (MPH or KPH) and the rear axle ratio (3:31, 3:54, etc.). The relationships are given on page 284 of the J.30 Spare Parts Catalogue (June 1963).

The sticker found on speedometers when supplied from the factory. Here the sticker is seen on an NOS sedan speedometer, as seen by the 140 MPH limit, as opposed to the 160 MPH limit on an E-type. Also the third warning light for low fuel is not present in the bottom center, as on E-types.

This early speedometer shows the blue bulb filters of E-types up to about 1966. Later, the color was changed to green.

This speedometer calibrated in miles per hour was standard for cars going to countries using the English system.

Speedometers calibrated in kilometers per hour were standard for cars going to continental Europe and other countries using the metric system.

The early tachometers were marked "RV 7403/02."

TACHOMETER

At least two types of tachometers were fitted. The early were marked "RV7402/02" and the later "RV7413/03." This change occurred at 850288/9, 876116/7, 860028/9 and 885205/6, as noted on page 285 of the *J.30 Spare Parts Catalogue (June 1963)*.

About February 1962, at chassis numbers 850288/9, 860028/9, 876116/7 and 885205/6, the tachometer was changed.

At chassis numbers 850701/2, 861168/9, 879323/4; and 888542/3, about November 1963, the clock in the tachometer was changed to one fitted with a rectifier. The clock dial is marked CE.1111/01 (except for a few early ones that were marked CE.1111/00 in error). A black sleeve indicates that the clock is fitted with a rectifier.

Somewhat later tachometers were marked "RV 7413/03."

SECONDARY INSTRUMENTS

Three of the secondary instruments, water temperature, oil pressure and fuel level have small white markings printed on their faces, likely part of model numbers. These are hidden from normal view by being recessed behind the lip of the face piece, or hood, in front of the back plate. Some of these markings are shown here.

Likely all 3.8-liter E-types were fitted with fuel gauges marked "BF2200/01." This marking has been seen on both the left and right side of the gauges. It appears most earlier cars had the marking on the left.

1 It appears likely all 3.8-liter E-types were fitted with BT2200/00 water gauges.

2 Earlier oil pressure gauges were marked "PE2300/01."

3 Later oil pressure gauges were marked "PE2300/02."

4 "BF2200/01" marked on the left of a fuel gauge.

5 "BF2200/01" marked on the right of a fuel gauge.

A fuel gauge marked "BF 2200/02."

A fuel gauge marked "BF 2200/10."

The authors have not observed any part numbers on the faces of ammeters.

Two fuel gauge variants; the one on the left has no "3/4" marking, while the one on the right does. Generally, the authors have not seen "3/4" marking on 3.8-liter fuel gauges, but more research is needed to see if and when it may have appeared. 875026, 875045, 875109, 875122, 875130, 875157, 875206, 875258, 875274, 875954, 876163, 876319, 876577, 876602, 877102, 879032, 879152, 879406, 879725, 1E32437 do not have the 3/4, but 1E17271, 1E75436BW, 1R27925, 2R13987, 1S20001 (a Series 3 V12) do. Some of these cars were restored, but it does appear that the "3/4" marking came about during 4.2-liter production.

SWITCHES AND CONTROLS

The May 1961 issue of *Road & Track* stated that "The fan, of course, has its own switch on the instrument panel." The authors have never seen such a manual control switch either in illustrations or on cars, and this is the only reference to it of which they are aware. An automatic thermostatic switch was used and is discussed from pages 215 to 217.

In about August 1963, the turn signal/headlight-flasher switch was changed at chassis numbers 850725/6, 861197/8, 879550/1 and 888766/7; about August 1963, the turn signal/headlight-flasher switch striker plate was changed at chassis numbers 850725/6, 861197/8, 879550/1 and 888766/7; about March 1964, the turn signal/headlight-flasher switch clamp bracket was changed from being a part of the switch to being part of the steering column at chassis numbers 850810/1, 861460/1, 880870/1 and 889819/20; and about May 1964, the striker for the turn signal/headlight-flasher switch was changed at chassis numbers 850858/9, 861604/5, 881281/2 and 890317/8.

The very early brake warning lights had red plastic lenses. Note that the lens here has been melted and distorted by the heat of the warning lamp bulb. This is typical of these early lenses and is likely why they were later replaced with glass lenses.

INDICATOR LIGHTS

It is likely that a few of the early cars were fitted with a reverse-engagement light on the dash above the heater controls.

A light above the heater controls is seen in various illustrations of early prototype coupe interiors. In the late 1960s or early 1970s, an early roadster was observed with a clear-lens light in this location that lit up when reverse was engaged. The chassis number was not recorded and no other one has been observed by the authors, but this was likely a reverse-engagement warning light as illustrated in the early pictures.

Some early brake-warning light lenses were red plastic and would melt when the bulb was left on for a long time. These lenses were later replaced with glass lenses.

From research of surviving cars: Chassis numbers 875026 and 875109 had the plastic lenses and 875954, 875958 and 876052 had the glass lenses.

A later brake warning light with the red glass lens. This lens could stand up to the heat of the bulb.

CIGAR LIGHTER

The cigar lighter came in basically two types. The early type is of the sort generally seen in Jaguars manufactured in the 1950s, with an all-plastic handle section, as opposed to the later plastic handle with a conical metal collar, as seen on the later lighters. The later, multi-piece unit is of a smaller diameter than the early unit. The early and late lighters are not interchangeable in the sockets.

The *Spare Parts Catalogue* indicates that at chassis numbers 850168/9, 860009/10, 875589/90 and 885050/1, in late fall or early winter of 1961, the cigar lighter was changed. The nature of the change was not specified. Then at the transition from outside to inside bonnet latches, at chassis numbers 850091/2, 860004/5, 875385/6 and 885020/1, earth cables were added for the cigar lighter.

The later, small-diameter cigar lighter. The early and late lighters are not interchangeable in their sockets.

The early, large diameter cigar lighter.

IGNITION SWITCH AND KEY

A single key was used for the ignition and the door locks and it was changed late in 3.8-liter production. Both early and late keys are made by Wilmot-Breeden, but the early type is the round-headed FS, while the late type is the square-headed FP. The three numeric digits following the alphabetic prefix apparently represent the key pattern.

About March 1962, a cable for the steering column lock connector to the instrument panel wiring was introduced along with the combined ignition switch-steering column lock for cars going to Germany. This occurred at chassis numbers 876664/5 and 885566/7. Changes at chassis numbers 850587/8, 860862/3, 878036/7 and 886753/4 (and 876665-878036 and 885567-886753 for Germany only): the lock and ignition switch assembly on the steering column was changed from Neiman to Waso Werken and a cable was introduced to connect the steering column lock connector to the instrument panel wiring.

Opposite side of the round-headed Wilmot-Breeden FP-type key.

The square-headed Wilmot-Breeden FS-type key was used on later cars.

The round-headed Wilmot-Breeden FP-type key was used on the early cars.

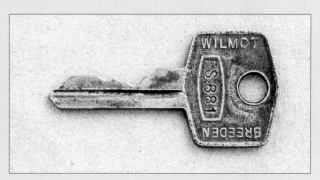

Opposite side of the square-headed Wilmot-Breeden FS-type key.

GRAB HANDLE

At chassis numbers 850708/9, 861174/5, 879342/3 and 888566/7, about May 1963, the grab handle and its fixings were changed and its position was slightly changed.

It is noted on page 20 of *All About the Jaguar E-type* that a "chrome plated grab handle is unique to early show and press cars." This would not, then, likely apply to any production cars. The authors have never seen such a grab handle.

STEERING WHEEL AND COLUMN

On the early cars, the steering wheels were round in cross-section, lacking the scooped-out thumb trough and with exposed aluminum on the inner circumference. The

authors are not aware of any deviations from this design in the early cars. Later cars had a steering wheel with a scooped-out thumb trough running around the inner front of the wood ring and with no aluminum showing on the wood section. The cross-section of the early wheel is much fatter than that on the later wheels.

From research of surviving cars: chassis numbers 875954, 875958, 876289, 876577 and 885733 had the fat cross-section wheel and 879325 and 887576 have the scooped-out wheel.

About March 1962 at chassis numbers 876664/5 and 885566/7, a cable for the steering column lock connector to the instrument panel wiring was introduced (for Germany only). This was the introduction of the combined ignition switch-steering column lock for cars going to Germany.

There were several changes in the steering column at chassis numbers:

- 850547/8, 860646/7, 877487/8 and 886213/4, about June 1962, the lower tubular-shaft steering column was changed to a one piece forging and the seal where the shaft passes through the dash was changed;

- 850587/8, 860862/3, 878036/7 and 886753/4 (876665-878036 and 885567-886753 for Germany only), about October 1962, the upper-steering column assembly was changed and felt bearings were replaced with Vulkollan polymer bearings;

- 850587/8, 860862/3, 878036/7 and 886753/4 (876665-878036 and 885567-886753 for Germany only), the lock and ignition switch assembly on the steering column were changed from Neiman to Waso Werken.

- 850810/1, 861460/1, 880870/1 and 889819/20, about March 1964, the turn signal/headlight-flasher switch clamp bracket was changed from being a part of the switch to being part of the steering column;

- 850818/9, 861480/1, 880982/3 and 889966/7, about April 1964, the upper steering column bearings were changed from Vulkollan to Elastollan.

The authors have seen E-types, up to an 877 prefix on the left-hand drive roadsters, with steering wheels with the structural aluminum exposed on the inner circumference of the wheel. Thus, these early wheels were used for sometime. The cross-section of the wheel was circular. The authors are not aware of any variations in this design while it was in use in the early cars.

Later steering wheels had a thumb groove cut in the wood and the aluminum support ring was completely embedded in the wood. The cross-section of the early wheel is much fatter than that on these later wheels. A steering wheel from a 4.2-liter car is shown here, but is representative of the later 3.8-liter style wheels.

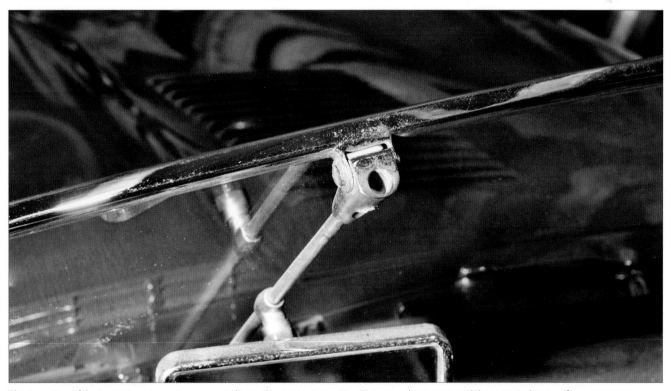

Front view of the locking steering column, as fitted to 3.8-liter German market cars.

Rear view of the 3.8-liter locking steering column.

PEDALS

The clutch pedal was changed at chassis numbers 850232/3, 860020/1, 875858/9 and 885104/5. At chassis numbers 850474/5 and 860374/5 (except 860365), about May 1962, the accelerator pedal assembly was changed, apparently to facilitate heel-and-toe operation.

About May 1962, the brake power lever and pedals were changed, apparently to increase the mechanical advantage, at chassis numbers 850474/5, 860374/5, 876998/9 and 885870/1 (except 860365).

At chassis numbers 850807/8, 861445/6, 880834/5 and 889779/80, in about March 1964, the brake pedals were changed to improve attachment to the pedal shaft and a tab washer was added to the pinch bolt.

MIRROR AND MOUNTS

The upper retainer for the roadster rearview mirror mounting rod on some early cars had an extra plate, or spacer, screwed to it. Later cars had a single piece.

This early plate appears on the car with chassis number 875026 but not on 875109. It is a small detail and does not show up well in photographs, so it is difficult to find evidence of it in any references.

About February 1963, the interior mirror assembly was changed at chassis numbers 861056/7 and 888066/7.

This top view of the two-piece top mirror mount shows the spacer's position between the mount and the top windscreen frame.

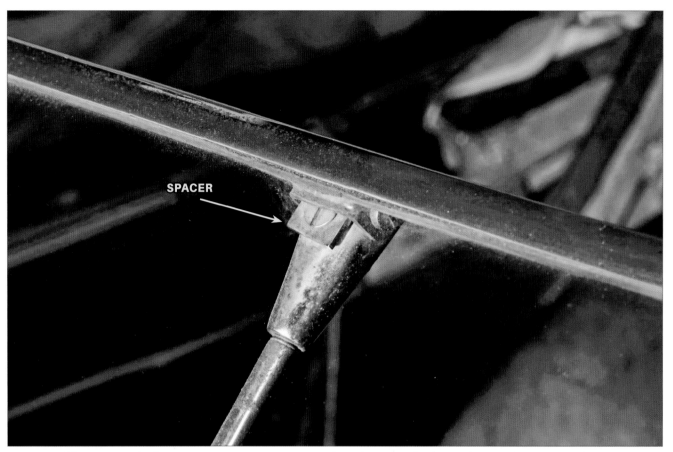

Front view of the top mount for the rear view mirror mount on a very early roadster. Note the chromed spacer plate screwed in between the mount and the windscreen.

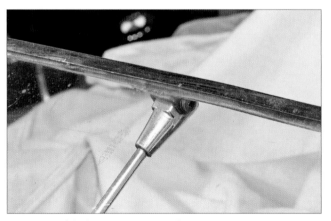

Front view of the later one-piece roadster mirror rod mount.

This one-piece roadster mirror rod mount was introduced early in production and is typical of most roadsters. Note that the thick section is wider than on the early mount.

INTERIOR LIGHTS

The screw for the interior light was changed at chassis numbers 860478/9 and 886013/4.

HANDBRAKE LEVER

The authors are not aware of any design changes to the handbrake lever.

DASH TOP

The early cars had dash tops that were much thinner than those on later cars. It is not clear how long this was continued.

From research of surviving cars: Chassis numbers 875958 and 876052 had the flat dash top, while 879325 had the fat dash top.

The early cars had this flat dash top.

The fat dash top of the later cars.

DEFROSTER DUCTS

The plenums supplying the defrost vents, or ducts, on the padded dashboard (the screen rail fascia assembly) varied during 3.8-liter E-type production. The earliest configuration used three plenums to feed all the vents; two long plenums on the ends and a short one in the middle. These plenums were typically made of two halves, stapled together and retained on the dash top by metal tabs spot-welded onto the dash top frame. It appears the earliest plenums were white plastic, while early on this was changed to black. In some cases, they were attached to the corrugated flexible delivery hoses with black tape. For example, illustrations of right-hand roadster 850003 (page 178, *All About the Jaguar E-Type*) showed white plastic plenums and the tape. Left-hand roadster 875026 has white plastic plenums as well. There may have been exceptions and overlap to the various types of plenums.

The later configuration was to use five plenums of similar size, one for each vent. The authors have only seen these later plenums in black plastic. These units have always been observed as two halves joined together by plastic

welding and without staples. They are retained in the metal frame of the dash top by being inserted from the top side and held in place by a flange; there are no spot-welded metal tabs retaining them.

See additional information on the grills used over these plenums in Chapter Six, *Features Relating to Both 3.8-Liter and 4.2-Liter Cars*.

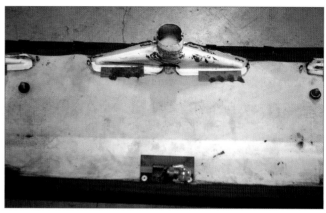

An early white plenum clearly shows the staples and the spot-welded on brackets that hold the early plenums in place. Later plenums are passed through the steel dash frame and do not need these retaining brackets.

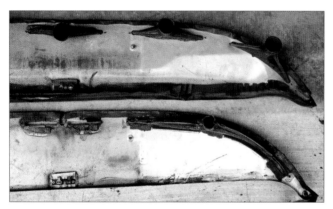

Late and earlier-type dash tops. On the top of the illustration is a later-type dash top with five defroster plenums (from a 1966 4.2-liter coupe, but representative of the later 3.8-liter type) and on the bottom is an earlier-type top with three plenums.

This later black heater plenum is held in place by a molded-in flange located on the other side of the insertion hole in the metal dash top frame. A bit of this flange can be seen sticking out of the hole (by mistake during assembly) on the left-hand side of the plenum.

A close-up view of an earlier plenum molded in white shows the staples used to hold the two halves of the early plenums together. Staples have been observed on both the early black and early white plenums, although they are much more prominent on the white plenums.

DASH MATERIALS AND TRIM

There are several variations in the dash trim materials used both for the center dash and the two outer sections.

The earliest standard for the center of the dash was the aluminum trim with a dot pattern etched on it. Around the 1963 model year, the patterning on the aluminum trim was changed to a stamped-in, or embossed, cross pattern. The final version of the trim on the instrument center section was not aluminum, but black vinyl, as used on the rest of the dash.

At chassis numbers 850609/10, 860912/3, 878301/2 and 887131/2, about October 1962, the pattern embossed on the aluminum trim used on the instrument panel was changed. This is very likely the change from the etched dot pattern to the embossed cross pattern.

What is apparently one of the early Experimental Department cars may have had black center trim, in the manner of a Mk 2 sedan. In *Car and Driver*, May 1961, a very early roadster is shown with black center trim, as opposed to the usual etched dot pattern aluminum trim. This car is pictured in many places in the magazine and, also judging from *Jaguar E-Type: The Definitive History*, it appears to be chassis number 850002. It is not clear from these pictures whether the center section is painted black, or trimmed in black material.

The leather trim appears to have come in on the lower part of the console before the aluminum trim was replaced on the front part of the console and the center section of the dash.

At chassis numbers 850751/2, 861253/4, 879802/3 and 889029/30, about September 1963, the front finisher panel was changed from embossed cross pattern aluminum to black trimming.

There were variations to the vinyl trim used on the outer two sections of the dash. A relatively-flat and porous pattern has been seen on left-hand drive roadster 875026. It is quite different from the usual wrinkled pattern seen on most cars. The authors are not sure how many other early cars (if any) had this same pattern, but some pictures in the literature of Experimental Department cars show a high degree of reflectivity on their dash coatings suggestive of this relatively-flat material.

A view of the porous textured dash covering material on a very early car. This may not have been standard on all early cars.

The typical wrinkled textured dash covering material as found on later cars.

With the possible exception of a few Experimental Department cars, the early 3.8-liter E-types had this aluminum trim with a dot pattern etched on it used to trim the central instrument panel and the top of the console. Note the very flat tops of the circular dot regions and the rough surface in between them. It appears this surface was generated by mask-printing the circles and etching. In any case, all original etched dot pattern aluminum trim the authors have observed have this sort of finish.

Later on in production (about model year 1963), this cross pattern aluminum trim was used. The aluminum is raised up on the edges of these elongated indentations, suggesting they were created by embossing. Based on the authors observations, this pattern remained in use until model year 1964 when the lower console was covered in leather and the central instrument cluster was trimmed in the same black polymeric material used on the rest of the dash.

There were additional dash trim changes. On the later cars, a curved, chrome trim piece was at each end of the dash, where it joined the L-post trim.

Another change was the addition of chrome mounts on the grab handle.

The last style of center dash trim used on the 3.8-liter cars was black vinyl, as used on the Series 1 4.2-liters.

This view of a later dash shows the chrome trim used at the L-posts and the later-type chrome grab-bar mounts. This picture is from a 4.2-liter car, but is the same configuration as the late 3.8-liter cars.

LEFT: This is a view of dot pattern aluminum trim commonly seen in recent years on restored cars. This is likely a reproduction material. Differences between this material and the earlier dot pattern aluminum trim shown in the other pictures in this section are that the circular dot regions are domed and often burnished (likely by handling) on the highest region of the domes. The area between the circular regions, the interstitial region, does not show the etched pattern, but is relatively smooth. In some instances, this interstitial region shows slight parallel lines or scratches. Thus, it is likely this pattern was made by an embossing process. The authors have never seen any material like this on a part known to be original from the factory.

On the early cars, the dash top butted directly against the L-post trim and there was no chrome trim at the ends of the grab handle.

GLOVEBOX

The earlier form of the 3.8-liter glovebox inserts were fabricated from fiberglass. Fiberglass boxes have been seen with both thin and thick wall-thickness. They have also been seen with a wide or a narrow flange, or lip, running around their periphery to hold the box into the dashboard opening.

It was observed that chassis numbers 875026 and 875109 had the fiberglass glovebox, while 875954, 876289 and 876577 had the cardboard glovebox.

View showing the inside of a fiberglass glovebox insert. The interior is finished to be smooth and does not show seams, as were evident in the later fabricated cardboard gloveboxes.

View of the inside of a cardboard glovebox insert. The opposite sides of the rivets are evident on this inner surface, as well as the seams and folds. The inside was coated with a black material that gave a velvet-like surface finish.

Top-view of a fabricated cardboard glovebox insert, showing the rivets used to hold the sections together and the bends and seams created when the cardboard insert was fabricated.

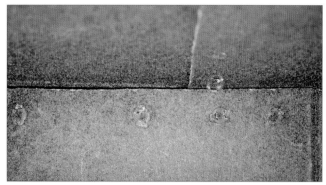

Close-up view of the inside of a very late cardboard glovebox insert, this one from roadster 879032. This very original car still shows much of the felt-like finish. Also, the rivets are somewhat less pronounced than the authors have generally seen on earlier cars. This may be a natural production variation, or may suggest an improved assembly process.

SUN VISORS

The mounts for the sun visors in the coupes underwent numerous small changes during production (the 3.8-liter roadsters did not have sun visors). The base of these mounts is roughly lozenge-shaped, with a raised boss, or mesa, with a hole to retain the pivot of the visor arm. They are mounted to the roof of the car, just above the top of the windscreen, by screws passing through two holes on opposite sides of the base. The raised boss extends forward on the base roughly in two intersecting inclined planes terminating at a point (somewhat rounded) opposite the pivot hole. The pronounced boss of the early visor mounts was similar to that found on later Mk 2 sedans, although in the case of the Mk 2 sedans there were three mounting holes instead of two.

As production continued the shape of this boss evolved, becoming shorter, lower and less pronounced.

It appears that all E-types had two mounting holes for the base plates, while the Mk 2 sedans had three. Otherwise the mounts are similar.

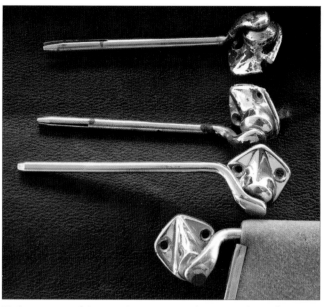

Various stages of the sun visor mount evolution are shown here. At the bottom, with visor attached, is the bracket from 885013 showing the most pronounced boss. It leads from the edge of the base (up in the picture) to the arm attachment point. The bolt seen on the bracket is a later repair and should not be present. Above this lowest bracket are brackets with progressively lower and less pronounced bosses. The trend seems to be that as production progressed the bosses got lower and the outline of the footprint of the boss became less pointed at the top.

On the right is the visor bracket from 885013 and on the left is a somewhat later bracket. The progression of the "softening" of the triangular raised boss, or stanchion, shows in this comparison. Again, the bolt showing on the bracket on the right is a later repair and should not be present.

There were changes in the backs of the visor mount brackets as well. The early bracket from 885013, on the right in the picture, shows a flat base with the recess in the back of the stanchion restricted to the area immediately around the retaining bolt. The later bracket, on the left in the picture, shows the broader recess behind the lower and wider stanchion.

Brackets from later Mk 2 sedans are similar to those used in the E-types, but can be distinguished by having three holes.

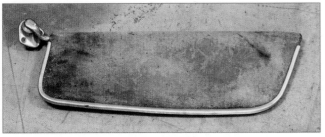

The visors used in E-types are different from those used in Mk 2 sedans. The upper visor is from a Mk 2 and the lower is from E-type 885013.

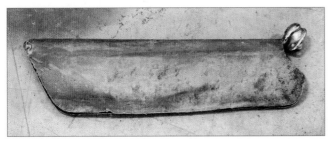

This earlier visor is likely to be from a 1962 or 1963 era E-type, based on the shape of the triangular raised stanchion on the boss.

This later E-type visor has no trim around the edge and shows the feature of a protrusion of the form of the visor under the pivot point. This protrusion was not a feature of the earlier cars.

CONSOLE FRAME, TRIM AND COMPONENTS

On a few of the very-early cars, likely produced by the Experimental Department, the console was quite different from the early production cars. Some of the unusual features are square speaker grilles, no ashtray above the radio, fewer rivets on the chrome strip around the shift boot and a rectangular ashtray (or perhaps cubby) on the lower part of the console next to the parking brake. These features tend to show up as a group. *Jaguar E-Type: The Definitive History* pictures all these features together, and Porter states that they are of "the interior of one of the two Fixed Head prototypes with several curious features in evidence."

There were many changes in the console area after production began in earnest. Three types of ashtrays were used. The first of these was a chrome rotating type with a simple oblong shape. It was used in this form for the first few years of production and then two "wings" were added to the top of the oblong shape. Porter includes a view of a winged ashtray on a car with a black center dash, so apparently the black dash covering came in before the winged ashtray was discontinued.

Sometime after the console was changed to the covered version with the armrest-storage box, the ashtray was changed again to the drawer type as used in the Series 1 4.2-liter cars.

It has been observed that cars chassis numbers 860084, 876052, 876577 and 879093 had the wingless ashtray, while 879325 and 889076 had the winged ashtray.

About May 1963, the ashtray was changed at chassis numbers 850695/6, 861149/50, 879291/2 and 888512/3. This is likely the addition of the wings to the oblong rotating ashtray. About January 1964, the ashtray was changed again, at chassis numbers 850785/6, 861383/4, 880614/5 and 889503/4 and that the new one is not interchangeable with the old. This is likely the institution of the large, rectangular ashtray.

Similar to the trim change of the dashboard center section, the front and bottom console trimming underwent changes. The first change was in the pattern used on the aluminum. The circular pattern was replaced with the cross pattern, exactly as in the case of the first center-dashboard trim change. In the second change, the trim on the front and bottom consoles was changed from aluminum to a material matching the interior color of the car. However, instead of the vinyl trim used on the later dashboard center sections, the trim was leather. The trim changes from aluminum to leather did not occur at the same time for both front and bottom console sections. The lower console was trimmed in leather before the aluminum was replaced with leather on the front console. This is seen, for example, in the top picture on page 14 of the left-hand drive coupe 887868.

About October 1962, at chassis numbers 850609/10, 860912/3, 878301/2 and 887131/2, the patterns embossed on the aluminum finisher panels on the assembly above the gearbox and on the assembly over the gearbox and driveshaft cover were changed.

At chassis numbers 850736/7, 861215/6, 879760/1 and 888858/9, except for 850725, 850727, 879531, 879543, 789545, 879546, 879553, 879556, 879562 (these cars come before the listed change, so it is likely that "except for" means the new consoles were fitted to these earlier cars before they were made standard), about August 1963, the console was changed to a new one that had an armrest with storage space. At chassis numbers 850751/2, 861253/4, 879802/3 and 889029/30, about September 1963, the front finisher panel was changed from embossed aluminum to leather and at chassis numbers 850786/7, 861388/9, 880630/1 and 889525/6, about March 1964, the radio panel part of the console was changed.

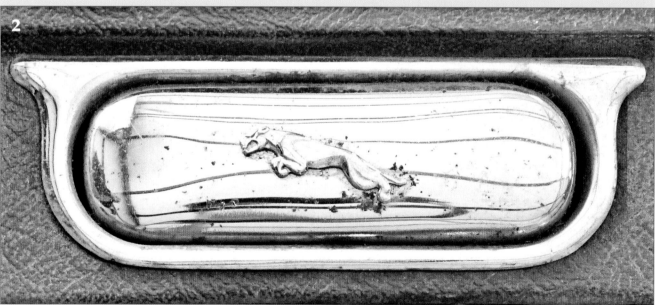

1 The earliest ashtrays had an oblong shape.

2 Later, two small "wings" were added to the upper part of the ashtray. Perhaps this was to help determine which side was up during assembly, as some of the early ashtray frames were inserted upside-down.

3 View of the early type ashtray from the top. This is the same general layout for both the early non-winged and later winged types. This is the closed position.

4 View of the early type ashtray from the top in the open position, showing how the ashtray swivels out. This ashtray unit has been installed in the correct orientation; when they are installed upside-down a flange from the mount overhangs part of the ashtray aperture.

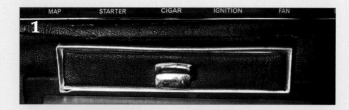

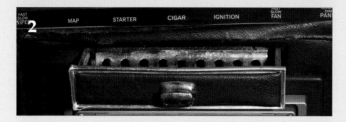

1 *The last style of 3.8-liter ashtray was the sliding-tray type, as used in the early 4.2-liter cars. This one is in the closed position.*

2 *The sliding-tray type ashtray in the open position.*

3 *This console has leather trim on the front and chrome speaker grilles, suggesting it was about a mid-1964 model year unit (the very late 3.8-liter consoles had the non-chrome speaker surrounds found on the Series 1 4.2-liter cars). The leather trimming appears to be original and, interestingly, the dot pattern aluminum of the earlier design is underneath the leather. Perhaps this is a unit that was re-trimmed by an owner and it does not represent a factory configuration. However, it appears original and raises the question of the factory reworking earlier parts to upgrade them for use on later cars. This would have been a rework of a quite earlier console, as the dot pattern is underneath, not the later stamped-in cross pattern.*

4 *The aluminum trim on the early consoles followed the progression of the center dash, coming first in the dot pattern and later in the cross pattern. This is the early dot pattern material.*

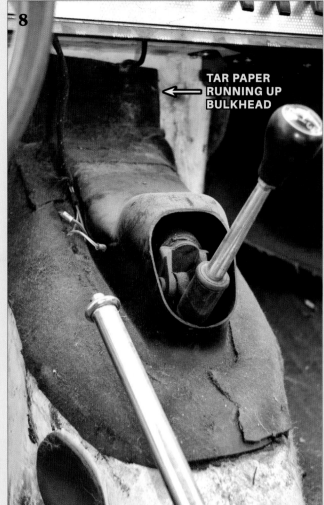

TAR PAPER
RUNNING UP
BULKHEAD ←

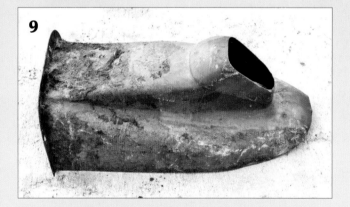

5 This close-up view of the dot pattern aluminum trim on the center console of left-hand drive roadster chassis 875026 shows the details of the forming of the aluminum and the use of the piping on the early cars.

6 The later consoles were trimmed in leather and had an armrest-storage area at the rear. There were several stages to the introduction of this configuration, some without armrest, some mixing aluminum and leather. The authors have not yet deduced a sequence to this and feel there may be cases where a feature, for example leather on the lower console, that came in and then production went back to aluminum for a while. More research is needed to sort this out, but, in any case, what appears in this illustration seems to be the final state of the 3.8-liter console configuration.

7 The plastic transmission covers came in both white and black. This is a white version.

8 This black plastic transmission cover from a very original 1962 coupe, chassis 885056, has apparently not been removed from the car since the tar paper was applied at the factory. Note the tar paper running up the bulkhead of the body tub toward the front of the black plastic cover.

9 Steel transmission covers were also used. This unit is not affixed all around its periphery with screws going into the transmission tunnel, but has a lip on the rear that slips under the rear part of the transmission tunnel aperture. The cover is then affixed by a few screws at its front lip. No screw holes are seen along the lateral sides of this cover.

Back view of the steel transmission cover in an inverted position. The tang or lip is showing at the left. It is spot-welded to the steel cover.

A later transmission cover that is affixed by screws around the periphery instead of using a tang. This cover also shows a rubber boot screwed to the edge of the shift lever aperture. This boot is not seen in the fully-trimmed interior, but sits below the leather boot. This particular cover may have come from a 4.2-liter car, but there is evidence such covers were used on late 3.8-liter cars; late 3.8-liter body tubs have been seen with screw ports around the periphery of the transmission tunnel aperture.

When no radio was fitted this blanking plate was installed over the aperture. It was comprised of a rectangular backing piece covered with interior trim material in the center. The edges had the same style as the edges of the typical factory- or dealer-fitted radio.

Back view of an installed blanking plate on an etched dot pattern aluminum trimmed 3.8-liter console.

The NOS blanking plate without the central vinyl trim, showing the construction and mounting holes. It was made of stamped, chromed sheet steel.

Back view of the NOS blanking plate showing its stamped sheet steel construction.

Throughout 3.8-liter E-type production this shift-knob was used. It had a black plastic main body (possibly phenolic) with a threaded brass insert for screwing onto the shift lever, against a locknut. The top had a glued-on clear dome with the shift pattern painted on the inside. This design was a break with the knobs used on the XK-series sports cars, which were single-piece black plastic with the shift pattern on top and threaded inserts. With the introduction of the 4.2-liter E-types a spherical single-piece black-painted knob was introduced. It had the shift pattern cast into the top.

A region to the front right of the shift boot housing on 879032, a low-mileage and well preserved 1963 roadster, showing the embossed cross pattern aluminum trim from several angles. Also note the piping and the relatively common flaw of the string protruding from the center, in the lower right of the picture.

Another view of the dot pattern aluminum trim (likely recently-made reproduction material). This time it is seen on the top of the console, next to the handbrake. The domed characteristic of the dots noted earlier is clear here.

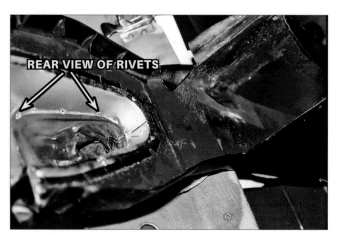

Interior view of an unrestored early roadster console, showing the rear view of the rivets holding the leather retaining ring.

A leather-covered console, with later-type pull-out ashtray. This is of the style of late 3.8-liter cars and early 4.2-liter cars. The speaker grilles, without chrome surrounds, as seen here, were introduced in late 3.8-liter production.

Inside view of the late-type console showing the Blaupunkt radio installation. In this instance two speakers were used. Single-speaker however, were likely to have been the standard configuration used by the factory and/or dealerships.

View looking up in the right-hand side footwell of 879032, a well preserved roadster. The two large chrome-plated steel thumbscrews retaining the console are evident on the left of the picture, to the right of the speaker grille. This is also a good view of the edge trim of the carpet and under-dash trip, as well as the fasteners.

UNDER CONSOLE AREA

The transmission cover over the large opening in the transmission tunnel came in different types. These pieces were made of molded plastic and they came in black and white. Pressed and fabricated sheet steel was also used.

Roadster chassis number 875109 had a transmission cover made of metal. The style is different from those found on some 4.2-liter cars and it differs from the plastic covers in several ways. Its mounting at the rear is by a tang that goes under the rear edge of the transmission tunnel aperture. Chassis number 889076, a late coupe, had this same type of metal cover. The covers are affixed with sheet metal screws all around. Coupe 885056 has a black plastic cover.

The round plugs used to plug the gearbox inspection holes on the left side of the transmission tunnel came in at least two types. Some of the early cars had three-piece fabricated sheet steel covers instead of the later rubber ones.

From research of surviving cars: Chassis numbers 875026 and 875109 had the metal inspection hole covers, while 860084, 889076 and 890061 had the rubber covers.

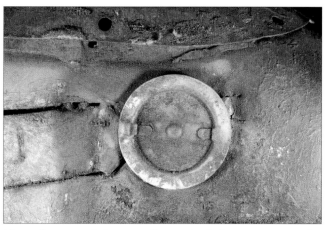

The earliest transmission-tunnel inspection hole covers were made of steel. The disc was held in place by a spring riveted to the center of the plate. This is the cockpit-side view.

This transmission-side view of an early metal transmission tunnel inspection-hole cover shows the three-piece construction, with a deflecting metal bow that retains it in the hole.

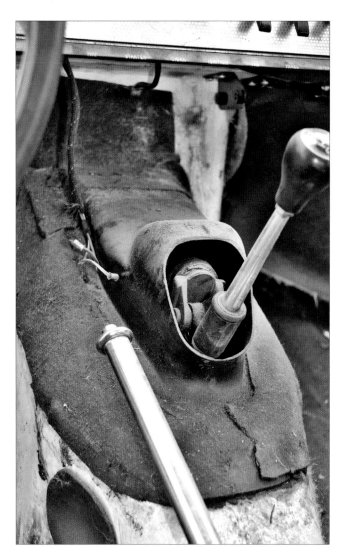

The black plastic transmission cover on coupe 885056.

Cockpit-side view of a later one-piece rubber transmission-tunnel inspection hole cover.

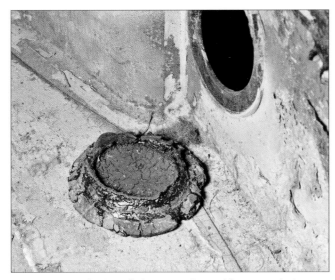

Transmission-side view of a later one-piece rubber transmission-tunnel inspection hole cover. The rubber has deteriorated significantly here.

CARPETS AND INTERIOR TRIM

There are a few references about leather being employed for the trim, as well as the seats. For example, *The Autocar*, March 17, 1961, states "leather is used throughout for the trim…" In *Jaguar Sports Cars*, Skilleter says, "Leather was employed for the trim, except for the carpeted areas and the headlining…" The authors are not aware of any other evidence that this ever occurred. Leather was used for the seats, shift boot and early heel pads, but most of the other trim was not leather.

The headliner color was gray or beige for cars without a green interior, and green for cars with a green interior.

As with other areas of the car, there are numerous pictures of prototypes, or very early production cars, with unusual features. Unusual interior trim is shown running up the pillars on a prototype roadster in *Car and Driver*, May 1961. Chrome trim strips are absent on the doors of a very early car on that issue's cover. The lower chrome strip is absent on one of the prototype coupes in *Jaguar E-Type: The Definitive History* and 885002 is shown with both chrome strips.

The luggage compartment mat in the coupes was originally two pieces, but later it was changed to one piece. On a few very early cars, the small piece of the two-piece mat had a small tab on the forward end, presumably to lift it up.

One of these 3.8-liter interior trim changes was the introduction of covers over the coupe rear-door hinges. The early cars had bare hinges while the later cars had covers over the hinges.

Changes by chassis number for this section are:

- ▶ 850357/8, 860175/6, 876581/2 and 885503/4, Flintkote was added to the front floor and the front carpets were changed;

- ▶ 860478/9 and 886013/4, about May 1962, the headlining, including the cantrail and rear trim panels, the panel assembly for trimming the windscreen header rail and the trim panel assembly for the windscreen header rail were all changed;

- ▶ 850526/7, 860580/1, 877355/6 and 886092/3, about June 1962, changes were made to the mat assembly on the floor behind the seats, the mat assembly on the rear bulkhead panel and the moquette face piece for the lower bulkhead panel, the casing assembly below the quarter light, the hinged extension for the luggage compartment floor and the support rail assembly for the hinged extension in its lowered position;

- ▶ 861092/3 and 888256/7, about August 1963, the mat assembly on the luggage compartment floor changed from a two-piece to a one-piece unit;

- ▶ 861098/9 and 888301/2, about August 1963, the trim panel for the shut pillar, the casing assembly at the side of the luggage compartment floor and the hinged extension assembly for the luggage compartment floor were all changed.

- ▶ 850723/4, 861188/9, 879495/6 and 888697/8, in about June 1963, armrests were added to the doors;

- ▶ 850713/4, 861178/9, 879422/3 and 888657/8, about June 1963, a trim panel was fitted to the hinge face of the door and was retained by the door light-switch striker;

- ▶ 850751/2, 861255/6, 879892/3 and 889053/4 (and some prior cars), about September 1963, the front carpets were changed to a type with a plastic heel pad;

- ▶ 850771/2, 861324/5, 880411/2 and 889346/7, about November 1963, the carpet fasteners were changed;

- ▶ 850808/9, 861445/6, 880839/40 and 889786/7, in about March 1964, the interior door trim was changed.

An early car without an armrest on the door.

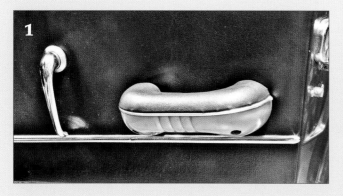

1 *This 4.2-liter Series 1 armrest from a two-seater is of the sort used on late 3.8-liter cars.*

2 *The early coupes had a two-piece mat in the luggage area. The large section was in an L shape, as seen here.*

3 *The early coupe rear-door hinges were without covers. It is likely these uncovered hinges often fouled against the contents of the luggage area.*

4 *Later on, moquette-trimmed covers were added to the hinges.*

5 *The small section of an early two-piece floor mat. The two brackets sticking through the left side of the mat were likely added after the car left the factory.*

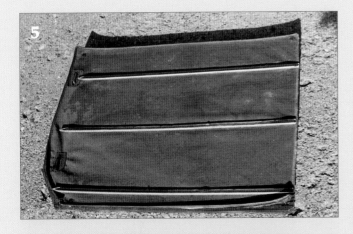

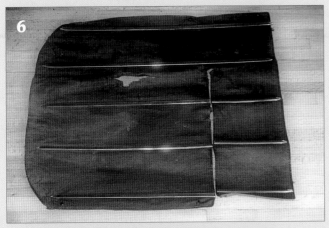

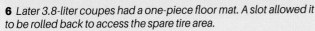

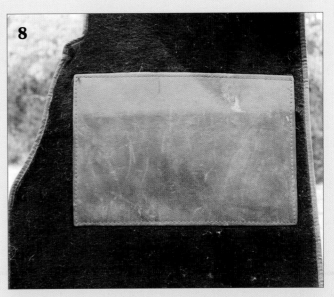

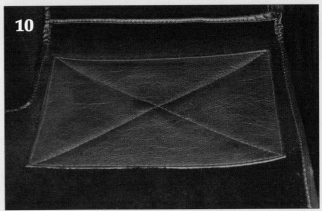

6 *Later 3.8-liter coupes had a one-piece floor mat. A slot allowed it to be rolled back to access the spare tire area.*

7 *Back view of the carpet from coupe 885056. The body number, 1055 (indicating coupe body V1055) is seen twice in chalk or, more likely, crayon.*

8 *An original carpet from coupe 885056. Note that it lacks the two diagonal lines of stitching that are often seen in reproduction carpets. It is not clear if this diagonal stitching pattern was originally used or not.*

9 *An original carpet from roadster 879032. The protective pad here may be Hardura rather than leather. Interestingly, it is installed below the surface of the cut-pile carpeting and appears in a frame of edge-trimmed material.*

10 *A diagonally-stitched protective pad in a restored car. The authors are not sure if cars were delivered from the factory with such stitching.*

SEATS AND MOUNTS

The seats on some Experimental Department cars were different from those in production cars. They had flat, squared-off shape to the seat back and, in some instances, different stitching arrangements. After these few early cars, two seat types came to be standard: the small-radius or narrow-back seats and the large-radius or wide-back seats. It appears that the narrow-back seats were used on roadsters and the wide back seats were used on the coupes. Some early coupes were fitted with roadster seats. Chassis number 860005 is fitted with the narrow-back seats. Apparently some seats were finished in suede, although the authors have never observed this.

Seat cushions in 1961 cars had thin padding, which was improved for 1962.

Some early seats had coarser grain leather. In *The Jaguar E-type: A Collector's Guide*, referring to a picture showing coarse-grained leather, Skilleter stated, "This 1961 roadster has the rather unusual large-grain pattern leather, which was sometimes used in early cars." The same reference states, "pre-1962 cars had 'unfortunately placed' beading across the seat back which could become an annoyance on long journeys," and that, "Trim shop messed around with different sorts of padding in different places…"

The early seats had short mounts, allowing only a small adjustment range. For these early seats, the longitudinal spacing of the four bolts holding the seats to the slides is shorter than the spacing found on later cars. This change is likely the one that is recorded in the literature as occurring at chassis numbers 850526/7, 860580/1, 877355/6 and 886092/3, where it is noted that about June 1962, the seat slides were changed.

The seats used on roadsters had a small radius of curvature at the top.

The coupe seats had a large radius of curvature at the top. Apparently, a few coupes were fitted with roadster seats.

The early cars, with short seat adjustment range, had mounts a narrow bolt spacing of the seat mounting, as in the locking-side lower seat track shown here. A later seat track is shown on the top, with wide bolt spacing between the mounting bolts. After the range of seat adjustment was increased, the mounts were changed, and the mounting bolts were farther apart.

Seat tracks from later (top) and earlier (bottom) seats, showing the increase in bolt spacing that took place.

Early-type "LEVEROLL-" markings on the end of an adjuster lever.

Later-type "A.W. CHAPMAN, LTD," "LEVEROLL," and "LONDON S.W.6" markings on the end of an adjuster label.

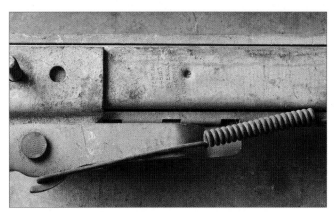

"PATENT NO. 648182, 'LEVEROLL', A.W. CHAPMAN, LTD., LONDON S.W.6" stamped on the top sliding section of a locking part of a seat track.

The same legend on the bottom side of the bottom part of the track.

HOOD OR CONVERTIBLE TOP, FRAME AND HARDWARE

On the earliest cars, the outer two convertible top clasps were necked-down. The later outer clasps had more uniform and thicker cross-sections. It is likely this change was made to increase the strength of the clasps, which must have broken easily.

Chassis numbers 875026, 875109, 875186 and 875251 were seen to have the necked-down clasps and 875407 had a single necked-down clasp (it may have come this way, or the other one may be a replacement).

RIGHT: *The central convertible top clasp. This apparently only came in one basic form and did not go through a change from the necked-down form to the thicker form, as did the side clasps.*

From the delicate appearance of the early necked-down convertible top clasp, it is evident why not many survive.

Another view of an early necked-down convertible top clasp.

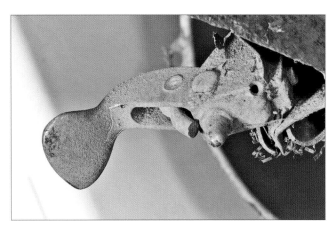

An early necked-down convertible top clasp that has broken off, as many have. The small cross-section of the clasp is clear here.

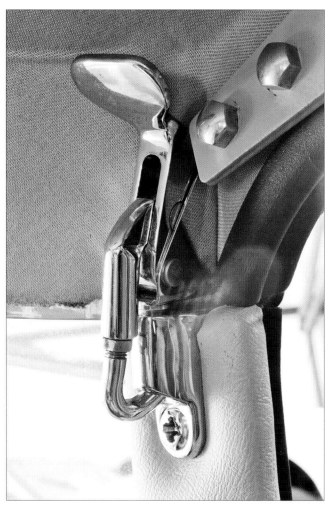

The thicker convertible top clasps, as found on most Series 1 cars, were much more durable.

HOOD, OR CONVERTIBLE TOP, CLOTH AND WINDOW

The convertible top material changed from the early mohair cloth material to a plastic material. The plastic convertible top material was introduced at about the same time as the introduction of the open headlights in late 4.2-liter production in 1967 (the Series 1.25 cars).

In the top of the convertible top, there is a long bag of shot in a damping tube.

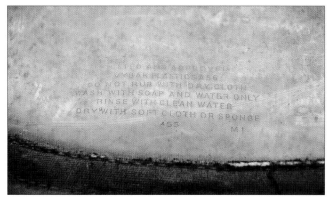

The warning and markings found on the lower left of the convertible top rear window.

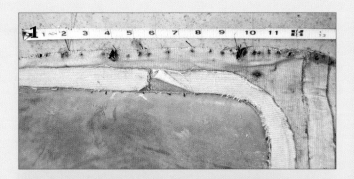

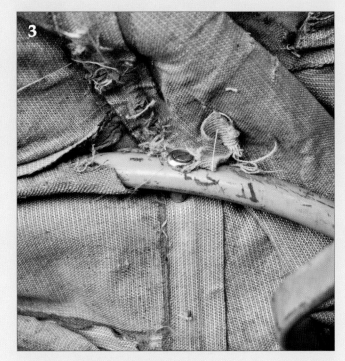

1 The rear of the convertible top was typically fastened to the rear wooden tack strip by a series of small tacks. Their locations are compared here with a ruler, marked in inches.

2 Close-up of mohair material of the convertible top.

3 View of the interior material used on the convertible tops. Also seen here is a section of the frame, showing the paint color.

4 A close-up of the fabric used to cover the steel section at the front of the convertible top frame. Also seen here is the early-type large diameter hole with trim for the canopy rail strap to pass through when restraining the top in the folded configuration.

5 Close-up view of one of the top-retaining tacks, with a ruler for size. This one measures about one-half inch long.

6 View of the heads of one of the retaining tacks, against a ruler. Its diameter is a little more than 1/8 inch, but these diameters seem to vary somewhat.

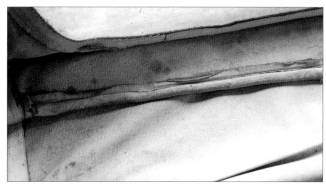

View looking up, with the rear window toward the top of the picture, of the anti-drumming shot-filled tube running laterally across the inside of the convertible top.

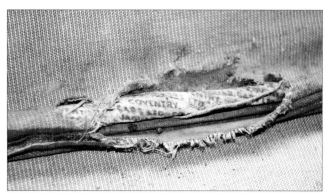

Inside view of the shot-filled bag sewn in the convertible top. The inner wrapper is labeled "JAGUAR CARS LTD. COVENTRY." One of the balls of shot is seen below the bag.

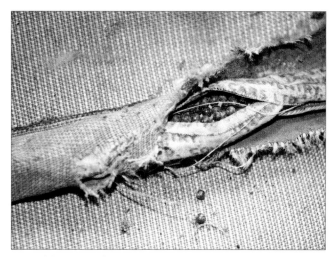

View of the inside of the bag, showing the shot inside.

The front of one of the clasps found on either side of the top. Also illustrated is the texture of the material, stitches and small pop-rivets used around the inside of the frame running around the window.

Back view of the clasp, also showing a close-up of the outside of the convertible top material and stitching.

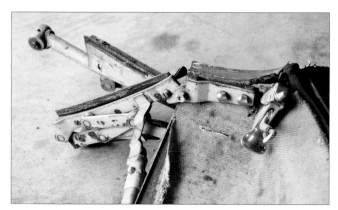

General view of some of the convertible top frame hardware. The later-type non-necked-down convertible top clasp is seen on the right. To its left are two of the chromed domed fasteners. Other original fasteners are seen further to the left, including the chromed domed nut on the cross-member showing toward the bottom of the picture.

Early (top, from roadster 875472) and late (bottom) of the front cowling (or canopy rail) of the convertible top frame. Most notably, the holes for the top retaining straps are in different locations and are of different sizes (the early hole being noticeably larger).

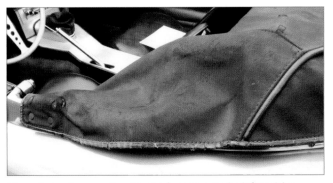

View of a boot cover, showing the fasteners, to the left and the piping and stitching.

The convertible top cover supplied from the factory with left-hand drive roadster 875026. This is a mohair material with black piping. Note the three retaining straps used to retain the leading edge of the cover, in contrast to later vinyl covers that had two straps (the one in the center was no longer used). Based on observations, it appears the transition from three to two straps occurred sometime around the time of the transition from mohair to vinyl.

HOOD, OR CONVERTIBLE TOP COVER

The convertible top cover came in various color combinations. One combination illustrated in early photographs is a black cover with red piping on a white outside latch car with a red interior. Some early black-and-white pictures also illustrate dark covers with both light and dark piping. On the early cars, three clasps on the bulkhead fastened the boot cover, instead of two on the later cars.

At chassis numbers 850934/5 and 881864/5, about October 1964, the convertible top cover was changed.

Inside view of the convertible top cover supplied with 875026. The soft beige material in the middle was apparently only used for a short period before a more durable material was introduced. The body number was typically written in what appears to be crayon on the convertible top covers and here "1044," matching the top cover to body R1044, is still lightly showing on the right and left of the beige material. This writing is shown more clearly in other pictures.

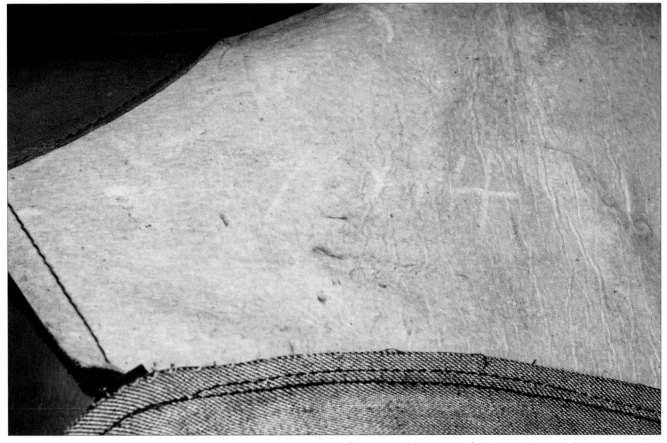

View of the driver's side (left side) "1044" crayon markings on the inside of the convertible top cover for 875026. These markings were much more pronounced when first observed in the early 1970s.

View of the passenger's side (right side) much larger "1044" markings on the 875026 cover. As with the other 1044 markings on this top, these have faded with time.

Close-up view of the fabric and stitching on a mohair convertible top cover.

The driver's side (left side) of the inside of the convertible top cover from left-hand drive roadster 875954. By this point in production the newer central inside trim had been introduced on the convertible top covers, as seen here in contrast to the cover from 875026. This newer material is more glossy and durable. Note also the number "2202," indicating body number R2202 but without the prefix, is crayoned on the black pad on the side instead of in the middle. Note also the interior color, black, is crayoned on the cover as well.

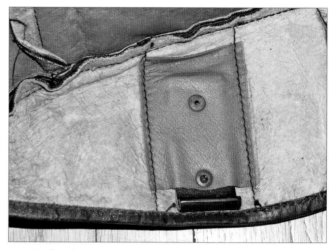

Details of the fasteners and construction of the region of the top cover where the clips are located.

An outside view of a convertible top cover from a 1963 roadster. Note here that the piping is red, the same color as the interior of car 879032 from which this cover came.

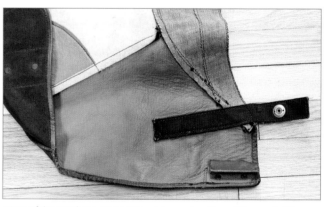

View of the stitching, materials and construction of the end of the convertible top cover. The strap containing a TENAX snap (that attaches to the top of the interior side of the B pillar) is also seen here.

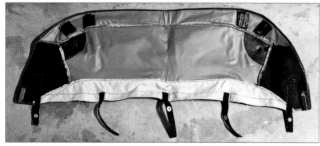

An interior view of the convertible top cover from 879032. Note again the body number, "5711," indicating body R5711, written in crayon on the black patch on the upper right of the cover, suggesting the body number marking went at least to this point.

Outside view of the TEXAX snap fastener on an outer retaining strip of the cover.

Inside view of the TEXAX snap fastener on an outer retaining strip of the cover.

Details of the clip on the outer edges of the cover and its fasteners. This clip goes over the front portion of the rear bodywork, just behind the door aperture. These clips are leather covered, at least on the early cars.

Outside view of a "LIFT THE DOT" fastener on one of the three retaining strips on the leading edge of the cover.

Inside view of a "LIFT THE DOT" fastener on one of the three retaining strips on the leading edge of the cover.

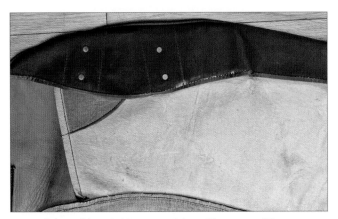

General view of the stitching, materials and fasteners of the cover from another view.

HARDTOP MOUNTING EQUIPMENT

The *J.30 Spare Parts Catalogue (June 1963)* states on page 322 that the hardtop assembly was available on right-hand drive roadsters from 850024 and onward and on left-hand drive roadsters 875027 and onward. On the

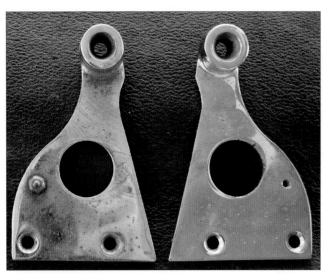

Conventional hardtop mounts.

Hardtop mounts exhibiting the section with a smaller radius. These mounts are early and appear to be as they left the factory.

same page it is noted that the first type hardtop fitting kit was listed for cars 850024 to 850091 and 875027 to 875385 and the second type of fitting kit was listed for cars 850092 to 850455 and 875386 to 876974. At this transition point the tap plate (BD.21191/1) and retainer for tap plate (BD.21191/2) were omitted, suggesting that nuts were built into the bodywork for retaining the mount after this point. No mention is made to fittings for cars 850456 and subsequent, or cars 876975 and subsequent.

From observations it appears that, in any case, the hardtop mounts were not always fitted to cars after 850023 or 875026. The following is a listing of some observations of cars both before and after the listed chassis number for the introduction of the hardtop mounts (850023/4 and 875026/7):

Cars not observed to have hardtop mounts:
- 875014
- 875026 (unrestored)
- 875049 (restored)
- 875109 (unrestored)
- 875122 (restored)

Early roadsters did not come with mounting brackets for the hardtop. They became available as an option after a few cars were produced.

Later cars came fitted with mounting brackets for the hardtop. These were also apparently retrofitted by dealers when hardtops were ordered for cars without these brackets. This illustration is from a Series 1 4.2-liter roadster, but is representative of the 3.8-liter hardtop mounting brackets.

- 875157 (restored)
- 875258 (restored)
- 875272 (restored)
- 875274 (restored)
- 875837
- 876319
- 876482 (unrestored)
- 879406

These cars were observed to have the mounts:
- 875038 (restored)
- 875045 (restored, but the brackets were reported to have been on the car in 1977, before the restoration)
- 880913

So, as expected, the hardtop mounts were not always fitted after they were made available as an option.

This would be consistent with the observation that some early cars, apparently 875003 (the New York Show car) were fitted with hardtops and presumably had mounts.

One variation the authors have seen on hardtop mounts is a second radius of curvature in a part of the circular section in mounts fitted to the car, behind the door jamb.

This variation is illustrated in the two figures on the right side of the previous page.

At chassis numbers 850356/7 and 877430/1, in about July 1962, the hardtop mounting brackets were changed.

T-KEY STORAGE MOUNT

On at least some outside latch cars, there were clip mounts to store the T-key when not in use. The mounting

The two spring clips were used to store the T-key on a very early car. Pouches were apparently also used. These clips are located on the right rear of the console. On the very early prototype cars they may have been located in front of the right door in about the same location where the inside bonnet-release handle was to be located later (when the bonnet latches were moved inside). A picture of 885002 showing the clips mounted in such a location, on the right-hand side door pillar (apparently before the car's restoration), is shown in the July 1999 issue of Jaguar World.

clips appear to be the same as those used to hold the jack rod in the boot. In Porter's *Original Jaguar E-Type*, a T-key is shown stored on the right side of the console, but in a small bag (on a restored car). On page 32 of Jenkinson's *Jaguar E-Type 3.8 & 4.2 6-cylinder; 5.3 V12*, a T-key mount is shown mounted with clips on the right bulkhead just in front of the right-hand side door in an *Autocar* line drawing. On page 141 of *All About the Jaguar E-Type*, by Paul Skilleter Books (this page is a reprint from a July 1999 *Jaguar World* article entitled *E-type 9600 HP*) the T-key clips for 885002 are shown on the right bulkhead inside the cockpit, just to the left of the door hinges. In the same article it states "The 'T' handle used to operate the locks normally lives in a small pocket behind the right-hand seat," but notes 885002 is an exception.

Chassis number 875026 had the clip mount on the right rear of the console.

INTERIOR RELEASE

The authors are not aware of any design changes to the interior bonnet latch release mechanism.

BOOT RELEASE

The cable release that opens the roadster boot is operated by pulling a black plastic knob in the right rear of the cockpit. No design changes are known.

The black plastic boot lid release in the right rear of the cockpit.

BODYWORK
COUPE BODYWORK CHANGES

Note that in this section, as throughout the book, the terms "right" and "left" refer to the car's right and left, that is, right and left as seen from the driver's perspective when seated in the car. This is the usual convention, as cited, for example, on the cover page of SECTION A, GENERAL INFORMATION of the Jaguar factory service manual, Publication number E/123/5.

Rear view of the bodywork and taillight of 885008 showing the valley between the coupe superstructure and the top of the wing terminating before the taillight. This results in a relatively straight leading edge on the taillight. This was typical of early coupes.

A view along the taillight of early coupe 885018 showing the slight curve in the leading edge of the taillight. As with early coupe 885008, the valley between the top of the wing and the coupe superstructure terminates before it reaches the taillight.

The later coupes had the valley or crease continuing further back toward the rear of the car than on the early cars. This is most evident in the shape of the leading edge of the taillight assembly. Instead of curving slightly, it has a slight bulge to accommodate the crease. This is a photograph of a 4.2-liter car, but shows the shape of the later 3.8-liter cars.

On early coupe bodywork, there is a valley (or crease) where the top of the rear wing meets the coupe greenhouse. On the early 1961 coupes this valley terminates before it reaches the taillight. Thus, the sheet metal coming up to the leading edge of the taillight is rounded, but does not show a crease. Consequently the early coupe taillights have a relatively straight leading edge. This is seen in the top right figure on page 101. The early 1961 taillights appear quite similar to 2+2 taillights, that also have a relatively straight leading edge.

On later coupes, the crease continues into the leading-edge of the taillight. Thus the taillight has a slight bulge forward at its leading edge.

Howe has also noted the different rear coupe bodywork shape above the rear lights.

FIREWALL

While the transition from outside latch cars to inside latch cars took place at a specific point (after 500 cars, at right-hand drive roadsters 850091/2, right-hand drive coupes 875385/6 and left-hand drive coupes 885020/1) the cars produced before and after this transition show a progression of changes related to the bonnet latch location switch-over point (from outside latch to inside latch). Most of these progressive changes are evident in the right-most and left-most sections of the firewall and in the small vertical curved sections of the bulkhead on the very far left and right. These sections are the part of the bulkhead curved outward to follow the curved shape of the sides of the body.

These changes were:

▶ a group of three holes for attachment of the mounting bracket for the locking hook mechanism (for inside latch cars) was on the firewall

▶ a slot was provided in the firewall to pass the connecting rod used to control the latch pivot used with the inside latches

▶ two bolt holes appeared before the outside/inside transition on lower outer bulkhead. Their purpose was to retain an upcoming stop to be used in the inside latch configuration

▶ the pop-riveted rubber bonnet stop of the early cars was retained for a while after the adoption of inside latches

BONNET STOP

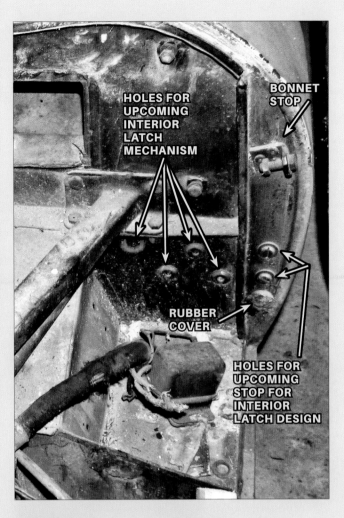

HOLES FOR UPCOMING INTERIOR LATCH MECHANISM

BONNET STOP

RUBBER COVER

HOLES FOR UPCOMING STOP FOR INTERIOR LATCH DESIGN

Left-hand drive coupe 885009 shows none of the precursor features for the outside-latch configuration (thus is a Generation 1 configuration): no holes for mounting the upcoming mounting bracket for the locking hook (for inside latch operation), no hole for the upcoming con rod to operate the locking hook, and no holes for the upcoming bonnet locating-pin receiver bracket (for the bonnet locating peg of for the interior latch design) on the lower part of the outer bulkhead. Note that it also does not have the hole in the lower part of the outer bulkhead.

ABOVE RIGHT: Interestingly, 885013 (only four left-hand drive coupes later than 885009) shows all the outside latch precursor features: all the holes for the upcoming interior latch mechanism (the three pivot-mount holes and con rod hole on the firewall), and the holes for the upcoming stop for the interior latch design (the bolt holes on the lower outer bulkhead). It also shows a rubber cover, or plug, for the hole in the outer bulkhead. Being an outside latch car, it shows the mount for the outside latch on the sill, and the upper bonnet stop on the outer bulkhead. Note that while 885013 is only four left-hand drive coupes after 885009, it is 291 engines (R1426-9 from R1135-9) and 8 coupe bodies (V1025 from V1017) later.

RIGHT: This view of the left side of inside-latch coupe 885056 (looking toward the back of the car), shows these features:

▶ The mounting bracket for the locking hook

▶ The con rod to operate the locking hook (seen just coming through its hole in the bulkhead)

▶ The bonnet latching hook and the bonnet locating peg receiver bracket

▶ The bonnet locating-peg receiver bracket.

However, being a Generation 2 car, the vestigial components of the external latch operation are also visible:

▶ Two screws to retain the external bonnet latch mechanism

▶ The rubber bonnet stop, pop-riveted on near the top right of the picture

The rubber plug for the outer bulkhead hole also shows here. This apparently has no relation to bonnet latch configuration.

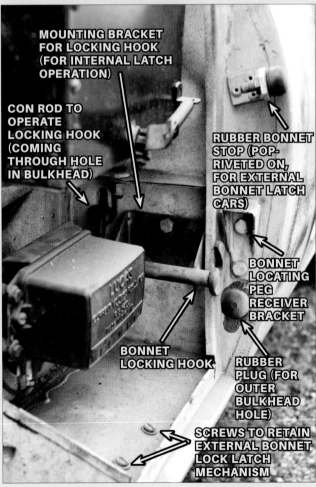

MOUNTING BRACKET FOR LOCKING HOOK (FOR INTERNAL LATCH OPERATION)

CON ROD TO OPERATE LOCKING HOOK (COMING THROUGH HOLE IN BULKHEAD)

RUBBER BONNET STOP (POP-RIVETED ON, FOR EXTERNAL BONNET LATCH CARS)

BONNET LOCATING PEG RECEIVER BRACKET

BONNET LOCKING HOOK

RUBBER PLUG (FOR OUTER BULKHEAD HOLE)

SCREWS TO RETAIN EXTERNAL BONNET LOCK LATCH MECHANISM

Here roadster 879032 shows only the inside latch features and none of the outside latch features. Thus, it is a Generation 3 configuration. As typically seen on the later cars, it has a rubber plug in the hole in the lower part of the outer bulkhead.

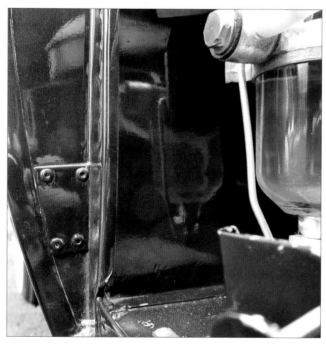

The restored left-hand drive outside latch roadster 875045 shows the early-type cover, held in with four pop-rivets, for the hole in the lower part of the outer bulkhead. As expected for an early car, 875045 shows no precursor features for the outside latches. Unrestored 875026 has the same cover and also shows no precursor features. These are Generation 1 cars.

▸ two holes on the lower sill (just next to the top of the sill) to retain the outside latch bracket were still present after the transition to the inside latch configuration.

Another feature of note is a hole in the outer bulkhead, sometimes with a rubber plug, sometimes covered by a plate held on by four pop rivets and sometimes not present at all. The presence and configuration of this hole is not apparently correlated with the latch mechanism components.

When no comments about a particular feature in the following list are given, it indicates that no information was available on that aspect of the car. In collecting this data it was noted that possibly the outside latch precursor features on inside latch cars and the inside latch precursor features on outside latch cars, may have come mostly in groups. That is, perhaps there were basically three body configurations supplied to the factory, which the authors refer to here as Generation 1, Generation 2 and Generation 3:

▸ Generation 1: configured for outside latches only

▸ Generation 2: configured for both outside and inside latches

▸ Generation 3: configured for inside latches only

These Generation 1, Generation 2 and Generation 3 configurations address only the bonnet latch mechanism and rubber stops; they do not contain information on the presence or absence of a lower outer bulkhead hole and its different covers. Cars produced by the Experimental Department are apparently of a unique configuration outside this system. It also seems some cars have body configurations between the three generations, *e.g.* 875157 and 875258 (both restored). More research is needed to better understand the progression here.

The engine, body and transmission numbers for the cars are listed below next to the chassis numbers (when known) for making apparent the approximate position in overall production (somewhat indicated by the engine numbers) and in the roadster or coupe body series (depicted by the "R" and "V" body numbers).

In addition, the list indicates whether the car has been restored or not. Here "restored" means the car appears to have been substantially or completely dissembled, suggesting it probably underwent extensive rework of the sort that disturbs a car's original state.

Right-hand drive outside latch roadsters:

For these cars, the two holes on the sill for retaining the outside latch bracket are present, and not mentioned in the descriptions following:

▸ 850008 (engine R1030-9, body R1021, restored): no holes on firewall for pivot, rubber plug in hole in outer bulkhead (on RHS only, no hole on LHS), no bolt holes on lower outer bulkhead, rubber bonnet detent on outer bulkhead.

- 850034 (engine R1157-9): no holes on firewall for pivot, no hole in outer bulkhead, no bolt holes on lower outer bulkhead, rubber bonnet detent on outer bulkhead.

Left-hand drive outside latch roadsters:

For these cars, the two holes on the sill for retaining the outside latch bracket are present, and not mentioned in the descriptions below:

- 875009 (engine R1020-9, body R1016, restored): no holes on firewall for pivot, rubber plug in hole in outer bulkhead, no bolt holes on lower outer bulkhead, rubber bonnet detent on outer bulkhead.

- 875026 (engine R1037-9, body R1044): no holes on firewall for pivot, no slot for pivot con rod, four pop rivets retaining cover over hole in outer bulkhead, no bolt holes on lower outer bulkhead, rubber bonnet detent on outer bulkhead.

- 875038 (engine R1078-9, body R1067, restored): no holes on firewall for pivot, no hole in outer bulkhead, no bolt holes on lower outer bulkhead, rubber bonnet detent on outer bulkhead.

- 875045 (engine R1071-9, body R1068, restored): no holes on firewall for pivot, four pop rivets retaining cover over hole in outer bulkhead, no bolt holes on lower outer bulkhead, rubber bonnet detent on outer bulkhead.

- 875109 (engine R1138-9, body R1129): no holes on firewall for pivot, no hole in outer bulkhead, no bolt holes on lower outer bulkhead, rubber bonnet detent on outer bulkhead.

- 875122 (engine R1168-9, body R1142, restored): no holes on firewall for pivot, no hole in outer bulkhead, no bolt holes on lower outer bulkhead, rubber bonnet detent on outer bulkhead.

- 875130 (engine R1169-9, body R1189, restored): appear to be no holes on firewall for pivot and no hole in outer bulkhead.

- 875157 (engine R1255-9, body R1251, restored): no holes on firewall for pivot, rubber plug in hole on outer bulkhead, two bolt holes on lower outer bulkhead, rubber bonnet detent on outer bulkhead.

- 875206 (engine R1326-9, body R1295, restored): three holes on firewall for pivot, rubber plug in hole on outer bulkhead, two bolt holes on lower outer bulkhead, rubber bonnet detent on outer bulkhead.

- 875258 (engine R1390-9, body R1254, restored): no holes on firewall for pivot, rubber plug in

hole on outer bulkhead, two bolt holes on lower outer bulkhead, rubber bonnet detent on outer bulkhead.

- 875272 (engine R1301-9, body R1372, restored): three holes on firewall for pivot, slot for pivot con rod, rubber plug in hole on outer bulkhead, two bolt holes on lower outer bulkhead, rubber bonnet detent on outer bulkhead.

- 875274 (engine R1395-9, body R1373, restored): three holes on firewall for pivot, slot for pivot con rod, rubber plug in hole on outer bulkhead, two bolt holes on lower outer bulkhead, rubber bonnet detent on outer bulkhead.

- 875331 (engine R1464-9, body R1443 on tag, R1442 on commission plate, restored): three holes on firewall for pivot, slot for pivot con rod, rubber plug in hole on outer bulkhead, two bolt holes on lower outer bulkhead, rubber bonnet detent on outer bulkhead.

Left-hand drive inside latch roadsters:

For these cars, the three holes on the firewall to retain the inside latch pivot, the slot on the firewall for the latch con rod to pass through are present, and not mentioned in the descriptions below. Mention of the two holes on the lower outer bulkhead is referring to holes for the locating-pin receiver bracket.

- 875472 (engine R1624-9, body R1604, restored): two holes on sill for outside latch bracket, rubber plug in hole on outer bulkhead, two bolt holes on lower outer bulkhead, rubber bonnet stop on the upper outer bulkhead in several places where this string is repeated.

- 877102 (engine R5122-9, body R3621, restored): no holes on sill for outside latch bracket, rubber plug in hole on outer bulkhead, two bolt holes on lower outer bulkhead, rubber bonnet detent on outer bulkhead, no rubber bonnet detent on outer bulkhead.

- 879032 (engine RA1100-9, body R5711, restored): no holes on sill for outside latch bracket, rubber plug in hole on outer bulkhead, two bolt holes on lower outer bulkhead, rubber bonnet detent on outer bulkhead, no rubber bonnet detent on outer bulkhead.

Left-hand drive outside latch coupes:

For these cars, the two holes on the sill for retaining the outside latch bracket are present, and not mentioned in the descriptions below:

- 885004 (engine R1002-9, body V1004, restored): no holes on firewall for pivot, no rubber bonnet detent on outer bulkhead.

- 885005 (engine R1009-9, body V1005, restored): no holes on firewall for pivot, apparently four holes for pop rivets for retaining a cover over hole in outer bulkhead, no rubber bonnet detent on outer bulkhead.

- 885009 (engine R1135-9, body V1017): no holes on firewall for pivot, no slot for pivot con rod, no hole on outer bulkhead, no bolt holes on lower outer bulkhead, rubber bonnet detent on outer bulkhead.

- 885013 (engine R1426-9, body V1025): three holes on firewall for pivot, slot for pivot con rod, rubber plug in hole on outer bulkhead, two bolt holes on lower outer bulkhead, rubber bonnet detent on outer bulkhead.

- 885018 (engine R1447-9, body V1022): three holes on firewall for pivot, slot for pivot con rod, open hole on outer bulkhead, two bolt holes on lower outer bulkhead, rubber bonnet detent on outer bulkhead.

Left-hand drive inside latch coupes:
For these cars, the three holes on the firewall to retain the inside latch mounting bracket for the locking hook, the slot on the firewall for the latch con rod to pass through, and the two holes on the lower outer bulkhead for the locating-pin receiver bracket are present, and not mentioned in the descriptions below:

- 885056 (engine 1816-9, body V1055): two holes on sill for outside latch bracket, rubber plug in hole on outer bulkhead, rubber bonnet detent on upper outer bulkhead.

- 885066: two holes on sill for outside latch bracket, hole on outer bulkhead, no rubber bonnet detent on upper outer bulkhead.

- 885130 (engine R2400-9, body V1128): two holes on sill for outside latch bracket.

- 885154 (engine R2499-9, body V1175): two holes on sill for outside latch bracket, rubber plug in hole on outer bulkhead, no rubber bonnet detent on upper outer bulkhead.

- 889560 (engine RA4?15-9, body V6929): no holes on sill for outside latch bracket, rubber plug in hole on outer bulkhead, no rubber bonnet detent on upper outer bulkhead.

- 889859 (engine RA5054-9, body V7322): no holes on sill for outside latch bracket, rubber plug in hole on outer bulkhead, no rubber bonnet detent on upper outer bulkhead.

BODY TAGS

Body tags on at least some of the early cars made by the Experimental Department were made from small rectangular plates of aluminum, with the body number apparently hand-stamped with a punch. These early tags may have been affixed to the firewall with screws or pop rivets. Very early in production, approximately when the few Experimental Department-built cars ended, the body number tags were changed to the standard Jaguar pressed sheet steel tags with rounded edges. As with other Jaguars of these period, these were held in place by two pop rivets. Ian Howe pointed out that on these pressed steel stamped plates, the prefix letter ("R" for roadsters and "V" for coupes) is of a smaller font than that used for the letters following it. This appears to generally be true of these plates for E-types as well as for some or all other Jaguars from around the period of E-type production.

The location of the body tags was initially on the firewall, above the brake and clutch reservoir mounting bracket on the upper right side of the firewall. The location was moved to the left bulkhead in the boot at or about the time of the transition from outside to inside bonnet latches. It was also about this same time that the body number was crayoned onto the right front firewall, in the general region where the old plate had been.

Also, as seen with other numbers recorded on the commission plate (engine and transmission numbers), the numbers stamped on the commission plate and those on the body tags are often close but not matching (this is discussed in the section on serial number anomalies on page 438).

The location of the pressed-steel body tags on the firewall of the early production cars varied somewhat, being mounted generally above the left side of the reservoir bracket, but sometimes to the right side of the bracket.

This is a listing of the locations of body tag locations on some early cars:

- 875009 (engine R1020-9, body R1016): on left (restored)

- 875026 (engine R1037-9, body R1044): on left

- 875045 (engine R1071-9, body R1068): on left (restored)

- 875109 (engine R1138-9, body R1129): on left

- 875119 (engine R1156-9, body R1184): on left (restored)

- 875206 (engine R1326-9, body R1295): on left (restored)

- 875258 (engine R1390-9, body R1254): on left (restored)

- 875472 (engine R1624-9, body R1604): in boot (restored)

- 885008 (engine R1116-9, body V1015): on right (restored, but was seen to be in this position before restoration)

- 885009 (engine R1135-9, body V1017): on right

- 885013 (engine R1426-9, body V1025): on left

- 885018 (engine R1447-9, body V1022): on left

- 885066 (engine R1986-9, body V1097): in boot

Interestingly, what is stated to be (and looks like) the original commission plate on early coupe 885002 is shown located on top of the right side sill (the typical location for standard production 3.8-liter E-types) on page 138 of *All About the Jaguar E-Type*. The tag does not look as if it has been moved.

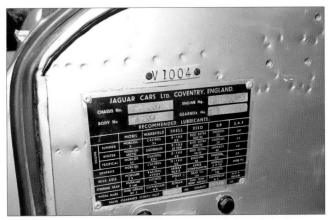

At least some of the early prototypes had body number tags fabricated from aluminum and mounted on the right-hand side of the firewall. The current restorations of 885004 and 885005 show this configuration. The body number tag on this restored car is held on with screws.

After the Production Department began building the cars the tags had changed to pressed sheet metal. The authors are not sure at what point this took place, or if there were overlap between the two systems. This is unrestored 875026 (engine R1037-9) showing the tag mounted above the left-hand side of the pop-riveted reservoir mount.

A body number tag mounted above the left-hand side of the welded brake reservoir mount on 885013.

On 885009 (engine R1135-9, body V1017) the body number plate was mounted above the right-hand side of the reservoir mount.

FOOTWELL RECESSES FOR BRAKE ASSIST MECHANISM

Both right and left side footwells had a recess to make clearance for the brake power-assist mechanism. On

Earlier cars had the recess for the brake system comprised of a pressed-in feature in the footwell, seen here as a dip located to the right of the leading edge of the middle blanking plate (to its left side in the picture, which is looking toward the rear of the car). The pipe in the lower right of the picture is an exhaust header for an American V-8 that had been installed in the car.

early cars this was comprised of a small dip near the leading edge of the top of the footwell. At sometime in production a second depression, oblong in shape, was included behind the first. This is not illustrated here, but is shown on page 5 of Howe's "Early E-type Spotters Guide 2" in *The E-Type*, Issue 78, May 2011. This arrangement with two recesses appears to be a precursor to the single long recess, comprised of two-pieces of sheet metal, seen on later cars.

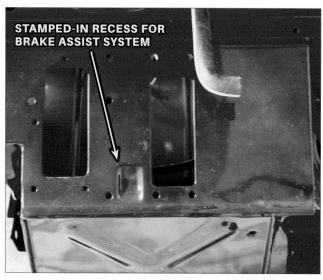

On the right-hand side, the recess is not easily seen on left-hand drive cars, but shows clearly here between the open clutch and brake apertures on the left-side footwell of 875472 when it was undergoing restoration.

The later-type brake recess port shown on a left-hand footwell.

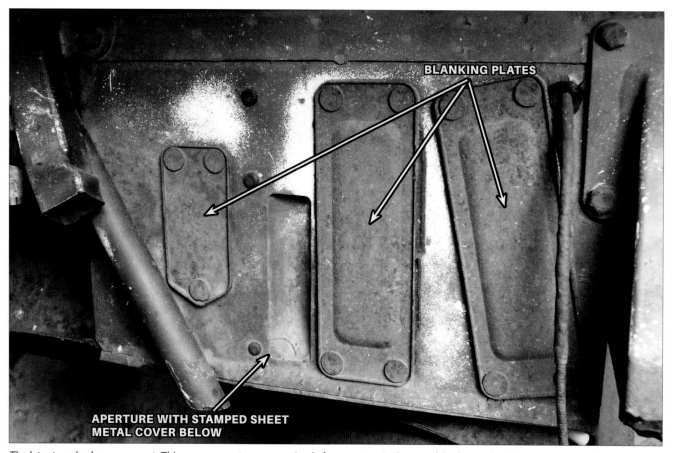

The later-type brake recess port. This arrangement was comprised of an aperture in the top of the footwell with a stamped sheet metal cover attached from below.

FIREWALL MOUNTING OF THE WINDSCREEN WIPER PARK-POSITION ADJUSTMENT KNOB

The windscreen-wiper park-position adjustment knob is mounted on a protrusion on the left-hand side of the firewall. On a very few of the first production cars this protrusion was made from a separate piece of metal, and was spot-welded into a hole in the firewall. Subsequent to these few cars, the protrusion was stamped directly into the firewall sheet metal itself, removing the need for attachment of a separate piece. The multiple-piece arrangement appears to have been used on only a few very early cars before being replaced by a single-piece configuration. The authors have observed the early

Underside view of the brake-recess plate on the right side footwell, looking up from the floor toward the top of the footwell. The construction of the plate spanning right and left apertures is evident when seen from below.

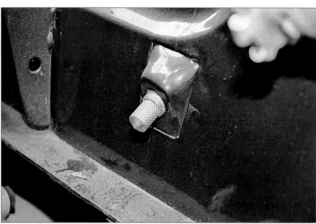

The protrusion in the firewall sheet metal for the windscreen-wiper park adjustment knob changed in early production. This protrusion on the firewall of 850008 (engine R1030-9, body R1021) is fabricated from a separate piece attached to the firewall. In this picture the retaining nut for the adjustment knob is not fitted.

Top view of a brake-recess plate on the top of the left-hand side footwell.

Somewhat later in production, but still very early, 885008 had the adjustment knob retained in a stamped section of the firewall.

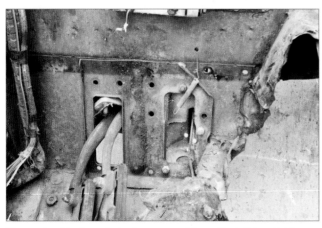

The underside view of a brake-recess plate on the left-hand side, also seen from below.

885018 (engine R1447-9, body V1022) shows the same single-piece stamping for the adjustment knob.

multi-piece protrusion on 850008, which had a pressed-in protrusion. 850034, 875014, 875026, 875038 (restored), 875109, 885008, 885009, 885013 show a pressed-in protrusion. The multi-piece protrusion is seen in a line drawing in Figure 38, on page 36 of the Jaguar Service Manual, publication number E/123/5.

On 875472 the single-piece stamping is seen clearly when the knob has been removed.

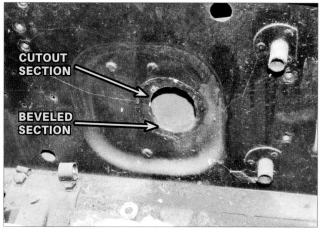

This right-hand side power-brake accommodation hole on left-hand drive coupe 885009 has a beveled section on the bottom, but has a cutout section with sharp edge on the top.

885013 shows a fully-beveled hole, in the late style.

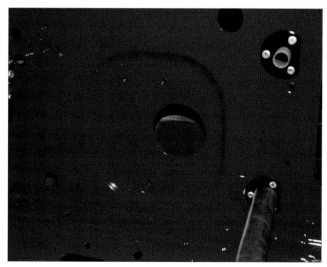

The authors have not observed any cutting on later brake servo clearance holes. This view from 875472 is typical.

BRAKE SERVO CLEARANCE HOLE IN FIREWALL

There were different types of holes in the firewall for the power brake assist mechanism. Generally, some of the earlier holes had rough edges, with the later having beveled edges. This is discussed on page 7 of Howe's "Early E-type Spotters Guide 2" in *The E-Type*, Issue 78, May 2011.

BRAKE SERVO CLEARANCE HOLE COVER

The brake servo clearance hole on the passenger's side of the firewall on 3.8-liter cars (where no brake mechanisms were fitted) was covered by a steel cover held on by pop-rivets. On early cars, there were three pop-rivets holding the plate on, 120-degrees apart with one rivet at the top of the plate. Later, four pop rivets were used, 90-degrees apart, again with one at the top. The number of rivets from a sample of a few cars appears below. As before, the other commission-plate numbers are given so as to roughly place the car in the overall sequence of production. It is also again noted when a car is restored, or if it has otherwise clearly been disturbed from its original state.

- 875026 (engine R1037-9, body R1044): 3
- 875109 (engine R1138-9, body R1129): 3
- 875274 (engine R1395-9, body R1373): 3 (restored)
- 875472 (engine R1624-9, body R1604): 4 (restored)
- 876602 (engine R3736-9, body R2984): 4 (restored)
- 885005 (engine R1009-9, body V1005): 3 (restored)
- 885009 (engine R1135-9, body V1017): 3
- 885056 (engine 1816-9, body V1055): 4
- 885066 (engine R1986-9, body V1097): 4

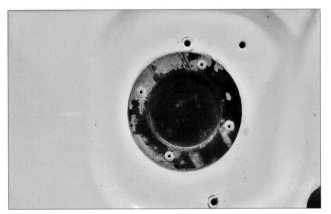

The three-rivet brake hole cover still showing some of its original black paint, and the typical unpainted rivets.

Four-rivet brake hole cover seen on 885066. Here the original black paint and unpainted rivets are well preserved.

On one early car, 850008, the cover plate found in place before restoration was made of aluminum instead of steel and was fastened with three rivets. This is the authors' only observation of an aluminum cover.

No reservoir bracket is seen on restored 885005. The same is true for restored 885004.

BRAKE AND CLUTCH RESERVOIR MOUNT ON FIREWALL

On right-hand drive cars the brake and clutch fluid reservoirs were mounted on the firewall. Except for the very first few cars, possibly only those made by the Experimental Department, there was a reservoir-mounting bracket affixed to the right-hand side of the firewall on all cars, whether right-hand drive (where the reservoirs were mounted on the bracket) or left-hand drive (where the bracket was unused).

875026 has eight rivets on the reservoir bracket.

On 875206 the bracket is spot-welded. The small hole just to the left of center (to the right in the picture) with pulled-up edges, is likely not original.

At least some Experimental Department cars had no reservoir bracket. The two restored cars 885004 and 885005 show the lack of a bracket. Shortly thereafter the brackets were fitted to all cars. Initially, the brackets were affixed to the firewall by two rows of pop rivets (along the top and bottom flanges). In all observed cases, this mounting arrangement used four pop rivets per row, for a total of eight.

Data from individual cars:

▸ 850008 (engine R1030-9, body R1021, restored): held on by eight screws, but was likely pop-riveted on before restoration

▸ 850034 (engine R1157-9): welded

▸ 875009 (engine R1020-9, body R1016, restored): pop-riveted

- 875026 (engine R1037-9, body R1044): pop-riveted

- 875045 (engine R1071-9, body R1068): pop-riveted

- 875109 (engine R1138-9, body R1129): welded

- 875119 (engine R1156-9, body R1184, restored): welded

- 875206 (engine R1326-9, body R1295, restored): welded

- 875258 (engine R1390-9, body R1254, restored): welded

- 875472 (engine R1604-9, body R1604, restored): welded

- 885009 (engine R1135-9, body V1017): welded

- 885013 (engine R1816-9, body V1055): welded

- 885066 (engine R1986-9, body V1097): welded

875009 (engine R1020-9, body R1016) shows a relatively thick section of flange above the body number plate, but has a thin section of flange at the right-hand side (shown at the left in the picture). The brake/clutch reservoir mounting bracket (only used to mount reservoirs on right-hand drive cars, and unused on left-hand drive cars such as this one) has always been seen by the authors, on original cars, painted the body color. The black paint seen on this restored car is almost certainly incorrect. Likewise, they have seen the round cover to the far right of the picture in black paint only, so the white color (matching the body color) is likely in error on this restored car.

Left-hand drive roadster 875206 (engine R1326-9, body R1295) has the flange thick all the way across to the right end.

BONNET SEALING RUBBER RETENTION FLANGE

It has been noted that the flange along the top of the firewall retaining the rubber sealing gasket at the back of the bonnet was thicker on some earlier cars than it generally was on later cars (*e.g.* page 5 of Howe's "Early E-type Spotters Guide 2" in *The E-Type*, Issue 78, May 2011). A long thick flange is seen also. While research shows this effect to some extent, the flanges are often of different heights on different places along the firewall, making the thickness somewhat difficult to define and any progression over time difficult to characterize. More data will be gathered.

The following is a listing of cars with thickness of the flange noted. As the flanges are often bent and as the thickness of the flange can change along the firewall, this data is somewhat subjective; no exact measurements were taken and some of the listings of thick, medium or thin might be classified in a different category by a different observer.

- 875009 (engine R1020-9, body R1016): thick

- 875026 (engine R1037-9, body R1044): thick

- 875045 (engine R1071-9, body R1068): thick

- 875122 (engine R1168-9, body R1142): thick

- 875206 (engine R1326-9, body R1295): medium

- 885008 (engine R1116-9, body V1015): medium

- 885009 (engine R1135-9, body V1017): thin

- 885013 (engine R1426-9, body V1025): medium

- 885018 (engine R1447-9, body V1022): thin

- 885056 (engine R1816-9, body V1055): thin

- 885066 (engine R1986-9, body V1097): thin

DRAIN HOLES IN FUEL FILLER NACELLE

The drain holes in the fuel filler nacelle are discussed in the section "Fuel Filler Recess, Cap, Lid and Hinge".

STRENGTHENING RIB IN REAR BULKHEAD

The central strengthening rib on the panel behind the seats was not present on early cars. This is noted on page 9 of Howe's "Early E-type Spotters Guide 2" in *The E-Type*, Issue 78, May 2011 and has been observed by the authors on many cars. Based on observations over the years it appears this dip was introduced somewhere around about chassis number 875190 or so.

Initially, it appears, the central section of the rear bulkhead was without a strengthening rib. This picture also well illustrates the straight rear bulkhead behind the seats, as discussed elsewhere.

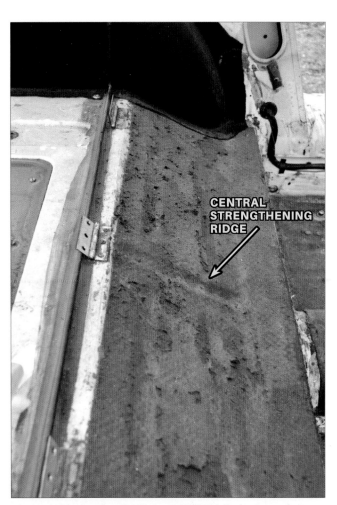

The rear of the interior of LHD coupe 885056 shows the central strengthening ridge beneath the original tar paper covering.

STRENGTHENING RIBS IN BOOT

The strengthening ribs pressed into the sheet steel boot panels on the perimeter of the boot (behind the beige finishing panels) were found in both inset and relieved types. This is noted, for example, on page 9 of Howe's "Early E-type Spotters Guide 2" in *The E-Type*, Issue 78, May 2011.

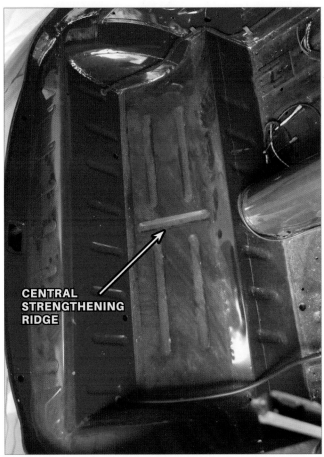

The central strengthening rib showing on chassis no 875472. The authors have only seen these ridges protruding into the area of the rear subframe, and never up into the area of the cockpit. That is, they have always appeared dished-in when viewed from inside the cockpit.

The boot-side panel recesses on 875026, showing inset stamping.

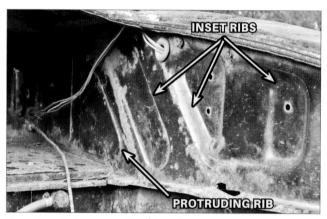

Inset boot stampings showing on 875472.

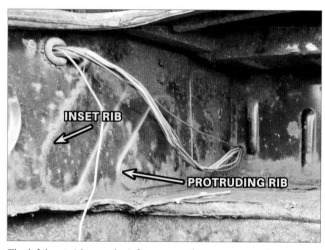

Stamping reinforcement ribs in the right boot side panel of left-hand drive roadster 876319. There is a protruding rib toward the front of the car, but three inset ribs further toward the rear.

INSET RIBS

PROTRUDING RIB

INSET RIB

PROTRUDING RIB

The left boot side panel reinforcement rib stampings, with a protruding rib toward the front of the car and an inset rib toward the back, again on 876319.

BONNET

WINGS (FRONT FENDERS)

There were many detail changes in the wings of 1961 and 1962 cars. In addition to the well-known change from outside to inside bonnet latches, there were numerous changes in the details of various fasteners, brackets and hardware. Some are shown here.

About October 1961, at chassis numbers 850091/2, 860004/5, 875385/6 and 885020/1, the bonnet and front fenders assembly was changed and the bonnet latch was moved inside. This is the transition point of the first 500 cars.

BUMPER STOP MOUNT

On the left is a wing the authors suspect is an NOS replacement for use with an outside latch car. It appears from the crude gas welding that the bumper stop above the outside latch mechanism was added later. Note that the vertical metal flange (oriented horizontally in the picture) used to attach the fender well to the wing is not quite perpendicular to the main line of the bottom of the trailing edge of the wing, likely an indication of the flange being glued rather than welded, as it would be if it was a wing produced at the time of initial outside latch production. The wing on the right is an earlier outside latch wing not showing the bumper stop mount.

GUSSET

The triangular gusset seen in the wing at the left, at the juncture of the trailing edge of the wheel arch and the straight trailing section, is a later feature. It is not seen on the earlier wing on the right.

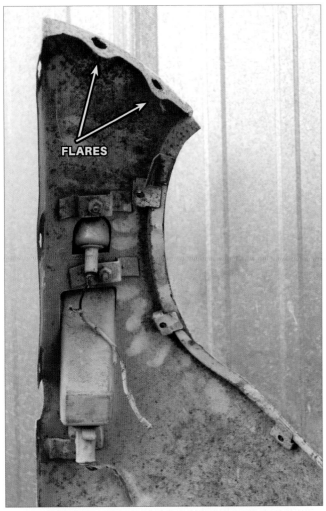

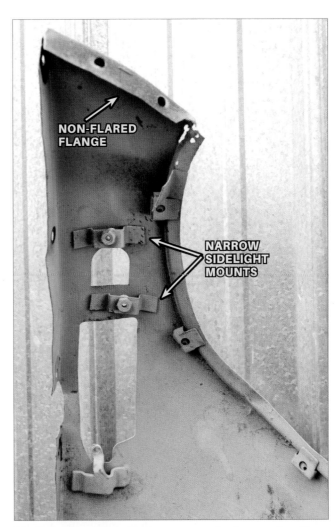

The wings on early cars, approximately during the production time of the outside latch cars, had flares in the flanges. These were located at the location of the holes for the bolts that are used to attach the wing to the bonnet center section. These flares are showing here on left-hand drive coupe 885008's original right wing. Note also the straps holding the bolts retaining the side/flasher lamp are wide on this early car.

The flares around the bolt holes seen on early wings are absent in the panel-attachment flange of this later bonnet. It appears the flares were discontinued perhaps sometime before the end of outside latch production. The retaining straps for the side/flasher lamp mounting bolts are narrower here than the early ones seen in the picture of the wing from early coupe 885008.

BONNET CENTER SECTION

On very early cars a weld seam is found running laterally inside the bonnet center section and also in the bottom panel of the belly pan. This seam line is apparently more prominent on earlier cars and seems to be found in slightly different positions along the longitudinal axis of the car. The authors do not know at what point this feature was discontinued. This feature is noted by Howe.

On most early cars the body number is stamped on the stiffening bracket at the back of the juncture of the right wing and the bonnet center section. While many cars show this, the practice appears to be inconsistent. Body numbers as late as R1604 have been stamped in this location, but many times they appear to have not been stamped. Perhaps these stampings were made to permit mating up of the correct bonnet with the chassis on the assembly line. The body numbers on the earlier cars were on a tag pop-riveted on the top right area of the

firewall, so the two numbers would have been easy to see together when joining the bonnet. On later cars with the body number attached in the boot, the body number is often written in crayon on the firewall near the location where the body number plate used to be attached. This crayon number could play the same role as the tag did earlier. One unusual case is coupe 885056, that has body tag V1055 located in the luggage compartment, but has 1081 stamped on its apparently-original bonnet.

The welded-in louvers are a well-known feature of the early cars and were only in production for a few months. Afterward, the louvers were pressed directly into the bonnet center section.

Some early cars show spot welds on the outside surface of the bonnet where the wheel wells fasten to the inside surface of the bonnet.

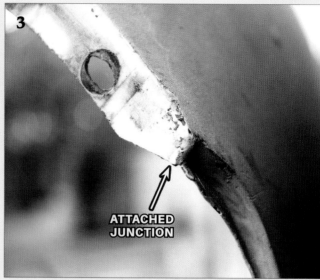

ATTACHED
JUNCTION

NON-ATTACHED
JUNCTION

1 Multiple large diameter holes on the flange between the intake aperture and headlight nacelle on an early car.

2 After the very earliest bonnets with large holes and flares, came bonnets with larger holes but no flares. Later, bonnets had smaller bolt holes and still no flares.

3 There were detail changes on bonnet construction over time. Here the juncture of the two flanges on the bonnet center section at the lower corner of the headlight aperture have been joined together.

4 Here the juncture of the two flanges on the bonnet center section at the lower corner of the headlight aperture have not been joined together on this later bonnet center section.

5 On early cars a joining weld ran laterally across the bonnet and shows on the inside. This is a view looking up inside the intake aperture of restored left-hand drive roadster chassis number 875009. This is also seen on some belly pans. Later the bonnet was comprised of fewer separate pieces and there is no weld line seen.

6 Another view of the joining weld on the front of the bonnet. This one is from the unrestored coupe 885056.

7 The rear terminating edge of the bulge on this restored early 3.8-liter car comes sharply back, in a manner the authors have never seen on 3.8-liter cars known to be original.

8 In all original 3.8-liter cars observed by the authors the terminating edge of the bulge in the bonnet center section lies in the same vertical plane as the back edge of the wings. In addition, all vent trim pieces at the back of the bulge have had planar faces, as shown here.

9 For comparison with the 3.8-liter cars, here is the rear of the bonnet of P1R42679. This car is in very original condition and shows a forward-taper on the terminating edge of the bulge. This feature have been seen on other Series 2 cars as well, but never on a Series 1 car. The chrome vent trim at the back of the bulge on this car is planar, showing no curvature (not seen in this figure).

10 For reference, here is the terminating edge of the bonnet bulge on V12 roadster 1S20001. This car also has a planar grille on the rear of the bulge. The car is in very original condition, with its full history known.

JOINING WELD

At chassis numbers 860478/9 and 886013/4, about June 1962, the bonnet and its hinges were changed.

From research of surviving cars: Chassis numbers 860005, 875407, 875967 and 876052 had the welded-in louvers, while numbers 876577, 885576, 885733 and 885980 had the pressed-in louvers. The outside latch car, chassis number 875186, had pressed-in louvers. This is an anomaly and probably the center section of the bonnet was replaced in the past. It is somewhat curious, though, as there is no apparent evidence of damage to the front fenders, which still have the outside bonnet latches.

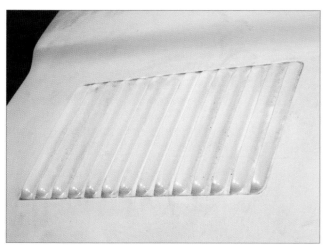

Welded-in bonnet louvers were characteristic of the early cars.

Inside view of the welded-in louvers. Note the louver section is not merely a flat piece spot-welded in, but has been fabricated into a box section before installation in the bonnet center section.

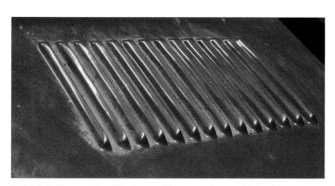

Later 3.8-liter cars had the bonnet louvers stamped into the center-bonnet section sheet metal. These louvers are from 4.2-liter E-type 1E14959, but are representative of the stamped-in louvers.

Inside view of the stamped-in louvers from left-hand drive roadster 879032.

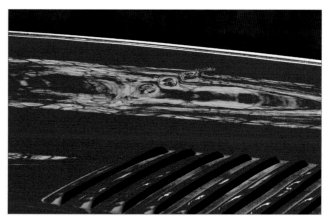

The early bonnets often show the effects of spot-welding of the duct and diaphragm panels to the center panel. These can appear as dimples on the outer surface of the center panel. Later bonnets had the duct and diaphragm panels glued in, so this effect is not seen. This outside view looking across the center panel of the bonnet of an outside latch car clearly shows spot welds above the right side wheel well baffle.

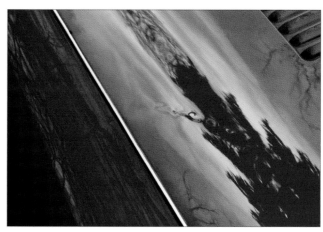

Another view of the bonnet spot welds, this one looking down. Here the sweep of the spot welds across the bonnet center panel and out to the top of the right fender can be seen.

BONNET BELLY PAN

The belly pan of early cars had a single small hole under its leading edge, roughly in the center. This was discontinued shortly into production. Later, the institution of the automatically-tipping license plate mechanism necessitated an oblong hole toward the front of the belly pan to permit the connecting rod to pass through.

The recess on the trailing edge of this belly pan from 885056 (to accommodate the bonnet hinges) has the pulled-in edges seen on early cars. On later cars, the edges were basically parallel or somewhat flared out. In addition, this is the only belly pan observed with both the oval hole (for the license plate tipping connecting rod to pass through), as well as the small round hole seen on early belly pans.

This is a 1963 belly pan showing the later-type flared-out edges on the bonnet-hinge recess. It also shows the standard single oval hole to accommodate the license plate tipping con rod.

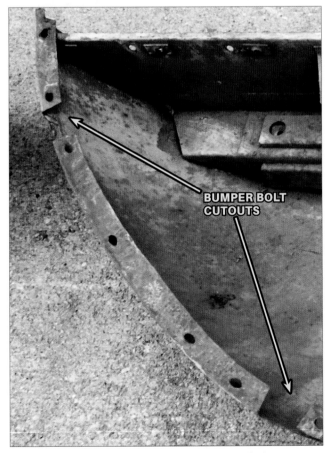

The more neatly cutout apertures to accommodate the bumper attachment bolts seen on a 1963 belly pan. Contrast this to the crude cutouts shown for early coupe 885056.

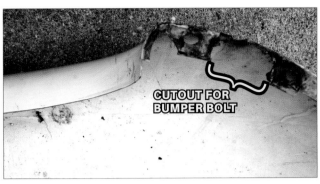

The crude cutout on the panel fastening flange to accommodate bumper-mounting bolts is seen here on early coupe 885056. These were more neatly cut out on later cars.

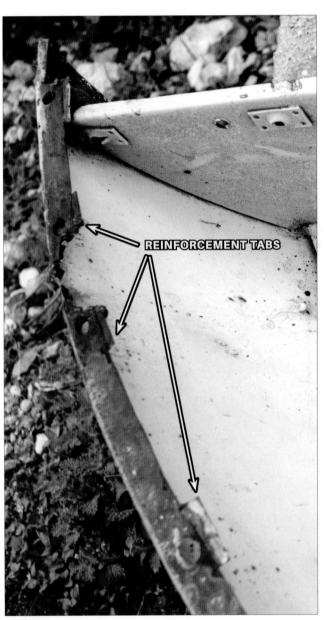

On earlier belly pans there were reinforcement tabs under some of the attachment-flange bolt holes. This feature is shown here on 885056. This appears to have extended throughout the welded-in louvers and it appears the holes were generally larger on the outside latch cars.

A close-up view of the reinforcement tabs on the belly pan of 85056.

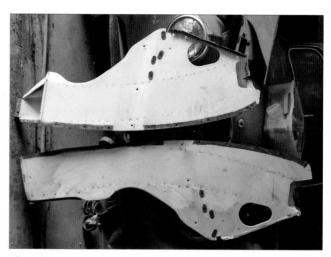

These bonnet panels from 885056 show the spot-welds seen on early bonnets.

BONNET INNER PANELS, HARDWARE AND TRIM

Brace at the juncture of the rear of the bonnet center section (to the top far left in the picture) and the rear of the right wing on 875157, showing the body number stamping 1251.

The early type headlight-sealing rubber was a narrow U-channel section with relatively sharp edges that fitted around the headlight cover glass. The rubber-and-glass assembly then sat in the recess around the headlight glass aperture in the bonnet.

On later belly pans there were no reinforcement tabs under the holes.

Later cars had this headlight cover sealing gasket with a more complex cross-section than earlier seals.

The early-type bonnet-hinge bearing protruding from the front subframe. This was a boss with threaded protrusion. The hinges pivoted on the bearing or boss. The bearing was fixed in the transverse tube.

Another view of the early-type bonnet hinge mount, with the bonnet-hinge bearing permanently affixed to the front subframe lateral ends.

The later-type bonnet hinge mount on the front subframe had a removable bonnet-hinge bearing that was retained in the transverse tube by a bolt.

View of the later-type bonnet hinge mount with the bonnet-hinge bearing and its retaining bolt removed, as would be done to remove the bonnet and hinges as an assembly (without the necessity of removing the hinges from the bonnet, as was required of the earlier design shown in the figure to the left).

A bonnet-hinge bearing with retaining bolt through the center, removed from a later-type front subframe.

The early-type domed-headed rivets on the bonnet balance link assembly (lower) and the later flat-headed rivets on the balance link above.

A typical flange permanently attached to the upper front subframe arm. This is one of the attachment points for the bonnet balance link assembly.

On a few very early cars, likely some or all of the cars produced by the Experimental Department (rather than the Production Department) the attachment point on the upper front subframe arm for the bonnet balance link assembly was clamped on with bolts. Perhaps this acted as a means of adjustment. In any case, it was discontinued very early on, after only a few cars were made.

BONNET HINGES AND LIFTS

Several changes are listed for this area: at chassis numbers 850238/9, 860138/9, 876457/8 and 885384/5, the bonnet hinge and front cross-member of the front frame were changed about February 1962; and at chassis numbers 860478/9 and 886013/4, about June 1962, the front subframe assembly and hinge were changed.

It was observed that unrestored cars 875026 and 876482 have the early-type thin hinges. Even 879032, a 1963 model year car, had thin hinges.

1 The early-type bonnet hinges had a thin section around the pivot point and tapered corners on the bracket. It appears that these brackets were painted the body color.

2 The later-type bonnet hinges had a thicker section around the pivot point and more sharp corners.

3 Three styles of bonnet hinges, the later thicker types to the left and the early thin type to the right.

4 This fabricated sheet steel bracket was bolted just next to the left-hand side bonnet lift in order to retain the electrical cable running from the subframe to the bonnet. As seems to be often the case, the cable is not running through the clip.

BONNET LATCHES

On the first 500 cars, the bonnet latching mechanism was operated from outside the bonnet with a T-key. Subsequently, the mechanism was changed to one operated from inside the cockpit without a key. This transition is the most easily observable of the changes from the first 500-cars to the later cars and, has been noted, this occurred about September 1961 at chassis numbers 850091/2, 860004/5, 875385/6 and 885020/1. This transition is discussed further in the "Firewall" section.

Three holes in the firewall to mount interior latches were introduced before the latches were changed to inside-operated types. They are plugged with white plugs.

For a period after the latches moved into the cockpit, the two screws used to retain the catch on the body on each side were continued. From research of surviving cars: Chassis numbers 860084, 875427, 875954 and 876052 have these screws on each side.

1 *With the introduction of the inside bonnet latches, the catch was mounted on the bonnet.*

2 *The early bonnet latch mechanism was found on the inside of the front wing, retained by four slot-head screws.*

3 *The catches for the early mechanism were bolted to the tops of the front sills.*

4 *The inside latching mechanism (the mounting bracket for the locking hook, and the hook itself) was bolted to the firewall.*

5 *The two retaining screws for the outside bonnet latch on the body were continued sometime after the bonnet latches were moved inside.*

The latch control handle was mounted in front of the doors.

RUBBER STOPS

As part of the exterior bonnet latch setup, rubber stops were mounted on the firewall where the bonnet came up against it.

In Martinez and Nory's *European Automobiles of the 50's and 60's*, there are two clear pictures of an early inside latch car with the rubber stops of the outside latch setup. This is likely to be indicative of how the car left the factory because the car is a quite original example and this would be an unusual and difficult part to fit as a modification. Number 860005 has these rubber stops, while 876052 does not have them. This is discussed in much more detail in the Firewall section beginning on pages 102 to 107.

The rubber bonnet bumpers of the outside latch cars were mounted on these brackets.

REAR TUB SHEET METAL, FIREWALL AND UNDERSIDE

About May 1962, the following components are cited to have been changed at chassis numbers 860478/9 and 886013/4:

- ▶ rear fender assembly
- ▶ tail panel below the boot lid
- ▶ boot gutters
- ▶ casing assembly at the rear side of the luggage compartment floor
- ▶ roof panel assembly
- ▶ windscreen header panel assembly
- ▶ scuttle top panel and windscreen pillars
- ▶ cantrail panel assembly
- ▶ drip bead on the cantrail panel assembly
- ▶ windscreen pillar assembly
- ▶ underframe
- ▶ closing panels under the screen pillars
- ▶ outer sills
- ▶ roof panel
- ▶ rear fenders
- ▶ boot lid

Changes for chassis numbers 850526/7, 860580/1, 877355/6 and 886092/3:

- ▶ body underframe assembly
- ▶ floor assembly
- ▶ rear end body shell

Other changes listed for the rear tub were:

- ▶ seal assemblies at the rear of the wheel arches were changed about March 1963 at chassis numbers 850655/6 and 879023/4
- ▶ the body underframe assembly and floor assembly were changed at chassis numbers 860580/1 and 886092/3
- ▶ the rubber buffer cushioning the bonnet sides in the closed position was discontinued (incorporated as part of the new inside latch) sometime shortly after chassis numbers 850091/2, 860004/5, 875385/6 and 885020/1

COCKPIT SHEET METAL

The most well-known change in the cockpit sheet metal was the introduction of the sunken footwells and the recessed rear bulkheads, on both the driver's and passenger's sides. While the E-type prototype E1A had sunken footwells, the footwells of the early production E-types were flat. This and the welded-in louvers, are two often-quoted features of early E-types.

In Jaguar Sports Cars, Skilleter stated that "all the 1962 E-types incorporated footwells in both driver's and passenger's side of the cockpit and an indentation made in the rear bulkhead on both models also allowed more rearward travel for the seats." This suggests Skilleter considered flat floor cars as 1961 models.

In late winter 1962, at chassis numbers 850357/8, 860175/6, 876581/2 and 885503/4, the floor assembly was changed to include footwells. Note that the *J.30 Spare Parts Catalogue (June 1963)* lists chassis numbers 876381/2 instead of 876581/2, the numbers given in other sources. A Jaguar service bulletin lists the body numbers for the change as OTS: 2879/2889, FHC:1635/1647.

An April 23, 2014 posting on the E-type UK website forum (http://forum.etypeuk.com) carried a copy of *Service Bulletin*, Number N.15 dated May 1962 stating that, in connection with the "dished footwell" (*i.e.* the design following the flat floor): "This modification can be carried out to earlier cars at the customer's request and cost. All the necessary parts and detailed fitting instructions are available from the Jaguar Service Division, Coventry. See also Service Bulletin No. L.18." Thus, some earlier flat floor cars may have been converted to dished floors at the factory or dealerships.

Other listed changes are the retainers for the cantrail seals were changed at chassis numbers 860478/9 and 886013/4; about June 1962, the body underframe assembly, floor assembly and rear end body shell were changed (including modifying the rear bulkhead of the body shell to include recesses to allow the seats 1-1/2 inches more rearward travel), at chassis numbers 850526/7, 860580/1, 877355/6 and 886092/3; and the body underframe assembly and floor assembly were changed at chassis numbers 860580/1 and 886092/3.

1 *An inside view of the flat floor of an early car.*

2 *An outside view of the flat floor of an early car.*

3 *Early in production these sunken footwells were introduced to increase room in the cockpit. This is the inside view, from the cockpit.*

4 *Outside view of the sunken footwells on a later car.*

DOORS

RAIN TROUGHS

Rain water entering along the front of the door was caught by a trough attached to the top of the door frame. Some of these drains were pop-riveted on and some were spot-welded. It appears the earlier design used pop rivets. In addition, on earlier cars there was a small hole on the slanted section below the trough to catch water. In both cases, the water was directed through the door and out drains at the bottom.

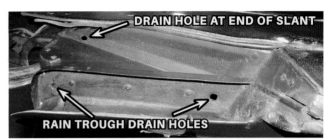

Rain trough on early roadster 875026 showing drain holes at the front and back, as well as the third drain hole on the end of the slanted region below the trough.

Side view of the same scene showing the shape of the sheet metal trough. The raised forward region on the lower hole can also be seen. Presumably this helped guide water into the lower hole.

5 The straight rear bulkhead area behind the seats on left-hand drive roadster 875026.

6 Another view of the straight rear bulkhead area behind the seats in left-hand drive roadster 875090, with all trim and seats removed.

7 Later in 3.8-liter production, the rear bulkhead was indented to increase seat travel. This illustration is from a 4.2-liter car, but is representative of the 3.8-liter indented bulkhead.

The region of the lower door drain hole from early roadster 875088 (engine R1132-9, transmission EB237JS, body R1140). Note the hole is not tipped toward the rear of the car (up the slant) as seen in 875026, but instead apparently has a deposit of material (lead?) in front of the hole. This helped guide water into the hole. This is usually accomplished by raising the metal on one side of the hole. The authors have only seen this in this one instance and suspect it may not be a factory feature.

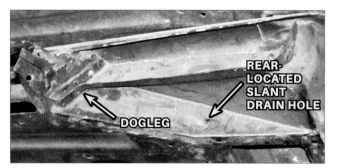

The later door water troughs had a dogleg continuation on their rear end. This extended the region where water leaking between the door and body-shell was trapped (to then be directed out the bottom of the door). Note that in this instance, the hole in the lower slanted section of sheet metal (below the water trough), has been moved from its prior position near the front of the slanted section, rearward to near the middle. Based on observations this feature likely was introduced 1963.

In this case, the rear shroud is not present and the drain hole can be seen.

This view of a door from a 4.2-liter car shows the dogleg to the rear of the trough and trim on the lower slanted region. There is no hole in the slanted region, or if there is, it is covered over. Possibly some late 3.8-liter cars had this feature, but it may have come in with the 4.2-liter cars.

Two shrouded lower door drains on the lower trailing edge of the door on roadster 875109 (engine R1138-9).

BOTTOM DOOR DRAINS

Water collected in the door through the trough and holes along the leading edge, around the glass, or in any other manner, could exit through drains along the bottom edge of the door. In order to prevent the rubber seal around the door from blocking these drains, hoods or shrouds were placed beneath them to permit the water to exit on the outside of the rubber seals. These shrouds were held by pop rivets.

On coupe 885056 (engine R1816-9) the lower leading edge of the door has only one drain and shroud.

Two drain hold shrouds on the leading bottom edge of the door of roadster 875109, held in place by pop-rivets.

Coupe 885056 has a single shrouded drain hole on the trailing edge as well. It appears this feature continued to the end of 3.8-liter production.

INNER DOOR SKIN

On earlier cars the holes to retain part of the window regulator assembly were doubled. That is, while only four holes were needed, two sets of four were drilled, shifted in register from each other by about an inch. Only one set of four was used to retain the window regulator. This was later changed to a single set of four holes, all of which were used. In addition, early doors had four elongated holes along the top, three toward the rear and one toward the front. On later doors the second from rear-most hole was omitted and only three holes appeared.

An early inner door skin from roadster 875088, showing the eight holes for the window regulator (just to the left of the door latch hole in the middle of the door). The four oblong holes along the top of the door are apparent here as well.

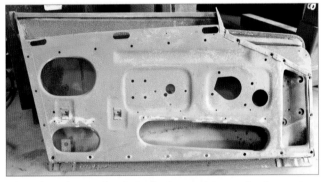

A later door showing four holes for the regulator mechanism and only three oblong holes along the top of the door.

Close-up of the eight-hole feature with window regulator mechanism bolted in place. In this instance, likely from roadster 875198, rubber plugs have been placed on the two extra rear-most holes.

Another eight-hole configuration. In this case (unrestored coupe 885056) the two rear-most extra holes are taped over with what appears to be electrician's tape.

DOOR TOP SECTION

The top section of the outer door skin was comprised of two pieces on early cars. This was later changed to a single-piece arrangement.

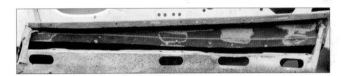

Inner view of the top section of an early door showing the seam where the two sheet metal sections were welded together. Likely this door is from 885008.

Close-up view of the seam between the two outer door-skin pieces on coupe 885056.

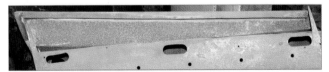

An inner view of a later, single piece door skin without a seam.

REAR OF DOOR

The trailing edge of the door on restored coupe 885008. Here the top edge of the outer skin is thin, as opposed to the doors of later coupes that had a thick filled-in top section. This thin skin at the top has been observed on 885008, 885009, 885013 and 885018.

Comparison of a thick top trailing edge of a later coupe, on the left, with the thin edge of an unrestored door from 885008. These are the only two types of top trailing edge coupe door features of which the authors are aware.

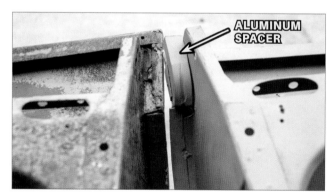

An early coupe door with the thin top trailing edge on the left, contrasted with a roadster door on the right. The roadster doors had an aluminum spacer fastened on the inside edge of the top trailing skin of the door. On the outer side of this was the chrome trim piece running across the top of the door.

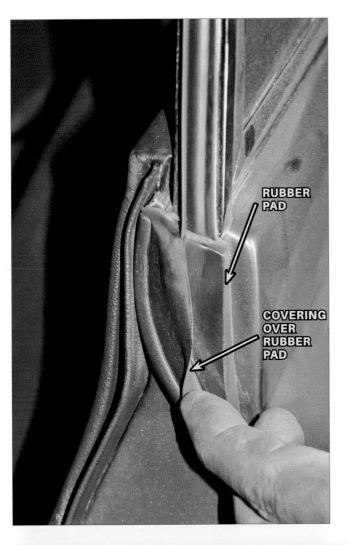

LEFT: *The top front of a striker face of coupe 885008 (after restoration) showing the rubber pad directly below the vertical B-pillar. The covering rubber is pulled back here to better show the rubber pad. These pads filled the region behind the thin trailing edge of the tops of the early coupe doors and acted as gap fillers. In later coupes this rubber feature was absent and the top of the trailing edge of the door was filled-in, as shown in other pictures in this section.*

RUBBER PAD

COVERING OVER RUBBER PAD

BELOW: *Close-up view of the aluminum spacer on the top trailing edge of the left door of left-hand drive roadster chassis number 875026. On the left is the end of the chrome trailing trim piece running along the top of the door.*

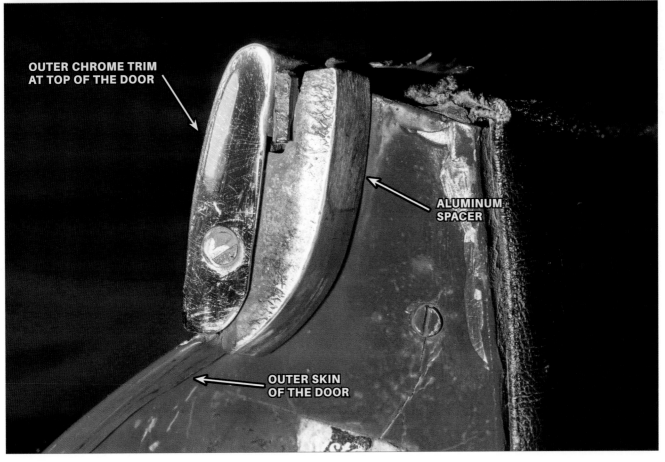

OUTER CHROME TRIM AT TOP OF THE DOOR

ALUMINUM SPACER

OUTER SKIN OF THE DOOR

DOOR HINGES

Early door hinges had grease nipple fittings to lubricate the hinges. This was omitted on later doors.

Early hinge with grease fitting.

Later hinge mechanism without grease fitting.

Views along the rotation axis of early (top) and later (bottom) door hinges.

The earliest type door hinge, showing the grease nipple for lubricating the pivot shaft. There is only one set of holes for the detent arm to attach to the hinge, showing on the upper right surface of the hinge (in the picture), making it suitable for one side of the car only.

The next style of door hinges also had holes for attaching the detent arm on one location on the hinge, making the hinges only suited for one or the other sides of the car. It also had a hole next to the pivot point, but it was not threaded for a grease nipple.

Later the door hinges did not have any fitting for a grease nipple and had two sets of detent holes drilled, suiting the hinge casting for use on either side of the car. Note also here the heavy bosses on the right and left of the region where the pivot shaft goes.

Side views of three types of door hinges. On the left is a hinge with a grease nipple, as typically found on outside latch cars. In the middle is a later hinge that was in production roughly through the run of flat floor cars. The right hinge is for a later 3.8-liter car. Note on the right-most hinge that there are two sets of holes for the door detent arm, making the hinge suitable for use on either side of the car. The earlier hinges are only appropriate for one side.

DOOR COVERS AND PADDING

On earlier cars the padding between the door inner skin and the trim panels was made of a matted fiber material, while on later cars rubber disks were used. This may have been a change that occurred when the 4.2-liter models came out, or it may have been a late 3.8-liter production change.

View of the padding on the right door of coupe 885056, showing the matted fiber pads.

About May 1962, at chassis numbers 860478/9 and 886013/4, the door shells and hinges were changed. Skilleter cites this change with chassis numbers 860475/6, instead of 860478/9. At chassis numbers 850506/7 and 877201/2, about May 1962, the door shell assembly was changed. Some cars before these chassis numbers were also modified.

DOOR HINGES AND SUPPORTS

About May 1962, the door shells and hinges were changed at chassis numbers 860478/9 and 886013/4. Skilleter cites this change with chassis numbers 860475/6 instead of 860478/9.

DOOR LATCHES

The authors are not aware of any design changes.

BOOT SHEET METAL

The recess for the backup light in the rear inside of the boot floor changed on the early cars. On early cars it was pop-riveted and on later cars it was welded. Cars chassis numbers 875026 and 875109 had the pop-riveted recesses, while 875254 and 876052 had the welded-in type.

A similar change occurred in the first support rail to the right of center on the boot floor. On early cars, it is pop-riveted in, while on later cars it is welded in. The change for the support rail occurred before the change in the backup-light recess. Chassis numbers 875026 had the pop-riveted rail, while 875109 had the welded-in rail.

The support panel for the boot lid aperture was changed at chassis numbers 860478/9 and 886013/4.

There were variations in the drains in the trough around the boot aperture on the early roadsters. The earliest cars had a single, centrally located drain, while the later

The backup light recesses in the boot floor were pop-riveted on the very early cars. Note here that the center support rail is also pop-riveted. Also note the handle for the early turret jack held by two clips on the welded-in rail.

Later on, the recess for the backup light was still pop-riveted, but the center support rail was welded.

In the last configuration, both the recess for backup light and the support rail were welded in.

The rubber plug in the access hole in the number-plate panel. These were found on later 3.8-liter cars, but this illustration is from a 4.2-liter.

Early boot apertures had a single drain hole near the middle.

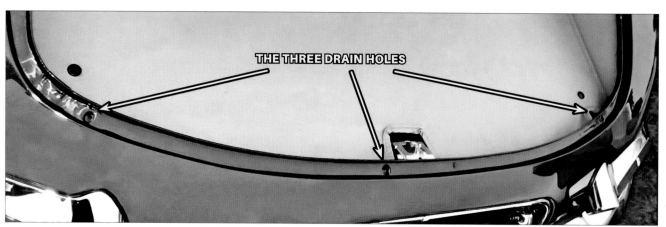

For a while three drain holes were used in the in the boot lip. It appears the three-hole design was produced for a short period between the one- and two-hole designs. This is left-hand drive roadster chassis number 875045.

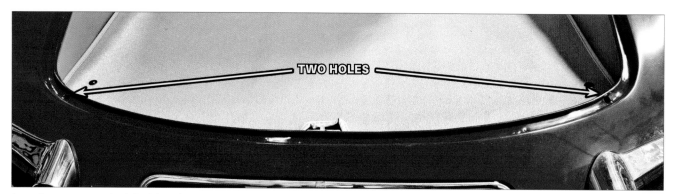

Later, boot apertures had dual drain holes.

cars had two drains, one at each rear corner. There was also a period when three drains were used, one in the middle and the two corner ones. The change from the single center drain tube to two tubes on the right and left is cited as occurring at chassis numbers 850117/8, 860006/7, 875520/1 and 885032/3, about October 1961. Chassis numbers 875026, 875109, 875251, 875254 and 875407 had a single center drain hole; numbers 875045, 875186 and 875223 had three drain holes; and numbers 875954, 875958, 876052, 876289 and 876577 had two holes. The boot mat for the three-drain-hole car, chassis number 875223, has recesses for the three drains in it. It appears to be a factory-original mat.

At chassis numbers 861615/6 and 890339/40, about May 1964, the rear casings at the side of the luggage compartment floor were changed.

BOOT LID

The casing assembly on the boot lid was changed at chassis numbers 860478/9 and 886013/4.

BOOT HINGES AND SUPPORTS

ROADSTER BOOT HINGES

The roadster boot lid hinges came in three types. The earliest type is a single, thin-aluminum casting. The next

version had dual, thin-aluminum sections that appear to be made by welding together two of the early, thin walled hinges. Lastly, the conventional, thick-aluminum cast hinges were used.

From research of surviving cars: Chassis number 875026 had thin hinges; numbers 875109, 875166, 875179, 875186 and 875407 had double hinges; and numbers 875254, 875954, 875958, 876052, 876289 and 876577 had thick hinges.

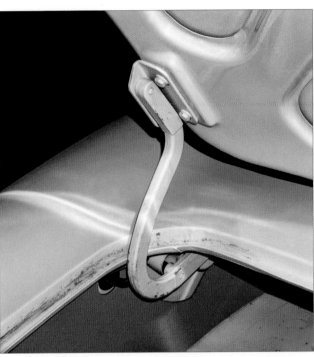

The final configuration of the roadster boot lid hinges was a fat aluminum casting. This type was used throughout the remaining production.

The very early roadsters had thin boot lid hinges. These probably did not hold up well, as the design was quickly changes to a dual-support arrangement.

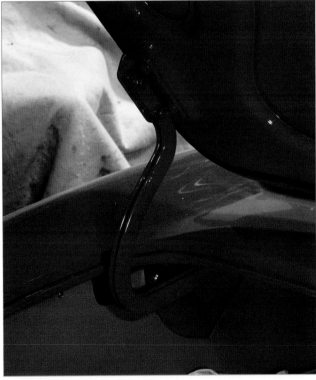

The dual, thin-aluminum roadster boot lid hinges were introduced early on, but were not used long.

Chassis number 875254 seems out of place; perhaps the hinges were changed at some point.

Changes at chassis numbers 850767/8 and 880290/1, in about January 1964, a hole was added to the number-plate panel at the rear to allow access to the boot lid latch in case the release cable should break, using a right-angle 3/16-inch diameter rod. A rubber seal was inserted in this hole.

COUPE REAR HATCH HINGES AND PROP

The hinges for the coupe rear hatch door were made in two varieties. The early-type hinges were fabricated and have sharp edges and the later hinges were cast and are rounded. Cars chassis numbers 860084 had the early fabricated hinges and 889076 had the late hinges.

The Jaguar E-Type: The Collector's Guide shows an early coupe, produced by the Experimental Department, with unusual springs on the rear door and no boot lid prop.

The boot lid hinge assembly was changed: the prop supporting the boot lid in the open position, the pivot bracket on the boot lid for the prop and the bracket on the body receiving the prop were all changed. The striker and safety catch for the boot lid lock were changed. This occurred at chassis numbers 860478/9 and 886013/4.

About December 1962, the boot lid prop and its bracket were changed at chassis numbers 861013/4 and 887316/7.

The prop is typically chromed, but one is seen in black on the Geneva car in *Jaguar E-Type: The Definitive History*.

Later on, the coupe rear-door hinges were cast. These cast hinges are from a 4.2-liter coupe, but are representative of those from late 3.8-liter cars.

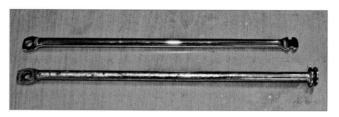
Coupe rear-door stays. The bottom stay shown here is from coupe chassis number 885009. This stay is about one inch longer than the upper stay from coupe 885008, which otherwise has the same appearance. The bottom stay with the two parallel disks on the end is the earliest type observed by the authors. It is possible some coupes earlier than 885008 may have had stays of the early type as shown on the bottom, but painted black instead of chromed. The upper stay in the picture is the later type. It is found in a notched and non-notched version. The notched variant was likely used later in production than the one shown here.

The rear-door hinges on the very early coupes were fabricated and had an angular look.

A collection of different stays. The one on the left is the early type. Apparently sometimes these were black. Later the second design was adopted. After this one of the side flanges was removed, which was likely to make insertion in the seat (the bracket on the body to receive the prop) easier.

FUEL FILLER RECESS, CAP, LID AND HINGE

The drain holes in the fuel-filler nacelle were located in different locations on the early and later cars. On early cars the drain hole was toward the front while later it was toward the rear. This is noted on page 9 of Howe's *Early E-type Spotters Guide 2* in *The E-Type*, Issue 78, May 2011. However, in addition, on some very early cars there was also an additional hole toward the back left of the nacelle. This is seen, for example, on 875014 and 875026. In the case of 875026, the hole had a plastic plug, similar to that used elsewhere on the body.

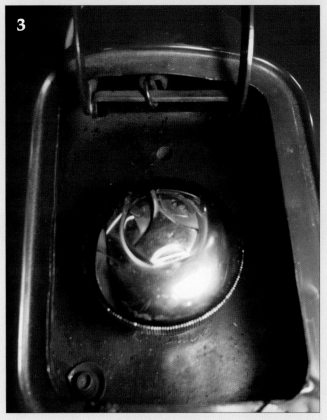

1 *The front drain hole in the fuel filler nacelle on left-hand drive roadster 875109. The locking gas cap shown here and in Figure 2 is probably not a factory-supplied unit.*

2 *This view of the rear of the nacelle on 875109 shows the absence of the second hole sometimes found at the left rear of the nacelle floor.*

3 *The fuel filler nacelle of some early cars had two drain holes; one at the front and one at the back. This view of 875026 shows the front hole and a plug that was fitted to the rear hole. The rear hole is hidden by the flange at the lower left of this picture.*

This detailed view of the rear of the fuel filler nacelle shows the second hole near the rear, as well as the cut-off plug that was used to cover it.

View of the rear fuel filler drain hole with the plastic plug in place. This is the same type of plug as used elsewhere on the body. The edge has been cut off to fit in the hole.

RIGHT: Interestingly, the two holes with rubber pad inserts are absent on left-hand drive coupe 885056. This is likely a mistake at the factory rather than an intended production modification. This same lack of holes and pads has been seen by the authors on other cars as well, including left-hand drive roadster 879406. Compare this picture to the top two pictures on this page with two rubber pads inserted in holes (only the pads are seen as they fill the holes) on the rear lip of the gas cap opening.

The later fuel filler nacelle in left-hand drive roadster 875272 with hole positioned toward the back. Also note the trough embossed around the hole.

The 3.8-liter cars came with two types of fuel filler, or gas, caps. The early cap was fabricated from chromed steel and was fitted to many British cars of the period. The later cap was a casting with fluted edges. Chassis numbers 860084 and 875026 were fitted with the fabricated cap.

There are different variants of these early fabricated caps. They are found with vent holes in the center of the top and without the vent. The reeding around the edge is seen in different variations. There are original and reproduction (or after-market) caps. Based on observations, it may be that the caps with the tighter, more pronounced reeding are the original type, but this is not certain. This is still being researched, as is the question of whether or not the central vent hole is a characteristic of original caps. Perhaps both varieties were supplied from the factory.

The later cast caps, with fluted edges, are also seen with and without central vent holes. As in the case of the fabricated caps, it is not now clear which was originally shipped on E-types from the factory, or if both were used.

The fuel filler box and its lid were changed, about May 1962, at chassis numbers 860478/9 and 886013/4. *The Jaguar E-type: A Collector's Guide* cites chassis numbers 860475/6 instead of 860478/9.

At chassis numbers 850907/8, 861722/3, 881705/6 and 890721/2, about October 1964, the gas cap was changed. This may be the end of the reeded edge chrome-steel fabricated cap and the beginning of the cast fluted cap.

A fabricated cap from a restored car. While this is likely a modern replacement cap, it does show the less-pronounced and less dense reeding. This cap also does not show the central vent hole.

Top view of a fabricated cap showing the central vent hole. Around the hole is what appears to be a silver paint; this is not a normal characteristic of these caps.

What is very likely the original cap supplied with left-hand drive roadster 876163 (still unrestored and largely unaltered from its original configuration), showing the well-pronounced and dense reeding around its periphery. Note that this cap does not have the central vent hole.

Top view of a fabricated cap showing the absence of a vent hole. This cap from a very early roadster shows medium-density, relatively deep and pronounced reeding.

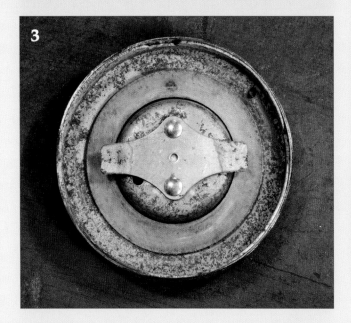

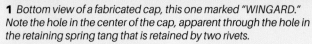

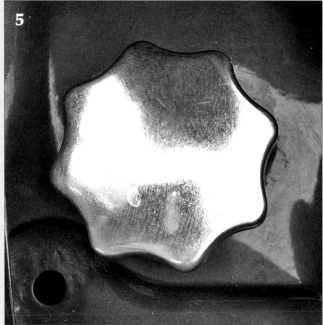

1 Bottom view of a fabricated cap, this one marked "WINGARD." Note the hole in the center of the cap, apparent through the hole in the retaining spring tang that is retained by two rivets.

2 Close-up of the "WINGARD" label.

3 Bottom view of another fabricated cap, this one not carrying a manufacturer's name (at least none is apparent). In this case, there is no central hole. This cap has its sealing gasket in place.

4 Close-up view of the bottom of a fabricated cap, showing how the inner section is pressed into the outer chromed steel cover. What appears to be a braided cable is showing through the hole on the left-hand side of the picture.

5 A later-type cast fluted fuel cap. This one does not have a central vent hole on the top.

6 Another cast fluted cap. This one has a central vent hole on the top.

BOOT PANELS, MAT AND FLOORING

The shape of the roadster boot mat and the plywood flooring in both the coupes and roadsters were altered at the rear to accommodate the change in the water drain locations. Cars were produced with one, two and three boot drain holes.

The Jaguar E-type: A Collector's Guide notes that at chassis numbers 860580/1 and 886088/9, about July 1962, the strikers for the luggage floor hinged extension latches and the rubber buffers for the extension in its raised position were changed.

BOOT LID SEALING RUBBER

The sealing rubber on the early roadsters was glued to the boot lid itself, while on later cars it was fastened around the edge of the boot aperture.

The literature notes that at the extensive rework of the coupes at chassis numbers 860478/9 and 886013/4, the sealing rubber around the rear hatch aperture was changed from one piece to two pieces.

On later roadsters, the sealing rubber was on the inner lip of the boot aperture.

On the early roadsters, the boot sealing rubber was mounted on the lid.

JACK HANDLE MOUNTS

In some early cars, the handle to the Shelly screw-type jack (a long steel rod) was stored in two clips mounts in the bottom of the boot. The mounts were screwed on the side of the first support rail to the right of center on the boot floor. These clips appear to the same type as used to mount the T-key on the right rear side of the console on some early cars.

From research of surviving cars: Both chassis numbers 875026, 875090 and 875109 had these clips.

EXTERIOR AND INTERIOR COLORS

The following listing is compiled from several lists published in various literature. These lists were similar, but not identical. The format of the table is exterior color/associated interior colors.

EXTERIOR/INTERIOR COLORS 1961 AND 1962

- ‣ Black/Red, Gray, Light Tan, or Tan
- ‣ British Racing Green/Suede Green, Beige, Light Tan, or Tan
- ‣ Bronze/Beige, Red, or Tan
- ‣ Carmen Red/Black, Biscuit, or Red
- ‣ Claret/Beige
- ‣ Cotswold Blue/Dark Blue
- ‣ Cream/Black, Cream, or Red
- ‣ Imperial Maroon/Tan
- ‣ Indigo/Red or Light Blue
- ‣ Mist Gray/Red
- ‣ Opalescent Dark Blue/Dark Blue or Red
- ‣ Opalescent Dark Green/Suede Green, Beige, Tan, or Light Tan
- ‣ Opalescent Gunmetal/Dark Blue, Light Blue, Red, or Beige
- ‣ Opalescent Silver Blue/Gray or Dark Blue
- ‣ Opalescent Silver Gray/Red, Light Blue, Dark Blue, or Gray
- ‣ Pearl/Dark Blue or Red
- ‣ Sherwood Green/Suede Green, Light Tan, or Tan

EXTERIOR/INTERIOR COLORS 1963 AND 1964

- ‣ Black/Red, Gray, Light Tan, or Tan
- ‣ British Racing Green/Suede Green, Beige, Tan, or Light Tan
- ‣ Bronze/Beige, Red, or Tan
- ‣ Carmen Red/Black or Red
- ‣ Cotswold Blue/Dark Blue
- ‣ Cream/Black
- ‣ Mist Gray/Red
- ‣ Opalescent Dark Blue/Dark Blue or Red
- ‣ Opalescent Dark Green/Suede Green, Beige, Light Tan, or Tan
- ‣ Opalescent Gunmetal/Dark Blue, Light Blue, Red, or Beige
- ‣ Opalescent Maroon/Maroon or Beige
- ‣ Opalescent Silver Blue/Gray or Dark Blue
- ‣ Opalescent Silver Gray/Red, Light Blue, Dark Blue, or Gray
- ‣ Pale Primrose/Black or Beige
- ‣ Pearl/Dark Blue or Red
- ‣ Sand/Black or Beige
- ‣ Sherwood Green/Suede Green, Light Tan, or Tan

While these were the standard color combinations, there were variations.

Cans of touch-up paint may have been supplied with some cars. An example of this is seen in the December 1961 *Car and Driver*.

TOOLS

A listing of the tool kit items is given in the *J.30 Spare Parts Catalogue (June 1963)*:

- ‣ Jack and handle
- ‣ Hammer (copper and rawhide)
- ‣ Budget lock key (T-key)
- ‣ Bleeder tube
- ‣ Valve timing gauge
- ‣ Grease gun
- ‣ Feeler gauge
- ‣ Screwdriver for contact breaker points
- ‣ Tire valve extractor
- ‣ Tire pressure gauge
- ‣ Adjustable spanner
- ‣ Pliers
- ‣ Tommy bar (short)

- ▶ Box spanner (spark plugs and cylinder head nuts)
- ▶ Box spanner (9/16x5/8 inch SAE)
- ▶ Box spanner (7/16x1/2 inch SAE)
- ▶ Box spanner (3/4x7/8 inch SAE)
- ▶ Open-ended spanner (11/32x3/8 inch AF)
- ▶ Open-ended spanner (9/16x5/8 inch AF)
- ▶ Open-ended spanner (1/2x7/16 inch AF)
- ▶ Open-ended spanner (3/4x7/8 inch AF)
- ▶ Tommy bar (long)
- ▶ Screwdriver
- ▶ Special wrench (for handbrake adjustment)

A fan belt is included in this list. It is not included, however, in the tool list found in the *J.30 Spare Parts Catalogue (June 1963)*. Also, a paper-wrapped grease gun is included in the kit, but is not listed here.

HAND TOOLS AND ROLL CASE

Possibly a few of the early Experimental Department cars may have been fitted with the sedan-style round wood-and-steel tool kits. Production cars appear, from the beginning, to have been fitted with flexible tool rolls, as is usually associated with E-types. The roll case is shown on a car claimed to be 875012 in the December 1961 *Car and Driver*. Car 875026 came with a roll case.

The open-ended wrenches came from different manufacturers. On various Jaguars the authors have seen them marked with a T over a W in a circle: "GARRINGTON," "SSP," "SNAIL BRAND," and "EAGLE," instead of "JAGUAR" with "CHROME VANDIUM" on the opposite side and "SHEFFIELD ENGLAND" on either sides of "EAGLE." Pliers have been seen marked "SHEFFIELD-MADE IN ENGLAND."

There seems to be a lot of variety in the tools and it is not clear if any particular wrench is correct for any particular year of car. On chassis number 875026, the

A typical tool kit from a 3.8-liter car. This one is from left-hand drive roadster chassis number 879032, a very original car, and is likely to be as delivered with the car from the factory. This kit is used here to serve as a reference point from which to look at variations in tools supplied with 3.8-liter cars throughout production.

original wrenches are of the T over a W in a circle and Garrington type.

There are variations in the types of tire gauges supplied in E-type tool kits: some are marked "DUNLOP" (marked "6J") and others have the Jaguar wings symbol. It is not clear which, if either, of these is correct for a specific year car. It appears the Dunlop is the correct gauge for the earlier cars and perhaps all 3.8-liter cars had the Dunlop gauge. These were supplied in many tool kits for Jaguar sedans pre-dating the introduction of the E-type.

A combination screwdriver (Phillips head and conventional) was introduced at chassis numbers 850647/8, 861070/1, 878936/7 and 888138/9.

For European cars fitted with earless knock-off hubcaps, the tool kit included a large brass wrench that fitted around the hubcap and allowed hammer-blows to tighten or loosen the cap. This is a different tool from the one used on late 4.2-liter cars.

Another specialty tool found in only the early kits was the Allen wrench used to adjust the early, manually adjusted parking brakes. Interestingly, it appears this tool was supplied in 3.8-liter tool kits very late into production, at least as late as 1963 left-hand drive roadster 879032. It may have been included in some 4.2-liter kits as well.

Back view of the 879032 tool roll.

From 879032 kit, a 7/16" 1/2" "TW" open end wrench.

Reverse side of the 7/16" X 1/2" "TW" open end wrench, showing the "JAGUAR" marking.

From 879032 kit, a 9/16" X 5/8" Garrington open end wrench.

From 879032 kit, the reverse side of the 9/16" X 5/8" Garrington open end wrench, showing the "JAGUAR" marking.

From 879032 kit, a 9/16"X 5/8 and 7/16"X 1/2" box spanners. Note that these spanners are marked in the middle, rather than on the ends. It is likely that the end-marked spanners are the later ones. This kit from 879032, a 1963 model year car, is the latest the authors have seen with center-marked spanners.

From 879032 kit, the box spanners were designed to nest inside each other to save space in the tool kit.

From 879032 kit, the spark plug wrench.

From 879032 kit, the large tommy bar.

From 879032 kit, the small tommy bar.

From 879032 kit, the convertible screwdriver. It can be converted from Phillips to standard by sliding in a new end. The standard blade is shown. Earlier screwdrivers were not convertible and had the standard end only.

From 879032 kit, the Phillips insert for the convertible screwdriver.

From 879032 kit, the pliers.

From 879032 kit, the Garringtons adjustable wrench. Note the "S" on the end of the word. These were likely the later 3.8-liter adjustable wrench type.

From 879032 kit, the reverse side of the Garringtons adjustable wrench.

From 879032 kit: A "6J" "DUNLOP"-marked tire pressure gauge.

From 879032 kit: Back of the 6J air gauge, showing patent numbers and "MADE IN ENGLAND."

From 879032 kit: It appears the air-pressure gauge sometimes or always came in a clear plastic bag.

From 879032 kit: Somewhat surprisingly, the Allen key for adjusting the early manual adjusting parking brake mechanisms (what was discontinued about October 1961 at chassis numbers 850089/90, 860003/4, 875331/2 and 885014/5) was still supplied in the kit for 879032. Perhaps this tool was supplied all the way through 3.8-liter E-type production.

From 879032 kit, the early tire-valve tools were brass. Later they were changed to yellow plastic.

From 879032 kit, this is what the authors believe is the representative contact-breaker screwdriver. There are many reproductions of this that vary in numerous ways, especially centering on the rivet in the middle.

From 879032 kit: From 879032 kit: reverse view of the contact-breaker screwdriver.

From 879032 kit, the feeler gauge kit.

From the 879032 kit, the usual cam-timing tool supplied for years with all XK-engined cars.

From the 879032 kit, the Dunlop brake-bleeder hose can.

From the 879032 kit, the grease gun with instructions wrapped around it in the usual manner that these were supplied in for sometime.

CHANGES

Page 274 of the J.30 Spare Parts Catalogue (June 1963) lists the change from this early fixed-shaft screwdriver, shown here, to the combination screwdriver (with Phillips head and conventional shafts) as occurring at 850647/8, 861070/1, 878936/7 and 888138/9. The later combination screwdriver from the toolkit from 879032 is shown earlier.

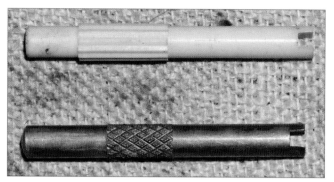

Later on in 3.8-liter production the brass tire valve (shown here on the bottom) was replaced by the yellow plastic type (shown here on the top).

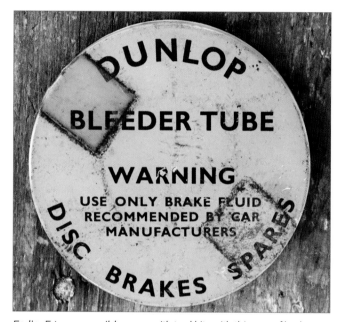

Earlier E-types possibly came with tool kits with this sort of brake-bleeder tube tin.

Earlier E-type tool kits came with "GARRINGTON" (as opposed to "GARRINGTONS") adjustable wrenches.

Opposite side of the early Garrington wrench. The authors have seen other adjustable wrenches, for example those marked "GEDORE" and "BAHCO" (the latter marked as made in Sweden) that are likely from sedans. They have seen no evidence for adjustable wrenches being delivered with 3.8-liter cars at the factory other than those carrying either the "GARRINGTON" or the "GARRINGTONS" markings.

LEFT: *It appears that the later socket wrenches had their sizes stamped on the opposite ends, as shown here, rather than in the middle.*

BELOW: *This sort of sedan toolkit is often cited as appropriate for very early E-types. This tool kit sits in the center of the spare tire. While it is possible one or a few of the Experimental Department cars may have been fitted with these (maybe only for a photo shoot), the authors have seen no evidence these were ever supplied by the factory with production E-types.*

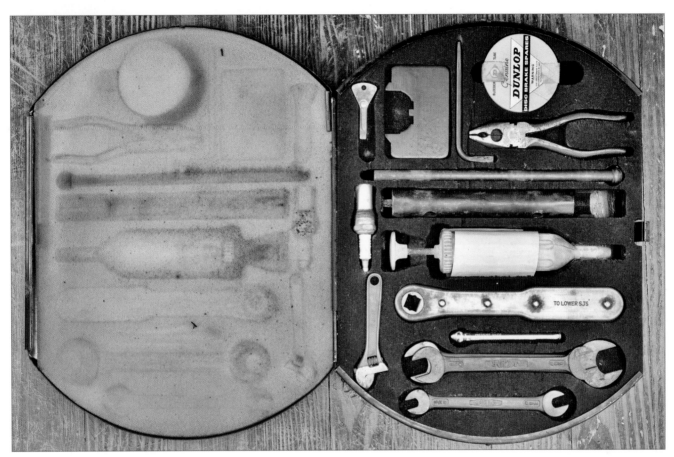

HAMMER AND WHEEL-REMOVAL TOOLS

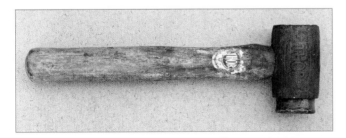

ABOVE: *The initial type multi-piece knock-off hammer had brass on one side and a roll of rawhide on the other.*

RIGHT: *Close-up of the hammer head showing the cast "THOR" markings, as well as the label on the handle. The recessed area on the left side of the head is where a roll of rawhide was housed when the hammer was originally supplied.*

The hubcap removal tool for the European earless hubcap. When standard knock-off hubcaps, with the typical ears, were used, this tool was not supplied.

Inside view of the earless hubcap removal tool showing the rectangular recesses. This is a different design than that used for the tool for the post-1968 earless knock-off hubcaps.

JACK

SHELLY JACKS

The first type of jack fitted to E-types was the Shelly jack. This jack was comprised of a cast-iron base and aluminum top, with a three-tier telescoping set of two concentric threaded tubes with a concentric threaded rod in the center.

There are several different types of cast markings, some raised and some inset. On the front of the jacks the authors have seen "SHELLY" in cast raised characters on a lozenge-shaped boss, with raised cast "LJ225" below the SHELLY mark on an oblong boss. Sometimes there are two characters below the LJ225, such as "59" or "61," that may be casting year marks. "CA265, BH, PROV PAT" is on the opposite side. Variations in these markings for a collection of Shelly jacks are tabulated below.

RIGHT: A typical early Shelly jack. This one is from roadster 875026.

BASE CAST MARKING	CONFIGURATION OF TOP	OTHER MARKINGS	CHASSIS OF ORIGIN
LJ225 59	No buttress	Possible inset "6" between "bh" and "prov pat"	875026
LJ225 59	No top	No other marks	Unknown
LJ225 61	Buttress	Possible inset "1" above "shelly"	876163
LJ225	No top	Possible inset "6" between "bh" and "prov pat"	876319
LJ225	No buttress	Inset "1" between "bh" and "prov pat"	885056
LJ225 61	No buttress	Inset "5" above "shelly"	Unknown
LJ225	No buttress	Inset "6" between "bh" and "prov pat"	Unknown

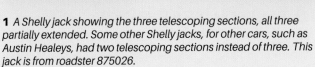

1 A Shelly jack showing the three telescoping sections, all three partially extended. Some other Shelly jacks, for other cars, such as Austin Healeys, had two telescoping sections instead of three. This jack is from roadster 875026.

2 From our observations, it appears that the early Shelly jack heads did not have a supporting buttress for the latching-pin boss.

3 The support buttress leading from the latching-pin boss to the handle insert aperture is evident on this jack head from roadster 876163.

4 Despite its other similarities, the jack on the left is not from an E-type as it does not have the recess around the top section that is attached to the bottom with a clip. The jack on the right showing the recess is from roadster 876319.

5 Markings on the jack from coupe 885056. The oblong boss has LJ225, but no two-digit suffix.

6 The same non-XKE jack as featured in caption 4, above, showing LJ225 59 on the boss. The authors suspect it is likely that the two digits are the last two numbers of a date, perhaps the casting date. If so, this jack base would have been cast in 1959.

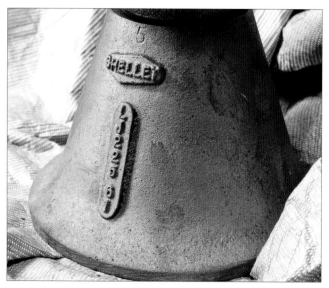

View of the front of a lower casting with "LJ225 61," possibly indicating a cast year of 1961. This one has an inset "5" above the "SHELLY" marking on the lozenge-shaped boss.

Reverse view of the jack from coupe 885056 showing the CA265, BH, PROV PAT markings, likely with an inset character "1" between the "BH" and "PROV PAT."

This jack has an inset "6" between the "BH" and "PROV PAT."

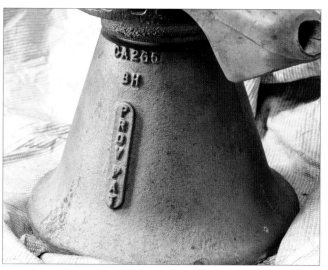

A jack with no apparent inset markings.

View of the underside of a Shelly jack showing the nested threaded posts in their stowed position. Also evident here is the relieved area of the top aluminum casting around where the ratcheting rod goes in.

METALLIFACTURE JACKS

Later in 3.8-liter E-type production the cast iron and aluminum Shelly jack was replaced by a sheet metal fabricated Metallifacture jack. This jack was used on late 3.8-liter cars and on early 4.2-liter cars.

An unusual looking screw-type jack with an angular top section is pictured in *Jaguar E-Type: The Definitive History*, but this may be a machined replacement top. The design of the original rounded tops was weak where the turning rod went in and are often found cracked and it is possible this angular top is an improved replacement made outside the factory.

The authors have seen this jack in two variants: those with the markings "METALLIFACTURE, PATENT APPLIED FOR," and "METALLIFACTURE, PATENT No 903079." The "PATENT APPLIED FOR" jacks are likely the earlier type, although given how many E-type components are out-of-order in the production sequence, this may not be the case. Possibly the two types overlapped in their being supplied to cars during E-type production.

A Shelly screw jack appears to be shown in a storage bag in *Car and Driver* magazine, December 1961. The authors have not seen any other evidence for storage bags for the early jacks.

About June 1962, the jack was changed to the cantilever type with integral handle and the container for the jack was introduced, at chassis numbers 850548/9, 860660/1, 877518/9 and 886246/7.

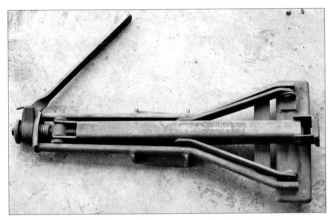

The Metallifacture fabricated jack with attached handle. Later ones used during 4.2-liter production had a detached handle. It appears that all the Metallifacture jacks came with a storage bag (not shown here).

A Metallifacture jack, with "PATENT APPLIED FOR" markings.

A Metallifacture jack with "PATENT No 903079" marking.

T-KEY

The T-key is listed, without any change notes, as part of the tool kit in the June 1963 *Spare Parts Catalog*. It probably came only in the kits for the 500 cars with outside bonnet latches, but given the idiosyncrasies of E-type production it is possible the cessation of its inclusion in the toolkit may have occurred before or after this point in production, or there may have been cases where it had stopped being supplied, then was supplied again, then stopped again. In any case, its inclusion in the kit ended somewhere around the bonnet latch transition point.

The correct T-key is cast steel with a cylindrical cross-section. A key that is now frequently seen with early cars is the one with a teardrop cross-section (of the sort often seen on Triumph cars), but it is not clear that it ever came with the early cars.

The question of T-key location, whether it was part of the kit or carried in mounts, is discussed earlier in this chapter.

The original bonnet T-keys had a cylindrical cross-section top.

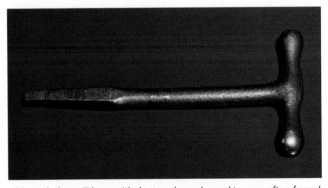

Although these T-keys with the teardrop-shaped top are often found with early cars, they were probably never supplied by the factory, but included new with other British cars.

3.8-LITER ENGINE, DRIVETRAIN AND CHASSIS COMPONENT CHANGES

T his chapter analyzes the changes made to the engine, drivetrain, chassis and other mechanical parts during the full production run of 3.8-liter E-types from 1961 to 1964.

ENGINE: CYLINDER BLOCK

Cylinder block changes in the literature include the notes that at engine numbers R7194/5 (about October 1962), the dowels between the bearing caps and the cylinder block were enlarged and that at engine numbers RA6024/5 (about April 1964), the cylinder block was changed to mount the new lower-timing chain intermediate damper. It is also noted that two tapped bosses were added about May 1964.

ENGINE BLOCK PART NUMBER LOCATION AND STYLE

As with many of E-type components, the blocks carried a part number. While this number was typically a fully cast mark, in many cases some of the numerals cast in the block were ground off and others stamped on. This occurred at the factory or at the foundry.

The block part numbering system was somewhat complex. The 3.8- and 4.2-liter six-cylinder block numbers carried the most common part number prefix, "C." In some instances the "C" was followed by a period, and in others the period was absent. Different block part number locations were used on 3.8-liter E-type blocks during production. The numbers were initially located directly above the oil filter on the right side of the block and later further forward on the block and higher up (sometimes so high the tops of the numerals were machined off when the block deck was machined). The letters "FF" are often found near the part number.

Here, as in many other cases, there are discrepancies between the *J.30 Spare Parts Catalogue (June 1963)* and the cars as produced. On page 1 two engine-block numbers are cited: C.17212/1 for early cars (from engine numbers R1001 to R7194) and C.19291 for later cars (engine numbers R7195 and subsequent). Neither of the authors has ever seen evidence of an E-type leaving the factory with a block marked C.17212/1 or C.19291. A best estimate of the part numbers used on 3.8 E-type blocks fitted to cars, as they shipped from the factory, is given below. This data is compiled from direct observations of cars, or from other references as cited.

While the authors have no evidence of a car leaving the factory with block part number C.17212/1, they do have some information on two instances of blocks with cast block part numbers C.17212/1 fitted to E-types. Roadster 875169 was recently reported to be fitted with a block with the cast part number C.17212/1 and apparently no serial number stamp on the top of the oil filter boss (the standard location). This same combination, a car fitted with a C.17212/1 block with no serial number stamp, was seen one other time as well. The authors postulate that the C.17212/1 part number given in the *Spare Parts Catalogue* refers to a replacement block supplied by the factory for early cars, not to any block that was ever fitted to a car at the factory. This would explain both of the instances of the C.17212/1 blocks not having serial numbers stamped on them; they could have been fitted to the cars as correct and official replacement parts, as specified in the *Spare Parts Catalogue*. After all, the *Spare Parts Catalogue* may be just that, a listing of spares for repairing the cars and replacing damaged parts and not specifically a listing of parts fitted to the cars when they left the factory (*cf.* the discussion below on the intermediate timing chain sprocket). In any case, this does not address the issue of what the actual differences may be between, say, a C.17212/1 "spare" block and a C.17523 block fitted at the factory. This is material for future research. With this preface, the examination of the part numbers found on engine blocks of production E-types begins.

It appears that the earliest E-types, possibly most of those produced by the Experimental Department before the Production Department took production over, used Mk 2 sedan 3.8-liter blocks, numbered C.17200. On page 196 of Porter's *The Most Famous Car in the World* is a photo of the block apparently fitted to coupe 885002 when Porter received it. The block serial number is not clear, but the cast part number "C.17200, FF" does appear to show on the block, located in the usual location for early blocks, on the vertical section of the right side of the block, above the oil filter mount.

On the top left of page 82 of Skilleter's article "77 RW" (pp. 80-85, V. 13, no. 4, May 2001 *Classic Jaguar World*) a block cited to be R1001-9 is shown. It appears to have the cast part number "C.17200." On the top of page 84 of the same reference the block is shown again, painted and again apparently showing the "C.17200" number. In this picture the serial number is visible and appears to be R1001-9.

Engine R1004-9 has "C.17200" cast in the block, in the usual spot above the oil filter mount. Unexpectedly, block R1470-9 (which may now reside in England) was observed to also have the part number "C.17200" cast in. This is a very late block serial number to carry the "C.17200" part number; many blocks with earlier serial numbers carry the "C.17523" part number. For example, blocks with serial numbers R1030-9, R1037-9, R1157-9, R1423-9 and R4432-9 have "C.17523" blocks. However, the case of R1470-9, if correct, is not too remarkable, as out-of-order discrepancies such as this occur with other numbering sequences in E-type production (see, for example, the discussion of head-numbers *vs.* engine numbers below).

The R1470-9 part number may have occurred as a result of stocking and transportation. Blocks may have been loaded in a truck at the foundry, for transport to the factory, with the earliest-produced blocks in the back of the truck and the latest-produced nearest the truck loading door. Upon removal, the latest-produced blocks would be removed first and perhaps go to serial number stamping first, thus roughly reversing, or at least to some extent scrambling, the order of the cast marks (the part numbers and pour dates) and the serial number stampings.

After these first few cars, the block part number was changed to "C.17523." Based on observations, this number seems to have been used until about engine number R6000-9, at which point the block part number C20012 began to be used (Mk X engines also carry the block part number C20012). The "C.17523" number appears to have been initially fully cast in, for example on engines R1030-9 and R1037-9.

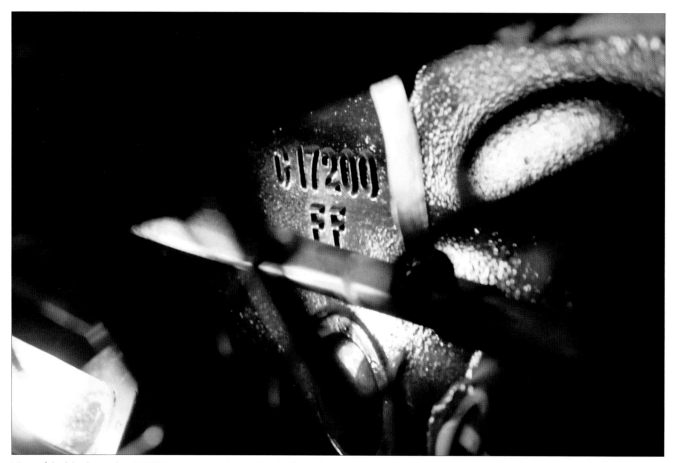

View of the block number C17200 cast on engine R1004-9. The authors are not aware of any instances of the C17200 number being stamped in (either fully or partially) on any E-type blocks. In this case there is no period after the "C" in the part number and the "FF" is located below the part number.

1 *View of the block part number C.17523 on engine R1241-9. On this early block the part number is cast in, rather than stamped in. Note the "FF" is located above the part number in this case, and a period is located between the "C" and the number. Note also that, as in the case of some other block part numbers, the part number C.17523 does not appear in the Spare Parts Catalogue.*

2 *A stamped-in "C 20012" part number on block number RA3074-9, located in the forward upper section of the right-hand side of the block.*

3 *A fully stamped-in "17523" block number, with wide number spacing. Here "FF" is above the number and if there was a period after the "C", it has been ground off. This is from engine number R1423-9.*

4 *Another fully stamped-in "C.17523 " block number, with close number spacing. Here there is a period after the "C." This is from engine number R4432-9.*

5 *A stamped-in "C 20012NC" part number on block. This is block number R8305-9.*

6 *A cast "C 20012" part number, with no period after the "C" and "FF" on the same line to the right of the part number. This number is located to the upper right of the position where the earlier C.17200 and C.17523 where stamped. This is block serial number RA1908-9.*

On some later cars the cast "C" was left from a prior number, that was originally cast in and subsequently ground off, and the numerals "17523" were stamped in its place. The authors have no information on what this earlier number may have been. Stamped-in "17523" part numbers are seen, for example, on blocks R1423-9 and R4432-9.

The table below shows the progression of block part numbers, along with the engine serial numbers and, when available, the numbers stamped on the top rear of the block (the "block numbers"), the three-letter stampings on the front left of the block (typically matching those on the timing chain cover and other places on the block), the

ENGINE NUMBER	BLOCK PART NUMBER	REAR STAMPING	CHAIN COVER and BLOCK	BLOCK CAST DATE	MARK LEFT OF BLOCK DATE	NOTES
3.8-liter E-type blocks						
R1001-9	C.17200,FF	x	x	x	x	From reports, not examined
R1004-9	C.17200,FF	x	x	9-11-60	x	
R1030-9	FF,C.17523	x	x	16-2-61	x	
R1037-9	FF,C.17523	B823	AXE	27-2-61	M2	
R1157-9	FF,C.17523	x	x	x	x	From reports, not examined
R1241-9	FF,C.17523	L465	x	9-2-61	M2	
R1423-9	FF,C.(17523)	M412	NOY	4-7-61	O2	
R1470-9	C.17200	x	x	x	x	From reports, not examined
R1620-9	x	number not clear	x	6-6-61	O2	From reports, not examined
R1816-9	x	x	x	29-8-61	x	
R1986-9	FF,C.(17?)	P590	x	18-9-61	S2	From reports, not examined
R2765-9	x	x	x	x	S2	
R4143-9	x	x	TMQ	09-1-62	D5?	
R4432-9	FF,C.(17523)	Y782? Y782?	WXQ	18-2-62	U6	
R5800-9	FF C(17523)	x	x	15-3-62	x	From reports, not examined
R6470-9	FF,C.(17523)	x	x	x	x	
R8305-9	FF,C.(20012NC)	AJ30?, ZA30?	27-9-62	x		
R8607-9	x	K367	x	x	x	
R8627-9	FF,C.(20012NC)	x	x	x	x	
R8878-9	FF,C(20012NC)	x	x	x	x	From reports, not examined
RA1908-9	C20012 FF	x	x	4-3-63	E	
RA2017-9	C20012FF	AU305	TFS	x	No mark	Block number on upper front of block
RA3074-9	C(20012) FF	AX588	AJD	21-5-63	HF J	
RA5259-9	C.(20012)FF	BE576	SFR	6-11-63	x	
RA5516-9	x	x	TMB	19-8-63	HFF R	
3.8-liter Mk X blocks						
ZA2636-9	FF,C.18582	x	x	x	x	
ZA7367-9	C20012FF	x	x	13-12-62	x	
ZB1804-8	C(20012)FF	x	EJE	12-7-63	N	
ZB2006-8	C(20012)FF	BA672	FLF	13-8-63	HF L	

In the notation used here, characters within parenthesis have been stamped with a punch in the location where cast numbers were ground off. Commas in the "Block Part Number" column of the table indicate where the characters were split between two or more rows on the engine block. An "X" means the marking is not known.

cast pour date and the characters cast into the area to the left of the pour date. Data on similar blocks, those from the straight-port S-type 3.8-liter engines fitted to Mk X sedans, are included. To avoid confusion, please note that the correct terminology for the "straight-port" engines fitted to the XK-150S, the E-type and the Mk X sedan is "S-type engine," and the terminology is used throughout this book. Special note of this is made to avoid confusion with the "S-Type" Jaguar sedan or its engine, which are different objects than the straight-port "S-type" engine.

Based on this data, it appears the transition from number 17200 to 17523 occurred very early in 1961 and that the transition to stamped-in 17523 numbers occurred around April 1961. The 20012NC numbers appear to have come in late in 1962 and the "NC" suffix was apparently dropped by April 1963.

ENGINE BLOCK POUR DATE MARKINGS

As with most XK engine blocks, the 3.8-liter blocks typically had what appears to be the pour date, or casting date, cast into the lower left side of the block, just in front of the dipstick aperture boss. While most 3.8-liter blocks have a casting date, some do not. Based on observations, the authors estimate that up to ten percent of the blocks do not have casting dates. When the dates do appear, they follow the format "DD-MM-YY." If a day or month is a single digit entry, the authors have never seen leading zeros used.

The date casting varies in appearance. It seems all date castings have a bar above and below the date and often there are recesses, bosses or other marks, to the right and left of the date. Generally it appears that the earlier date castings, to sometime in 1962, have somewhat shorter and thicker bars above and below, often with rounded edges. Later date castings tend to be longer, have sharper corners and generally have more features to the right and left of the date. Sometimes they are boxed-in on the right side. Overall, these are crude markings and there is a lot of variation. Sometimes the dates are hard to read.

This September 27, 1962 casting date mark shows the early features clearly.

A later (March 4, 1963) date mark showing the longer bars and sharper edges. This one has a partially-closed frame on the right and a large dip to the left of the "4."

A 3.8-liter block showing no date casting. In addition, there are no alphabetic characters in the further left regions forward of the dipstick.

A February 18, 1962 casting date, showing the thicker bars and rounded corners.

An August 19, 1963 casting date mark, this one boxed on both ends. The "6" being incomplete on its lower left and appearing somewhat like a "5" is the sort of defect not infrequently seen in the characters of these markings.

CHARACTERS TO THE LEFT OF POUR DATE

Large, cast characters are often found in the region to the left of the date castings (that is, more toward the front of the engine). Generally within a few inches forward of the date, or farther forward, about halfway up the block. These positions are not exact and there is a lot of variation to the locations. Sometimes the characters are applied in a casual manner, tipped at large angles, in some cases. They sometimes show the small round features found in other castings (*e.g.* the head) that may be pins of some sort used in the casting master die to hold the labels in place. The characters further to the front of the block have been observed by the authors as "HF" and "HFF," but others may have appeared.

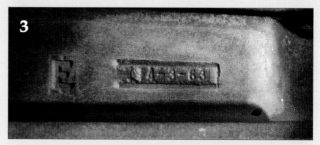

1 *The "M2" appearing here is typical for a very early block. This one is dated February 9, 1961.*

2 *A "U6" marking on a February 18, 1962 block.*

3 *This "E" on a March 4, 1963 block clearly shows the dots or pins often found on cast marks. These are common on the "A" and "Z" characters cast into the cylinder head valleys as well. Likely these are artifacts of some means of attaching the character shape to the mold master.*

4 *A "G" is seen in the later (August 31, 1964) block. Note the date is framed on the right here. The "G" is somewhat further forward and unusually tipped forward.*

5 *An overview of a block showing the "HF" characters located well in front of the "J" just in front of the date.*

6 *"HFF" characters located in the central region of the block.*

ENGINE NUMBER STAMPINGS

The engine number, R1004-9, R1030-9, *etc.*, was stamped in many places on the engine (sometimes without the trailing compression ratio designation), including the engine block itself. Other locations include the head, crankshaft and flywheel. Throughout 3.8-liter production this number was stamped on the top of the oil filter boss on the lower central region of the block. The details of the characters used in making this stamping are covered in Appendix: Labels and Marks section. Note that the periods used in engine numbers in the literature (e.g. page 3 of the *J.30 Spare Parts Catalogue (June 1963)*, for example R.1037-9, do not appear in any stampings the authors have seen. The stamping in this case is: R1037-9.

An engine-number stamping on 3.8-liter block RA3074-9, showing its typical location on the oil filter boss.

TIMING CHAIN COVER STAMPINGS

Three capital letters are typically stamped on the upper left front of the block and these generally correspond to

The "AJD" letters stamped on the upper-left side of the engine block of RA3074-9, matching those on the timing chain cover.

letters stamped on the upper left side of the timing chain cover. Perhaps these are the initials of the engine builders but the authors have no evidence for this and feel it is unlikely given that they have never seen an instance of the same series of letters repeating. Alternatively it is speculated that the letters were used as a means of matching the timing chain cover to the block at the time the cover and block were faced off together. The markings could permit matching the cover to the block during re-assembly when the engine was subsequently built up after the machining operations. This is especially likely, since generally matching letters are stamped on the lower face of the block, next to the main bearing caps and on the main bearing caps themselves. These items, too, would be fitted to the block for machining and subsequently removed for engine assembly. So here, too, the markings would assist in keeping the caps together with the engine upon which they were initially machined. More research is needed to determine if in fact this is the case.

The letters "AJD", with unknown significance, are stamped on the upper left face of the timing chain cover on engine RA3074-9. As seen in subsequent pictures, these same letters are stamped on several other places on the block and other components.

"AJD" is stamped on each of the main bearing caps of engine RA3074-9.

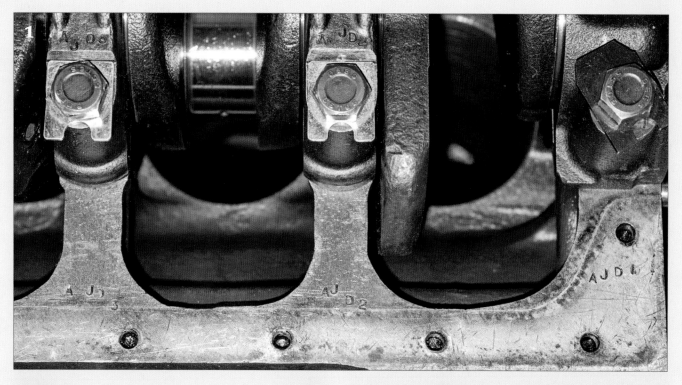

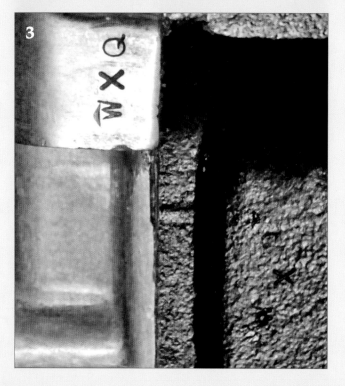

1 The letters "AJD" appear on the bottom face of the engine block RA3074-9, next to each main-bearing saddle.

2 Another set of stamps on the upper left front of the block, paired with those on the timing chain cover. Here the letters face forward and the block stampings are behind the rib at the front of the block.

3 Stamps with letters facing rearward, on both the block and the cover. The letters on the cover and on the block face are generally found to face the same way. Here again the letters on the block are stamped behind the front rib of the block.

4 Letters facing upright on both the cover and the block. This is a case where the block stampings are on the rib itself. While these letters have been observed in many different orientations (upright, lying to the left, and lying to the right), the authors have never observed them stamped upside-down.

BLOCK NUMBER STAMPINGS

In a manner similar to the head-numbers stamped at the rear of the cylinder heads, the blocks carried alphanumeric stamped markings at their rears as well. The marking were stamped on the rear face of the block, typically in the upper right region.

RIGHT: *An "L465" stamp on block R1241-9.*

Block RA3074-9 shows an "AX588" stamping.

BLOCK PAINT

On some unrestored engines retaining their original paint, the engine number stamped on the top of the oil filter boss can be seen to be painted over by a white or light beige paint. Perhaps this was used to make the numbers more legible for tracking during the production process. The presence of subtle features such as this paint is another argument for preservation instead of restoration; how many of these markings may have been destroyed by restorers who did not even notice them. If this light paint were not chronicled here or elsewhere, the entire fact of its existence could have eventually been inadvertently lost through obliteration by the restoration process.

An example of the light-colored paint over the engine number on the block on R6470-9.

This late 3.8-liter engine, RA5516-9, provides another example of the light-colored paint over the engine number.

CYLINDER HEAD AND CAMSHAFT COVERS

CYLINDER HEAD NOMENCLATURE

In this book the term "head-number" is used to refer to the number stamped on the raised stanchion at the rear of the head valley. The authors assume this rear number is the actual head-number, likely assigned to the head as it arrived at the factory from the foundry. By contrast, the engine number is stamped at the front of the head, on the back of the timing chain gallery. This is the same number that also appears on the block, flywheel, crankshaft and commission plate.

CYLINDER HEAD PAINT

The XK S-type engines were designated "gold top,"

and the cylinder heads were painted a color to denote this. Initially, for the 3.4- and 3.8-liter XK-150S cars (the first to be fitted with the S-type engine, though it was subsequently used also in E-types and Mk X sedans) the head was painted a different color from that seen on later 3.8-liter cars with the S-type engine. It was not the bronze-like metallic gold of the later cars, but rather an orange-pumpkin color (originally so described by Haddock in presentations, articles, and his 1991 Jaguar E-Type Six-Cylinder Restoration and Originality Guide).

The Winter 1974 issue of The Milestone Car contains a black-and-white photo of an early cylinder head with what is likely to be the pumpkin-colored head, as the glossy finish of the paint is that of the pumpkin-colored paint and not that of the metallic paint. Both colors indicated the "gold top" S-type engine.

A letter from the factory to the owner of E-type chassis number 876052, dated September 30, 1987, states that there was only one type of gold paint used on the cylinder heads: "With regard to cylinder head color for your vehicle, our records quite clearly indicate only one specification for the 3.8-liter model: Bradite Old Gold paint - 2991 Air Drying." However, in light of the above evidence, it is likely their records are incomplete.

The authors have observed numerous unrestored cars with S-type engines retaining original paint of both in the early pumpkin color and the later brassy gold color. The extent of the paint on the heads includes the valley between the cams, up to the cam covers along each side, and at the front up the vertical face of the back of the timing chain galley, stopping at the top. At the rear of the valley the paint continues down the back of the head to where the head meets the block. The rear of the head is painted laterally out to both sides of the back of the head. On the intake side the paint stops at the back of the head, while on the exhaust the regions between the exhaust manifolds and the exhaust-side cam cover is

Head VS2090-9 from an XK-150S, the first application of the "gold top" S-type engine. All XK-150S cars have pumpkin-colored head paint.

XK-150S head VS2090-9 showing the pumpkin-colored paint not only in the valley, but also along the region between the exhaust manifold and the exhaust cam cover. Observations of XK-150S and both 3.8- and 4.2-liter E-types shows the early pumpkin, or later brassy gold paint, in these two regions and never above the intake manifolds or on the front of the head in the recess below the breather cap. Many restored cars have been painted in these regions with pumpkin or gold paint.

Furthest forward extent of the paint toward the front of the head on the exhaust side. The paint stops right about where the polishing begins.

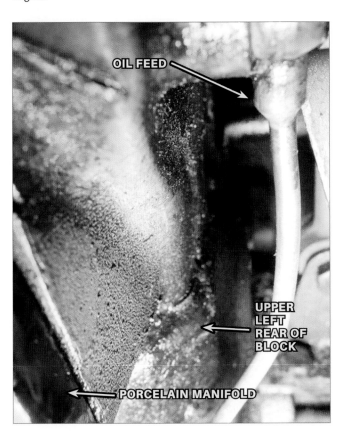

painted. The authors have never observed paint on the intake side of the head (on the right, below the intake cam cover) or anywhere on the front face of the head. Of the latter, particularly note no paint has been seen in the recessed area below the breather cover where nuts secure the head to the front timing chain cover. Particular note is made of where paint has never been observed, as many restored cars have been painted in some of these areas. The authors do not wish the situation to become more clouded for future observers as information continues to be lost due to the restoration of original cars.

The early pumpkin-colored paint used on early XK-150S heads and early 3.8-liter E-type heads. This is E-type engine R1037-9.

View of pumpkin-colored paint on the rough-cast surface between the exhaust manifolds and the exhaust cam cover.

LEFT: Pumpkin-colored paint on the rough-cast back surface of the head. The black porcelain of the rear-most exhaust manifold can be seen on the lower left of the picture. The left side oil-feed to the exhaust cam is seen on the upper right and the black-painted engine block is in the lower center part of the picture.

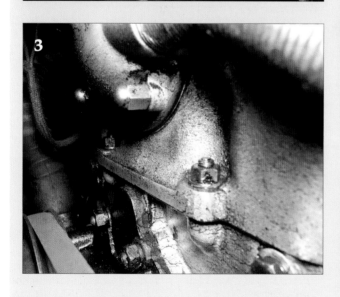

Based on observations, the pumpkin-colored paint was used as late as engine R2550-9. There may also have been overlap between the two types of paint. From research of surviving cars, chassis numbers 860005 (engine R1522-9), 875026 (engine R1037-9), 875090 (engine R1086-9), 875186 (engine R1289-9), 875283, 876052 (engine R2447-9), 885056 (engine R1816-9) had pumpkin paint. Car 876163 (engine R2765-9), 876319 (engine R3081-9) had the later metallic paint.

ENGINE-NUMBER STAMPINGS ON THE HEAD

The engine number, such as R1004-9, R1030-9, was stamped in many places on the engine, including the heads. The head stamping was located at the front on the back of the timing chain gallery located. This area was used throughout 3.8-liter production. See also Chapters One and Eight.

CYLINDER HEAD PART NUMBER AND OTHER CASTING MARKS

During 3.8-liter E-type production the heads carried the part number C.14957. The same number was used on all XK-150S cars with electrical tachometer drives (this includes 3.4- and 3.8-liter engines). In addition to the part number, there were other casting marks and stampings on the heads and these casting marks vary among heads. One sample of seven C.14957-type cylinder heads showed six of the seven carrying the WM7286 foundry mark (WM, William Mills, was one of the foundries that cast E-type heads, along with WYF, West Yorkshire Foundry), four had three-digit numbers cast in (two 214s, one 224 and one 225) and five had "V" stamps (one V2, two V3, two V15). Several from the sample had single-digit numerals, one had a "213JAG" stamp, two had "*78" cast in and one had "T3" stamped in. More data needs to be collected to better see the distribution of these and other markings and more work is needed to understand their meanings.

OPPOSITE:

1 *Paint on the back of the head on the right (intake) side. Observations indicate that the paint stops at the juncture of the rear rough-cast surface and the point of the machined-off face where the intake manifolds attach.*

2 *The unpainted region between the front intake manifold and the rear of the timing chain gallery at the front of the head.*

3 *The unpainted recess at the front of the head, below the crankcase breather housing where the two nuts retain the head to the timing chain cover. The authors have seen instances of these nuts with black paint on them.*

4 *R1423-9 is another early head with pumpkin-colored paint.*

5 *R1816-9 showing the early paint.*

6 *Later brassy paint showing on R3018-9.*

7 *Late 3.8-liter E-type engine RA4415-9 showing the brassy paint. The paint appears darker here than typical due to dirt.*

3.8-liter production heads carried the cast part number C.14957. This was the same number of the later XK-150S engines with the electronic tachometer drive. Prior to this the XK-150S engines had a cable tachometer drive that had two bolt holes instead of the three used in the C.14957 head. The WM7286 foundry mark may be an inside designation at William Mills foundry. The authors do not know what the other markings designate.

Another C.14956 head. It has the same WM7286 mark and in this case "225."

*This C.14956 head has a "*78" mark, meaning unknown.*

Another C.14957 head, this with "214" cast in.

One of the oval "JAG" stamps, lower center, found on the heads. It is stamped here on one of the four raised areas on the bottom face of the head. The horizontal line seen about 3/4 of the way up the raised area is where the final facing-off of the head took place at the factory. The region below this was not subject to the facing-off and was left raised up above the main face of the head.

Very frequently when heads are faced-off during restoration the four raised areas are brought down to the new surface of the head. In this process, the markings stamped in these raised areas are lost and the head can be seen to have been reworked by the absence of the four raised areas. This is another example of the many ways the originality of a car is degraded and information is lost by reworks and restorations.

TABLE OF 4.2-LITER HEAD MARKINGS

CHARACTER CAST IN VALLEY	ENGINE NO.	JAGUAR HEAD PART NO.	HEAD NO.	FOUNDRY PART NO.	FOUNDRY
Z	7D53022-9	C24540	CH499	C2143	WYF
Z	7E11567-9	C26200C	CX462	C2143	WYF
Z	7E1221-9	C.14957/1	BF463	C.1186	WYF
A	7E3025-9	C(24540)	BE341	WM7286	WM
Z	7E3845-9	C(24540)	CD182	C.1186	WYF
Z	7E8760-9	(26200)	CN831	C2143	WYF
6	Un-stamped	P39209	FU829	CP2626	WYF
Z	Un-stamped	C(26200/)1	DU48	C2143	WYF
None	Un-stamped	P36677A	M518	WM7286	WM
Z	Un-stamped	C2(62)00-2	EJ462	C2143	WYF
None	Un-stamped	C28300-A	IG423	WM7286	WM
A	Un-stamped	C28300	CE340 (GE340?)	WM7286	WM

On the top of 3.8-liter E-type heads, in the central region of the valley between the two cams, there is typically a single capital alphabetic character cast in. The authors have seen "A" and "Z" (possibly the "Z" may be an "N"), but do not know the meaning of this marking. However, based on observations it appears that the "A" mark was used on heads cast at the William Mills foundry and the "Z" was found on heads cast by the West Yorkshire Foundry. The table above is a listing of observations of this character, along with some other head-numbers. This information is from 4.2-liter heads and some from XK engines other than those from E-types, but it shows the correlation of the letters cast in the head valley to the foundry.

The following is a listing of some head casting letters related to the engine numbers upon which they were observed:

Engine Number	Head Casting Letter
R1037-9	A
R1301-9	Z
R1464-9	A
R1956-9	A
R3081-9	Z
R8305-9	A
RA1100-9	A
RA2017-9	Z
RA3074-9	A

An "A" cast into the central valley of the cylinder head. The small, surrounding rectangle, as well as the circle above the "A" are typical.

A "Z" or "N" cast into the cylinder head central valley.

CYLINDER HEAD WATER JACKET PORTS

It appears all 3.8-liter heads had single oblong water jacket ports on the head face, to the right and left of the combustion chambers, in the manner of prior XK heads and of the initial 4.2-liter heads. By contrast, later 4.2-liter heads had two shorter, oblong holes replacing each of the single long oblong holes of the 3.8-liter and early 4.2-liter cars.

CYLINDER HEAD COOLING PLUGS BETWEEN INLET PORTS

The 3.8-liter E-types, as well as XK-150S cars, had two ports into the cooling jacket of the head, one between each pair of fuel-mixture inlet ports. These were plugged with screw-in plugs of brass or copper. It appears this practice ran throughout 3.8-liter S-type engine production, but stopped or tapered out during 4.2-liter S-type engine production, as is detailed in the 4.2-liter change section.

One of the two brass screw-in plugs from engine R2206-9. These were used on the ports between the three sets of dual inlet runners on the head of all 3.8-liter cars. In prior XK engines there were no plugs in this region and only an open port, since the intake manifolds were single-piece units covering this area. These plugs were found, however, on early 4.2-liter E-types, but later omitted since the one-piece 4.2-liter intake manifold covered these ports up.

HEAD-NUMBER STAMPINGS

The head-number stampings at the rear of the valley of the head seem to roughly indicate the order of heads being used for engine construction at the factory. This head-number continued to appear on the heads after stamping the engine number (found stamped on the back of the timing chain gallery at the front of the head) was discontinued about the time of the introduction of the Series 1.5 in 1968. The 3.8-liter blocks had the engine numbers stamped on the back of the timing chain gallery throughout their production.

While the heads came from two foundries, William Mills (designated by "WM") and West Yorkshire Foundry (designated by "WYF"), it appears the head-numbers were stamped on the rear of the heads in a single sequence, spanning and interleaving the heads arriving from both foundries. That is, it appears that there were not two separate sequences of rear head-numbers, one for each foundry, but only one sequence. Thus, it seems likely these numbers were stamped on at the Jaguar factory.

Interestingly, the appearance of the cast stanchion upon which the head-numbers were stamped seems to come in two types: the William Mills heads generally have a wider and slightly more irregular shaped stanchion, while the West Yorkshire Foundry stanchions are generally not as wide and have sharper corners. In addition, evidence of two flat-head screw marks is often found on either end of the stanchions on William Mills heads. This is probably a consequence of how the stanchion was attached to the master form used to create the molds for casting the heads. Sometimes these marks are extremely pronounced and other times difficult or see, or perhaps absent. The slots in the screw head impressions are found in different orientations, indicating there were likely several mold masters or perhaps changes in one mold master. West Yorkshire Foundry heads do not appear to show evidence of screw marks on the stanchion. On a related subject noted earlier, very short cylindrical protrusions, essentially circular dots, are often observed adjacent to other cast characters on both head and blocks. Like the screw-head impressions, this is likely an artifact of the means used to hold the forms for these characters onto the mold master. These show in the illustrations of some of the cast characters seen in this book.

This rear-stamping stanchion from S-type engine VS2090-9 from an XK-150S has very pronounced screw markings.

The stanchion on R1004-9 shows the same screw orientation as engine VS2090-9.

Another view of the rear-marking stanchion, this one from R1037-9, cast at William Mills. Note that the position and direction of the screw slots here compared to VS2090-9, are identical, or very close, to each other.

The stanchion on RA6464-9 seems to shows two screws at the right and left edges, as seen on the earlier cars.

The stanchion on R4143-9 does not show screw marks. Note also the shorter lateral extent and the sharper edges.

The stanchion on R8607-9 seems to show a single screw mark in the center.

Cylinder head changes in the literature include the notes that at engine numbers R2599/600 (about December 1961), the sealing port at the left rear of the cylinder head was changed, at numbers R2599/600 (about December 1961), the cover for the left-hand (exhaust) camshaft was changed, at numbers R3690/1 (about March 1962), the head stud holes in the cylinder head gasket were enlarged and that at numbers R6723/4 (about September 1962), the inlet valve guides were lengthened.

Changes noted for the "RA" sequence include a change at engine numbers RA2971/2 (about September 1963), of the material of the exhaust valves. At numbers RA5648/9 (about March 1964), *The Jaguar E-type: A Collector's Guide* notes a change in the chamfer and oil drain holes below the control ring of the pistons (to reduce oil use).

It is noted that at engine numbers RA5736/7 (about April 1964), the cylinder heads on E-types and Mk X cars were made the same, but it is not clear if this means the E-type head was changed or not.

At RA7323/4 it is noted that about August 1964 engine-lifting brackets were added to the cylinder head. Some head studs had to be made longer.

SUMP AND DRAIN PLUG

While XK engine sumps were made from both cast aluminum and stamped and fabricated sheet steel up to the time of the E-type, all E-type sumps were cast aluminum. On early cars these cast sumps were smooth. This is in contrast to the pans on later cars, which had cooling fins cast into them. Neither of the styles of cast aluminum pans were polished. The *J.30 Spare Parts Catalogue (June 1963)* does not designate a change for this part. The authors suspect the non-finned sumps went approximately to engine R7500.

Research of surviving cars indicates chassis numbers 860084 (engine number R3137-9), 875026 (engine number R1037-9) and 885748 (engine number R4276-9) had smooth sumps, while 876289 had the finned sump.

At engine numbers R5399/400 (about June 1962), the sump filter basket was changed to have four semi-circular cutouts. The sump drain plug changed to steel about September 1962, at engine numbers R6417/8. An unspecified change in the sump drain plug about March 1964 occurred at engine numbers RA4573/4.

Some of the early sumps were possibly painted black. This may have been the case on chassis number 875026 (engine number R1037-9).

The left side of an early non-finned sump.

The left side of a later finned sump.

STARTER MOTOR

The authors are not aware of production changes to the starter motor during 3.8-liter E-type production.

ENGINE MOUNTS

The literature records that about December 1961, at chassis numbers 850168/9, 860009/10, 875590/1 and 885050/1, the support bracket for the rear engine mount was changed. This is likely the Metallistic mount from which the bell housing mount hangs.

CRANKCASE BREATHER

The corrugated aluminum breather pipe venting the crankcase fumes out the bottom of the engine compartment, a holdover from the XK series, is a feature of the first 500 E-types.

At one point, 885002 was fitted with a breather venting in D-Type fashion, from the camshaft covers themselves. This was apparently one of two or three engines fitted to 885002 by the factory and is not representative of the production configuration. *Classic and Sportscar* magazine, April 1986, stated that this was "a special D-Type breathing arrangement" on chassis number 885002 and that it, along with other modifications, was used to make this press car a better performer. This is not a typical feature of the early cars.

The crankcase breather arrangement was changed from the corrugated tube to a rigid pipe feeding into the air intake plenum. This occurred at the end of the production of the first 500 cars, *i.e.* at chassis numbers 850091/2, 860004/5, 875385/6, and 885020/1. This is reported as having occurred about October of 1961. It also involved a change in the front cover on the cylinder head.

This corrugated crankcase breather pipe from one of the first 500 cars, chassis 875026, is of the same type used on the XK Jaguars, attaching at the front of the cam chain gallery. It vents crankcase fumes out the lower left side of the engine compartment.

View down the early-type crankshaft breather pipe, showing its exit through a cutout in the bottom aluminum engine compartment panel.

ALUMINUM
BREATHER
CASTING

After the first 500 cars, the
crankcase breather was routed
through the carburetor intakes.
This is the top view of the
aluminum breather casting
that attaches to the front cover
breather housing.

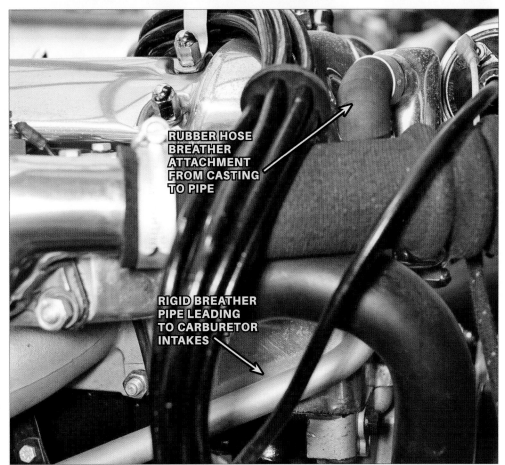

RUBBER HOSE
BREATHER
ATTACHMENT
FROM CASTING
TO PIPE

RIGID BREATHER
PIPE LEADING
TO CARBURETOR
INTAKES

As with the earlier vent, the
through-the-carburetor
crankcase breather pipe
originated at the front of the
camshaft chain gallery.

However, there are differences.
This one came out the right side
of the engine, ran through a
rubber hose breather attachment
from the casting to the pipe,
and was routed through a rigid
breather pipe leading to the
carburetor intakes.

This is where the later vent attaches to the air cleaner.

OIL FILTER ASSEMBLY

A change in the oil filter occurred about March 1964 at engine numbers RA4974/5 and the implementation of a plastic ring impregnated with magnetized metal particles to replace the metal magnetic ring in the oil filter assembly about August 1964 at engine numbers RA6833/4.

TIMING CHAIN COVER

The literature indicates a change in the bolts securing the timing chain cover to the cylinder block at engine numbers R1509/10 and again at engine numbers R1845/6. The former change occurs at the point at which the dynamo mounting bracket, pulley and fan for the dynamo pulley were changed, so it is likely associated with this mounting change. About August 1964, at engine numbers RA6419/20, the front timing cover was changed so that the oil seal could be changed without removing the cover.

CRANKSHAFT DAMPENER AND PULLEY

The change from the aluminum crankshaft pulley to the cast iron version is reported as occurring at engine numbers R1458/9 in October 1961. The change from the single V belt to the duplex dual-V fan-belt, with associated changes in the crankshaft pulley, generator pulley and water pump pulley is reported as occurring about June 1962 at engine numbers R5249/50.

There was a change in the crankshaft dampener about May 1964 at engine numbers RA6453/4.

The early crankshaft-dampener pulleys were aluminum.

The later crankshaft-dampener pulleys were cast iron.

OIL DIPSTICK

The dipstick is reported to have changed about February 1963 at engine numbers R9699/700. This may be the change illustrated in the figures here.

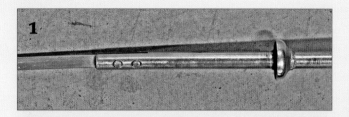

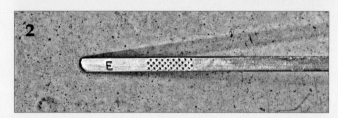

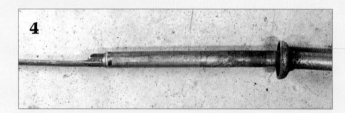

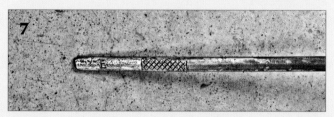

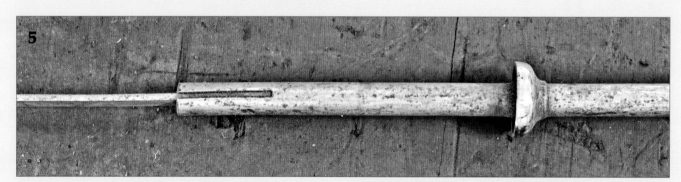

1 *View of flat dipstick showing retaining rivets.*

2 *Acceptable-oil-level markings on the front side of a flat dipstick. Note the "E" marking at the end.*

3 *Back side of the flat dipstick end. Similar pattern to the front, but without the "E" mark. Note that the patterns on the flat dipstick shown here are a diagonal array of stamped-in rectangles.*

4 *Later on, the dipstick was made of half-round stock. It was inserted into a hole in the end of the handle, next to a second short piece of half-round stock and soldered in.*

5 *Side view of the early flat dipstick. The flat stick is inserted into a slot in the handle and retained with two rivets.*

6 *End view of soldered-in dipstick showing the two half-round sections inserted and soldered into the hole. The long half-round section is toward the back of the picture, and the short half-round section is toward the front.*

7 *Front view of the end of a half-round dipstick. Note the acceptable-oil-level markings for this dipstick are comprised of a stamped-in crosshatch, with termination lines on the high and low level ends. It carries the same type of "E" marking as typically found on the flat dipstick.*

8 *Back view of the end of a half-round dipstick. The authors have never seen oil level markings in this region.*

OPPOSITE: *This legend is cast into the brass handle at the top of the dipstick.*

CRANKSHAFT, CONNECTING RODS, BEARINGS, CAPS, PISTONS AND RINGS

Numerous changes are cited in the literature. These include a reduction in the big end connecting rod bearing clearances, about February 1962 at engine numbers R3161/2, about September 1962 a change in the connecting rods and pistons to implement a chamfer on the inner edge of the upper pressure ring and the introduction of a two-part scraper ring at engine numbers R7103/4, at this same point the connecting rods had an oil spray hole added near the small end (these were marked with yellow paint near the rib) and at engine numbers R7194/5 about October 1962, the dowels between the bearing caps and the cylinder block were enlarged.

The crankshaft was changed about October 1962 at engine numbers R7308/9.

At about February 1963, the main bearing cap bolt lock washers were changed at engine numbers R9520/1.

About August 1964 the scraper rings on the pistons were changed for 8.0:1 and 9.0:1 compression ratio engines. The new rings were Maxiflex 50 and the change occurred at engine numbers RA6745/6.

In late 1963, new oil control rings were introduced and they reduced oil burning.

CRANKSHAFT

The literature reports that the 3.8-liter E-type crankshafts underwent a change at engine numbers R2563/4, related to the change in the rear main seal. Likely this is the point at which the seal from the spiral oil retainer to the rope seal. The *J.30 Spare Parts Catalogue (June 1963)* indicates a change from part number C.4808/1 to C.18350/1. The authors have seen the C.18350 marking on crankshafts; they have only seen the C.4808 marking on some early crankshafts.

There was another change in the crankshaft, not listed in the *J.30 Spare Parts Catalogue*, where it underwent an increase in the width of the webs. This is seen in the figures. Based on observations it is likely that the difference in the webs occurred around engine numbers R8500 or so.

Views looking forward on late (on left) and early (on right) crankshafts. Based on observations it is likely that the difference shown here from the narrow crank pin web (on the right) to the wide crank pin web (on the left) changed around engine numbers R8500 or so; it is not listed in the J.30 Spare Parts Catalogue (June 1963). This picture also illustrates the very different shapes of the counterweights between the two crankshafts, but, as discussed in the text, this is likely not indicative of the transition between the early and late crankshaft types.

CRANKSHAFT COUNTERBALANCE WEIGHTS

The 3.8-liter crankshafts had counterbalance weights as an integral part of the crankshaft, which, excepting the oil gallery plugs, was of a single-piece design. The authors have seen the counterweight sections of the crankshaft ground to very different shapes, but have not been able to correlate this with any particular production date, serial number or part number transition point. It is not likely the differences in the counterweight shapes between the late and early crankshafts illustrated in this section relates to the early-to-late crankshaft transition.

Views looking backward on early (on left) and late (on right) crankshafts, again showing the change in the width of the webs. As in the previous figure, great variation between the counterbalance weights is seen between the two crankshafts, but this is apparently not indicative of the web-reinforcement change.

Close-up view of the narrow crankpin web on an early-type crankshaft.

Close-up view of the wide crankpin web on a later-type crankshaft. This change occurred during 3.8-liter production and continued throughout 4.2-liter production. The oil-channel plug is missing from the crankshaft illustrated here.

REAR MAIN SEAL FEATURES

The *Spare Parts Catalogue* states that at engine numbers R2563/4 the rear main seal was changed from the non-gasket type to employing a rope gasket for a seal. The authors observe that the earlier crankshafts had a more pronounced grooved helix at the end of the crankshaft to direct the oil back into the sump. Later crankshafts appear to have a less pronounced helix, apparently relying more on the rope seal to retain oil in the engine.

The rear main seal region on early crankshaft R1038-9 shows a tight helical pitch and deep grooves in the helix.

The rear main seal area on late crankshaft RA3074-9 shows a milder helical pitch and shallower helical grooves.

Profile view of the rear main seal area of early crankshaft R1038-9, showing a deep-groove, tight-pitch helix.

Profile view of the rear main seal area of late crankshaft RA3074-9, showing a shallow-groove, milder-pitch helix. The oil thrower to the right of the helical region appears to have the same outside diameter at the peak as the earlier crankshaft, but the dip to the rear is deeper.

ENGINE SERIAL NUMBER STAMPINGS ON CRANKSHAFTS

As with several other major engine components (the block, cylinder head and flywheel), the crankshaft typically had the engine serial number stamped on it. This stamping is located on the rear side of the number one (rear-most) counterbalance weight, just adjacent to the rear main-bearing cap.

Engine number RA3074, less the "." and the "-9" suffix denoting the compression ratio, stamped on the rear-most counterbalance.

Another view of an engine number stamped on a crankshaft. This one is from engine RA5336.

CRANKSHAFT MARKINGS

E-type crankshafts carried other markings besides the engine number. As in the cases of the block and cylinder head, some were cast and some were stamped-in.

This view of a later-type crankshaft has the part number, C.18350, cast in to one of the webs. The "/1" suffixes given in the J.30 Spare Parts Catalogue (June 1963) is not included. Other markings are shown here as well. The authors have not seen the C4808 part number on any of the earlier crankshafts.

One of the casting marks observed on a crankshaft. The authors do not know what this number represents.

VALVES, VALVE GEAR, CAMSHAFTS, CHAINS AND SPROCKETS

The intermediate timing chain sprocket assembly changed from a two-piece design to a single-piece design in about October 1961 at engine numbers R1075/6. This is likely the change discussed on page 28 of the *J.30 Spare Parts Catalogue (June 1963)* where part number C.2309, 20-tooth intermediate sprocket at the bottom of timing chain and associated part number C.2307, 28-tooth intermediate sprocket at the top of the lower timing gear are both superseded by part number C.17154. Perhaps because the two parts serve the same function, the *Spare Parts Catalogue* does not cite the engine number at which the change took place. This supports the authors' supposition of the *Spare Parts Catalogue* being a listing of spares for repairing the cars and replacing damaged parts, and not specifically a listing of parts fitted to the cars when they left the factory. This might account for so many changes listed by serial number coming from other sources (often *Jaguar E-Type: The Definitive History* and *Factory-Original Jaguar E-Type*) than the *Parts Catalogue*.

Other changes listed in the *Spare Parts Catalogue* include the introduction of a hole at the base of the inlet camshaft about August 1961 at engine numbers R1216/7, a change in the oil-thrower at the rear of the exhaust camshaft at engine numbers R2599/600, a drilling in the inlet camshaft to reduce cold-starting noise about May 1962 at engine numbers R5000/1, a change in the intermediate damper assembly for the upper timing chain about June 1962 at engine numbers R5532/3, a change in the vibration damper for the lower timing chain about November 1962 at engine numbers R8138/9 and a change in the lower timing chain intermediate damper (the new damper was positioned differently and was attached to two tapped bossed on the cylinder block) about May 1964 at engine numbers RA6024/5.

OIL PUMP AND OIL DELIVERY SYSTEM

The size of the oil pump was increased in June 1961 at engine numbers R1008/9 and that about May 1964, at engine numbers RA6603/4, a support was added to the first intermediate bearing cap to support the oil delivery pipe, replacing a lock washer used on the cap earlier.

The Parts Catalogue notes that the oil pump was changed and the oil suction pipe was changed to 3/4 inch instead of 11/16 inch about June 1963 at engine numbers RA2077/8.

FUEL SYSTEM: CARBURETORS AND MANIFOLDS

At engine numbers RA2463/4 the needle valve and seat in the carburetor float chamber was changed to Delrin acetal resin and changes were made in the lid and hinged lever. In *The Jaguar E-type: A Collector's Guide*, Skilleter cites a date of about June 1963 for this change. Porter, in *Jaguar E-Type: The Definitive History*, cites a date of about April 1964 for the change. Based on these dates it is likely the engine numbers of this change are RA5463/4 instead of RA2463/4.

About January 1964, at engine numbers RA4115/6, the throttle spring bearings in the carburetors were changed to an impregnated plastic material.

CARBURETORS: SUCTION CHAMBER ASSEMBLIES

Suction chamber dampener caps in the earlier 3.8-liter E-types the were brass with a white metal coating. These brass dampener caps were stamped with an "O." The cap on the dampeners was changed from copper to black plastic around 1963. Roadster chassis number 876577 (engine R3653-9) had the brass carburetor tops, while chassis numbers 879325 (engine RA1769-9) and 887576 (engine R8910-9) had the plastic dampener caps. The authors have never seen an original car with a brass cap with "OIL RESERVOIR," with or without an "O," on an original E-type.

The necks on the tops of the suction chambers, where the dampener assembly screws in, were shorter on E-types than on previous HD8 carburetors used on XK-150s or, subsequently, on Mk X sedans.

OPPOSITE:

1 An early-type dash-pot dampener cap made of brass and still showing most of its original white metal coating. It is very unusual to see this much of the original coating still present. Often, none is left.

2 A brass carburetor dampener cap with "OIL RESERVOIR" stamped on the top. This one does not have an "O" stamp, although sometimes they do. This picture is from a Mk2 engine. Typically these markings are found on earlier XK cars and some sedans. The two lines running horizontally across the cap are scratches and not part of the cap marking.

3 A later-type black plastic dash-pot dampener cap.

4 Sometimes the plastic dash-pot assembly caps are found in this light tone. This tone may be the result of the plastic resin fading with time, or perhaps they are later replacements. As with the black plastic caps, the "AUC 8115" marking is molded on the cap.

5 This black plastic cap appears to be lighter in the middle. Perhaps this is the way it was made, but it may represent a stage in the aging process.

6 The suction chamber from an S.U. HD8 carburetor from an early E-type. Note the brass dash-pot cap and low neck of the casting into which it is screwed.

7 This view of the top of the suction chamber of an S.U. HD8 carburetor of an XK-150S shows the early long-neck design used prior to the E-type and subsequently on Mk X sedans. Contrast the length of the top of the suction chamber, where the dash-pot assembly screws in, to the same section of the suction chambers on the other pictures in this chapter, which are much lower. This suction chamber has the early-type brass dash-pot cap. Later on, the dash-pot caps were made of black plastic. These sometimes failed and let the dash-pot dampener rod protrude out the top of the cap.

CARBURETORS: FLOAT CHAMBER TAGS

The inside-threaded bolts retaining the caps on the three S.U. HD8 carburetor float chambers had aluminum tags located under them. These tags protrude out from the bolts, and are stamped with characters. The authors have no evidence for any S.U. carburetor fitted to an E-type leaving the factory without these tags, in spite of the fact that neither the *Spare Parts Catalogue*s (*J.30, etc.*), nor the Service Manuals show them in the exploded views of carburetor components. These tags have been referred to as an "Identity Label," an "S.U. part number," an "ID tag" a "reference number," and a "Carburetor Specification." Possibly these tags denote the configuration of the carburetor (perhaps the particular needle valve used, the setting of the float level, *etc.*). The markings on the tags changed as E-type production went on, perhaps reflecting changes in the setup of the HD 8 carburetors. The prefixes on the designations for carburetor sub-assembly components from the *J.30 Spare Parts Catalogue* (*June 1963*) are mostly "AUC," with some "AUD," (as seen on various of the S.U. carburetor tags) and they are followed by four digits. For example, Jaguar part number 8760, Return Spring, is referenced on page 32 of the *J.30 Spare Parts Catalogue (June 1963)* as AUC.2020, and part number 8765 is referenced as AUD.2093. The number on the tags on the E-type float chambers, though, had three digits instead of four, as might be the case if they indicated the entire carburetor configuration. A sub-assembly part might have more digits to break out more detail.

The authors have observed that on early 3.8-liter cars all three of the tags were the same, each labeled "AUC946." Later on they carried a suffix letter, "R" for rear, "C" for center and "F" for front. From observations of unrestored cars the authors have seen tags without suffixes on 875026, 875087, 875122 had one without suffix and two with (perhaps one was replaced) and 885056, a very original coupe, had suffixes on all three. Engines R1956-9 and R3653-9 each had two tags remaining, with suffixes.

Page seven of the JCNA Judges Guide (Stevenson, Bob, Chief Judge, Jaguar Affiliates Group of Michigan, *JCNA Series 1 E-type Judge's Guide*, www.jcna.com/library/tech/e-type1.pdf) states that the tags read "AUC946 F, C and R," but the early tags did not have the F, C and R suffixes. It is also noted on page seven that, "These tags changed to read AUD112 sometime between engine number RA3577 and RA4296. It's very possible that this change took place at RA4116 as mentioned in SB B.24, but at this time, 7/09, the authors are not certain."

Tuning S.U. Carburetors, Third Edition, SpeedSport MotoBooks, Middlesex, England, 1975 (no author cited) discusses the different S.U. carburetors used on many cars. They refer to the three-digit number as a "specification," (pages 85 and 87) and refer to the four-digit number as a "part number" (page 87), consistent with the speculations above. On page 94 they refer to the Jaguar V12 E-type having AUD547 specification carburetors. On page 98 they refer to the 3.8-liter E-type having AUD112F, AUD112C and AUD112R specification carburetors and the 4.2-liter E-type having AUD227F, AUD227C and AUD227R specification carburetors.

The authors have observed an AUD227C, possibly originally a light green color, found on an E-type (but likely not an original).

An early float-chamber tag with the "AUC946" designation and without prefix. This is from roadster 875026, that also carries the other two similar tags. Note the large font of the characters. This was reduced for at least some of the AUC946 tags with suffixes.

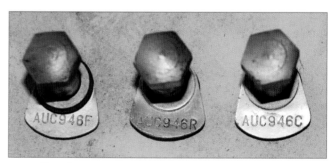

A set of later float-chamber tags from coupe 885056 showing the suffixes. The"AUC946" carries suffixes "F", "C" and "R," indicating their position on the carburetors: Front, Center or Rear carburetor. The tags are out of order in the picture.

OPPOSITE BOTTOM LEFT: *A rear tag with suffix, on engine R3653-9 from roadster 876577. Note the unusual double stamping of the "R" over a previously-stamped "C." The same type of stamp appears to have been used for the "R" as that which stamped the other letters, so it is likely this is a factory error and correction.*

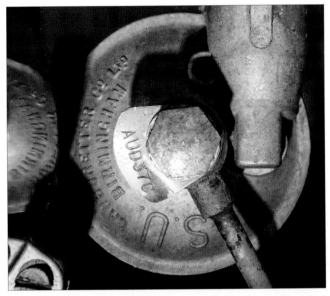

This blue tag from a Mk X sedan shows some of the variety found in these tags. This one is "AUD37C," a two-digit number.

A bare aluminum AUC865 tag on an E-type. This is a restoration and this tag is likely not original.

An example of the sort of variety one can find in the carburetor float-chamber tags. In addition to various alphanumeric stampings, they come in several different colors, including green, red and blue. The authors have never seen colored tags on an original E-type.

A tag with AUD112F, potentially in a dark color. This is the marking seen on later 3.8-liter E-types.

CARBURETORS: FLOAT CHAMBERS

Float-chamber tops on the 3.8-liter cars and many, if not all, Series 1 4.2-liter cars, had a blind hole cast in them, just adjacent to the fuel-inlet boss on the cast top. This hole is likely a remnant from when spring-loaded brass push-shafts were used in this location to depress the float in the chamber below.

This view of a float chamber top from an S.U. carburetor from an MGTF produced in the mid 1950s shows what is sometimes called a "tickler" rod, in brass, inserted in the round hole cast in the float-chamber cover (cf. https: //en.wikipedia.org/wiki/Carburetor for a discussion). These brass rods, typically found on earlier S.U. carburetors (before the period of the E-type), depressed the float chamber when they were pushed down, thus releasing the needle-and-seat valve in the float-chamber.

Some of the earlier float-chamber tops had three residual blind holes showing in the casting. Note the "AUC4261" cast marking on the cap, not seen in the companion shot of the single-blind-hole cap here. The authors have seen this type of cap with three blind holes mainly on 1961 cars (whether XK-150S, Mk IX, or E-type).

CARBURETORS: BODY STAMPINGS

In addition to the markings on the float-chamber tags, the bodies of the carburetors themselves were stamped. Typically alphanumeric characters were stamped on the tops of the flanges of the downstream ends of the carbure-tors, next to where they bolt to the intake manifolds. There have been various speculations as to what these represent, including a dating system; the authors suspect that this is correct. Some examples are given here. More research is needed.

The blind hole cast into the cover of the float chamber of this HD8 carburetor is typical of the early 3.8-liter E-types and it seems this ran into, if not through, 4.2-liter Series 1 S.U. carburetor production. It is almost certainly left over from the earlier S.U. carburetors that had a spring-loaded brass shaft in this location to depress the float.

A "T5" marking on the manifold-side carburetor flange on roadster 875026. As is typical, the same stamp is seen on all three carburetors. Note also the series of "P" characters often found on the manifold nuts. Note also the orientation of the nuts, with the beveled edges of the six junctures of the flats facing out. The authors suspect this was the standard configuration, but are not sure this was necessarily consistent.

A "U3" stamping on engine R1956-9. Unusually, there are two "U3" stamps on this same flange. The other two carburetors are also stamped "U3," but are not double-stamped.

This sand-cast S.U. carburetor, made in the 1950s before E-type production, is labeled "N13."

This carburetor has a "D12 6" stamp, using two groupings of alphanumerics.

INTAKE MANIFOLDS: AIR BALANCE PIPE

The air balance pipes of the early type, before the change to the simplified throttle linkage at engine numbers R2933/4, were similar, but not identical to, those used on XK-150S cars. For example, E-types used a manual choke, while XK-150S cars and the Mk X sedans (that both used the S-type engine), used a starting carburetor. The starting carburetor fed into two ports in the bottom of the air balance pipe. While bosses were supplied in the castings on E-types for these two ports, they were not drilled out, while on XK-150S and Mk X cars they were.

Here the air balance pipes for a 3.8-liter E-type, in the back and for an XK-150S, in the front. Resting on each balance pipe is the control rod from the carburetor from associated car. Note that the XK-150S control rod is straight while the E-type rod is kinked. It appears these kinked E-type rods were used only on cars with the early-type multi-piece throttle linkage, as shown on the bottom of page 188. When the simpler throttle linkage system was introduced the rods appear to have reverted to the straight type. Also evident here are the two holes in the XK-150S balance pipe where the pipe to the starting carburetor feeds into the balance pipe. These holes are absent in the E-type balance pipe because a choke was used instead of a starting carburetor for E-types.

INTAKE MANIFOLDS: WATER OUTLET PIPE

The water-outlet pipe connecting the three intake manifolds changed very early in production. Initially the area behind the blanking plate was dipped in, while later it was flat. Based on observations, it appears the dip in the water outlet pipe was a feature on engines up to about engine R1138-9 (left-hand drive roadster 875109). Unrestored cars 875026, 875086 and 875100 showed the dip or depression and cars 875090, 875122 and 885056 did not. Of course the change may not have come at an exact point and there may have been overlap between the two types of outlet pipes. Interestingly, XK-150S cars do not have this dip.

It has been suggested that the few very early cars produced by the Experimental Department did not have the dip in the water outlet pipe. Coupe 885004 does not have this feature (but the car has been worked on or restored), but restored coupe 885005 does have the dip. Coupe 885002 apparently had two or three engines fitted. *Jaguar E-Type: The Definitive History* shows a picture of an engine stated to be fitted by the Experimental Department, perhaps E5020-9 (pages 68 and 72), that appears to show a dip in the manifold. An illustration of Experimental Department roadster 850003 before restoration on pages 162 and 173 of *All About the Jaguar E-type* appears to show the

Later water-outlet pipes were flat in back of the blanking plate.

The early water-outlet pipe on the intake manifolds had a dipped-in region just in back of the blanking plate.

dipped-in manifold. The engine is stated to be R1001-9 on page 173.

Another difference in the S-type XK engine between the XK-150S and Mk X cars and the E-type cars is the sensor to actuate the starting carburetor. On the XK-150S and Mk X cars, with a starting carburetor, the sensor is located in the port at the top of the water outlet pipe. E-types had a manual choke instead of a starting carburetor, and had a blanking plate fitted over the sensor port.

Triangular blanking plate over the water temperature sensor on a water outlet pipe from an E-type.

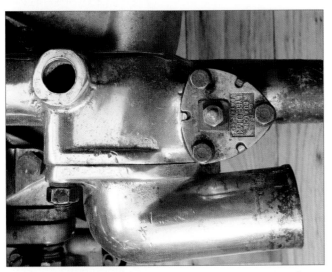

A Mk X sedan water outlet pipe with water temperature sensor for activating the starting carburetor.

INTAKE MANIFOLDS

The intake manifolds used on S-type engines for XK-150S and Mk X cars differed from those used on E-types. The former did not have the curve found in the manifold flow path used on the E-types, but rather had relatively straight flow ports. In addition, at least some Mk X manifolds had the carburetors attached by a spring-loaded arrangement

on each of the four bolts retaining the carburetor flange.

Left-hand drive roadster chassis number 875026 (engine R1037-9), may have never had its intake manifold apart. On this car, the chrome hex nuts holding the manifolds to the head, the air and water manifolds to the intake manifolds, and the carburetors to the intake manifolds are all oriented so that the beveled edges of the nuts face

The intake manifolds are another difference between the XK-150S S-type XK engine and those used in 3.8-liter E-types. On the left is the relatively straight XK-150S manifold and on the right is the more curved E-type manifold. Note that the XK-150S carburetors are held at an angle to the right face of the head, while the E-type carburetor flanges are parallel to the head.

Bottom view of an XK-150S intake manifold, on the left and an E-type manifold on the right. It appears that each of these manifolds was the only type used for the XK-150S and E-type, respectively. Note the part-number characters are smaller on the E-type manifold as compared to the XK-150S manifold.

Earlier XK S-type engines, as used on XK-150S cars, as well as those used on Mk X sedans, used the electric starting carburetor shown here between the front and middle carburetor. All E-types had manual lever-operated chokes.

outward, and the sharp edges face inward. See the illustration on the lower right of page 184.

The Jaguar E-type: A Collector's Guide notes that at engine numbers RA7175/6, about October 1964, the intake manifold gasket was changed from cupronickel to a tin-plate material.

THROTTLE LINKAGE

About January 1962, at chassis numbers 850248/9, 860020/1, 875910/1 and 885124/5, changes were made to the spacing collar and washer on the accelerator pedal assembly and to the accelerator-pedal lever assembly itself. About the same time, at engine numbers R2933/4,

The later throttle linkage was greatly simplified, with the three control arms permanently fixed to a single rod. The center pivot was discontinued.

The throttle linkage on the early cars, this one from chassis 875026, was a complex arrangement, having many redundant adjustments. Each of the three carburetor control arms was separately clamped to one of two round rods, allowing separate angle adjustments for each arm. In addition, the relation between the two rods could be set using the corrugated steel clamp connecting them. On XK-150S cars, a solid cast clamping collar was used instead of the steel corrugated clamp.

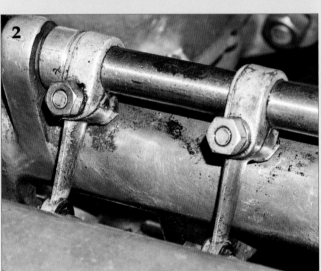

1 *Slave shaft lever on an early throttle linkage showing the part number 4054. Note the last digit is stamped on over a cast digit. This is typical and agrees with the listing in the Spare Parts Catalogue which gives the part number AUC.4054 for the lever.*

2 *Two slave shaft levers showing wear-through of the white-colored metal plating they had when supplied from the factory. This is typical, as in the case of the suction-chamber damper caps on the carburetors. Often both the levers and caps are seen with no plating remaining, but it appears they were all plated when delivered from the factory.*

3 *Comparison of an E-type control rod connecting the throttle linkage to the carburetors on the E-type (on top, part number C.17635) and on an XK-150S, lower.*

4 *The corrugated sheet steel coupling link (part number 4833, AUC4334) as used in the early E-type multi-piece throttle linkage. From observations and research, it appears this linkage was used on all early multi-piece throttle linkages. The authors have never observed the cast crimped coupling link used on the XK-150S cars on an original E-type.*

5 *Detail of the washers, nuts and bolts retaining the corrugated sheet steel coupling link.*

the three-shaft slave shaft design to operate the throttle was altered to a two-shaft design.

The three bent steel control rods (part number C.17635) between the linkage and carburetors for E-types differed from the linkages for XK-150S cars with a similar XK S-type engine. The E-type control rods had a kink in them and the linkages for XK-150S cars were straight.

The early throttle linkage employed three control levers, bolted to the throttle slave shafts, to actuate the steel rods connecting to the carburetors. The entire mechanism was actuated from the rear slave shaft by a rod running to the firewall. While typically there were three such control levers bolted to the slave shafts, one for each carburetor, an additional vestigial control lever has been observed (more than once) on the rear slave shaft. These rods may have been a hold-over from when a similar linkage was used on XK-150S cars, and an extra lever was used to activate the throttle linkage (seen in the illustration below). A very early E-type engine with such an extra lever attached is seen on page 68 of *The Most Famous Car in the World*.

This restored multiple-piece throttle linkage on an XK-150S shows the throttle control rod bolted on the rear slave shaft between the rear and middle control rod levers. On the E-type linkage the control is through a third slave shaft (part number C.18905) extending from the linkage on the air balance pipe to the firewall.

Close-up of the XK-150S throttle control lever on the left and the cast coupling on the lower right (with two clamping bolts and nuts showing). On early E-type linkages the coupling is made from folded sheet steel (see figure 5 on page 189).

FUEL FILTER AND LINES

The fuel bowl bracket changed both in shape and in the orientation in which it was installed.

The bracket for mounting the fuel filter to the frame was changed about October 1961 at chassis numbers 850091/2, 860004/5, 875385/6 and 885020/1. This is the end of the first 500 cars, a transition point between outside and inside bonnet latches. It appears the bracket was changed to avoid fouling of the fuel filter assembly on the new inside latching mechanism.

REINFORCING IMPRESSION IN THE MOUNTING BRACKET

A later-type fuel bowl mounting bracket with reinforcing impression. It is mounted in the later manner, facing up. It appears the bracket was oriented upward to permit the fuel sediment bowl assembly to clear the new inside bonnet-latch mechanism when it was adopted

LEFT: Initially the fuel bowl brackets were installed facing down, as shown here on 875026. This bracket carries its original gray paint and is of the early type without a reinforcing impression stamped in. The vertical component of the bracket is also significantly shorter than the later type brackets (although this is not evident from the picture).

Front and back views of four different fuel sediment bowl bracket types, illustrating the various sorts that were in use. Note the presence or absence of the reinforcing dip and the use of one or two holes on the side of the bracket that bolts to the bulkhead flange and frame member.

AIR CLEANER

Very early in production, the seam flange running around the outside edge of the triangular fiberglass air cleaner plenum was decreased in size. From research of surviving cars: Chassis number 875026 had the wide flange, while 875235 had the narrow flange.

About October 1961, at chassis numbers 850091/2, 860004/5, 875385/6 and 885020/1 (the end of production the first 500 cars) the base assembly for the air-intake box was changed to accept a new-type vent.

The wide sealing flange on an early air-filter plenum.

The narrow sealing flange of a late air-filter plenum.

RIGHT: *This view of a later sump removed from the car shows the increased length and the seams on either end where it was brazed together. Though not visible here, the left-hand side has female threads. On these later cars, the filter was attached to the bottom of the fuel pump intake pipe. This particular sump has a small drain plug on the bottom (the second nut on the far left), a feature on the later version of this sump.*

GAS TANK

The cylindrical drain plug or sump seen on the bottom of the gas tanks of later E-types is absent on some of the very early cars (possibly just some of those from the Experimental Department). When the cylindrical drain plug first appeared, it was a multi-piece unit, but about October 1961, at chassis numbers 850091/2, 860004/5, 875385/6 and 885020/1 (the end of production of the first 500 cars), the gas tank assembly was changed to adopt the one-piece sump. When the early sump was fitted, the gas tank had female threads and the sump had the male. This was reversed for cars fitted with the later sump.

An early multi-piece gas tank sump removed from the car. Note the male threads. The bottom part of this sump (on the left side of the picture) unscrews from the cylindrical body to permit the spring and collar to be inserted and removed.

This disassembled view of the inside assembly of the early multi-piece sump shows the bottom cap on the left, the spring in the middle and the collar for the fuel-pump intake pipe on the right. The filter is not shown.

End view of the later version of the inside-thread sump showing the drain plug end on.

The gas tanks on the early cars had female threads to retain the sumps. The intake pipe on the bottom of the fuel pump is showing here.

View of an early sump in situ *on the bottom of the gas tank.*

The gas tanks for the later cars had male threads to retain the sumps. Here the intake pipe on the bottom of the fuel pump, with its filter bag, is showing protruding from the sump attachment port on the bottom of the gas tank.

FUEL PUMP, MOUNT AND LINES

All 3.8-liter cars had submerged fuel pumps. However, the fuel pump and its bracket in the gas tank on the first 500 cars were different in many ways from later pumps, as seen in the figures. At the end of first 500 production, about October 1961, *i.e.* at chassis numbers 850091/2, 860004/5, 875385/6 and 885020/1, the fuel pump, bracket, pipe and filter bracket were changed. This is the transition from the early to the late fuel pump, as seen in the figures.

 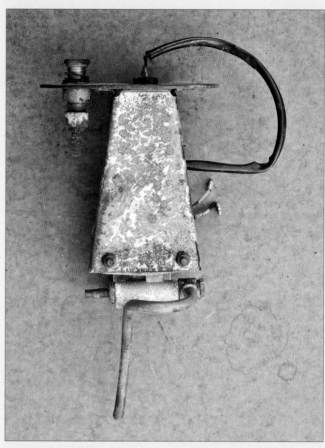

Front (left) and back (right) views of an early fuel pump on its early bent sheet metal mounting bracket. This one is from left-hand drive roadster chassis number 875109.

LEFT: *A side view of another early fuel pump, this one from left-hand drive roadster 875026, showing the disk-shaped screen filter, somewhat similar to the filters used in the dual gas tanks of MK X sedans. The authors have only seen one instance of this, on 875026, but have not seen many original fuel pumps from cars this early. If this was the initial standard, it was replaced very early on in production with the diagonally-cut pipe that extended down into the screw-on sump assembly.*

ABOVE: *Front view of the same pump from chassis 875026 showing the disk filter and cast and stamped on markings, including the "4 61" date code.*

LEFT: *The short braided-wire sleeve covering the electrical wires to the pump. This one is from an early-type pump. Characteristically for the early pumps, its two ends, while parallel to each other, are offset. This is not the case for sleeves from later-type pumps where the alignment of the aperture on the cover and the pump electrical connection port are not so offset as on early pumps.*

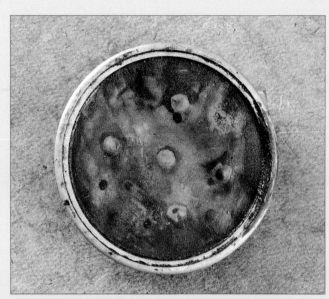

Top view (left) and bottom view (right) of the disk-type filter as seen on the pump from 875026.

Front view (left) and back view (right) of a later-type fuel pump on post mounting. Note the lead seal on the wire on the right-hand side top of the pump.

In about January 1962 the fuel pipe from the pump and its bracket were changed, with the attachment of the line to the pump by a banjo fitting at chassis numbers 850254/5, 860026/7, 876030/1 and 885160/1; about January 1964, the fuel pump was changed (an increase in operating pressure) at chassis numbers 850785/6, 861385/6, 880618/9 and 889509/10; and about October 1964 the feed pipe filter to the fuel pump was changed, at chassis numbers 850934/5, 861780/1, 881863/4 and 890847/8.

In summer or early fall of 1962, the fuel line from the pump to the gas tank outlet connection was changed from the Vulkollan material to Nylon, at chassis numbers 850526/7, 860583/4, 877354/5 and 886094/5.

The early-type in-tank fuel pump apparently was supplied with different intake pipe configurations. In many cars the intake pipe was a straight un-filtered line with a diagonally-cut end.

Front view (left) of an early-type pump, with pressure regulator cover and impeller cover removed. Note it has both cast and stamped in ("78388 B" and date code "4 61") characters. Note also the characteristic domed top. The back view of an early-type pump shows the cast arrow mark denoting the direction of rotation of the disk impeller.

Front view (left) of a late-type pump housing with pressure regulator cover removed gives a view into the flow ports. The back view (right) of a later pump shows the arrow denoting rotation direction of the impeller. This arrow is much larger than the direction arrow on the early pump. It is also raised, as opposed to the inset arrow on the earlier pump.

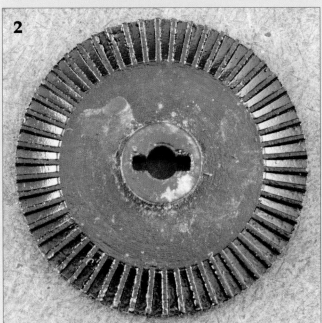

1 While the pressure regulator cover on the early pump was unmarked (all marks were on the main cast body of the pump), the regulator cover of the later pump, as shown here, carried part number and date-stamp information.

2 A view of the polymeric impeller located at the bottom of both early and late pumps. The authors have seen these impellers in a decomposed state, as if they dissolved. This one appears to be in good condition.

3 The small armature that drives the impeller on the submerged Lucas pumps. This one is from a later-type pump; the authors are not aware of variations between the armatures of the early and late pumps.

4 This view of an NOS fuel pump from a Mk X sedan shows its disk-shaped filter. Note that it has a different mount to the pump than seen in the disk-filter seen on an E-type. Note also the braided power cable is substantially longer than that used on the E-type pump.

FUEL LEVEL SENDER UNIT

The Fuel level sender unit mounted in the top of the gas tank came in at least two types. The later type had a small blind hole in the top and the early type had no hole. Left-hand drive roadsters chassis numbers 875026 and 875109 had the early sender, without holes and 879325 had the later type with holes.

The Fuel level sender units on the early cars did not have holes cast into them.

Later Fuel level sender units had blind holes cast in them.

IGNITION COIL AND BRACKET

An extension assembly for the coil bracket was added about October 1961 at chassis numbers 850091/2, 860004/5, 875385/6 and 885020/1, the transition from outside to inside bonnet latches.

Two styles of wire-retainer caps were used on the coil. While the retainers used on the distributor caps were slightly shorter, they are found in both varieties.

Later replacement Lucas coils can differ markedly from those originally fitted. See additional information in Chapter Six, FEATURES RELATING TO BOTH 3.8-LITER AND 4.2-LITER CARS.

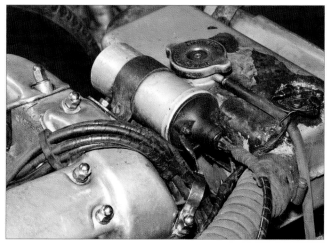

The standard coils originally fitted were produced by Lucas and had black plastic insulating end-caps.

The month and year of manufacture ("1 59") of this original Lucas coil were stamped on the case.

DISTRIBUTOR

The Parts Catalogue notes the distributor and vacuum suction pipe were changed about April 1963 at engine numbers RA1381/2. The distributor was changed on 9.0:1 compression ratio engines, about July 1964 at engine numbers RA6833/4 and that about October 1964 the distributor was changed on 8.0:1 compression ratio engines at engine numbers RA7201/2. The note about the change in the vacuum suction pipe is likely related to the change from the screwed connection to the use of a section of rubber tubing pushed on to a non-threaded tube.

The early distributor from the opposite side.

The early distributor, type 40617D. Note that the terminal for the contact-breaker points connection to the coil is a screw terminal, rather than a spade connector. A spade connector is attached to this screw terminal and the coil line female connector presses on this.

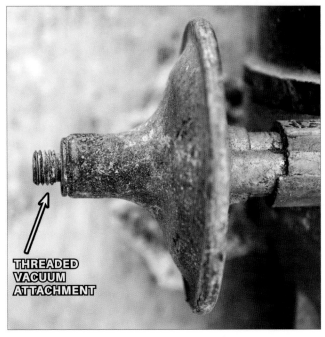

THREADED VACUUM ATTACHMENT

On the earlier distributor, the attachment point for the vacuum line from the front carburetor is threaded.

The part number markings, arrow to denote rotation direction and date on an early distributor.

The later 40887 distributor. Note the rounded cap and the presence of several axially-oriented support fins cast into the lower part of the distributor body just above where it inserts into the block.

The later distributor from the opposite side. Note that the waterproof collar is installed on this example. The authors have not seen these used on 3.8-liter cars.

The vacuum timing adjust attachment point on the later distributor has a tube protruding from it upon which a short rubber hose presses. This is a press-fit only, since the attachment is through a non-threaded tube. The short hose acts as a connector to the vacuum line from the carburetor.

The part number and date stampings on a later distributor.

INSUATED
FEED-THROUGH
MOUNT

This late 3.8-liter E-type engine distributor shows the insulated mount for the contact-breaker feed-through by itself (as opposed to being integrated in the waterproof collar.

Another example of a later 40887 distributor on a late 3.8-liter engine.

DISTRIBUTOR ROTOR, CAP AND WIRE RETAINERS

The seven spark plug wire retainers on the top of the distributor cap and the one on the coil came in at least two types. On the early cars these retainers came with tightly spaced grooves. Later cars had retainers with widely spaced grooves.

Rubber sleeves were fitted to the spark plug wires where they enter the distributor cap, about August 1963, at engine numbers RA2289/90.

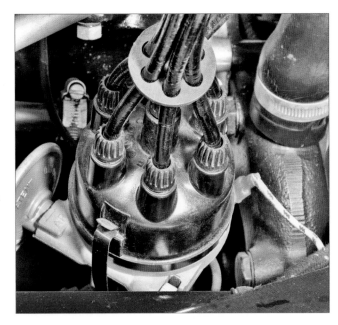

RIGHT: *The early distributor cap has a roughly cylindrical and squared-off appearance. Note the early-type high-tension wire retainers on this distributor cap.*

The later distributor cap has a roughly spherical shape. This one has the circular black plastic collar (waterproof cover) between it and the distributor body, but this is a later feature of 4.2-liter cars around April 1965 (see 4.2-liter section). When this cap first came in it seated directly on the distributor body without this collar.

A typical rotor, as originally supplied with the cars.

Side view of a standard original rotor.

This after-market rotor was a replacement used in many cars about twenty years ago. It functions, but is not of the original design. Other non-original pattern variants exist as well.

The early spark plug wire retainers for the coil and distributor cap had small slots and an abrupt taper at the end.

The later spark plug wire retainers had wide slots and a more gradual taper.

SPARK PLUG WIRES AND ORGANIZERS

The spark plug cable organizers on the early cars were comprised of a chromed steel ring, black plastic discs and a rigid, dark-brown plastic sleeve. In later cars the wires were housed in a flexible, black plastic sheath (the discs and rings were no longer present) and a single narrow organizer was used.

The wire and retainer routing and configuration vary on early cars. Sometimes the wires were routed over the surge tank hose (running from the front of the exhaust

An early spark plug organizer retained on the lower front-most stud of the intake cam cover, as appears to be typical for outside latch cars.

LEFT: *Left-hand drive roadster chassis number 876319, a very original car, shows the spark-plug retaining cable mounted on the intake cam. It is bolted to the left, front-most stud of the cam cover over the camshaft itself (as opposed to the part of the cover over the chains). This is the fourth stud from the rear of the cam cover.*

The early spark plug cable organizers consisted of a chrome ring and black plastic discs with six holes in them. In this case the disk has slipped out of the ring. Generally there are several disks. This one is from 875090, an outside latch car with corrugated crankshaft breather on the left side of the engine, in exception to the suggestion in the text that this location was used to avoid the breather. The suggestion may still be correct; inconsistency is common in the way features changed over time in E-type production. While the car is very original, of course the ring could have been moved during repairs.

This spark plug wire guide was used on the later engines. Here it is seen in conjunction with the black-plastic sleeve organizer.

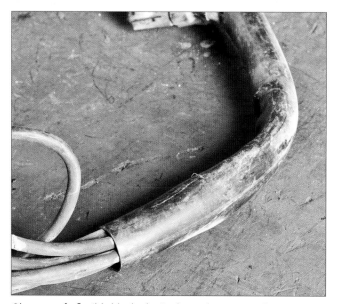

Close-up of a flexible black-plastic sleeve that was used to organize the wires.

The sleeve organizer on left-hand drive roadster 879032 showing a typical routing over the front of the cylinder head.

manifold assembly to the right rear of the header tank) and sometimes under it. In addition, the chrome retaining ring has been observed fastened on various locations on the right-front cam-cover retaining studs. It appears the earlier cars had the ring mounted to the front lower stud holding down the camshaft-chain galley section of the cam cover. Later, the ring seems to have been typically bolted to the front-most top stud on the section of the cam cover over the cam itself (as opposed to those over the cam-chain gallery). This may be a result of the change in the crankcase breather. The breather moved from the left side of the engine (the corrugated aluminum tube) to the right side of the engine (the multi-piece assembly with the steel pipe running from the front of the head to the air cleaner intake). In the process of this change, the chrome spark plug wire retaining ring may have been located upward to avoid fouling with the breather tube.

About March 1962, at engine numbers R3854/5, the spark plug cables were increased in length and rerouted. The spacers for the spark plug leads were changed.

About April 1964, at engine numbers RA5633/4, the spark plug cables were changed and about August 1964, at engine numbers RA7323/4, the spark plug cables had to be lengthened to accommodate the new engine-lifting brackets.

SPARK PLUG CAPS

The spark plug caps on early cars are round, with the word "CHAMPION" written in a circular fashion. This same cap, or one that is extremely similar, was also supplied to other British cars, for example, late 1950s or early 1960s BMC Minis. Some later 3.8-liter E-types were fitted with the oval-top type, with "CHAMPION" written in a straight line across the top and a later type has "CHAMPION" molded across the top inside a bow-tie shape. E-type chassis numbers 875026 (engine numbers R1037-9) and 876052 (engine numbers R2447-9) had the circular caps and 876577 (engine numbers R3653-9) had the bow-tie types.

A more common form of the spark plug cap in a nearly oval shape, showing the "CHAMPION" lettering.

The earliest cars had spark plug caps with circular "CHAMPION" lettering on the top and a dot in the center. This is a view of early roadster 875026.

The final form of the spark plug caps had this bow-tie shape. Typically, the raised section was painted white.

These oval-top caps found on the very original coupe, 885056, do not have "CHAMPION" marked on them.

In some cases, the bow-tie caps are found without paint. It is not clear if they were perhaps sometimes supplied this way or not, but they have been observed, as in this case, without any apparent trace of paint.

SPARK PLUGS

The spark plugs were Champion N.5, according to the specification sheet in *The Motor*, May 22, 1961 and in the *J.30 Spare Parts Catalogue (August 1961)*. However, in the *J.30 Spare Parts Catalogue (June 1963)*, the part number UN.12Y is given. *Car and Driver*, December 1961, commented about using N.5 plugs for the street and N.3 for racing. The Service Manual E/123/5 lists UN.12Y, with N.3 for racing.

At engine numbers R9527/8, about December 1962, the spark plugs were changed to Champion UN.12Y.

Currently-available Champion spark plugs are not identical to the ones available earlier. The older-type plugs have machined top contacts, while the currently-available plugs may all have molded top contacts. The parting line from the mold is visible on the modem contacts.

COOLING SYSTEM: RADIATOR AND FAN SHROUD

The 3.8-liter E-type radiators were made of aluminum. While a few cases of brass radiators have been observed a on late 3.8-liter cars, it seems unlikely these were originally fitted at the factory. The radiators initially carried an aluminum plate on their tops, held on by four small dome-headed screws (rarely properly duplicated in restorations). Later on in production these tags were no longer fitted. It appears that the stamp-set for these tags at Marston Excelsior did not have an "L" of the same font as the other characters, as a larger-font "L" stamp is often used, as well as an upside-down "7" punch. The "ISSUE No" box seems to always be un-stamped. Other radiator variations included "L" of the same font as the other characters. The authors have seen a larger-font "L" stamp used, as well as the upside-down "7" used as an "L." "8" characters are of varying font size and are sometimes stamped upside-down.

The contacts on the tops of the original Champion spark plugs were machined.

The modern replacement Champion spark plug top contacts are cast and the parting line is evident.

This is the back view of an early aluminum radiator. The fiberglass shroud has been removed.

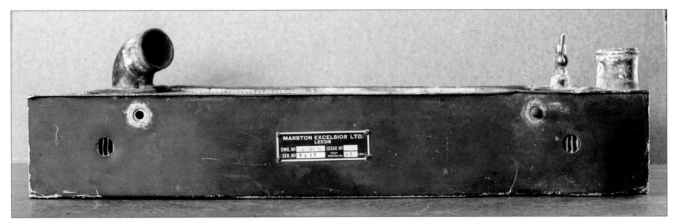

A view of the top of the radiator, showing the location of the serial number tag. Later 3.8-liter aluminum radiators did not have this tag.

CHASSIS NUMBER	RAD S/N	DWG NO.	PRESSURE TEST	ISSUE NO	NOTES
875026	217	ML185 8A	15	(Blank)	Large font "l" punch used, one "8" stamped upside-down
(Unknown)	873	ML185 8A	15	(Blank)	Large font "l" punch used
876319	x	x	x	x	No tag
876577	3017	ML185 8A	15	(Blank)	"L" is upside-down "7", two different-sized "8" punch fonts used
850034	2190 (over 2180?)	ML185 8A	15	(Blank)	"L" is upside-down "7", two different-sized "8" punch fonts used, one upside-down, "9" in 2190 may be stamped over an "8"
879032	x	x	x	x	No tag
x	2336	ML185 8A	15	(Blank)	"L" is upside-down "7", two different-sized "8" punch fonts used, one upside-down

The data is based on observations of radiators that appear to be original to the chassis numbers given.

The radiator tag for radiator 217, from roadster 875026, shows the large "L" stamp in the DWG. No box and the second "8" is stamped upside-down. As is typical of these tags, the ISSUE No box is empty; the authors have seen this on all original tags they have observed. Note the hemispherical domed flat-head screws retaining the tag to the top of the radiator.

The tag for radiator 873 has a large-font "L," and the second "8" is again upside-down.

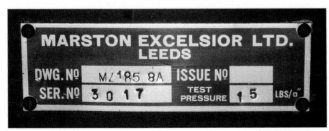

The tag for radiator 3017, from roadster chassis number 876577, has an upside-down "7" used to form the "L." Here, too, the second "8" is stamped upside-down.

The top plate of radiator 3017 shows two large holes in it, just forward and laterally out from the top support mounting-bolt hole. These large holes are present on radiators 217 and 873 as well. Some radiators, it seems later ones, had smaller holes or no holes at all in the top plate.

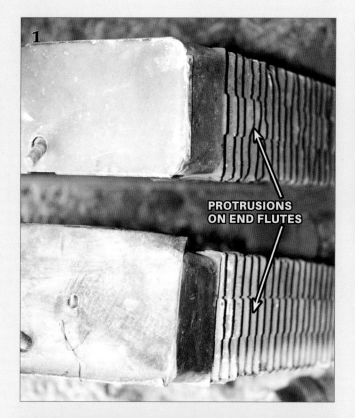

PROTRUSIONS
ON END FLUTES

1 The top radiator has the rounded corners generally seen on radiators with no bolt hole. In the lower part of the picture is a slightly earlier radiator with the typical sharper corners, and a bolt hole (in this case, a small hole - the very earliest radiators had a larger hole). Note that the flutes on both these later radiators have their central third protruding a little. This middle third of each flute is separated by notches on its leading and trailing edges. The authors have not seen these protrusions and their associated notches on early radiators.

2 View of the end flutes on an early aluminum radiator showing the absence of the protruding central one third of the flutes; they are uniform in lateral extent from the front to the rear of the car.

3 A view of a later-type aluminum radiator on coupe 889560, showing only the bolt holes and the rounded corners.

4 Interesting example from roadster 876602 showing the sharp corners and large bolt hole in the top plate, but only one hole in this case, on the right side. The car has been restored, so it is possible the radiator has been altered, with a hole being filled or the radiator replaced.

5 An example of one of the reproduction radiators available. Contrast this to the pictures of original aluminum radiators above. This one has flutes on the end, but they are too large, protruding outside the body of the radiator.

6 Another type of reproduction radiator. This one has flutes that are very thick, but do not extend too far out. This one has what appears to be the drain plug fitting on the top right, instead of the lower left, as in the originals.

7 This reproduction radiator has flutes machined into its aluminum lateral ends. The flutes in this design do not protrude beyond the footprint of the radiator, and in this sense more accurately simulate the originals than many reproductions. This is perhaps a reasonable replacement for use on a car until an original radiator is located, or for use while the original radiator is preserved dry.

8 Two later 3.8-liter E-type radiators that were not fitted with serial number tags. The lower radiator in this picture has two holes in the top plate, as did the earlier radiators, but these holes are smaller on this later radiator. The radiator on the top has only the two bolt holes in the top plate. Note the "4383" number printed in white paint on the top plate. This might be a serial number marking; it is later in sequence than the latest number the authors have seen on an aluminum tag, of 3017. Note also the rounded corners as seem to be typical on the later radiators, as well as the absence of the holes seen on the earlier radiators.

HEADER TANK

The header tank was changed and the flow was modified inside. The inlet was at the corner for the early cars and at the side for later cars. Left-hand drive roadsters chassis numbers 875026 and 875186 had the early tanks, while roadster 876052 had the later tank. The corner connection was observed on the very original left-hand drive roadster chassis number 879032. The side connector was seen on restored chassis number 879152 and restored 879244. However, the very original 879406 had the corner connector. Thus, it is likely the two parts were interleaved in production, as was the case for other components.

The *Spare Parts Catalogue* states that at chassis numbers 850656/7, 861090/1, 879043/4 and 888240/1, about March 1963, the radiator header-tank assembly was changed; the 4lb. pressure cap was changed to a 9lb. one.

Two early-type tanks, both exhibiting the corner-located inlet pipe. The one on the left is a reproduction. As is typical with most, or all, of the reproductions it has an especially wide flange.

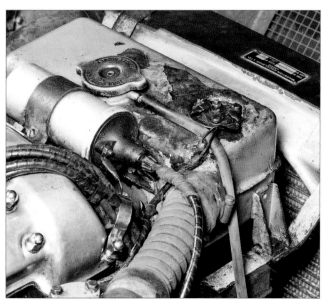

The later header tanks had the right-hand-side water-hose connection in the side of the tank, as opposed to the right-rear corner, as was previously the case.

The early header tanks had the right-hand connection on the rear corner.

WATER PUMP AND PULLEY

About June 1962 the pulley for the water pump was changed to the duplex type, with an associated change in the driving belt. The material of the pulley was also changed, from aluminum to cast iron. This occurred at engine numbers R5249/50.

There was a change in the water pump impeller at engine numbers RA3289/90 around September 1963.

Some of the early tanks had an especially narrow mating flange.

HOSES AND CLAMPS

See information on this topic in Chapter Six, FEATURES RELATING TO BOTH 3.8-LITER AND 4.2-LITER CARS.

About March 1963 the water hose between the engine water outlet and the header tank was changed and that this occurred at chassis numbers 850656/7, 861090/1, 879043/4 and 888240/1. At some point the header-tank hose was changed from convoluted to straight and perhaps this is what is being referred to here.

THERMOSTAT

About November 1962 a quick lift thermostat was fitted with a higher opening temperature. This occurred at engine numbers R8299/300.

CHARGING SYSTEM: GENERATOR (DYNAMO) AND BRACKET

At the transition from outside to inside bonnet latches, about October 1961 at chassis numbers 850091/2, 860004/5, 875385/6 and 885020/1, the generator was changed from part number 22531/A-C45.PV5/6 to part number 22902/A-C42.

The dynamo mounting bracket, pulley and fan for the dynamo pulley were changed at engine numbers R1509/10.

At R1844/5, about October 1961, at the introduction of the introduction of the automatic fan belt tensioner this link was changed and its name in the *Spare Parts Catalogue* was changed from "Generator Adjusting Link" to merely the "Generator Link."

Side view of a 22531 generator. This unit has been rebuilt and repainted. The unit is not fully re-assembled, and is missing the cover for the brushes on the left-hand side.

A 22531 generator in situ in restored coupe 885008. Note the larger outer diameter than the 22902 generator. The first style of a single-grooved pulley is evident here.

BEARING COVER

End view of the rebuilt 22531 generator. Note the large diameter rear-bearing cover.

A 22902 generator, as used in 3.8-liter cars after the transition from the first 500 outside latch cars to the later inside latch cars. Note the smaller outer diameter compared to the earlier 22531 generator. This generator shows the later-type double-grooved pulley.

PULLEYS AND BELT

The generator adjusting link was changed at engine numbers R1509/10.

About October 1961, the generator adjusting link was changed and a jockey pulley assembly was added. This change occurred at engine numbers R1844/5. Apparently, these were retrofitted to some early engines by Jaguar.

The fan belt was changed; the early fan belts were of the single-grooved type and the later belts were of the wide, double-grooved type. This change occurred about June 1962 at engine numbers R5249/50.

The carrier for the jockey pulley was changed at engine numbers RA1100/1.

At engine numbers RA1099/100, about March 1963, the automatic fan-belt tensioning system was changed and at engine numbers RA5885/6, about April 1964, the jockey pulley bracket was changed to have impregnated plastic bushes instead of the brass bushes that were used earlier.

Left-hand drive roadster chassis 875026 (engine number R1037-9) has an idler pulley mounted between the generator and water-pump pulleys, apparently used for tensioning the belt. This is not the usual spring-loaded jockey pulley of the later 3.8-liter cars. This early car is very original, but authors are not sure of the origin of this pulley, or whether it was fitted at the factory or not.

Side view of the manual adjuster mechanism.

This manual adjust fan belt system may have been used on a few very early cars. Note here, as well as in the other two pictures on this page, the reusable locknut on the bolt holding the top front bracket of the generator to its mount. This is one of the few places on the car that such a reusable locknut is used.

The upper mounting system for the early generators (before the automatic tensioner came in). Note in particular the spacer collar between the flange of the upper left hole in the front camshaft cover and the generator link. This component is sometimes omitted in restored cars. The generator link changed at engine-number transition R1844/5.

Later on, this auto-adjust fan belt system was introduced. It is comprised of a spring-loaded automatic tensioner pulley.

An early aluminum single-groove water-pump pulley, mounted on left-hand drive roadster chassis 876163.

A later double-grooved cast iron water-pump pulley from engine RA3074-9.

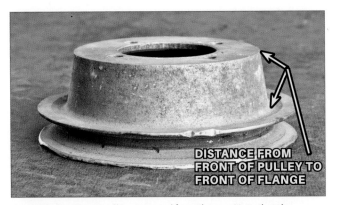

An early aluminum pulley removed from the car. Note that the distance from the front-edge of the pulley body (at the top of the picture) to the first groove for the fan belt is greater than on the double-grooved pulley shown below.

A later cast-iron double-grooved pulley from later 3.8-liter E-type engine, RA3074-9. It is painted in silver.

VOLTAGE REGULATOR AND BRACKET

The voltage regulator and bracket were changed (part number 37304A/RB.310 changed to 37331A/RB.340) at the point of onset of inside bonnet latches, at chassis numbers 850091/2, 860004/5, 875385/6 and 885020/1 about October 1961.

LEFT: *The RB.340 voltage regulator has a black plastic cover. It was used on most 3.8-liter cars.*

The first type of regulator, the RB.310 (Lucas version 37304. The number 37304 often carried a suffix, perhaps denoting variations over time) was used on the first 500 cars. The second type, the RB.340 regulator, (Lucas version 37331A), are easily distinguishable; the RB.310 regulators have an aluminum cover while the RB.340 have a black plastic cover. However, there are different versions of these two types of regulators; in addition to the 37304A variant, the RB310 comes in 37304B, 37304D, 37323B, 37332A, 37334B variants and possibly others. From observations of the first 500 E-types it appears only the 37304-type was used on these E-types.

The RB.310 variant number is stamped on the bottom flange of the regulator. On the left the model number, in this case 37304B. On the right is the voltage, 12V and date of manufacture, in this case October of 1960.

The aluminum cover immediately identifies the early RB.310 voltage regulator.

BATTERY, CABLES, TRAY AND MOUNTS

The battery was a Lucas tar-topped unit, part number C.16061, Lucas number 54028639-FRV.11/7A with six separate filler caps.

An interesting pair of battery photos are seen on page 243 of *Jaguar E-Type: The Definitive History*. The upper photograph shows an early prototype car with a battery with the "LUCAS" letters on the side highlighted in white. The lower picture shows a later 3.8-liter car with a non-highlighted battery.

At chassis numbers 850209/10, 860012/3, 875760/1 and 885085/6 two more rubber corner pads were added to the battery clamp in about November 1961.

About August 1962, the rubber pads under the corners and end of the battery clamp were changed to a single pad. This occurred at chassis numbers 850572/3, 860722/3, 877660/1 and 886381/2.

The cup- or helmet-type battery cable connector. This is the negative terminal, marked "-." The small hole of the side is for an additional connector. Sometimes these were for an accessory on earlier British cars. On the E-type there was apparently no application for this side hole.

ELECTRIC: WIRING HARNESS

About November 1962, the forward wiring harness was changed. This occurred at chassis numbers 850273/4, 861186/7, 878020/1 and 886748/9. The cable to the front lamp connector was changed about May 1962 at chassis numbers 850499/500, 860435/6, 877154/5 and 885970/1. This is the same transition as the horn change, so it is likely the change from the horn with the cable protruding through a grommet, to the horn with the two spade connectors.

At chassis numbers 850723/4 and 861186/7, about June 1963, there was a change in the front wiring harness.

COOLING FAN, RELAY AND SWITCH

The thermostatic switches operating the radiator cooling fan came in at least two types. The first type has a nut and bolt contact, with a spade connector bolted to it. The

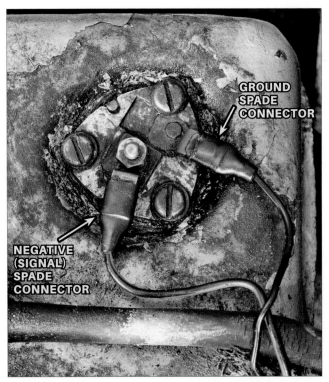

On early cars, the thermostatic cooling fan switch had the negative (signal) spade connector bolted to the center terminal. This one has the ground spade connector attached to the body of the switch.

Close-up of the top plate of another type of early thermostatic switch.

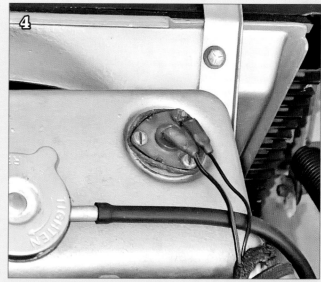

second type has a spade connector molded in the top. The second type is sometimes molded from red plastic and has the word Otter in stylized print molded in it. Chassis numbers 860005, 875026 and 876052 have the early switch. It is cited in the literature that at chassis numbers 850273/4, 861186/7, 878020/1 and 886748/9 the relay for the fan motor was changed and that this occurred in late 1962 or early 1963.

WINDSCREEN WASHER

The windscreen washing system used an electric motor driving a centrifugal pump. The pump was located in a small plastic reservoir at the bottom of the glass main reservoir. From a single operation of the washer switch on the dashboard, the fluid in this small reservoir was delivered to the windscreen through two nozzles. The motor was wired with power terminals ("+" or "A" and "-" or "C"), with the intermittent pulse delivered through a central terminal labeled "B." The "+," "-," "A," "B," and "C" designations were molded into the motor housing adjacent to the terminals. In addition to this marking, a green sticker was used with an "A" in a black background, a "B" in a black and green diagonal striped background, and "C" on a green background. This sticker appears to be peeled off a roll and cut with a serrated edge, in the manner of cellophane adhesive tape. Variations in this label are discussed on page 447.

The hard plastic motors that drive the windscreen-washing fluid from the bottle are comprised of a dark material that resembles a phenolic resin such as Bakelite. As with other Lucas components, these units carry a month and date code. This is imprinted on the rear face of the motor, beneath the three spade connectors.

1 *Side view of an early thermostatic switch showing the sensing chamber that protrudes into the header tank.*

2 *Later cars had a thermostatic cooling fan switch with the spade connector molded in, as seen on this Otter switch. This one has the usual beige plastic insulator with "OTTER" markings. It is dated September 1966, so while too late to have been supplied on a 3.8-liter car, it is representative of those that were.*

3 *Side view of an Otter switch showing the enclosure for the temperature sensor that protrudes into the header tank.*

4 *This thermostatic switch has a red insulator of a smaller diameter than often seen; this is likely an after-market switch.*

5 *The unusual plug-in connector on this later thermostatic switch has been observed on restored E-types; it is likely this is a later type that was never originally supplied from the factory on E-types.*

6 *A plug-in type thermostatic switch installed on a 3.8-liter E-type. Note the unusual tall connector mating to the switch. Note that the car's female spade connectors are attached to an adapter on the plug-in connector.*

7 *A later Otter switch, dated May 1973 (after the cessation of six-cylinder E-type production), with a black plastic insulator insert. Typically, when the late Otter switches were supplied on E-types the plastic was a beige color instead of black.*

A view of the rear of a windscreen-washer fluid pump motor, showing the "+," "-," "A," "B," and "C" markings molded in the housing, as well as the "A," "B," and "C" sticker.

A rear view of another windscreen-washer pump motor, this one showing a gold sticker with filling instructions. The part number, 78337E, voltage, 12V and date, 2-64, are imprinted into the rear face of the housing.

What is almost certainly the original windscreen-washer pump motor from 885056, again showing the green tape, part number, 78337B, voltage, 12V and date, 6-61 on the rear-most face of the motor. As is typically the case, there is no evidence of there having been a sticker with filling instructions.

The filler aperture cover, which also serves as a measuring cup carries molded-in instructions. The early covers are typically molded in a blue elastomeric material. Sometimes they are found painted black on the top. Later covers were molded in a black elastomeric material.

A blue elastomeric windscreen-washer bottle cover, painted black. This is an NOS unit and almost certainly painted at the factory, probably the Lucas factory.

This filler cap for the windscreen washer system is molded from the blue elastomeric material, but the top surface is a brownish color, perhaps an effect that occurred over time.

View of the underside of the cap shown in the previous picture. Here the blue color of the cap is evident beneath the brownish-colored top.

The filler cap was molded in a blue elastomeric material on the early 3.8-liter E-types (as well as Mk 2 and Mk X cars of the period). It was later molded in black. In some instances at least the blue caps were painted black on the top. The filler cap acted also as a measuring cup for additives, as indicated by molded-in characters on the top of the cap.

BRAKE LIGHT SWITCH

Some of the early brake light switches had spade connectors oriented horizontally instead of vertically. There were also flat-sided nuts and nuts with recessed corners. It appears the nuts with recessed corners were the early type. Other variants have been seen, including round or square cross-section electrodes and different heights and shapes to the plastic insulator top.

A NOS windscreen-washer pump motor with an NOS brass junction piece used between the pump-assembly driven shaft and the motor output shaft, supplied in its original packaging. This part is evident on the top of the pump assembly drawing in Plate 54 on page 309 of the J.30 Spare Parts Catalogue (June 1963).

An early brake light switch with horizontally-mounted spade connectors and recessed corners on the nut faces, from chassis 875026. This type of nut is also seen with vertical spade connectors.

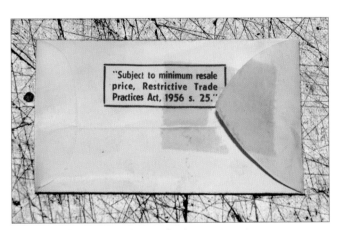

Back view of the NOS packaging for the junction piece.

This switch from chassis 875090 has flat-sided nut faces, an especially high plastic center section and square, rather than round, electrode cross-sections.

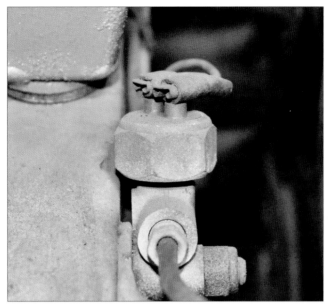

The switch from coupe chassis 885056 has flat nut faces, a flush plastic insulator and round cross-section electrodes.

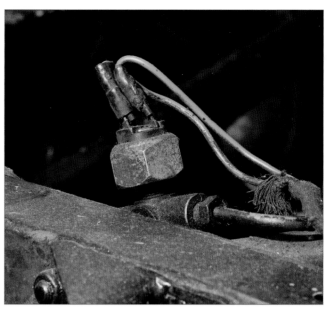

A typical brake light switch with vertically-mounted spade connectors.

Restored roadster 875472 is currently fitted with what appears to be a modern switch. Note the short axial extent of the nut section and the high center region of the plastic insulator. This unit has spade connectors, but these are not limited to modern-made switches; they were used on E-types during production.

HORN AND RELAY

The literature states that the horns were changed about May 1962 at chassis numbers 850499/500, 860435/6, 877154/5 and 885970/1. This is likely the change from the horn with the cable protruding through a grommet, to the horn with the two spade connectors.

TOP: *The early horn (on the left) and the later horn (on the right).* **ABOVE:** *Opposite side view of the early (left) and late (right) horns. Note the cable protruding out of the pressed-steel housing through a grommet on the early horn, vs. the spade connectors on the later horn.*

STARTER SOLENOID

At chassis numbers 850839/40, 861549/50, 881202/3 and 890234/5, about April 1964, the starter solenoid was changed to reduce water leakage.

TACHOMETER, PRESSURE AND TEMPERATURE SENDERS

The authors are not aware of production changes to these components.

BRAKES AND HYDRAULICS: BRAKE AND CLUTCH FLUID RESERVOIRS AND MOUNTS

The brake reservoirs on 3.8-liter cars came in several types. On the earliest cars the polymeric reservoirs were round with large, black plastic tops, marked "NIVOCODE". These caps were later replaced by hybrid caps, made of aluminum with black or white plastic tops. Lastly, the round reservoirs were replaced by rectangular ones, with the same hybrid tops.

The authors have observed some very early cars, for example left-hand drive coupe 885004, fitted with the aluminum with black plastic type top. While this car has undergone repairs or restoration, the owner has early photographs of the car showing this type of reservoir cap, suggesting this was the original configuration.

The floats on the reservoir caps came in at least two types. On some early caps, the fluid-level sensor float was a hollow unit made from a plastic resembling nylon. On later caps, the float was cork.

The clutch fluid reservoirs follow the pattern of the brake fluid reservoirs, going from round to square, but the cap on the early round type was metal. On later square reservoirs, the cap was made of plastic. In neither case did the clutch reservoir cap have electric sensors. Left-hand drive roadster chassis number 875026 has round reservoirs with the vertical-spade-connector black plastic caps and chassis numbers 875109 and 875235 have the round reservoirs with the horizontal-spade-connector black plastic-and-metal caps. Left-hand drive coupe 885056 is fitted with red horizontal-spade caps.

In Jaguar Publication *Jaguar 3.8 "E" Type Grand Touring Models Service Manual*, number E/123/5, on page O.7, in Figure 4, there is a line drawing of an early clutch reservoir with a cap like the early "NIVOCODE" brake reservoir caps. It appears identical, with the exception of the electric sensors, which are absent. The authors have seen no other evidence for such a clutch reservoir cap.

There are also drawings illustrating the metal clutch reservoir cap.

Many changes are listed in the literature for the hydraulic system. It is noted that at chassis numbers 850555/6, 860677/8, 877556/7 and 886282/3, about July 1962, the brake and clutch reservoir assemblies, including their mounting brackets, were changed and that at chassis numbers 877556/7 and 886282/3, the brake reservoir assembly and its bracket, were changed.

Jaguar International magazine, March 1986, notes that the mounting bracket for the fluid, reservoirs changed at chassis numbers 850565/6 and 860677/8, about July 1962.

At chassis numbers 850654/5, 861085/6, 878979/80 and 888184/5, it is noted in *The Jaguar E-type: A Collector's Guide* that about March 1963 the brake fluid reservoir caps were changed. The addition of a level indicator is also cited, but this must be an error, as the level indicators had been fitted before this time. A cover is noted as being introduced for the brake fluid reservoir cap at chassis numbers 850656/7, 861426/7, 888759/60 and 889696/7 about January 1964. Due to the date and the nature of the change, it appears that the right-hand drive roadster chassis number change point listed as 850656/7 should be 850806/7. This change appears to be listed only in *The Jaguar E-type: A Collector's Guide*.

About June of 1963, at chassis numbers 850729/30, 861203/4, 879576/7 and 888790/1, the filter in the clutch fluid reservoir was changed. There was a change in the protective caps for the brake fluid level indicators occurring at chassis numbers 850806/7, 861426/7, 880759/60 and 889696/7, about March 1964.

The earliest cars had cylindrical brake and clutch fluid reservoirs with vertical spade connectors in the caps. These black plastic caps marked "NIVOCODE," are apparently French Lockheed parts.

1 Close-up of the cap of an early brake fluid reservoir showing the "NIVOCODE" and Lockheed markings.

2 The earliest brake fluid floats were hollow, and appear to be made of nylon. The aluminum damping cover has been removed to show the float.

3 An early NIVOCODE cap with the aluminum damping cover still in place.

4 The second type of brake and clutch reservoirs were still round, but had horizontal spade connectors in the caps. These were constructed from plastic and metal. Initially, these caps were black.

5 The top view of the second-generation black reservoirs shows the simple lettering on the cap, only "SOVY" and "MADE IN ENGLAND."

6 The second-type caps also came in white. Note here the more complex lettering on the cap, as opposed to the early horizontal-spade connector.

1 *Some second-type caps were a red or pink color. Some may have started out red and faded to pink over time, as they have been observed in a range of shades. Again, these later caps have more complex lettering than the early caps. This particular cap has seen little use and is a bright red color.*

2 *A pair of red caps, these having seen some use and appearing in a lighter shade of red.*

3 *Another pair of red caps of lighter shade of red, almost a light pink.*

4 The third type of reservoirs was rectangular, but still had the horizontal-spade connectors. The caps seen here are a variant with a cylindrical boss in the center covering the level-sensing rod. It seems as if these caps were used at the same time as the caps without the bosses and that they were interleaved in production. The square reservoirs are commonly seen with the usual caps without the boss.

5 A close-up of the caps with the bosses. It appears these were only found on white caps. Note that the boss appears to be a separate piece of plastic from the cap. The fluid-level-sensing rod can be seen through the boss on the left.

6 A single rectangular bottle shown by itself without the mounting frame. The molded-in "FLUID LEVEL" marking is apparent. The hose clamp is not an original.

7 Very early on, the floats were changed to cork. The aluminum damping cover has been removed to show the cork. This is a red-cap top, but the cork appeared to come in very early on, right after the NIVOCODE tops were discontinued.

8 Rubber covers for the caps came in later in 3.8-liter production. It is likely these came in after the rectangular bottles were introduced.

9 A similar progression occurred for the right-hand drive cars, but the reservoirs were mounted on the firewall on the opposite side of the engine compartment. Here the round reservoirs are shown. This car is a race car and shows some modifications from the standard production configuration.

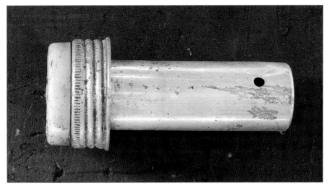

The aluminum damping cover over a cork float. This one on a white reservoir cover.

The round clutch reservoir had a pressed steel cap with no markings. Observations of very original cars suggest these caps were painted black, as is seen here. There have been reports of E-types fitted with similar caps, but with GIRLING markings. The GIRLING caps were used on a range of British cars at the same time as E-type production and were likely placed on E-types during repairs or restoration. The authors have never observed a car known to be original with a GIRLING clutch reservoir cap.

A steel GIRLING-marked cap. This one is from a Triumph TR-3. Note the reservoir is steel on this car. This is the type of cap that is attributed to be original for E-types, probably erroneously.

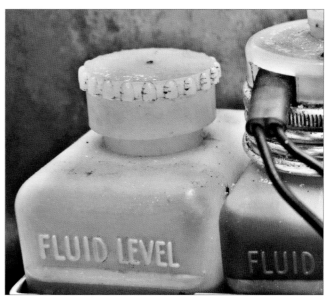

The clutch reservoir cap for the rectangular reservoirs was a polymeric material, likely the same as used for the reservoir itself.

This small pressed sheet metal cap has been observed two times on the later-type clutch fluid reservoir. In one instance (4.2-liter E-type chassis number 1E16928), the original owner stated the car came with the cap. It is shown here for reference and to elicit additional information on the topic.

BRAKE AND CLUTCH FLUID RESERVOIR HEAT SHIELD

The heat shield for the brake and clutch reservoirs in left-hand drive cars has a bend in it. Initially, cars were assembled with this bend at both the back and the front (perhaps by rotating it 90 degrees about the axis perpendicular to its main planar surface). *Jaguar E-Type: The Definitive History* pictures an unusual "tall" shield, bent forward at the top, on an early car, presumed to be chassis number 885002.

It is noted in the literature that the shield for the reservoirs was changed at chassis numbers 877556/7 and 886282/3.

HYDRAULIC LINES, SWITCH, CYLINDERS, SERVO AND ACTIVATION MECHANISM

The early cars had at least two types of brake light switches: those with horizontally-mounted spade connectors, and those with vertically-mounted spade connectors. These are illustrated in the "Brake Light Switch" section.

Numerous changes are listed as occurring during 3.8-liter production. These include a change in the clutch pedal, the bushing in the boss of the clutch pedal and the housing for the clutch pedal and brake pedal. The brass bush in the brake and clutch pedal housing was changed to impregnated plastic about December 1961 at chassis numbers 850232/3, 860020/1, 875858/9 and 885104/5, the brake master cylinder assembly changing at chassis numbers 876014/5 and 885155/6, the front and rear brake master cylinder assemblies being changed about February 1962 to give a more positive location of the rear spring support to the piston at chassis numbers 850254/5, 860026/7, 876014/5 and 885155/6 and the balance link for operation of the master cylinders changing about March 1962 at chassis numbers 850376/7, 860192/3, 876638/9 and 885571/2.

Other changes included the installation of an eccentric barrel nut to adjust the servo arm in the brake connecting lever to increase the mechanical advantage occurring about may 1962 at chassis numbers 850474/5, 860374/5, 876998/9 and 885870/1 (including 860365), a change in the clutch master cylinder to give more positive location for the main spring support to the piston, occurring about June 1962 at chassis numbers 850547/8, 860646/7, 877488/9 and 886218/9 and a change in the brake connecting lever between the pedal shaft and the plate of the servo bellows at chassis numbers 850649/50, 861079/80, 878963/4 and 888168/9 (including 860365).

BRAKE SERVO BELLOWS

The brake servos came in at least two types. The earlier type was marked "KELSEY-HAYES," and the later were marked "DUNLOP." The *J.30 Spare Parts Catalogue (June 1963)* lists only one type of servo and valve housing for all 3.8-liter E-types.

The vacuum test point (or check port) configuration is apparently associated with the transition of the valve housing. The check ports on the earlier type have an adapter extension piece (part 8725, VBO.10066), while the later have a bolt that does not protrude only slightly. In addition, the vacuum test point on the early Kelsey-Hayes type is located about half-way out from the middle of the valve housing, at about the 9:00 position (when seen from the front of the car looking back at the valve housing), while the Dunlop type has the test point located about half way out from the center at about the 1:00 position. As far as the authors have seen, these test valve positions seem to correlate with the Kelsey-Hayes and Dunlop type valve housings respectively.

The earlier Kelsey-Hayes valve housing. The long vacuum test vent is seen just to the left of the central brake connecting lever pivot point.

Close-up view of the early-type long vacuum testing take off port adapter extension (part 8725, VBO.10066).

An early Kelsey-Hayes valve housing removed from the brake assembly. In this view all cast inscriptions are showing, including "BELLOWS POWER UNIT # 41701" and "KELSEY-HAYES WHEEL Co., DETROIT, 32 MICH.," as well as some patent information.

Close-up view of the later-type short vacuum test point port adapter extension used on the Dunlop servo units. Note the location is higher up and on the opposite side from the vacuum test point port on the earlier Kelsey-Hayes units.

Some observations of valve housing types: left-hand drive roadsters 875026, 875109, 875090 and 876163 and coupe 885154 had Kelsey-Hayes servo unit, and left-hand drive roadster 879406 and coupe 889560 had the Dunlop servo unit.

Later in 3.8-liter E-type production the Kelsey-Hayes servo was replaced by the very-similar Dunlop unit, shown here. Markings include "BELLOWS POWER UNIT PT: No VB10000," and "FD2." The authors have seen both "FD1" and "FD2" markings on these bellows fitted to E-types.

This servo unit from a right-hand drive car shows an attachment plate at the top supporting a component of the throttle linkage. The plate spans the top of the rear plate of the servo unit and is bolted on both sides.

Rear view of the right-hand drive servo unit with throttle-linkage plate.

Comparison shot of the rear of a servo unit from a left-hand drive car without the throttle-linkage plate.

MASTER CYLINDERS

1 Small DUNLOP cast name on the side of the master cylinders was used on the early cars. Likely this was part number C.19968.

2 Later master cylinders had the DUNLOP cast into the top side, in larger letters than used for the side marking. This example carries a tag dated 5 62.

3 Another view of the later, larger DUNLOP cast on the top of a master cylinder. This one does not still have its aluminum tag and the full legend can be seen to be "DUNLOP 5/8."

The small DUNLOP lettering on the side of an early clutch master cylinder (in the foreground at the top of the picture). Note the lettering is oriented in a circumferential manner, rather than the axial orientation used for the DUNLOP lettering used on the early brake cylinders.

A later clutch master cylinder, with DUNLOP in larger letters oriented axially along the side.

BEARING TUBE RETAINING CONFIGURATION

The early flanged bearing tube at the side of pedal housing was held in place in the brake pedal housings with a single bolt, located on the bottom part of the flange. Later the design was changed to a configuration where two bolts were used to retain the flange. *J.30 Spare Parts Catalogue (June 1963)* indicates a change at 850232/3, 860020/1, 875858/9 and 885104/5, which is likely this part, as the brake pedal housing changed at the same point.

The early-type flange mount showing the single-bolt retention configuration.

The later-type flange mount on the bearing tube, retained by two bolts.

Later-type bearing tube mounting flange seen without bolts or circlip.

Another view of a later-type bearing tube mounting, this one shown without the bolts or circlip installed.

DATE LABELS ON MASTER CYLINDERS

The brake master cylinders typically had labels on them, including a date, as seen in the "Master Cylinder" section. Some early tags were hand inscribed, as shown here.

This early date label on the top master cylinder of roadster 875026 shows the date "22-4-60" hand inscribed on the aluminum tag.

The lower master cylinder on 875026 showing the same hand inscribing, with apparently the same date.

Later heater box ends were retained by fewer screws.

The early heater box ends were held in by three screws on the top, the bottom and the sides.

Left-hand drive roadster 875109 has locknuts used to retain the brake master cylinders to their mounting bracket. Note, in contrast, the standard nut used to retain the clutch master cylinder to its cast aluminum mount in the lower right of the picture. While the authors are not aware of changes in this configuration throughout 3.8-liter E-type production. Restored cars often do not have the correct types of nuts; this is one of the small details that are often inadvertently lost during restoration.

STEERING

The *Spare Parts Catalogue* lists several changes, in about March 1962, the spring, covers, plunger and so forth on the rack and pinion housing and the rack friction damper change (occurred at chassis numbers 850403/4, 860231/2, 876846/7 and 885735/6); about May 1962 the hardware for the rack and pinion assembly was changed; a two-stud mount was introduced for the rack thrust plate and the studs with locknuts replaced the two hexagon-headed setscrews (occurred at chassis numbers 850499/500, 860425/6, 877275/6 and 886045/6); and about July 1962 the three studs on the thrust plate and the mounting rubber for the rack and pinion were changed (occurred at chassis numbers 850558/9, 860691/2, 877578/9 and 886305/6).

HEATER

The screen filter on the top of the heater box seems to have come painted (or plated) both light and dark. The endplates on the early heaters are held on by more screws than on later cars. Car chassis numbers 860005, 875026, 875109, 875186, 875251, 875325, 875954, 875958, 876052, 876319, 876733 and 885733 have the early heater box and number 876289 has the later heater box.

BRAKE VACUUM SYSTEM

At least some of the vacuum reservoirs were marked with "TRICO" markings in white paint. The authors are not sure how prevalent this might have been, as the paint used for the lettering readily dissolves and washes off when wiped with gasoline. Many may have been lost during cleanings or the leakage of gas from the carburetors.

DRIVETRAIN: BELL HOUSING, FLYWHEEL, CLUTCH AND SLAVE CYLINDER

About April 1964 the clutch was changed to the Laycock diaphragm type and the flywheel was changed to accept either Borg & Beck or the diaphragm clutch and this occurred at engine numbers RA5800/1.

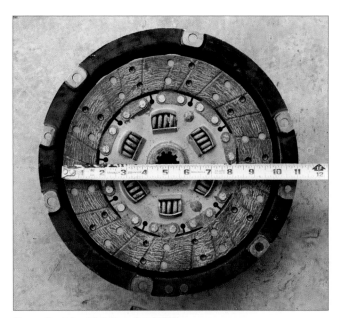

Opposite side of 3.8-liter clutch disk.

The first type of 3.8-liter pressure plate, 10-inches in diameter and with coil springs for compression.

Later 3.8-liter diaphragm-type pressure plate.

A 3.8-liter clutch disk.

Disk on later-type pressure plate.

TRANSMISSION AND MOUNTS

There were changes in both the transmission and the bell housing during 3.8-liter production. Early cast iron transmission cases changed significantly; the early transmission housings were marked "QUALCAST" in an oval. The mark was cast on the upper left-hand side of the case. It appears the Qualcast housings were used intermittently with the dated transmission cases. The authors have never seen markings that appear to indicate pour dates on Qualcast housings.

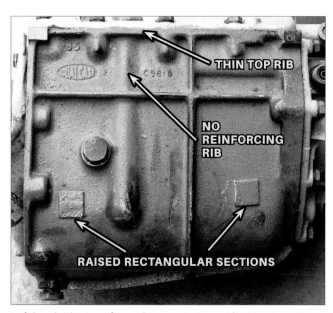

Left-hand side view of an early transmissions with a "QUALCAST" housing. Note the thinner reinforcing rib across the top lip and the lack of a reinforcing rib above and back from the level-check plug. While, as seen in the picture below, the cast-iron gearbox housings typically have pour dates, the authors have never seen a Qualcast housing with a pour date cast in it.

Left-hand side view of a later transmission housing. Note the pour date of "7 11 61" (November 7, 1961), as well as the thicker reinforcing rib across the top lip, as well as the additional reinforcing rib above and back from the level-check plug.

The next housing style had more and larger reinforcing ridges and did not show a foundry name. However, they carried cast pour-date marks. The date marks appear in at least two formats: numerals spaced out in three groups, "DD MM YY" and numerals all run together, "DDMMYY."

A close-ratio gearbox was offered as an option (see also Chapter Six, OPTIONS AND VARIATIONS). The close ratio E-type gearbox is identical to the XK 140 and XK-150 gearboxes, with the exception of the design of aluminum transmission top cover and aluminum rear mounting plate.

The cast aluminum bell housings came in at least two types: those with a flared starter motor extension and those with a non-flared extension. The non-flared were similar to, or the same as, those found on Mk 2 sedans. Non-flared housings were fitted to early 3.8-liter E-types, with the flared housings fitted to later cars.

Other possible bell housing variations include the presence or absence of recesses behind the throw out bearing pivot bosses and the shape, oval or round, of the bolt bosses inside the bell housing.

It appears that, at least for some early cars, the area of the bell housing where it bolts to the engine block, the area where it mates to the transmission, as well as the periphery of the aluminum transmission cover, were spray painted black. In some instances of early cars this paint is still apparent and a picture (in black and white) of a very early engine/transmission unit on the assembly line with a dark-colored paint in these regions is seen on page 163 of *Jaguar E-Type: The Definitive History*.

Another later-type housing, this one dated "231263" (December 23, 1963). It seems later housings have the pour date numerals run together without spaces.

Right-hand side of an early Qualcast transmission housing. As on the left-hand side, it shows a thin reinforcing rib across the top lip. Note also, there is no vertical support rib running between the two bolt bosses above the horizontal rib.

Right-hand side view of a later-type transmission housing. Note the thick top rib, as well as the vertical reinforcing rib running from the horizontal rib up to the top lip, between the two bolt bosses. Also note the cast number and two round bosses.

An early-type bell housing with a non-flared starter motor extension. This housing, or a very similar one was used on at least some Mk 2 sedans.

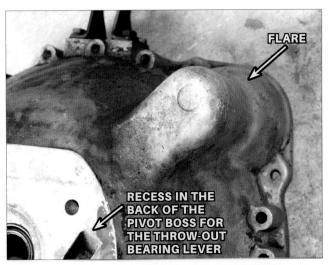

A later-type bell housing with a flared starter motor extension. This was used on most 3.8-liter E-types. Note the recess in the back of the pivot boss for the throw-out bearing lever in the back face of the bell housing. This recess is absent in early bell housings.

This fabricated sheet metal bracket held the speedometer cable in position. The bracket was located in the region where the speedometer cable passes by the bell housing bolts. This view is looking rearward from the left rear of the engine, across the top of the bell housing. The bracket is often missing, but this one is still in place on left-hand drive coupe 885056. It is mounted here on one of the upper left-hand side bell housing bolts and it still retains the speedometer cable.

Another example of the Speedometer cable retention clip. This one is mounted further down on the left-hand side of the bell housing on left-hand drive roadster 879406. It may have been relocated in the past. It appears not many of these survive and they do not seem to appear in the J.30 Spare Parts Catalogue (June 1963).

About January 1963, the rubber mounts at the rear of the gearbox were changed to a spring mount. This change occurred at chassis numbers 850648/9, 861061/2, 878888/9 and 888081/2, except for the chassis numbers: 850653, 850654, 861087, 878895, 878900, 878907, 878908, 878913, 878914, 878915, 878926, 878936, 878937, 878939, 878958, 878986, 879005, 879024, 879049, 888086, 888096, 888101, 888103, 888109, 888113, 888117, 888118, 888120, 888134, 888157, 888178 and 888238.

The rear end transmission cover and the speedometer driver gear were changed at gearbox numbers EB245/6JS.

At gearbox numbers EB1653/4 the dowel screws in the transmission gear-selection mechanism were changed.

The rear end cover of the transmission was changed at gearbox numbers EB8858/9JS. This change took place about February 1963 and was related to the change in the rear engine mounting.

Cars chassis numbers 850653, 850654, 861087, 878895, 878900, 878907, 878908, 878913, 878914, 878915, 878926, 878936, 878937, 878939, 878958, 878986, 879005, 879024, 879049, 888086, 888096, 888101, 888103, 888109, 888113, 888117, 888118, 888120, 888134, 888157, 888178 and 888238 were equipped with the rear end cover fitted to transmissions just prior to gearbox number EB8858JS.

Autocar magazine, May 14, 1965, stated that the 4.2-liter E-type with synchromesh gearbox was originally announced as an alternate model to the still-produced

3.8-liter E-type with the old gearbox. Thus, if late 3.8-liter cars were fitted with fully synchromesh gearboxes, it would have been very late in production. The authors have never seen an example of such a car.

The 3.8-liter cars used at least three types of transmission mounts. The first two types had sloped supporting surfaces, one on each side, for two cylindrical rubber mounts. The rubber mounts spanned from the sloped supporting surfaces on the top of the transmission mount to associated sloped surfaces on bottom of the rear of the transmission. The later-type mount, that continued on into 4.2-liter production, used a large central spring with a central rod.

The two sloped supports on the early mounts were fabricated from sheet metal and were supported by leading and trailing buttresses welded to the base plate. In the earliest mount both buttresses extended laterally from the inner location of the sloped supports outward only as far as the lateral termination of the sloped supports. On the later type, the leading buttresses were longer, extending further out laterally across the base plate.

The three types of transmission mounts. The latest type is at the bottom of the picture. The circular trough supports the spring and the rod goes through the central hole in the ring. The two upper mounts are the early types. The earliest variation, with short mount support buttresses, is in the middle. The second variation of the early mount is at the top with the leading buttresses extending further outward laterally.

OPPOSITE TOP: *The earliest form of the transmission mount, showing the leading and trailing buttresses terminating at the farthest lateral extent of the sloped support for the rubber mount. The rubber mount has bolts fused on each end and the lower bolt is attached to the mount through the hole in the sloped surface. Note the oblong hole on the far right is at an angle to the lateral direction.*

OPPOSITE BOTTOM: *The second form of the early mount, with the leading buttress extending laterally out to give an attachment region about twice as long as that of the trailing support buttress. Note the right-most hole on this mount is oriented with its long axis in a lateral orientation.*

DRIVESHAFT

About October 1961, the driveshaft was changed and its universal joints were enlarged. This change occurred at chassis numbers 850103/4, 860005/6, 875495/6 and 885025/6.

The driveshaft was changed and sealed-for-life universal joints were introduced. A gaiter was fitted to the sliding joint and the grease nipples on the universal joints and sliding joint were dropped, about May 1962 at chassis numbers 850479/80, 860386/7, 877044/5 and 885887/8.

DIFFERENTIAL

A temperature-sensing unit is mounted on an early car's differential drain plug in *The Jaguar E-type: A Collector's Guide*. The car was said to be part of the experimental test fleet. This does not represent a production feature.

In Plate 19 on page 83 of the *J.30 Spare Parts Catalogue (August 1961)*, the housing for the driveshaft bearings is shown without an O-ring seal, while in the revised Plate 19 on page 85 of the *J.30 Spare Parts Catalogue (June 1963)*, the housing is shown with an O-ring seal. This indicates the addition of the seal was a design revision that occurred between the initial *J.30 Spare Parts Catalogue (August 1961)*, and the reprint, *J.30 Spare Parts Catalogue (June 1963)*. One would then expect that the chassis numbers at which this transition occurred would appear in the June 1963 printing. However, no such revision is noted in the *J.30 Spare Parts Catalogue (June 1963)*. On page 83 the O-ring is inserted in the parts list between items 19-30 and 19-31 (as item 19-30A) without any note of the chassis-number transition point, as if the O-ring was present in all E-types from the beginning. This is just one more example of the anomalies found in the *Spare Parts Catalogues*.

The addition of an O-ring on the housings for the driveshafts in the rear end is noted to have occurred about November 1961. From research of surviving cars it was seen that chassis number 875109 had no O-ring, nor any groove for one.

A difference between the two versions of the *Spare Parts Catalogs* is that the *J.30 Spare Parts Catalogue (June 1963)* shows the small pin going in the center of the two shafts for the pinion mate gears. This pin is not shown at all in the *J.30 Spare Parts Catalogue (August 1961)*. This seems to suggest that early cars were not fitted with a pin, while later ones were. But there is no serial number information in either publication about when this took place.

FRONT SHOCK ABSORBERS

The original color of these shock absorbers was a grayish-blue. This is shown in the photograph.

The front shock absorbers were changed about February 1962 at chassis numbers 850321/2, 860121/2, 876394/5 and 885334/5.

Original paint (under a re-spray of black paint) on a front shock absorber.

On all cars metal tabs indicating the gear ratio were bolted to the differential housing. Some very early cars had an aluminum plate with a number on it pop-riveted to the bracing plate on the lower face of the main rear-suspension cross member. The authors are not sure what the number indicated.

The four locknuts holding the halfshafts and brake discs to the output flanges of the differential are found in different styles.

The *J.30 Spare Parts Catalogue (June 1963)*, lists numerous changes in the differential at chassis numbers:

- 879440/1 and 888672/3, about June 1963, for cars with 3.54:1 rear ends, the rear end was changed;

- 879460/1 and 888694/5, about June 1963, for cars with 3.31:1 rear ends, the rear end was changed;

- 850721/2, 861184/5, 879493/4 and 888705/6, about June 1963, for cars with 3.07:1 rear ends, the rear end was changed;

- 850736/7, 861225/6, 879820/1 and 889002/3, about September 1963, the 3.31:1 rear end ratio was made standard for all countries except Italy, France, Germany, Belgium, the Netherlands, the United States, Canada and Newfoundland;

- 879758/9 and 888966/7, about September 1963, the 3.07:1 rear end ratio was made standard for Italy, France, Germany, Belgium and the Netherlands;

- 879751 to 879808, 880025/6, 888952 to 888994 and 889123/4, in about September 1963, the 3.54:1 rear end ratio was made standard for the United States, Canada and Newfoundland;

- 850784/5, 861363/4, 880561/2 and 889451/2, about December 1963, the differential breather was changed to one with an extension tube on the differential cover.

CHASSIS: FRONT WHEEL HUBS

About August 1961 the stub axle carrier on the right-hand and left-hand front hubs was changed and a water deflector was added at chassis numbers 850047/8, 860001, 875132/3 and 885001.

A-ARMS AND PIVOTS

The A-arms came in two colors: silver and black. It seems that early cars had the black paint.

The front suspension assembly was changed about February 1962 at chassis numbers 850253/4, 860022/3, 875963/4 and 885142/3 and the again, about the same

time, at chassis numbers 850290/1, 860032/3, 876129/30 and 885209/10.

FRONT TORSION BARS

The authors are not aware of any design changes. These were finished in black.

FRONT ANTI-ROLL BAR

At chassis numbers 850707/8, 861171/2, 879331/2 and 888559/60, about May 1963, a keeper plate was added to the anti-roll bar bushes. It is not clear it this reference is to the front or rear anti-roll bar.

REAR WHEEL HUBS AND CARRIERS

Very early aluminum hub carriers have been shown painted in a dark color in various publications. Typically, though, these were bare aluminum.

An early smooth-sided hub (of the sort used on the first 500 outside latch cars) in situ on left-hand drive roadster chassis number 875026.

This is the smooth-sided hub, without any recess behind the area where the bearing is located.

STEP IN CASTING FOR BEARING

A later stepped (small bearing) hub carrier. The step in the casting for the bearing can be seen just intersecting the vent plug at the top of the picture.

DIPS IN SIDE OF CASTING

WATER THROWER

This later hub shows the water thrower as well as the horizontal dips in the side of the casting to the middle right of the picture. The water thrower was also seen on earlier hubs without this dipping in.

The outer rear hub bearings were enlarged about October 1961 at the transition to inside bonnet latches, chassis numbers 850091/2, 860004/5, 875385/6 and 885020/1.

About June 1962 the oil seals in the hub carriers, for the fulcrum shafts, were changed, at chassis numbers 850503/4, 860450/1, 877182/3 and 885984/5 and about September 1962 the rear hubs and hub carriers were changes to incorporate water throwers, at chassis numbers 850583/4, 860832/3, 877963/4 and 886685/6.

RADIUS ARMS, TRAILING ARMS AND HALFSHAFTS

The halfshafts were changed from a large diameter, hollow-tube construction to a small-diameter, solid tube construction. This occurred about July 1962 at chassis numbers 850549/50, 850552/3, 850554/5, 860657/8, 877534/5, 877544/5, 877549/50 and 886246/7.

Jaguar E-Type: The Definitive History reported that about December 1962 the grease nipples on the halfshaft universal joints were discontinued and the fitting hole was fitted with a plug.

About April 1963, various parts in the rear suspension, such as the wishbones, mountings at inner fulcrum shafts and the bracing plate, were changed. This occurred at chassis numbers 850678/9, 861105/6, 879131/2 and 888326/7.

Skilleter's *Jaguar Sports Cars* states that the rear shafts were given water shields in 1963 to protect the universal joints.

The roller-bearing seals in the halfshaft universal joints were changed and covers for the journal assemblies were added. This change occurred in late winter or early spring of 1964 at chassis numbers 850805/6, 861423/4, 880754/5 and 889688/9.

At chassis numbers 850824/5, 861520/1, 881152/3 and 890170/1, About April 1964, the front bush in the rear suspension radius arms was changed.

REAR SPRINGS, SEATS AND SPACERS

Some of the early springs, spacers and retainers differed from the standard early configuration that had packing rings at the top and the thick spring retainers at the bottom. For example, there are illustrations of early rear ends with very wide spring retainers on the bottom only in *Motor Racing*, April 1961 and in the May 15, 1961, *The Motor*. There is also a line drawing in *Motor Magazine*, March 15, 1961. In these illustrations, there are apparently no packing ring spacers on the top, as was used on the early cars.

About October 1961, the rear suspension coil springs and seats for the springs were changed and the aluminum packing piece at the top was dropped and the springs were lengthened, at chassis numbers 850136/7, 860007/8, 875541/2 and 885038/9.

From research of surviving cars: Chassis numbers 875026 and 875109 had upper spacers and thick spring retainers and on 875109 the rear springs appeared original and unaltered and were painted in a glossy black.

About October 1964 packing rings were added to the top of the rear springs at chassis numbers 850907/8, 861719/20, 881696/7 and 890714/5.

An early spring assembly with aluminum spacers in place at each end of the spring.

A later spring assembly without aluminum spacers.

Top view of a spacer ring from an early spring/shock absorber set.

Original paint on a rear shock absorber.

REAR SHOCK ABSORBERS

From research of surviving cars: On chassis number 875109, there were four very old and apparently original shocks labeled "GIRLING" and 64054324. These were painted a glossy gray color (which is standard for these shock absorbers).

The *Spare Parts Catalogue* states the rear shock absorbers were changed at chassis numbers 850321/2, 860121/2, 876394/5 and 885334/5.

Bottom view of a spacer ring from an early spring/shock absorber set.

Top view of original paint on a rear shock absorber.

REAR ANTI-ROLL BAR

From research of surviving cars: On chassis number 875109, the rear anti-roll bar and the two steel sheet metal brackets securing it to the rear tub appeared original and unaltered and were painted in glossy black.

About May 1963, a keeper plate was added to the anti-roll bar bushes at chassis numbers 850707/8, 861171/2, 879331/2 and 888559/60, but it is not clear if this reference is to the front or rear anti-roll bar.

BRAKES

While typically the brake calipers were plated in a silver color, some early ones may have been black (perhaps painted). From research of surviving cars: The rear calipers and cylinders of E-type chassis numbers 875026 and 875109 were plated with a silver-colored coating.

The *Spare Parts Catalogue* lists many changes to the brakes, in about December 1961, the front and rear

The early brake cylinders had a large retaining plate in the center for the adjustment rod. This plate, with six small holes in a ring around the center, was held into a recess in the bottom of the cylinder by crimpings around the edge (the rectangular indents showing around the circumference of the plate).

The later brake cylinders had a small retaining area for the adjusting rod.

brake caliper assemblies were changed from malleable iron to cast iron and the pistons were changed to have an integral backing plate, at chassis numbers 850253/4, 860022/3, 875963/4 and 885142/3; about September 1962, the setscrew and tab washer holding the rear calipers to the final drive unit were changed at chassis numbers 850577/8, 860740/1, 877735/6 and 886455/6; about June 1963, for cars with 3.54:1 rear ends, the rear brake discs were increased in thickness to 1/2 inch, the brake pad material was changed to Mintex M.59 and the rear calipers were mounted on adapter plates (as opposed to bolted direct), at chassis numbers 879440/1 and 888672/3; about June 1963, for cars with 3.31:1 rear ends, the rear brake discs were increased in thickness to 1/2 inch, the brake pad material was changed to Mintex M.59 and the rear calipers were mounted on adapter plates (as opposed to bolted direct), at chassis numbers 879460/1 and 888694/5; and about June 1963, for cars with 3.07:1 rear ends, the rear brake discs were increased in thickness to 1/2 inch, the brake pad material was changed to Mintex M.59 and the rear calipers were mounted on adapter plates (as opposed to bolted direct), at chassis numbers 850721/2, 861184/5, 879493/4 and 888705/6.

In *Jaguar Sports Cars*, Skilleter stated that in 1963 the brake pad material went from Mintex M.33 to Mintex M.59.

At chassis numbers 850290/1, 860032/3, 876129/30 and 885209/10 the brake pad material was changed.

The inside view of an early multi-piece brake piston. Note the plate retaining the self-adjusting mechanism is held to the piston body by two screws.

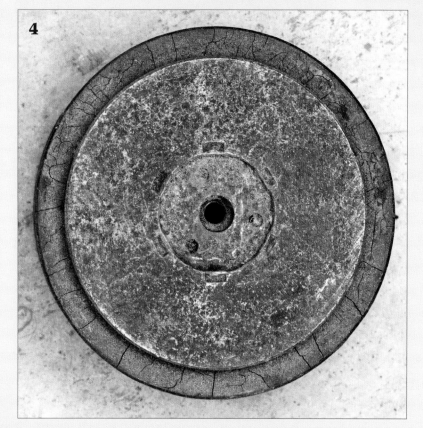

1 *A disassembled early multi-piece brake piston. The inner, brass center section is on the right and the steel section facing the pad is on the left.*

2 *Side of an early multi-piece brake piston.*

3 *Outer view (pad-side) of an early mulit-piece piston showing the brass rear section protruding through the center of the steel body.*

4 *The inside of a later one-piece piston.*

PARKING BRAKE

The handbrake assembly was changed to the auto-adjust type about October 1961 at chassis numbers 850089/90, 860003/4, 875331/2 and 885014/5.

There were several changes related to the parking brake during 3.8-liter E-type production, in about July 1962, the handbrake assembly on the rear brakes was changed, at chassis numbers 850550/1, 850552/3, 850554/5, 860663/4, 877534/5, 877539/40, 877566/7 and

The early manual adjust parking brake was adjusted with a small Allen key that was contained in the tool kit. The hole for the key can be seen in the lower right of this picture.

Later parking brakes were of the automatic-adjusting type. As the pads wore, a ratchet compensated for it. The mechanism is encased in the housing on the left and cannot be seen.

Overview of the early manual adjust parking brake mechanism, seen through the access aperture in the top of the sheet steel rear suspension cross member assembly. The parking brake pads (separate pads from the main pads of the hydraulic rear brakes) are seen in the lower center on either side of the brake disk, the parking brake operating lever is on the left (the left-most silver-colored piece), and the adjusting screw is in the middle, spanning the edge of the brake disk.

886262/3; the handbrake cable assembly was changed at chassis numbers 850554/5, 860663/4, 877566/7 and 886262/3; about August 1963, two fork ends replaced the compensator inner-lever link in the handbrake, at chassis numbers 850722/3, 861202/3, 879550/1 and 888759/60 (some sources cite chassis numbers 850727/8 rather than 850722/3).

FRONT WHEEL WELLS AND ENGINE COMPARTMENT UNDERSHIELDS

The aluminum sheet metal shield mounted on the bottom of the left side of the engine compartment was changed during 3.8-liter production. Initially the shields had a large cutout on the front to accommodate the crankcase-breather vent pipe that passed through on its way to the bottom of the car. While this type of crankcase breather was only used on the first 500 cars, the early-type shields were used well beyond the first 500. Late in production, the shield was changed and the cutout was reduced to a size only big enough to allow the plate to fit in the frame aperture. Later a canvas seal was used on one side of the shield.

What appear to be aluminum wheel wells are shown on an early car on the cover of *Car and Driver*, May 1961, but this is the only case the authors know of where the wheel wells appear to be of a different material or different design than the usual steel ones.

A canvas and rubber seal for the left-hand front frame undershield was introduced about April 1963 at chassis numbers 850680/1, 861120/1, 879159/60 and 888352/3.

At chassis numbers 850712/3, 861177/8, 879372/3 and 888611/2, about June 1963, the engine compartment undershields were increased in size and a cover was placed over the hole in the right-hand side shield (under the oil filter). The authors have not observed one of these covers.

The early left-hand side engine compartment undershield had a cutout on one corner to allow the crankcase breather pipe to pass through (seen on the lower right of this picture). This type of shield continued in use after the crankcase breather was changed to the later type.

A later left side engine compartment undershield without the vent cutout.

A late left-hand side engine compartment undershield with the canvas seal, showing along the bottom.

WHEELS, WEIGHTS AND HUBCAPS

Wheels came in painted silver, or chromed. In the *J.30 Spare Parts Catalogue (June 1963)*, both chromium wheels and wheels painted in stoved aluminum are listed and the chromium wheels are indicated as special order. For later U.S.-specification cars, however, the chrome wheels were standard.

The authors have seen evidence of a few cases of early cars with dark painted wheels.

Wheel weights are listed as available in the *J.30 Spare Parts Catalogue (June 1963)*, but no changes are denoted. The original wheel weights were rectangular in shape. The authors suspect these weights were used throughout the 3.8-liter production run, as similar weights were seen on a Series 1 4.2-liter car.

Cars shipped to Germany had earless knock-off hubcaps that required a special wrench for removal.

For racing a special wheel was offered for the rear.

Wheel weights had numeric weight markings. Various values were offered and some are pictured here.

The earless hubcap used on cars shipped to Germany. This is a different hubcap than those used on the post-1967 4.2-liters, which had three lobes rather than the two rectangular tabs seen here.

Outer view of the standard eared hubcap used on most 3.8-liter cars.

The hubcap removal tool for the European earless hubcap.

Inner view of a standard hubcap. This one is marked "1466, LH, AB," although there are variations to this. There are many different aftermarket hubcaps differing in many ways, including the "JAGUAR" lettering style and the markings on the inside. This is a subject for future research.

Inside view of the earless knock-off hubcap removal tool showing the rectangular recesses. This is a different design than that used for the tool for the post-1967 earless knock-off hubcaps used on E-types.

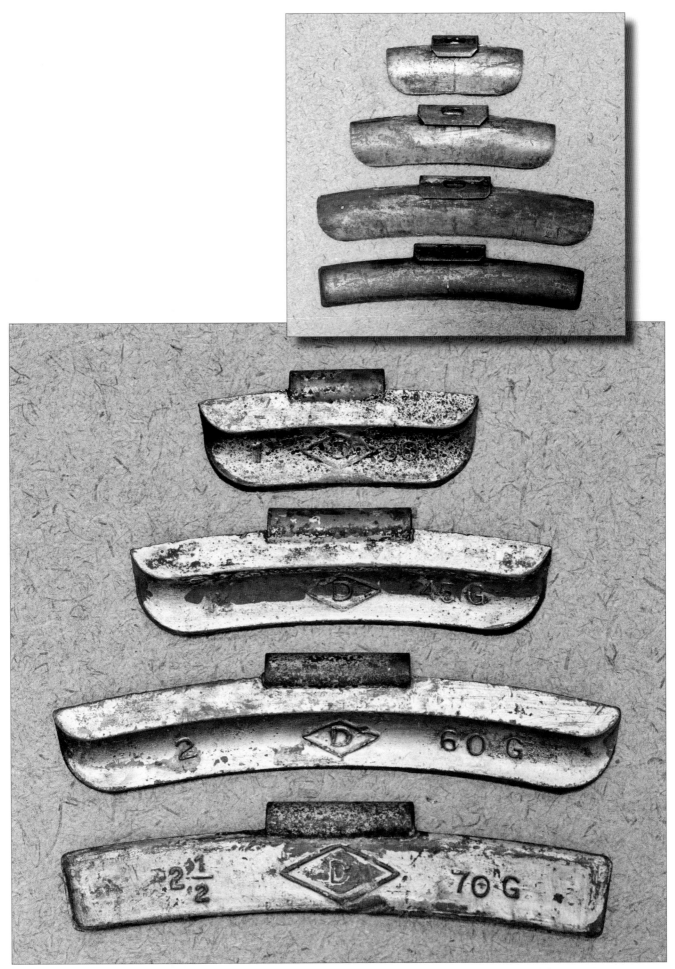

A collection of wheel weights marked with a "D" in a parallelogram. Based on observations, this is one of the types of weights the authors suspect was originally used on E-type wire wheels. It is possible the "D" stands for "Dunlop." INSET: The reverse side of the wheel weights.

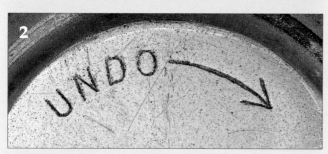

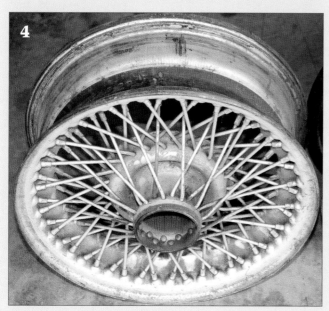

1 This hubcap differs in the design of the arrow denoting the UNDO rotation direction. Typically, these arrows are larger and of a different style.

2 Close-up of a standard UNDO-direction arrow.

3 Close-up of the small UNDO-direction arrow; this is atypical for E-type hubcaps.

4 The standard wheel in silver paint. The typical option was finished in chrome, as most of the U.S.-market were configured.

5 The rear optional steel wheel for racing.

6 This Borrani-type wheel with aluminum rim was another type of racing wheel used with E-types. It has been reported that this type of wheel was offered by the factory, or that the factory could get them fitted. The authors have no other documentation of this statement.

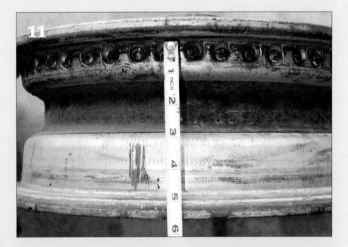

9 The inner rim of the optional steel racing wheel. Note the three-slot spoke nipples here. The red primer is likely an original factory finish. If so, these may be the original spoke nipples. It appears these racing wheels came out with the E-type in 1961.

10 The inner rim of the aluminum racing wheel.

7 Rear view of the Borrani-type aluminum racing wheel clearly showing the rim's aluminum construction.

11 Ruler showing width of a standard wheel.

8 The inner rim of the standard wheel. Note the black rubber strip seated in the lowest part of the wheel rim, protecting the inner tube from the ends of the spokes.

12 Ruler on optional rear racing wheel.

13 Ruler on alloy wheel.

A one-half-ounce wheel weight.

A one-ounce wheel weight.

A two-ounce wheel weight.

This is the wide whitewall type RS.5, as often used on U.S.-market cars, but sometimes in other markets as well. The tire was also offered in a blackwall.

TIRES AND TUBES

The 3.8-liter cars came with the recently introduced Dunlop RS.5 tires. These tires came in three types: blackwalls, and wide and narrow whitewalls. All were 6.40x15-inch Dunlop RS.5 tires. It appears the transition from wide whitewalls to narrow occurred about 1964, shortly before the introduction of the 4.2-liter model.

U.S. cars tended to have whitewalls and the English cars tended to have blackwalls.

One source, *Sports Car World magazine*, October 1963, cites the tires as Pirelli Rolle, but this is likely an error.

Rear of an RS.5 tire.

A two-and-one-half-ounce wheel weight. There is no "D" marking here, as discussed on page 249.

The standard tire for 3.8-liter E-types was a Dunlop RS.5. Dunlop R5 tires were recommended for racing, with different types for front and rear. The part number given on page 102 of the *J.30 Spare Parts Catalogue* (August 1961) for a Dunlop RS.5 tire, the standard tire for early E-types, is C.17422.

Typical "DUNLOP ROAD SPEED RS.5" lettering. Some small variations have been observed on original tires, but this lettering is typical.

Later on in 3.8-liter production the whitewalls offered on the RS.5s were narrower. Note the script lettering on this later tire.

Later on in production the lettering was changed to italic style. It appears this style was retained throughout the remainder of RS.5 production.

Tread pattern of an RS.5 tire. The authors have seen some variation in the exact pattern, but this pattern is typical.

The characters used for the labeling on this modern reproduction RS.5 are somewhat thicker than those seen on the originals. This is perhaps most evident in the "RS5" characters.

The "6.40-15" size-designation characters on an original RS.5 tire.

The tread pattern on this modern reproduction RS.5 is very similar to the original pattern. There appear to be variations in the types of reproduction tires.

In some instances the original RS.5s had this designation, in addition to the "6.40-15" information.

Some later, or possibly reproduction, RS.5 tires have this "6.40 H 15" designation instead of "6.40-15." In this case the "H" is smaller than the other characters.

4 This modern reproduction RS.5 has the typically thicker characters in the "NYLON" designation. Also seen here are more mold flash lines.

6 This trademark section from an RS.5 from a very early E-type shows the portrait in good resolution. It appears that on later tires the portrait is generally of lower quality. Note the legend below the trademark is in three lines, and the "MADE IN GREAT BRITAIN" legend.

6 This trademark region from a later original RS.5 shows the decrease in resolution of the portrait. The legend below the trademark is in two lines on this tire, and the legend reads "MADE IN ENGLAND".

7 On this modern reproduction tire the portrait trademark has been replaced by the modern Dunlop "D" in a chevron trademark. The three-line legend is used on this reproduction.

8 Here is an example of an apparently-original tire with the chevron trademark shown below the "DUNLOP ROAD SPEED RS5" legend. This is the back side of the tire.

1 Another modern reproduction RS.5. It is not clear if this tire was made by Dunlop or not. Note the "89H" lettering, "REPLACED BY" information.

2 Typical "NYLON" designation on an early original RS.5.

3 Italic "NYLON" on a later original RS.5.

9 *The front side of the same tire shown with the chevron mark below the main legend. Here the chevron trademark leads the main legend, which is in italic, as typically seen on later tires.*

10 *A typical yellow mark on an original RS.5.*

11 *This yellow marking is from a later, or possibly reproduction, tire.*

12 *This symbol is typical on original RS.5 tires. This tire was on a very early E-type.*

13 *Another view of the same symbol, this time with a star to the left.*

14 *A production code molded in an early RS.5 in a mold insert.*

A production code in a mold insert from a later, or possibly reproduction, RS.5.

"TUBE TYPE" designation on a modern reproduction RS.5. The authors have never seen this on an original RS.5 tire.

Another designation the authors have only seen on modern reproduction tires.

At least some modern reproduction tires carry this sort of additional information. Again, the authors are not aware of any such designations appearing on original RS.5 tires.

FRONT SUBFRAME

The lower rear mounts of the early front subframe assembly (part C.20352), *i.e.* the triangular tubular section bolted on the front of the front cross member assembly (part C.15014) came in two configurations. In the earliest configuration, the mounting flanges (steel plates with three holes each) on the rear ends of the lower tubes of the subframe were brazed on. Three bolts passed through these holes on both the right and left sides to hold the subframe to the cross member assembly. In the later mount design the junction between the mounting flanges and the lower tubes was strengthened by use of a longer plate. This longer plate still butted on the end of the tube, but it also folded back into a cradle shape that was brazed along the lower outer surface of the tube. Thus, the plates that bolted to the cross member assembly on each side were much more firmly attached to the lower tubes. Roadsters 875026, 875109, 876163 and 876319 were both fitted with unreinforced front subframes. The subframe on 875954 was reinforced.

This early-type lower front subframe mount did not have reinforcement along the bottom where it bolted to the front cross member assembly, but was only butted on the end of the tube.

Later 3.8-liter front subframes (and subsequent 4.2-liter frames) had this extension of the end attachment plate wrapping around the bottom of the tube to offer additional strength to the subframe mount.

Lower view of the later reinforced (left) and earlier unreinforced (right) front subframe attachment points. The two holes in the bottom of the reinforcement region on the later-type subframe are typical. Note also at the center top of the picture the late and early type bonnet-hinge attachments (discussed in detail elsewhere in this book).

The unreinforced front subframe lower tube attachment on left-hand drive coupe chassis number 885056.

Similar view, but of a reinforced lower front side-member assembly attachment plate from left-hand drive roadster 875954.

See information on the topic of painting of front subframe nuts and bolts in Chapter Six, FEATURES RELATING TO BOTH 3.8-LITER AND 4.2-LITER CARS.

In many instances the rear mounting flanges of the left and right front side-member assemblies had letters stamped on them. A range of stampings has been observed, whose meaning is not known.

The top outer rear mounting plates of the front-frame side members are sometimes seen with letters stamped in them. Here two "B"s are stamped in the mounting plate on 885056.

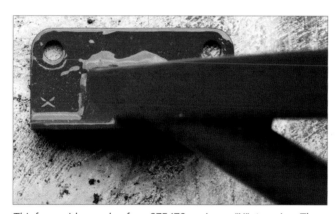

This frame side member from 875472 carries an "X" stamping. The authors have yet to determine the reason for these stampings, which typically are not present.

The outer right side of the right front-frame side assembly shows drips in the original paint on coupe 885056. The sag in the paint appears as if the member were upside-down when painted. This is consistent with the idea that, at least for sometime, the frame members were painted separately from the tub and later bolted on.

The aluminum undershield on the left-hand side retained a cutout for the corrugated crankcase breather vent pipe, for sometime after the vent pipe was discontinued (after the end the production of the outside latch cars). The clearance for this tube is seen in the shield on early coupe 885056, even though there was no vent pipe on this car.

Top section of the front cross member assembly on 875026, at the point where the cooling fan mount is cantilevered forward, shows the early fan wiring configuration with the wires routed down behind the motor. There is no hole and grommet in the motor mount assembly for the wire to pass through, as in later cars. This change occurred early in outside latch production.

The fan mount on 875109, showing the hole in the rear of the mount, near the front of the top element of the front cross member. It appears that rubber grommets were always inserted in these holes.

This top view of the cooling fan mount on 876319 shows the hole location and grommet clearly. The wire going through the hole is not the original.

The early-type bonnet hinge attachment point. The post with threaded end was attached to the end of the front subframe and required the hinges to be un-bolted from the bonnet for removal of the bonnet.

Early on the bonnet hinge attachment design was changed to this configuration where the post was inserted into the end of the front subframe, and held in place by a bolt. This enabled the bonnet to be removed without un-bolting the hinges.

The post and bolt used with the later-type bonnet hinge attachment design.

Comparison of the early (left) and late (right) bonnet-hinge attachment designs. This is an end view of the cross tubes of two front subframes, the early type on the left and the later type on the right. The smaller-diameter hole at the bottom of the recess on the right-hand side is a threaded hole into which the bolt screws.

An aluminum shield was attached to the rear of the front subframe cross member of 876163. It was held on by three bolted-on clips. Note here the later-type cross member with the boss attached near the middle to operate the front license plate retraction mechanism for later U.S. market cars.

Close-up of boss, mounted on the top of the front subframe cross tube, to operate the license plate retraction mechanism on later U.S. market cars. This is 875954.

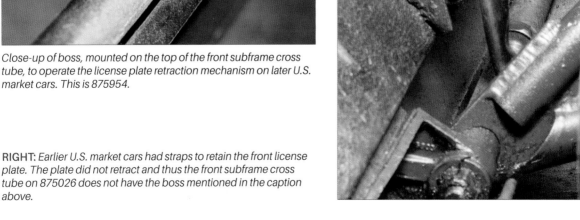

RIGHT: Earlier U.S. market cars had straps to retain the front license plate. The plate did not retract and thus the front subframe cross tube on 875026 does not have the boss mentioned in the caption above.

In the *J.30 Spare Parts Catalogue (June 1963)* it is stated that a different front subframe assembly is listed as used on all roadsters. The authors are not sure what sort of change to the front subframe this note is referring to.

About February 1962, the bonnet hinge was changed with an associated change in the cross-member of the front subframe, at chassis numbers 850238/9, 860138/9, 876457/8 and 885384/5. About June 1962, the front subframe assembly and hinge were changed, at chassis numbers 860478/9 and 886013/4.

In the June 1963 reprint of the *J.30 Spare Parts Catalogue* a different front subframe assembly (part number C.20352) is listed, than in the original printing of *J.30* (C.16942), but in neither case is a change a Left-hand drive.

REAR SUBFRAME, MOUNTS AND STOPS

The brace plate spanning the bottom of the rear suspension cross member, came in two types, as illustrated in this section. The rear suspension cross member or rear suspension cross member assembly, refers to the heavy-gauge sheet steel frame containing and supporting the differential, brakes and rear-suspension components. It is sometimes called a rear subframe.

About April 1963, the mountings for the inner fulcrum shafts changed, along with other parts in the rear end, such as wishbones, mountings at inner fulcrum shafts

and the bracing plate at chassis numbers 850678/9, 861105/6, 879131/2 and 888326/7. This is the point at which the large central aperture in the bracing plate (spanning the lower sides of the rear-suspension cross member) changed to a smaller one.

TUBING AND CABLES

The authors are not aware of any changes.

EXHAUST SYSTEM

The Parts Catalogue states that the welded-together exhaust tailpipe assembly was changed to a two-piece assembly about December 1961 at chassis numbers

NOS silencers in the early individual configuration. The crayon marks interestingly seem to show both the 3.8 part number C.17124 and also the 4.2-liter part number of 23869. Perhaps these were written on at a dealership or parts depot sometime after their manufacture.

An early rear end assembly bracing plate with the large hole.

A later rear end assembly bracing plate with the small hole. Note the outer shape of the plate is different from the earlier large-hole plate.

850178/9, 860011/2, 875607/8 and 885058/9 and that the bracket for the muffler was discontinued at chassis numbers 860175/6 and 885503/4.

About September 1963 the mufflers and their mounts were changed at chassis numbers 850754/5, 861270/1, 879989/90 and 889095/6.

The silencers, or mufflers, were probably supplied first as individual components and then as an assembly. This is illustrated in *J.30* (June 1963 A.L.1. reprint) in Plate 33 on page 155 where both the assembly and individual components are shown.

An unusual muffler mount, a sort of horizontal tang, is shown on an early car in *The Jaguar E-type: A Collector's Guide*.

REAR PIPES AND RESONATORS

The rear part of the exhaust system was a welded together unit on the early cars, while on later cars it was made up of separate pieces bolted together. The early welded-together resonator unit is shown in Jaguar Publication E/123/5.

The resonators on the early cars had longer large diameter sections than the later resonators. Within the early long large diameter section resonators, there are at least two

The two individual brackets offered with the silencers.

View of one of the folded sheet metal exhaust system clamps.

varieties: flat ends and pointed ends. Resonators with long, turned-down tips were also used on some very early cars.

The early resonators were welded together, not bolted as on later cars and they were larger than the later ones.

It is not certain that any 3.8-liter cars were fitted with the short large diameter section resonators (as fitted to Series 1 4.2-liter cars). *Jaguar International Magazine*, March 1986, seems to suggest they were and in *Jaguar E-Type: The Definitive History*, a picture appears to be illustrating such a late 3.8-liter car. However, this might illustrate a non-original car. A 4.2-liter car is shown with long resonators in the October 23, 1964 *Autosport* article "John Bolster

Tests the latest of a famous line – the 4.2-LITER JAGUAR E-TYPE," so, as was often the case with E-type variations, the resonator types may have overlapped in production.

Apparently, the length was modified to cut resonance. This may also be the reason for the various resonator types.

In December 1961 the welded-together exhaust tailpipe assembly was changed to a two-piece assembly. This occurred at chassis numbers 850178/9, 860011/2, 875607/8 and 885058/9.

The resonators on the early 3.8-liter cars had long large-diameter sections. Most had the squared-off tips seen here, but some early cars appear to have had more pointed tips on their resonators. While this is a restored car, these resonators were used on some early E-types.

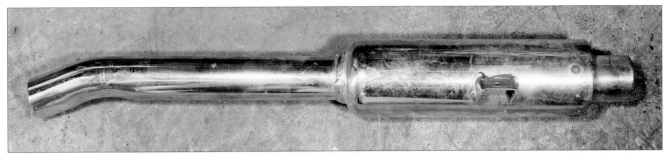

Possibly some later 3.8-liter cars may have had these short large diameter section resonators, as were typically used on 4.2-liter cars.

EXHAUST HEAT SHIELD

About January 1963, the heat shield assembly was changed, probably to accommodate the new gearbox mount, at chassis numbers 850648/9, 861061/2, 878888/9 and 888081/2. The *J.30 Spare Parts Catalogue* (June 1963) also states that the following chassis were fitted with

the early shield: 850653, 850654, 861087, 878895, 878900, 878907, 878908, 878913, 878914, 878915, 178926, 878936, 878937, 878938, 878958, 878986, 879005, 879024, 879049, 888086, 888096, 888101, 888103, 888109, 888113, 888117, 888118, 888120, 888134, 888157, 888178 and 888238.

4.2-LITER BODYWORK AND INTERIOR COMPONENT CHANGES

As in Chapters Two and Three, this chapter lists the production changes by component classification, rather than by order of serial number, but in this case for the 4.2-liter cars. The chapter covers the Series 1, 1.5 and 2, but treats only the changes within each of these three groups and assumes a working knowledge of the basic specification changes between these models. While the Series 1, Series 1.5, and Series 2 cars are all covered in this chapter, the differences between these models are not the subject of this chapter, and these changes are reviewed briefly in Chapter One. Occasionally, a model change difference is discussed or illustrated. This will occur, for example, whenever there is doubt as to whether they occurred exactly at a model-change boundary, and occasionally in other cases to help define the different 4.2-liter models. Thus, when discussing changes in a given area, such as the License plate Lights and Trim, it may be stated that no changes are known to have occurred, in spite of the fact that there were clearly changes in these components at the model-change boundary, in this example at the transition from Series 1.5 to Series 2 cars.

As in prior chapters, each figure illustrates the single, specific feature discussed in its caption. Any other features in the illustrations are incidental and may or may not represent the original state of the car.

EXTERIOR: HEADLIGHTS AND TRIM

The authors are not aware of changes to the headlight covers or trim during 4.2-liter Series 1 production, until the introduction of the first type of uncovered lights in 1967. Cleave notes (*JCNA Model Year '68 E-type Judges' Guide*, Stew Cleave, JCNA, 2006) that the chassis numbers at the transition to the Series 1.25 cars (the cessation of glass covers over the headlights, but otherwise basically

the cars retained Series 1 specifications) were listed as slightly different in the Build Records and the Spares Bulletins. He cites the Build Records numbers and Spares Bulletins as:

	BUILD RECORD	SPARES BULLETINS US/CAN	ALL OTHER
RHD Roadsters:	1E1863	1E1864	
LHD Roadsters:	1E14535	1E14532	1E15889
RHD Coupes:	1E21583		1E21584
LHD Coupes:	1E34120	1E34113	1E34550
RHD 2+2s:	1E50974		1E50975
LHD 2+2s:	1E77644	1E77010	1E77645

Then he notes this Spares Bulletin list states there are exceptions to the USA and Canadian cars:

Left-hand drive roadsters:	1E14534
	1E14536
	1E14537
	1E14540-1E14544
	1E14559-1E14561
	1E14590-1E14592
	1E14595
	1E14643
	1E14655
	1E14656
Left-hand drive coupes:	1E34114-1E34117
	1E34130
	1E34139
	1E34212
Left-hand drive 2+2:	1E77019
	1E77026-1E77029
	1E77048
	1E77059

Other slightly different numbers have been cited for the headlight cover change as well.

There are several references in the literature to the headlight covers being plastic (as was the case for the early 3.8-liter cars), for example in *Autosport* magazine, August 5, 1966. As in the case of similar comments made about the 3.8-liter cars, these references are likely in error.

Other notes on this subject in the literature include the statement that for right-hand drive Series 1 roadsters, the covered headlights were discontinued about October 1967 and that lights of 75-60 watt (versus the 60-60 watt of the 3.8-liter cars) were fitted to some early 4.2-liter cars.

During Series 2 production, the headlights were changed for cars exported to Belgium, Czechoslovakia, the Netherlands, Germany, Poland, Romania and Switzerland at chassis numbers 1R14065/6 and 1R28294/5. It is stated in *Original Jaguar E-Type* that the headlight trim finisher behind the headlight on the Series 2 cars was painted on cars exported to Australia.

All but some of the last Series 1 cars had covered headlights similar to those of the 3.8-liter cars.

RIGHT: *The first version of open headlights was fitted to some late Series 1 cars and to the Series 1.5 cars. The headlight itself was raised above the level of the bonnet and the chrome trim was changed. In addition, the small strip of chrome trim running from the front of the headlight recess to the top of the front bumper was discontinued.*

With the introduction of the Series 2 cars, the headlight assemblies were changed again. The lights were moved farther forward and the chrome trim was changed.

The front side lamps of the U.S.-specification Series 2 cars were not fitted to home-market cars. Part of the lens of this lamp is missing.

A rear side lamp on a U.S.-specification Series 2 car.

PARKING, BRAKE LIGHTS AND TRIM

The stop/tail/flasher lamps were red for Series 1 cars exported to the United States and red and amber for most other cars.

The stop/tail/flasher lamps were red for Series 2 cars exported to Canada, Greece, Portugal and the United States and were red and amber for most other countries.

With the introduction of the Series 2 cars, side lamps were included on export cars. Apparently, some early home market cars were also fitted with these side lamp units, but they were not operable. Typically, however, home-market cars did not have side lamps.

The side/flasher and stop/tail/flasher lamps for Series 2 cars were different for cars exported to Belgium and Japan; Canada, Greece, Portugal and the United States; and all other countries.

The side/flasher lights used a white lens for cars exported to Italy, Greece and Japan. The side/flasher lights were different for cars exported to France, although the lens colors were the standard amber and white.

Some Series 2 lighting changes were: the Series 2 side lamps were changed in some unknown fashion, but their colors remained the same, at chassis numbers 1R1392/3, 1R11051/2, 1R20485/6, 1R27050 and 1R35652/3; the stop/

tail/flasher lights were changed for cars exported to Canada, Greece, Portugal and the United States only, but the color of the lens remained red at chassis numbers 1R11973/4 and 1R27480/1; the side lamps changed for cars exported to Canada and the United States only at chassis numbers 1R13427/8 and 1R28054/5.

Side lamps are shown on one early Series 2 car, but are absent on another in *The Jaguar E-type: A Collector's Guide,* Skilleter stated that these "were fitted to many export cars and some of the early home-market deliveries." Side lamps are shown on an early left-hand drive Series 2 roadster pictured in *Road Test* magazine, February 1969, but are absent on a late right-hand drive Series 2 coupe (Australian specification) in *Modem Motor,* March 1971.

Early-type side/flasher lamp lens with all horizontal features in the triangular lens.

This second style of sidelight/turn signal lamp lens was introduced in early 1965. It replaced the unit with all horizontal features shown in the adjacent picture.

LICENSE PLATE LIGHTS AND TRIM

The authors are not aware of any changes in this area.

BACKUP LIGHT AND TRIM

The authors are not aware of any changes in this area.

WIPER ARMS, BLADES AND WINDSCREEN SQUIRTER NOZZLES

On the late steep-windscreen 2+2 cars, the dual, cowl-mounted squirter nozzles were replaced by a single dual-head nozzle mounted on the bonnet. In addition, these units had a frosted finish on the Series 2 cars. Other than this, the authors are not aware of any changes to the squirter nozzles within the basic model groups.

Motor magazine, January 13, 1968, claimed that the matte finish of the wiper arms and spindles was a result of complying with U.S. safety regulations which prohibited a polished reflecting surface. It is indicated there that this change came in with the Series 1.5, but no specific serial numbers are cited. An instance was observed of a late Series 1.5 car with a frosted wiper arm and a chrome nut and cowl (or "spindle"), perhaps an original configuration. An early Series 1.5 with this hybrid combination is pictured in *Jaguar E-Type: The Definitive History*. Two close-up views show a frosted arm, cowl and nut. Frosted wiper arms are shown on a late right-hand drive Series 2 coupe in *Modern Motor*, March 1971.

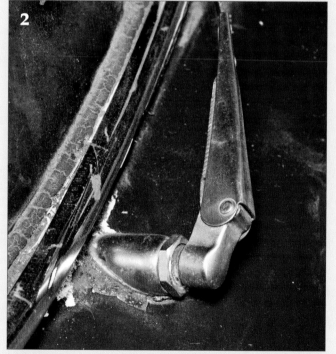

1 *The Series 1 cars had polished-chrome wiper arms and trim.*

2 *The wiper arms and trim on the late Series 1.5 and Series 2 cars had frosted chrome trim. This was required by U.S. specifications.*

3 *A combination frosted-chrome wiper arm with polished-chrome nut and cowl is from a late Series 1.5 car.*

4 *The wiper arm from a Series 2 car has both cowl and wiper arm in a frosted finish, and has the typical two rivets on the arm.*

5 *The wiper arm from a Series 2 car has both cowl and wiper arm in a frosted finish, and no rivets on the arm.*

6 *A windscreen-wiper arm from a Series 2 2+2. Note the frosted finish on the arm, as well as the cover for the drive arm. Also note the single rivet on the arm on the right. This is an exception to other models that typically have two rivets. Note also the cowl on the driveshaft is also frosted; on at least some Series 1.5 cars this cowl was chromed.*

7 *The Series 2 2+2 cars had a single dual-head squirter nozzle mounted on the bonnet.*

8 *The long polymeric tube for the washer fluid runs along the edge of the right wing and across to the bonnet-bulge where the dual squirter nozzle is mounted.*

9 *The single-nozzle squirter used on all six-cylinder E-types, with the exception of the bonnet-mounted dual squirter of the later 2+2 cars.*

10 *The dual squirter nozzle used on the bonnet of the later 2+2 cars.*

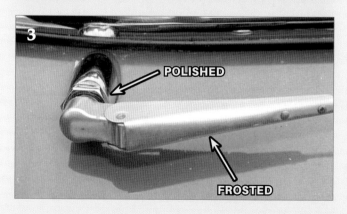

POLISHED

FROSTED

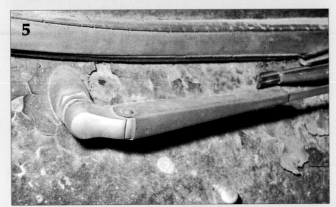

BUMPERS

At chassis numbers 1E1412/3, 1E11740/1, 1E20999/1000 and 1E32009/10, about March 1966, the rear bumper fittings were changed so that the bumpers could be removed from outside the car.

The early 4.2-liter E-type bumpers had inside mounts and could only be removed from inside the bodywork. This is a front bumper.

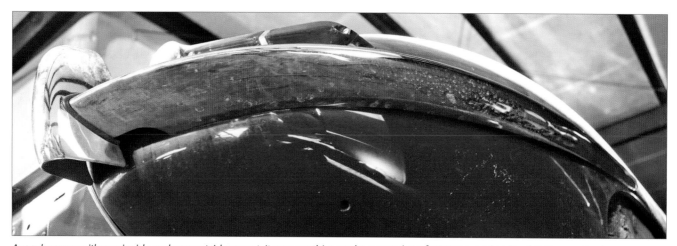

A rear bumper with one inside and one outside mount. It appears this was the second configuration, and earlier 4.2-liter cars had no access ports, in the manner of later 3.8-liter cars

LEFT: *Close-up of the second style of 4.2-liter rear bumper showing the single attachment-bolt access point at the rear. On early 4.2-liter cars (before about 1966) this access port was not present.*

OPPOSITE:

1 *An early front 4.2-liter car bumper showing no bolt access points.*

2 *A later front 4.2-liter car bumper showing bolt access points at the front and the rear.*

3 *An early rear 4.2-liter bumper showing only the rear bolt access point.*

4 *A later 4.2-liter bumper showing bolt access points at the front and rear. Note that the rear access point is larger than the single bolt access point found on the early 4.2-liter car bumpers.*

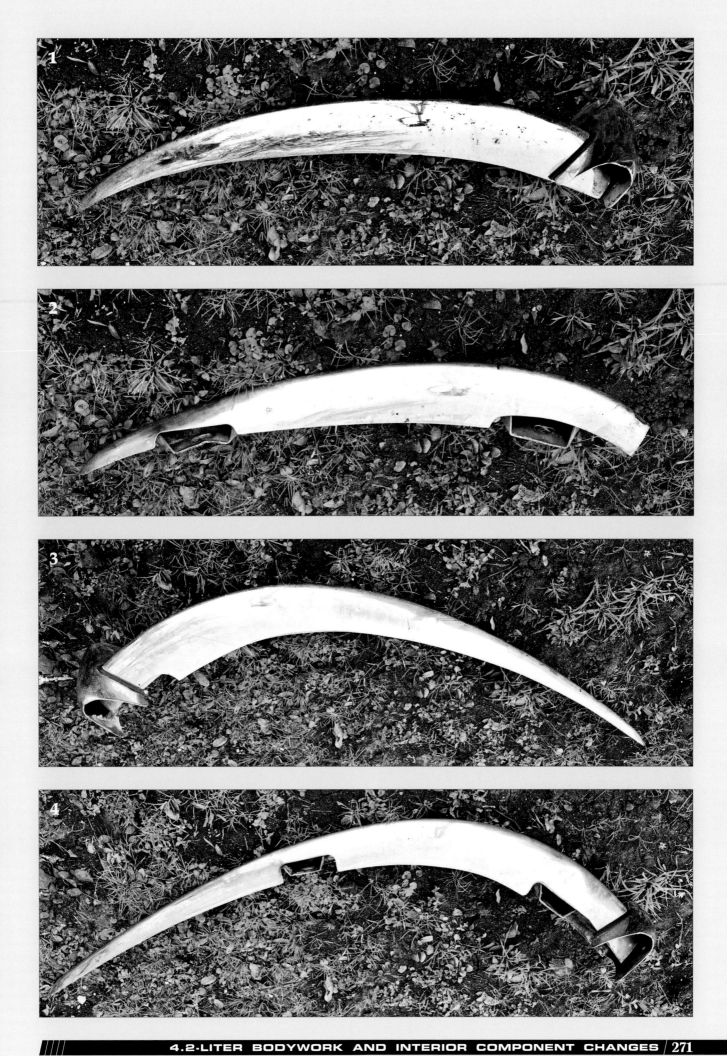

VENT TRIM

The vent trim at the rear of the bonnet was changed at the introduction of the Series 2 cars. The authors are not aware of any changes within the model groups.

DOOR HANDLES AND LOCKS

On the Series 1 two-seater cars, the lock was in the push button, while in the Series 1 2+2s, the lock was in a separate position below. The authors are not aware of any changes to this configuration.

Left side exterior door handle with the lock located separately from the push-button, below the handle. This configuration came in with the introduction of the 2+2, during Series 1 production for model year 1966 and likely ran up to Series 2 production.

Left side exterior door handle with lock in the button from a Series 2 2+2. This was a return of the locking configuration of the 2+2s to the standard configuration of the two-seater E-types.

TOP DOOR TRIM

About December 1966, the screws retaining the chrome beads at the top of the doors were changed to retainers and rivets. This occurred at chassis numbers 1E50121/2 and 1E75862/3.

CONVERTIBLE TOP TRIM

The retaining hooks for the convertible top cover (as mentioned in Chapter Two for the 3.8-liter roadsters) seem to have been present on all 4.2-liter roadsters.

OUTSIDE MARKINGS AND DECORATIVE TRIM

The Series 1 and Series 1.5 4.2-liter cars have the same grille bar as the 3.8-liter cars, while the Series 2 cars had a bar with an elongated escutcheon.

The boot lid markings of the 4.2-liter cars had, in addition to the "JAGUAR" badge, a "4.2" plate below and an "E-TYPE" badge above. Possibly some very early 4.2-liter cars only had the "4.2" and "JAGUAR" plates, as pictured in *The Jaguar E-type: A Collector's Guide*. In addition, *Motor Sport* magazine, April 1966, stated that the 4.2-liter E-types have "4.2-LITER JAGUAR" (they likely mean "4.2" and "JAGUAR") on the boot lid and no mention is made of "E TYPE" showing there.

In one instance, as illustrated in *Motor* magazine, October 31, 1964, a very early 4.2-liter coupe is fitted with only the "JAGUAR" badge on the rear door. In the January 1965 issue of *Motor Sport*, an early 4.2-liter coupe is shown with all three plates on its rear door.

On the last year's production of Series 2 cars, a plastic leaping Jaguar medallion was attached to the bonnet in approximately the same location as the exterior bonnet

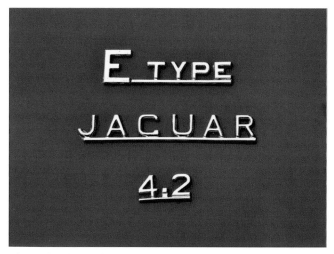

The 4.2-liter boot lid markings included the model name and engine displacement.

The pre-Series 2 4.2-liter cars had a round grille medallion, as used on the 3.8-liter cars.

With the introduction of the Series 2 cars, the grille bar was changed and an oval grille medallion was adopted in place of the earlier round medallion.

latches on the first 500 cars. This feature was not continued when the V-12 cars came out the following year.

Another feature of the last Series 2 cars was the introduction of chrome trim around the air intake aperture.

At chassis numbers 1E1711/2, 1E14582/3, 1E21472/3, 1E34146/7, 1E50709/10 and 1E77046/7, about January 1968, the motif bar and its rubber mountings were changed.

This plastic leaping-cat emblem from a 1971 car is located in approximately the same location as the outside latch mechanism had been ten years earlier.

As with all previous E-types, the Series 2 air intakes initially had no chrome trim around the outside.

The very late Series 2 air intakes had a narrow strip of chrome trim running around the edge. This was a precursor of the more elaborate Series 3 V-12 trim, which included an egg-crate grille.

WINDSCREEN AND PILLARS

The inclination of the windscreen of the 2+2 cars changed with the introduction of the Series 2 cars.

At chassis numbers 1E1657/8, 1E13386/7, 1E21388/9 and 1E33139/40, about March 1967, the windscreen glass was changed. This is likely a different change than the decrease in the incline of the front of the 2+2 glass.

1 The early 2+2 cars had a steep angle to the windscreen. This was a result of increasing the height of the roof.

2 The later 2+2 cars had an increased slope to the windscreen. This was achieved by moving the leading edge of the windscreen forward on the cowl.

SIDE WINDOWS, TRIM, FRAMES, WINDING MECHANISMS AND SEALING RUBBER

About February 1966, the coupe window frame seals were changed from felt to a flocked runner at chassis numbers 1E20952/3 and 1E31919/20. At chassis numbers 1E21311/2 and 1E32765/6, about September 1966, the regulator channel for the wind-up windows was changed.

WING VENTS

The authors are not aware of any changes.

REAR WINDOW

The authors are not aware of any changes.

FRONT LICENSE PLATE MOUNT

The U.S.-specification 4.2-liter Series 1 cars had the same connecting rod-actuated front license plate mount as the later 3.8-liter cars.

As in the case of the later 3.8-liter cars, those without the front license plate holder were still fitted with the connecting rod hole in the area beneath the air intake aperture.

INTERIOR: INSTRUMENTS AND CONTROLS

With the introduction of the Series 1.5 cars, the bezels of the instruments changed in cross-section from angular to semi-circular.

The speedometers were different for 2.88:1, 3.07:1, 3.31:1 and 3.54:1 rear ends and were offered in mile and kilometer calibrations.

Changes at chassis numbers:
- ▶ 1E1103/4, 1E10045/6, 1E20207/8 and 1E30033/4, about June 1965, the speedometer cable was changed.

- ▶ 1E1408/9, 1E11714/5, 1E20977/8 and 1E32008/9, about March 1966, the speedometers were changed to reflect a Dunlop tire change;

- ▶ 1E16537/8, 1E34944/5 and 1E77837/8, about July 1968, the water temperature gauge was changed to one with only zones marked on it, as opposed to the earlier calibrations.

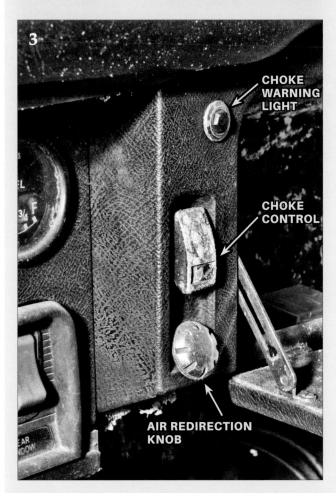

CHOKE WARNING LIGHT

CHOKE CONTROL

AIR REDIRECTION KNOB

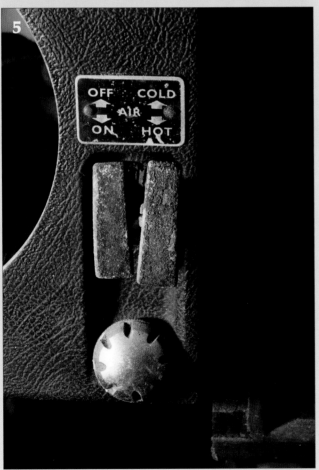

1 The instrument bezels on the Series 1 and Series 1.25 cars had the same triangular cross-section bezels used on the 3.8-liter cars.

2 The Series 1.5 and Series 2 cars had semi-circular cross-section instrument bezels.-

3 The late Series 1.5 and early Series 2 cars did not have the choke control label. Note the chrome air redirection knob below the choke control does not have any legend or arrow on it. This is likely the earlier version of these knobs. The choke warning light is at the top of the picture, with the choke control below, and the air redirection knob at the bottom.

4 Later in Series 2 production, a non-illuminated choke control label was introduced. The air redirection knob below the choke control is the labeled type, with "WINDSCREEN" and an arrow embossed on it.

5 The Series 1.5 and early Series 2 cars had a non-illuminated heater control label. These labels came in with the upgraded rocker switch dash, unlike the choke control labels, which were introduced after the new dash had been in production a while. A non-labeled air-redirection knob is used here.

6 Another unlabeled choke control, but the air redirection knob below the choke here has the legend "WINDSCREEN," and an arrow embossed in it. This is likely the later type of knob.

1 A heater control with a non-illuminated label and an air-redirection knob with "WINDSCREEN" and an arrow on it.

2 The late Series 2 choke-control labels were raised and illuminated from behind. The air-redirection knob, here carrying a molded-in label and arrow, is located below the choke control.

3 This heater-control knob is another, quite different, type. This type of knob was used on Series 3 V-12 cars, but potentially some late Series 2 six-cylinder cars as well.

4 As in the case of the choke control labels, the late Series 2 heater control labels were illuminated from behind. This late control also has a labeled air-redirection knob.

- 1R1351/2, 1R10536/7, 1R20424/5, 1R26834/5, 1R35563/4 and 1R42676/7, about October 1969, the clock battery was changed from a mercury-cell type to one operated by the car's battery. Some references cite chassis numbers 1R1350/1 instead of 1R1351/2 and numbers 1R24424/5 instead of 1R20425/6.

The change of the clock from the tachometer-mounted unit to the center-dash-mounted unit took place when the dash went over to toggle switches. This occurred at the transition from the Series 1.25 to the Series 1.5, and an early illustration of this is seen and discussed in *Motor* magazine, January 13, 1968. Two types of center-dash-mounted clocks were used: a "SMITHS" and a "KIENZLE." There appears to be some overlap between the two. The Kienzle type was generally being in use later in production, although the Smiths type has been seen on late cars, including some Series 3.

The early four-way flasher switches did not have a cover on the back, nor did they have an "ON OFF" label plate around the switch.

SWITCHES AND CONTROLS

A Series 1.5 roadster is shown with toggle switches and starter button in *The Jaguar E-type: A Collector's Guide* and Skilleter stated there that later Series 1.5 cars had the tumbler switches. However, the model designations have evolved since his book was written, and now what are considered Series 1.25 have toggle switches, and the new definition of Series 1.5 cars have all of them fitted with rocker (tumbler) switches.

The choke control assembly was different for Series 2 cars exported to Canada (including Newfoundland) and the United States (including Hawaii).

Series 2 cars had the four-way-flasher switch as part of the central row of switches and the indicator light between the tachometer and speedometer. The cable for the headlight flasher was different for cars exported to Italy.

Later four-way flasher switches had an "OFF ON" label added to the front. Even later, a cover was added to the back of the switch to cover the contacts and wiring.

Several chassis number related changes are listed in the literature at chassis numbers:

- 1E12024/5 and 1E32193/4, about December 1965, a hazard warning light (or four-way flasher) was fitted as standard. *The Jaguar E-type: A Collector's Guide* cites this change as occurring for U.S. cars in about July 1967;

- 1R7747/8 and 1R25430/1, the choke assembly was changed;

- 1R1775/6, 1R14120/1, 1R20952/3 and 1R28319/20, the headlight dip-switch was changed;

- 1E13804/5, 1E33688/9 and 1E76921/2, about July 1967, a cover was added to the four-way-flasher switch panel (for those cars with four-way flashers);

- 1E1457/8, 1E12033/4, 1E21206/7 and 1E32200/1, about September 1966, the turn signal-headlight flasher switch was changed;

With the introduction of the rocker switch dash during Series 1.5 production, the four-way flasher switch was located on the end of the central switch row.

The early Series 2 switch housings were flat. This is a view from a late Series 1.5 car.

The later Series 2 switch housing had two raised buttresses on either side of the headlight switches. Note the silver coating around the switches.

Another view of a later Series 2 switch housing. This one is for a car without a heated rear window, hence the unlabeled switch on the right-most position. Note also that the silver trim coating around the switches is not present here. The authors have seen other cases where it appears this coating was not originally on the switch housing from the factory.

The 4.2-liter Series 1 turn signal/headlight-flasher switch stalk was of the sort used on the 3.8-liter cars.

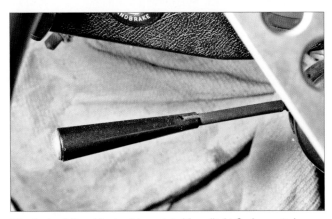

The Series 1.5 and Series 2 turn signal/headlight-flasher switch stalks had a tapered handle. The horn was now actuated by pushing on the end of the turn signal/headlight-flasher switch stalk, and not by pushing on the medallion in the center of the steering wheel.

- 1E1497/8, 1E12716/7, 1E21265/6 and 1E32691/2, about September 1966, the illumination color of the instruments and switch label strip was changed from blue to green;

- 1E2038/9 and 1E21783/4, about April 1968, the dashboard was revised, including the heater controls, choke and switches. A lid was added to the glovebox and the heater box was changed.

Illumination was added for the heater and choke controls in 1970. Before this, the heater was marked with a metal label and the choke was labeled with a similar metal label, or, in the early Series 2 cars, had no label at all. The movement of the horn button to the turn signal stalk came in with the Series 1.5.

The plastic housing for the row of tumbler switches in the Series 2 cars changed during Series 2 production. On the early Series 2 cars, this piece was flat in the center, while on later cars it had two buttresses on either side of the light switches.

INDICATOR LIGHTS

The authors are not aware of any changes to the indicator lights.

CIGAR LIGHTER

The authors are not aware of any changes to the cigar lighter.

IGNITION SWITCH AND KEY

Changes at chassis numbers 1R1084/5, 1R20094/5 and 1R35098/9. About December 1968, a steering column lock was fitted to right-hand drive cars. On some right-hand drive Series 1.5, cars this resulted in there being two ignition switches, one in the center of the dash and one on the steering column. A steering column with integral column lock is shown in the "Steering Wheel and Column" section below.

A column-mounted ignition switch.

At chassis numbers 1R9859/60, 1R26532/3 and 1R42381/2, about April 1969, the starter switch was changed to one that isolated some auxiliaries while the starter is cranking.

A key warning buzzer (that sounds when the key is in the ignition and the driver's door is closed) was new in 1970.

GRAB HANDLE

The authors are not aware of any changes to the grab handle.

STEERING WHEEL AND COLUMN

At least two types of steering wheels were used in the 4.2-liter cars: the polished wheel (with the scooped-out rim, as found on later 3.8-liter cars) found on Series 1 4.2-liter cars and the brushed-finish wheel found on Series 1.5 and Series 2 cars.

In *Motor* magazine, January 13, 1968 and in Porter's *Jaguar E-Type: The Definitive History*, it is claimed that the brushed-finish steering wheel was a result of complying with U.S. safety regulations, which prohibited a polished reflecting surface. It is indicated that this change came in with the Series 1.5.

All 4.2-liter steering wheels had the thumb-groove cut in the wood trim, as on later 3.8-liter cars.

As in the 3.8-liter cars, a locking steering column was available for some export Series 1 cars. Such a column was fitted to cars exported to Denmark, Germany and Sweden and also by special order.

In the Series 1 cars, the horn was actuated by pressing the escutcheon in the center of the steering wheel. These escutcheons had a chrome trim ring. For Series 2 cars, the horn was actuated on the turn signal/headlight-flasher switch stalk and the trim ring in the center of the steering wheel was black. The authors are not sure exactly when these two changes took place, or if the chrome-to-black trim ring change occurred simultaneously with the change in the location of the horn switch.

The energy-absorbing steering column came in with the Series 1.5 cars.

Listed changes in the steering wheel and column were at chassis numbers 1R1057/8, 1R20094/5 and 1R35098/9, the steering column lock and ignition switch assembly was fitted to right-hand drive cars; at chassis numbers 1R1084/5, 1R20094/5 and 1R35098/9, about December 1968, a steering column lock was fitted to right-hand drive cars; and at chassis numbers 1R1184/5 and 1R20263/4, the upper-steering column assembly was changed.

The Jaguar E-type: A Collector's Guide notes that at chassis numbers 1E1457/8, 1E12033/4, 1E21206/7 and 1E32200/1, about March 1966, the upper steering column was changed.

Early 4.2-liter cars had a polished finish on the aluminum of the steering wheel (as seen on the top), while later steering wheels had a brushed finish (as seen on the bottom).

With the introduction of the brushed-finish steering wheel, the trim ring around the narrow trim ring around the central horn button was changed from chrome (as seen in the prior picture) to black.

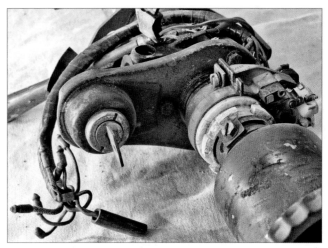

Series 1 cars had a chrome center trim ring directly surrounding the plastic "E-TYPE" horn push button.

Close-up view of a column lock.

A steering column with integral lock.

PEDALS

There were two types of pedal-box setups during 4.2-liter Series 1 production. The first type had a footprint compatible with the pedal-box apertures in the 3.8-liter cars. This design was changed in late 1965 to a more compact configuration and at this point the apertures in the top of the footwell were changed. The two types of pedal-box systems are very different in appearance and are not interchangeable. Due to the complexity of these units, several views of both early and late configurations are shown.

1 This is the right side view of the early 4.2-liter pedal box. It ran to about 1965. This early type is able to fit on a 3.8-liter car. The later version required a different aperture in the top of the footwell.

2 Right side view of the later 4.2-liter pedal box, with a smaller footprint. This design was introduced about 1965 and is not interchangeable with a 3.8-liter type pedal box.

3 Left side view of the early pedal box.

4 Left side view of the later pedal box.

5 Top view of the early pedal box. An electric tachometer-drive sender unit has been placed under the brake pedal to support the pedal box for photography; it is not related to the pedal box.

6 Top view of the late pedal box.

7 Bottom view of the early pedal box.

8 Bottom view of the later pedal box.

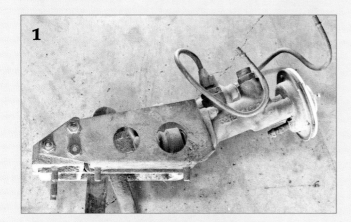

MIRROR AND MOUNTS

Series 1 cars had mirrors similar to those fitted to the 3.8-liter cars. The authors are not aware of the changes to the mirror within the 4.2-liter Series 1 cars. With the introduction of the Series 1.5, the mirror changed.

The interior mirror was different for cars exported to the United States and Canada.

Some Series 2 roadsters came with a mirror mounted on the sliding rod. It was similar to those found on the Series 1 cars, but with a different mirror mount.

This is another variant of break-away mirror that was used.

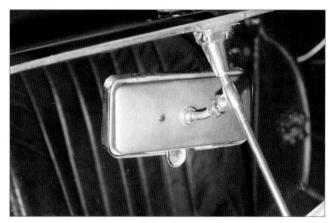

The Series 1 roadsters had a rod-mounted rearview mirror, of the sort used on the 3.8-liter roadsters.

Some late Series 2 roadsters had a rod-mounted mirror. The mirror and mount were different from those used on the Series 1 cars.

The Series 1 coupes had the roof-mounted rearview mirror, of the sort used on the 3.8-liter coupes.

INTERIOR LIGHTS

The authors are not aware of any changes to the interior lights.

HANDBRAKE LEVER

Changes at chassis numbers 1R35018/9 and 1R42038/9: The handbrake lever assembly was changed.

DASH TOP

The screen rail fascia and the defrosting equipment were changed at chassis numbers 1R1057/8, 1R7795/6, 1R20087/8 and 1R25430/1.

During Series 1.5 production, a break-away rearview mirror was introduced. It was to the inside surface of the windscreen. This mirror was also used on early Series 2 cars.

DEFROSTER DUCTS

About October 1969, a defroster-tube extension was fitted at chassis numbers 1R35649/50 and 1R42551/2.

DASH MATERIALS AND TRIM

The literature notes that the fascia panel assemblies were changed at chassis numbers 1R1392/3, 1R11051/2, 1R20485/6 and 1R27050/1.

At chassis numbers 1E1606/7, 1E13205/6, 1E21387/8 and 1E33149/50, about March 1967, the right-hand side scuttle top casing (under dash panel) was changed from Rexine-trimmed aluminum to fiberboard.

At chassis numbers 1E1685/6, 1E13724/5, 1E21442/3 and 1E33643/4, about March 1967, the center scuttle top casing was changed from Rexine-covered aluminum to fiberboard.

GLOVEBOX

The glovebox lid came in with the 2+2 cars. On the two-seater cars, it came in during Series 1.5 production, along with the rocker switches and other dash changes.

The Jaguar E-type: A Collector's Guide states that about April 1968, at chassis numbers 1E2038/9 and 1E21783/4, the dashboard was revised: The heater controls, choke and switches were changed. A lid was added to the glovebox and the heater box was changed.

SUN VISORS

Sun visors were introduced on the roadsters during Series 1 4.2-liter production at chassis numbers 1E12688/9, in late 1965 or early 1966. This change is not listed in any of the *Spare Parts Catalogue*s. It is not likely any Series 1.5 cars or Series 2 cars were supplied without sun visors.

At chassis numbers 1R1348/9 and 1R10522/3, the sun visor mechanism was changed.

At chassis numbers 1E20938/9 and 1E31787/8, about March 1966, a vanity mirror was added to the passenger's sun visor on the coupes; and at chassis numbers 1E1489/90 and 1E12687/8, about September 1966, sun visors were added to the roadsters.

An outer mount for a roadster sun visor. Note how the sun visor mounts merely bolted to the existing hardware.

A central mount for a roadster sun visor.

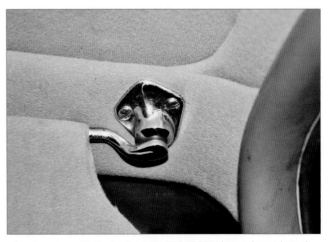

The visor mount in Series 2 coupe P1R42679 shows the wide and low triangular stanchion, the final evolution of these stanchions during 3.8-liter E-type production.

During Series 1 production, sun visors were introduced on the roadsters.

UNDER DASH TRAYS

At chassis numbers 1E50680/1 and 1E77376/7, about July 1968, the package trays were changed.

CONSOLE FRAME, TRIM AND COMPONENTS

During Series 1 4.2-liter construction, the boot on the shift lever changed. Initially it was of leather, in the same color as the seats, with a chromed-steel trim ring fastened with small rivets in the style of the 3.8-liter cars. About 1966, this was changed to an arrangement where the gearshift lever opening was reduced to a small circular aperture and a rubber boot was used in place of the leather to cover the hole. This arrangement was used for about a year, then the vinyl boot arrangement (of the Series 1.5 and Series 2) was introduced.

The literature states that at chassis numbers 1E1060/1, 1E10359/60, 1E20102/3 and 1E30349/50, the leather shift boot was changed to a rubber shift boot. *The Jaguar E-type: A Collector's Guide* states that about November 1964 the finisher panel on the gearbox was changed and the chrome bezel and chrome ferrule for the boot were deleted, but lists only chassis numbers 1E1060/1 and 1E10359/60 for the change.

About June 1965, the console was changed at chassis numbers 1E1201/2, 1E10847/8, 1E20501/2 and 1E30889/90. This may be when the vinyl shift boot was introduced. Some late Series 1 4.2-liter cars have been observed with the leather shift boot of the early Series 1 4.2-liters. However, no evidence for this was found in the literature.

About March 1967, the shift lever boot was changed to Ambla (a vinyl material) from the grommet (corrugated rubber boot) that was used previously, at chassis numbers 1E1685/6, 1E13588/9, 1E21441/2, 1E33548/9, 1E50585/6 and 1E76910/1. This is possibly the introduction of the third style of shift lever boot, as found on late Series 1 and early Series 2 cars.

The Series 2 cars had a vinyl shift boot with a smaller silver ring around it and the handbrake levers were different on the 2+2 from those fitted to the two-seater Series 2 cars.

At chassis numbers 1R35421/2 and 1R42400/1, about March 1970, the handbrake lever was changed to one with a different material in the pivot pin and lever and at chassis numbers 1R35656/7 and 1R43164/5, about January 1970, the automatic transmission selector lever was changed.

The shift knob on the automatic transmission was changed from spherical to elliptical on the Series 1.5 cars to increase its surface area and meet U.S. specifications.

With the change in the dash during the Series 1.5 production, the front section of the console also changed to the more padded version of the Series 2. About the time of the front console change that occurred during Series 1.5 production, the ashtray was changed and moved from the front console to a location in front of the armrest-storage area.

The storage area on the console was different on the 2+2s from the two-seater cars. The sidewalls were thicker on the 2+2 storage areas.

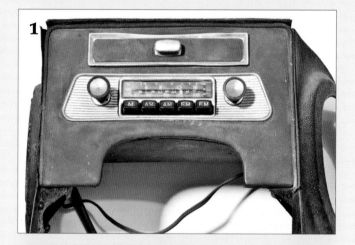

1 *The Series 1 console was the same as the late 3.8-liter consoles (with the possible exception of the speaker surrounds without chrome, that may have been used on some 3.8-liter cars). The Series 1 4.2-liter cars had a front-console-mounted ashtray, as seen here, in the manner of the late 3.8-liter cars.*

2 *Subsequent to the leather boot, a rubber shift-boot was introduced around model year 1966. The radio blanking plate here is not original, but the early pull-out ashtray is correct. This is a restored car and the upholstery is bulging out more than was the case originally.*

3 *Top view of an NOS rubber shift boot showing the flange at the base (not usually evident when the unit is installed) with its mounting holes.*

4 *Bottom view of an NOS rubber shift boot. These boots are sometimes referred to as "grommets" in the literature.*

5 *The Series 2 console used in cars not fitted with air conditioning. The rectangular plastic radio speaker grille is not original.*

6 One of the types of Series 2 consoles used in cars fitted with air conditioning. Note the metal console is painted in black crinkle-finish paint and has a cigar lighter on the lower right. Note also the discontinuity between the style of the front console and the long section running back between the seats, that is upholstered. Also showing here is the third style of shift boot, with a trim ring fitted around the inside of the aperture through which the shift boot extends, in contrast to the prior type where the trim went around the boot on the outside and was riveted on. This boot type is examined in more detail in following pictures.

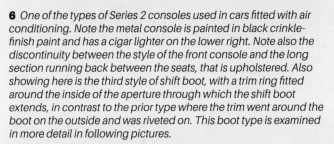

7 This radio blanking plate was used on some of the Series 2 consoles. Note its much simpler appearance in comparison to the blanking plates used on Series 1 cars (see the 3.8-liter section). These had chrome trim around the periphery simulating the trim used on the typical radios that were fitted.

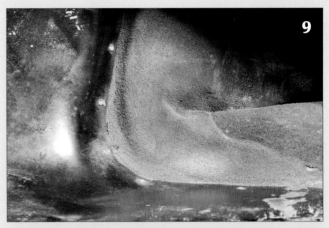

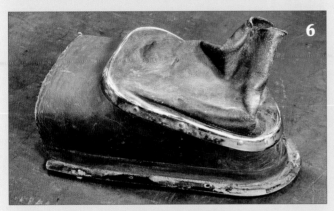

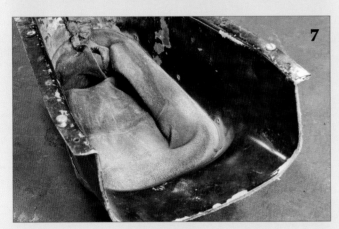

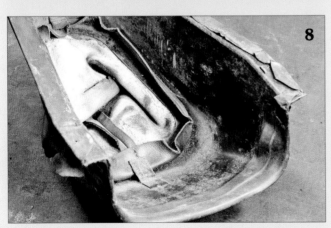

3 Another type of console used with when air conditioning and an automatic transmission was fitted. Note the absence of the cigar lighter on the console.

4 This shift knob was likely used throughout 4.2-liter production.

5 After the fitting of the rubber shift boots this vinyl boot was fitted. This coincides roughly with the introduction of the Series 1.5 cars. The trimming on the housing was vinyl as well, in contrast to the leather housing trim that as used on the first style of Series 1 4.2-liter leather shift boots.

6 The earliest form of the 4.2-liter shift boot was leather with leather covering on the base. The leather was glued to the black-painted sheet steel base. The chromed-steel ring retaining the leather shift boot was riveted on, in the manner of the 3.8-liter cars. This arrangement was followed by the rubber shift boot.

7 Interior view of the first style of shift boot. Both the boot itself and the trim on the housing are leather. Note, in contrast to the uncovered aluminum and at least some of late leather-covered 3.8-liter shift boots, the housing material is black-painted sheet steel instead of aluminum.

8 Interior view of the third style of shift boot. Note the vinyl trim and boot material. The boot material is cloth-backed. Note that the boot assembly is retained by a steel insert held in place by bent tabs on the front and back of the aperture, hence the absence of rivets on the ring surrounding the aperture on the top of the assembly (the side seen from the interior of the car).

9 Underside view of the first style of leather shift boot, showing the backs of the rivets holding the chromed steel retaining ring. The leather material on the black sheet steel housing are seen here.

10 Underside view of the third style of shift boot showing the retaining tab, retaining ring (showing under the vinyl boot trim in the center of the picture) and black-painted sheet steel housing.

1 Overview of one of the consoles used when air conditioning was fitted, showing also an air conditioning unit. Note that here the ignition key is incorporated in the air conditioning unit, rather than being located on the steering column.

2 Underside view of an air conditioning unit showing the air intake in the passenger's footwell (the round aperture at the lower right of the picture).

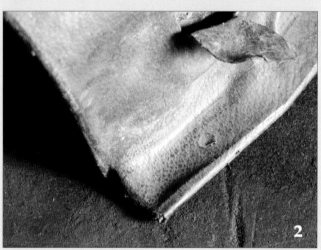

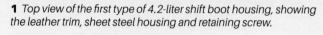

1 Top view of the first type of 4.2-liter shift boot housing, showing the leather trim, sheet steel housing and retaining screw.

2 Top view of the third type of 4.2-liter shift boot housing that came in at, or approximately at, the introduction of the Series 1.5 cars. Note the vinyl trim.

3 Outside view of the chrome retaining ring used on the first type of 4.2-liter shift boot, showing the retaining rivets and leather trim. The heads on these rivets on at least some early 3.8-liter cars were shaped like disks, with sharp edges, rather than rounded as seen here.

4 Inside close-up of the retaining rivets, black-painted sheet steel housing and leather boot used in the first type of 4.2-liter shift boots.

5 Close-up of the black-painted sheet steel housing and one of the flat-headed sheet metal retaining screws used to hold the housing to the base of the console in the first type of 4.2-liter shift boot designs.

6 View of the shift-boot arrangement used when an automatic transmission was fitted. The slot in which the lever slides had brush bristles protruding from the sides to seal off the area under the lever and cover.

7 When the Series 1.5 console was introduced the ashtray was moved from the front console to the lower section of the console running between the seats. The ashtray was located next to the parking-brake lever aperture.

8 Inside view of the console-mounted ashtray.

9 Vinyl-covered wooden cubby, as fitted to Series 2 2+2 cars. This is the later thick-walled console storage compartment.

10 Interior view of the thin-walled console storage compartment from a two-seater car.

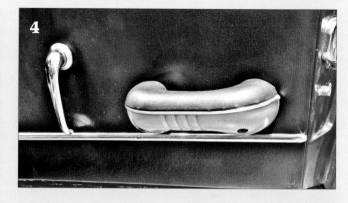

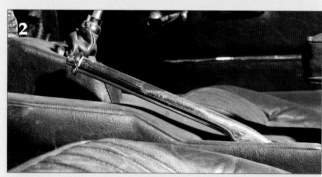

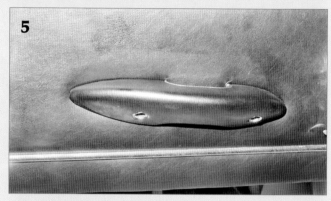

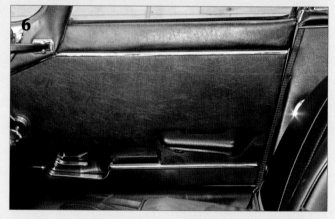

UNDER CONSOLE AREA

A rubber sealing plug was added to seal the gearbox apertures at chassis numbers 1E1225/6, 1E10957/8, 1E20611/2 and 1E30981/2 and about May 1970, the handbrake lever assembly was changed (the new one was longer and angled upward) at chassis numbers 1R35815/6 and 1R43923/4.

CARPETS AND INTERIOR TRIM

The door armrests changed several times during the 4.2-liter production. All the Series 1 cars had armrests, with different types for the two-seaters and 2+2s. During the production of Series 1.5 cars, the armrests were discontinued. Then, shortly after the introduction of the Series 2 cars, the armrests were reintroduced. The newer armrests were of a simpler and more pointed design than the earlier ones.

Armrests were added to the doors at chassis numbers 1R1325/6, 1R10334/5 (perhaps this should be 1R10534/5), 1R20390/1 and 1R26755/6.

The front of the doors, in the area where the door-light switch striker is located, was trimmed in the 4.2-liter cars. This area was not trimmed in the 3.8-liter cars.

In *The Jaguar E-type: A Collector's Guide*, states, when speaking of a Series 1 coupe, that the moquette was replaced with vinyl (moquette was used on early 4.2-liter cars) and the rear mat was changed to a one piece design. Later, this mat was replaced by trimming the panels directly in vinyl.

The 4.2-liter cars were fitted with false toe boards on the passenger's side. This may have been a feature of all 4.2-liter cars.

OPPOSITE:

1 Overview of the thin-walled console from a 4.2-liter two-seater car.

2 A hand brake lever from a two-seater car. This is of the sort used on 3.8-liter cars.

3 Hand brake lever from a 2+2 car. Notice the rib in the center and the cup-type release cap. Contrast the chromed sides of the console-mounted ashtray to the black crinkle finish used on the later ashtrays shown on page 293. The chrome-sided style appears to generally be the early style.

4 This 4.2-liter Series 1 armrest from a two-seater is of the sort used on late 3.8-liter cars.

5 A Series 1 armrest from a 2+2. Note the longer, tapered shape.

6 Late Series 2 armrests were molded in a single piece.

7 At least some Series 1.5 and early Series 2 cars did not have door armrests.

Changes at chassis numbers:

▶ 1E20116/7 and 1E30401/2, about February 1965, the casing assembly below the quarter lights was changed and the pocket assembly in the casing below the quarter lights was deleted. The cover assembly over the spare wheel and gas tank and forward luggage floor area were trimmed and the old luggage floor mat was done away with. The rear wheel-arch covers were changed from moquette trimmed to PVC trimmed. The hinged extension board and its support rail assembly were changed. Some carpets and Hardura mats and insulating felts and interior trimming were changed.

▶ 1E50422/3 and 1E76663/4 the trim panels above the rear door aperture and the headlining was changed;

▶ 1E21133/4 and 1E32267/8, in about September 1966, the hinged extension board in the luggage area was changed.

The moquette trimming found on the left and right sides of the boot, as used on early 4.2-liter coupes.

A view of late 4.2-liter coupe vinyl trimming.

Front view of a false toe board from a Series 1.5 car. Similar boards were used on Series 1 4.2-liter cars.

Front view of a false toe board from a Series 1.5 car.

SEATS AND MOUNTS

In the Series 2 cars, the early seats had smooth leather and the later seats had perforated leather. The trim on the seatbacks changed during 4.2-liter production; the early seats had moquette covering and the later seats had vinyl covering.

Changes at chassis numbers 1R1137/8, 1R8868/9, 1R20211/2 and 1R26004/5, in about May 1969, the perforated leather trim was introduced for the seats and the headrests were changed. The following cars were also fitted with the early seats: Chassis numbers 1R8870, 1R8871, 1R8873, 1R8874, 1R8875, 1R8876, 1R8877, 1R8878, 1R8879, 1R8880,

1R8881, 1R8882, 1R8883, 1R9029, 1R9042, 1R9069, 1R9070, 1R9077, 1R9147, 1R9169, 1R9172, 1R9174, 1R9185, 1R9195, 1R9255, 1R9328, 1R9244 (perhaps this should be 9344), 1R9350, 1R9396, 1R9419, 1R26002, 1R26007, 1R26010, 1R26022, 1R26023, 1R26025, 1R26028, 1R26033, 1R26051, 1R26053, 1R26057, 1R26069 and 1R26078.

▶ At chassis numbers 1R1301/2 (and some cars after 1R1277), 1R10151/2 (and some cars after 1R10114), 1R20365/6 (and some cars after 1R20354), 1R26683/4 (and some cars after lR26649), 1R35457/8 (and some cars after 1R35440) and 1R42559/60 (and some cars after 1R42539), about August 1969, the seat assemblies were adapted to take headrests as an optional extra, but chassis numbers 1R35457/8 and 1R42559/60 were not mentioned in the *Spare Parts Catalogue*.

▶ At chassis numbers 1E1011/2, 1E10312/3, 1E20079/80 and 1E30251/2 about January 1965, spacers were introduced at the front mounts of the seat slides where they attach to the floor.

▶ At chassis numbers 1E1039/40, 1E10337/8, 1E20097/8 and 1E30292/3, about January 1965, the fittings between the seat slides and the seat were changed and at chassis numbers 1E50660/1 and 1E76949/50, about July 1967, the upper squab of the back seat was changed.

▶ At chassis numbers 1E1418/9, 1E11802/3, 1E21037/8 and 1E32039/40, the trimmed base assembly of the seats and the screws and washers mounting them to the slides, were changed.

The smooth leather on a Series 1.5 seat is representative of the finish on early Series 2 seats.

Later Series 2 seats had perforated leather trimming.

Moquette-covered seatbacks were used on early 4.2-liter cars.

A vinyl-covered seatback on a later car.

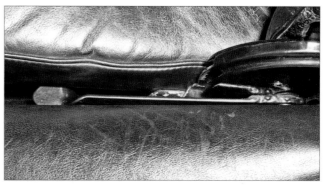

Later 4.2-liter seats had rake adjustment levers. This is the bent sheet metal type.

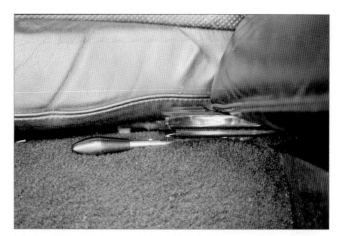

These adjustment levers with molded handles on a chromed shaft were another type of rake adjustment on 4.2-liter seats.

CONVERTIBLE TOP (HOOD), FRAME AND HARDWARE

The trim on most of the convertible top boards was a light-brown fabric. However, some Series 2 cars had black vinyl trimming.

A center convertible top clasp, as used on early 4.2-liter cars. This one is from a 3.8-liter car. Note the thin handle and thin section.

On some 4.2-liter roadsters, a label on the inner front area of the convertible top warned to move the seats forward before raising the top. This label was apparently not fitted to all 4.2-liter cars, as is evidenced by its absence in the illustration in *The Jaguar E-type: A Collector's Guide*.

The convertible top clasps of the Series 1.5 and Series 2 cars were different from the later 3.8-liter type. They had a thicker yolk and the central clasp was changed. The thicker-type clasps came in an early, sharp-edged style and a later, smooth-edged style. The second style is the common one.

1 A side convertible top clasp of the sort used on early 4.2-liter cars. This one is from a 3.8-liter car.

2 An early version of a thick center clasp from a Series 1.5 car. Note the sharp edges on the left of the fat section of the handle and the lack of a buttress on the handle on the left. This is the first stage in the evolution of the Series 2 clasps that have all sections thickened.

3 A top view of an early thick center clasp from a Series 1.5 car, looking from the top with the clasp in open configuration. Here the lack of a buttress on the handle is very evident.

4 One variant of a Series 1.5 thick side clasp. Note the somewhat abrupt transition between the handle and the body of the clasp.

5 Another variant of a Series 1.5 thick side clasp. This one has a smooth transition between the handle and the body of the clasp.

6 A late thick center clasp from a Series 2 car.

7 Side view of a late Series 2 thick center clasp. Note the very rounded edges and pronounced curvature of the handle and the cast buttress spanning the curve. This buttress was absent in the earlier thick-clasp designs.

8 Top view of a late Series 2 thick side clasp.

9 A Series 2 side clasp showing the same cast buttress as used on the Series 2 center clasps. Note the low frame profile. Contrast this to the high arched frame profile in Figure 10.

10 A Series 2 side clasp with a high arched frame. Contrast this shape to the frame in Figure 9. The authors have seen several variations in this component of the clasps over the period of E-type production.

11 The convertible tops on all 3.8-liter cars, and into 4.2-liter production, were made of mohair.

12 During Series 1 4.2-liter production, the convertible top material was changed from mohair to vinyl. This is a top from an unrestored Series 1.5 car.

4

8

5

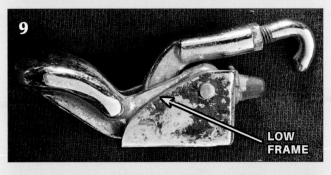

9

LOW
FRAME

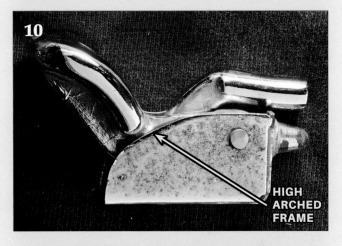

10

HIGH
ARCHED
FRAME

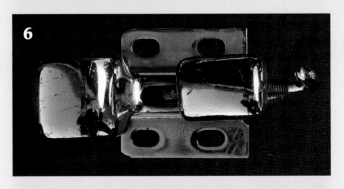

6

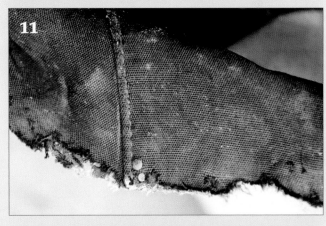

11

7

VERY
ROUNDED
EDGES

BUTTRESS

12

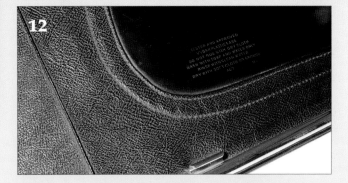

An outside view of the vinyl convertible top cover used throughout 4.2-liter production. Note that two straps are used to retain the leading edge of the cover, in contrast to earlier mohair covers that had three straps (an additional one was used in the center).

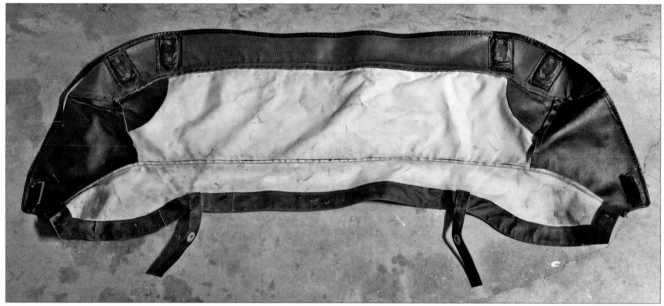

An inside view of the vinyl convertible top cover.

BONNET RELEASE

The authors are not aware of any design changes to the interior release.

BOOT RELEASE

With the introduction of the 4.2-liter cars, a lock was added to the boot release on the roadsters.

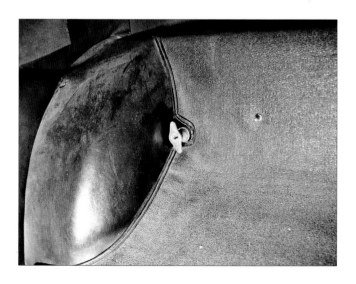

RIGHT: The lockable boot lid release in the right rear of the cockpit.

BODYWORK: FRONT FENDERS

At chassis numbers 1E1478/9, 1E12579/80, 1E21227/8 and 1E32631/2, about September 1966, the bonnet, front fenders, front bumpers and heater air-intake plenum were changed to the type as used on the 2+2s.

BONNET CENTER SECTION

At chassis numbers 1E1478/9, 1E12579/80, 1E21227/8 and 1E32631/2, about September 1966, the bonnet, front fenders, front bumpers and heater air-intake plenum were changed to the type as used on the 2+2s.

Autocar magazine, October 12, 1967, stated that the air intake aperture in the bonnet is "now single skinned." It is not clear exactly what is being referred to here. Other than this cryptic entry, the authors are not aware of any design changes.

When air conditioning was fitted, a portion of the inner wall of the heater plenum was recessed.

BONNET HINGES AND LIFTS

Changes at chassis numbers lR1187/8, 1R9569/70, 1R20269/70, 1R26386/7, 1R35352/3 and 1R42117/8: in about June 1969, the bonnet-lifting springs were replaced by a gas-filled cylinder.

A spring-loaded bonnet lift on a 4.2-liter car. This continuation of the 3.8-liter-type lifts was used on the early 4.2-liter cars. Near the end of the use of this type of lift cars were also fitted with the anchor points on the bonnet bulkhead for the soon-to-be-introduced gas-strut lift.

In order to accommodate air conditioning the inner wall of the heater intake plenum was recessed. This is a late Series 2 roadster.

A later gas-strut bonnet lift. These were used on the left side only, unlike the earlier spring lifts, which were found on both sides.

BONNET LATCHES

At chassis numbers 1E1423/4, 1E11885/6, 1E21075/6 and 1E32089/90 an O-ring was placed on the bonnet latch-operating rod to prevent vibration of the rod.

The safety catch on the Series 2 bonnets was found in one of two locations: in the center of the bonnet or on the right-hand side.

1 *The centrally-mounted bonnet safety catch on a late Series 2 roadster. In later Series 2 roadsters, but before the right-mounted catch came in, the provision for a right-mounted safety catch was made on the right side of the bonnet center sheet metal section, but not used. These extra bolts are not found on earlier cars.*

2 *This Series 2 2+2 bonnet has a right-mounted bonnet safety catch. Note the four bolt holes for the fitting of a central catch that was not installed on this car. Even though the design had moved to a right-mounted catch, these holes were left in the bonnet design.*

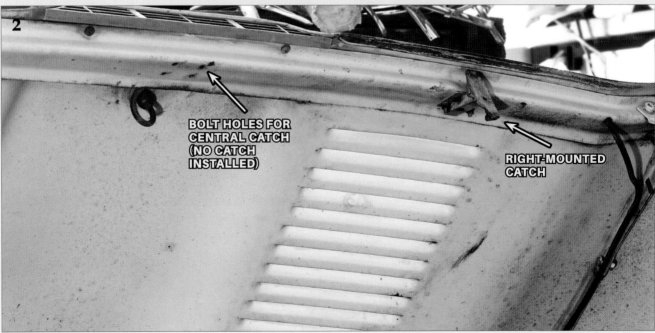

BOLT HOLES FOR CENTRAL CATCH (NO CATCH INSTALLED)

RIGHT-MOUNTED CATCH

RUBBER STOPS

The authors are not aware of any design changes.

REAR TUB SHEET METAL, FIREWALL AND UNDERSIDE

▸ The bodyshell underframe and rear end assembly were changed at chassis numbers 1E1069/70, 1E10425/6, 1E20116/7 and 1E30401/2 and about March 1965;

▸ At chassis numbers 1E20116/7 and 1E30401/2, bodyshell changes took place.

▸ The front closing panel assemblies for the cockpit and sills were changed about September 1965 at chassis numbers 1E1285/6, 1E11117/8, 1E20752/3 and 1E31170/1.

▸ In November 1965 sealing panels were added between the rear bulkhead panel and wheel arch valances, at chassis numbers 1E1333/4 and 1E11157/8.

▸ An attachment bracket assembly for the rear bumpers was introduced at chassis numbers 1E1411/2, 1E11727/8, 1E20995/6 and 1E32008/9.

Autocar magazine, October 12, 1967, mentioned that the rustproofing is said to be improved.

COCKPIT SHEET METAL

The cockpit panel assembly at the side of the gearbox was changed at chassis numbers 1E1060/1, 1E10359/60, 1E20102/3 and 1E30349/50.

At chassis numbers 1E1201/2, 1E10847/8, 1E20501/2, 1E30889/90, about June 1965, the driveshaft tunnel changed.

At chassis numbers 1E1225/6, 1E10957/8, 1E20611/2 and 1E30911/2 (and some previous chassis), about June 1965, a speedometer-drive access aperture, with cover, was added to the right-hand side gearbox side panel.

In June 1968 the U.S. Federal specifications for doors, casings and linings were adapted to right-hand drive cars.

DOORS

At chassis numbers 1E1692/3, 1E13951/2, 1E21450/1, 1E33774/5, about July 1967, the drain tray on the doors was changed.

DOOR HINGES AND SUPPORTS

The authors are not aware of any changes to the door hinges and supports.

DOOR LATCHES

The authors are not aware of any changes to the door latches.

BOOT SHEET METAL

The inspection plate over the rear brakes that was present on all 3.8-liter cars was included on 4.2-liter cars up until about 1966. At that point it was discontinued, and the holes in the boot above the brakes were no longer present.

In the October 12, 1967, issue of *Autocar*, the boot floor of a right-hand drive Series 1 roadster is shown without the brake inspection plate found on the 3.8-liter cars.

BOOT LID

The authors are not aware of any changes to the boot lid.

BOOT HINGES AND SUPPORTS

Both the 3.8-liter type stick prop and the later hinge-type prop were used on 4.2-liter coupes.

At chassis numbers 1E20851/2 and 1E31412/3, about November 1965, the coupe rear door support went from post-type prop to hinged-type prop.

The early 4.2-liter coupes had a post-type boot lid prop.

OPPOSITE: *Later in Series 1 production, the boot lid prop was changed to a hinged type.*

FUEL FILLER RECESS, CAP, LID AND HINGE

The gas tank and cap were changed at chassis numbers 1R1392/3, 1R11051/2, 1R20485/6, 1R27050/1, 1R35642/3 and 1R42849/50.

BOOT PANELS, MAT AND FLOORING

At chassis numbers 1E21133/4 and 1E32267/8, in about September 1966, the hinged extension board in the luggage area was changed.

The boot mat used on early 4.2-liter coupes.

The boot floor area of a late 4.2-liter coupe. The vinyl trimming is affixed to the floorboards.

BOOT LID SEALING RUBBER

The boot lid sealing rubber for all 4.2-liter cars was on the edge of the boot aperture, not on the lid.

EXTERIOR AND INTERIOR COLORS

As in the 3.8-liter section, the following listing is compiled from several lists published in various literature. These lists were similar, but not identical, so they have been combined to form a central list. Other sources contain basically the same information. As in the 3.8-liter section, the format of the table is exterior color followed by the associated interior colors.

EXTERIOR/INTERIOR COLORS 1965 TO SEPTEMBER 1967

▸ Black/Red Gray, Light Tan, or Tan

▸ Carmen Red/Black

▸ Cream/Black

▸ Dark Blue/Red, Light Blue, or Grey

▸ Golden Sand/Red or Light Tan

▸ Opalescent Dark Green/Suede Green, Beige, Light Tan, or Tan

▸ Opalescent Maroon/Maroon or Beige

▸ Opalescent Silver Blue/Gray or Dark Blue

▸ Opalescent Silver Gray/Red, Light Blue, Dark Blue, or Gray

▸ Pale Primrose/Black or Beige

▸ Sherwood Green/Suede Green, Light Tan, or Tan

▸ Warwick Gray/Red, Light Tan, or Dark Blue

EXTERIOR/INTERIOR COLORS SEPTEMBER 1967 TO JULY 1968

▸ Beige/Red, Suede Green, Light Tan, or Tan

▸ Black/Red, Gray, Tan or Light Tan

▸ British Racing Green/Suede Green, Beige, Light Tan, or Tan

▸ Carmen Red/Black, Beige, or Red

▸ Dark Blue/Red, Light Blue, or Gray

▸ Golden Sand/Red or Light Tan

▸ Opalescent Maroon/Maroon or Beige

▸ Opalescent Silver Blue/Gray or Dark Blue

▸ Opalescent Silver Gray/Red, Light Blue, Dark Blue, or Gray

▸ Pale Primrose/Black or Beige

▸ Warwick Gray/Red, Light Tan, or Dark Blue

▸ Willow Green/Gray, Suede Green, Light Tan, Tan, or Beige

EXTERIOR/INTERIOR COLORS AUGUST 1968 TO JULY 1969

- Ascot Fawn/Red, Beige, or Cinnamon

- Black/Red, Gray, Light Tan, Tan or Cinnamon

- British Racing Green/Suede Green, Beige, Cinnamon, or Tan

- Cream/Black

- Dark Blue/Red, Light Blue, or Gray

- Light Blue/Dark Blue, Gray, or Light Blue

- Pale Primrose/Black or Beige

- Regency Red/Beige or Gray

- Sable/Beige, Gray, or Cinnamon

- Signal Red/Black, Biscuit, Dark Blue, Red, Beige, or Cinnamon

- Warwick Gray/Red, Light Tan, Dark Blue, Beige, Cinnamon, or Black

- Willow Green/Suede Green, Gray, Light Tan, Beige, or Cinnamon

EXTERIOR/INTERIOR COLORS 1970 TO MARCH 1971

- Ascot Fawn/Red, Beige, or Cinnamon

- Black/Red, Gray, Tan, Light Tan, or Cinnamon

- British Racing Green/Suede Green, Beige, Tan, Light Tan, or Cinnamon

- Dark Blue/Red, Light Blue, or Gray

- Light Blue/Dark Blue, Gray, or Light Blue

- Old English White/Black

- Pale Primrose/Black or Beige

- Regency Red/Beige or Gray

- Sable/Beige, Gray, or Cinnamon

- Warwick Gray/Red, Light Tan, Dark Blue, or Cinnamon

- Willow Green/Gray, Suede Green, Tan, Light Tan, Beige, or Cinnamon

As in the case of the 3.8-liter cars, there were variations to the standards.

TOOLS

The 4.2-liter cars used a tool roll to contain the tools, similar to the 3.8-liter cars. A line illustration of the entire tool kit for a Series 1 4.2-liter car shown in Jaguar handbook E/131/6. Beneath the illustration is the following inventory of the tools:

- Jack

- Hammer (copper and rawhide)

- Hubcap removal tool

- Bleeder tube

- Valve timing gauge

- Grease gun

- Feeler gauge

- Screwdriver for contact breaker points

- Tire valve extractor

- Tire pressure gauge

- Adjustable spanner

- Pliers

- Tommy bar (short)

- Box spanner (spark plugs and cylinder head nuts)

- Box spanner 9/16x5/8 inch SAE)

- Box spanner 7/16x1/2 inch SAE)

- Box spanner 3/4x7/8 inch SAE)

- Open-ended spanner (11/32x3/8 inch AF)

- Open-ended spanner (9/16x5/8 inch AF)

- Open-ended spanner (1/2x7/16 inch AF)

- Open-ended spanner (3/4x7/8 inch AF)

- Tommy bar (long)

- Combination screwdriver

While the hubcap removal tool is listed as part of the kit, it was supplied only for cars with earless knock-off hubcaps. This large brass wrench fitted around the earless knock-off hubcap. Locked in place, it allowed hammer blows to tighten or loosen the hubcap. Note that this is a different tool from the one used on the earless knock-off hubcaps of prior cars, for example, those shipped to Germany (as discussed in Chapter Two).

While early cars had the iron, copper and rawhide hammer of the 3.8-liter cars, the later ones had a single-piece hammer. When the Series 2 cars came fitted with the Turbo Disk steel disc wheels (affixed by five bolts instead of a large central splined hub), a lug wrench was supplied with the tool kit.

There are variations within the tool kits. For example, there are various makers of the open-end wrenches. Moreover, the small adjustable wrench seems to be unique among the tools, in that it was often supplied by non-British firms. For some 4.2-liter cars and perhaps for some of the 3.8-liters, this wrench was made in Germany and perhaps other European countries.

Another variation is found in the 4.2-liter took kits is the brake-bleeder hose can, which was supplied by Lockheed or Girling.

In the *Series 2 Parts Catalogue (1979)*, an air-conditioner dipstick is listed as available for servicing the air conditioning.

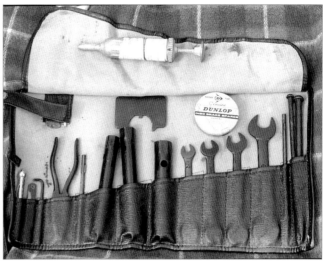

A 4.2-liter Series 1 tool kit. Note that in this particular kit the adjustable wrench is not present and the Allen key for adjustment of very early 3.8-liter handbrakes is included.

HAMMER AND WHEEL-REMOVAL TOOLS

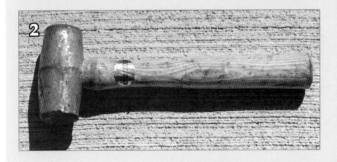

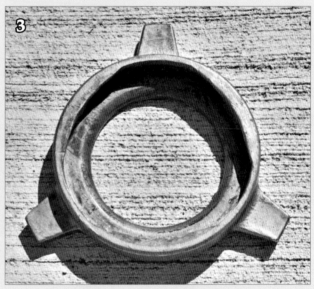

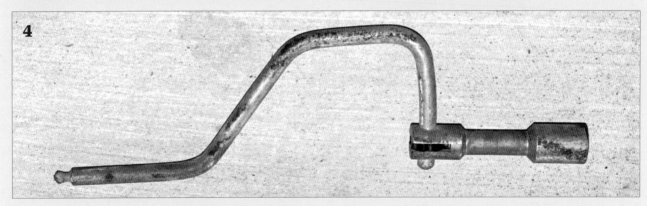

1 The early, multi-piece knock-off hammer had brass on one side and a roll of rawhide on the other. On this example the rawhide is missing. The main body was iron.

2 A late, single-piece knock-off hammer.

3 The knock-off removal tool for the Series 1.5 and Series 2 earless knock-off hubcaps. This hubcap tool is a different unit than the wrench supplied with some cars going to Europe (possibly just Germany) that had an earlier-type of earless hubcap. This earlier type is illustrated in the 3.8-liter section.

4 Cars fitted with the Turbo Disk wheels came with a lug wrench.

JACK

There were at least three styles of jacks. The first type had an attached handle, the second had a detached ratchet handle and the latest type had a detached handle that was made of a single rod bent into a crank shape. This is the type of jack used with the Series 3 cars and it was supplied with the late 1971 cars. All 4.2-liter car jacks were supplied with a bag.

1 *The early jack had an attached handle, in the manner of the late 3.8-liter cars.*

2 *The later jack had a detached ratchet handle. This illustration shows the later jack, but the ratchet handle is not illustrated here.*

3 *The last style of jack had a detached bent-rod crank handle (shown in a separate picture). This is the same sort used on the early Series 3 V-12 cars.*

4 *The bent-rod handle supplied with the last style of jack. This handle should be painted a gray color similar to that seen on the jacks shown on this page.*

5 *A typical bag used with the Metallifacture jacks.*

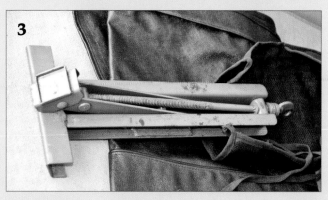

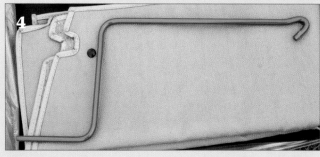

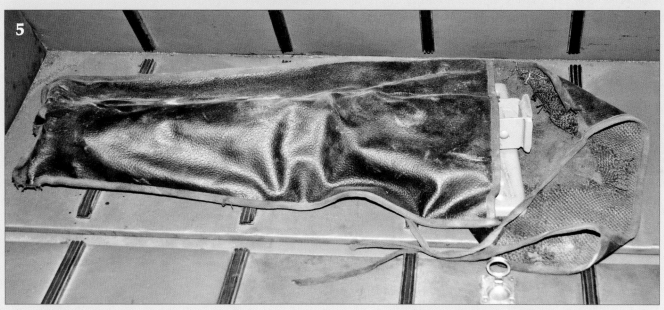

CHAPTER 5

4.2-LITER ENGINE, DRIVETRAIN AND CHASSIS COMPONENT CHANGES

This chapter covers changes made to the 4.2-liter E-type's engine, drivetrain, chassis and other mechanical parts.

ENGINE BLOCK PART NUMBER LOCATION AND STYLE

Based on many observations, engine blocks bearing these part numbers were supplied on 4.2-liter E-types:

    C21689
    C21689/1
    C26430
    C27880
    C28807
    C29040
    C29040/1

There may have been others, but it is likely this is the full list. The 4.2-liter OTS and FHC *J.37 Spare Parts Catalogue (November 1969)* lists only one cylinder block, C.24290, but this is a part number for a block assembly, not the bare block itself. Similarly, the *J.38 Spare Parts Catalogue (December 1966)*, also lists one cylinder block, C.26450, again as an assembly with no bare block part

number. The authors have never observed either C.24290 or C.26450 cast in or stamped on a cylinder block. The earliest observed 4.2-liter E-type block part number is C21689, seen on block from engine 7E1221-9.

The table on the following page shows the progression of block part numbers, along with the engine serial number and, when available, the numbers stamped on the upper rear of the block, the stampings on the front left of the block (typically matching those on the timing chain cover), the cast pour date and the characters cast into the area to the left of the pour date. Also included are data on similar blocks from the straight-head S-type 4.2-liter engines fitted to Mk X and 420G sedans.

The block from engine 7E1310-8 has part number C21689/1.

Engine 7E50896-9 shows block part number C26430. Note the commonly-seen effect of machining the top of the letters of the block number. This number is located at the top right front of the block.

ENGINE NUMBER	BLOCK PART NUMBER MARKING	REAR STAMPING	CHAIN COVER and BLOCK	BLOCK CAST DATE	MARK LEFT OF BLOCK DATE	NOTES
4.2-liter E-type blocks, OTS/FHC						
7E1221-9	FF C21689	A816?	x	x	x	
7E1310-8	FF C21689/1	A875	x	31-8-64	G	
7E4749-9	FF C21689/1	H51	x	1-3-65	N	
7E6466-9	FFC21689/1	x	x	x	x	
7E8263-9	C26430FF	x	x	11-2-66	AW	"AW" on right upper front
7E15808-9	C28(8)0(1)FF	x	x	5-12-67	D6	
7E17321-9	C28807FF	x	x	x	x	
4.2-liter E-type blocks, 2+2						
7E50086-9	x	R102?	x	6-1-66N (sic)	No mark	
7E50896-9	C26430FF	T519	x	24-3-66	No mark	
7E53417-9	C27880FF	AJ19	x	1-3-67	D1?	
7E53516-9	x	AK901	LER/?	31-3-67	D2	
7E60896-9	C26430FF	x	x	x	x	
4.2 S2 blocks						
7R5765-9	C29040/1	x	x	25-3-68	x	
7R14012-9	C29040 possible "/1"	BB820 side of block	x	5-3-70	1H4	"1H4" on lower rail; date on upper left
7R35669-9	x	B324	x	no date	A7	
4.2-liter MK X/420G blocks						
7D57540-9	C28( ) 0( ) FF	x	x	x	x	

In the notation used here, characters within parenthesis have been stamped with a punch in the location where cast numbers were ground off. An "X" means the marking is not known. The second column sometimes also includes the foundry markings (i.e. FF).

This C28807 block part number has had the second 8 and the 7 re-stamped. The authors do not know what characters were ground off before the stamping was done. This is engine 7E15808-9.

This block from Series 2 engine 7R5765-9 carries part number C29040. It is likely this was the last block part number used on 4.2-liter E-types.

ENGINE BLOCK POUR DATE MARKINGS

As in the case of the XK engines used on 3.8-liter E-types, most 4.2-liter engines had a pour date cast in. Initially this was in the same place as on the 3.8-liter blocks, on the lower left rear, just in front of the dipstick. Later it was moved to the upper right rear of the block. The cast characters located along the bottom left of the block, in front of the date, continued in 4.2-liter production. The longitudinal location of these characters varies, but typically the "HF" or "HFF" characters are located further forward on the block, as in the 3.8-liter case. One instance, 7E1221-9, has a single "F" cast in the forward position.

The "11-3-67" date on engine 7E53516-9 is preceded by a "D2" casting.

Pour date castings on the later blocks, such as this 25-3-69 date from Series 2 engine 7R5765-9, were cast on the upper right rear of the block. Interestingly, the style of the framing of the date is similar to that of the cast dates on the very early 3.8-liter E-types, with heavy bars above and below and no leading or trailing vertical components to the enclosure.

There are no characters in front of the 24-3-66 date on the block for engine 7E50896-9.

This 5-12-67 date on engine number 7E15808-9 is well boxed in. "D6" is cast in front. Note the two round pins or bosses above the "D" and the "6" characters. These are likely artifacts from pins or posts used to locate the forms for the characters on the block casting master.

On engine 7E50086-9 the date has an "N" suffix: "6-1-66N." The authors have only observed this suffix in this one instance.

This view of the Series 2 block from engine 7R14012-9 also shows no pour date mark on the lower left rear (it was on the upper right rear, typical for these later blocks) but has "1H4" cast in front of the area where the date was located on earlier blocks. There are no HF or HFF characters in the further forward region, as was often seen on 3.8-liter blocks. Note that this late block has five large core plugs (as opposed to the three plugs on earlier blocks) as well as having dipped-in features between the cylinders in the block outer wall (as opposed to the flat outer wall of earlier blocks).

The lower left rear of the block from engine 7R35669-9 shows "A7" cast in front of the dipstick hole boss.

ENGINE NUMBER STAMPINGS ON BLOCK

Similar to the practice used with 3.8-liter engines, the engine number, 7R5765-9, 7E50896-9, *etc.*, was stamped in many places on the components of the assembled engine (sometimes without the trailing compression ratio designation), including the engine block itself. In initial 4.2-liter production this number was stamped on the top of the oil filter boss on the lower central region of the block, in the same manner as the 3.8-liter E-types. The details of the characters used in making this stamping are covered elsewhere in this book. Later in production the engine number stamping on the block was moved to the outer face of the flange onto which the bell housing was bolted, on the left-hand side. While the earlier blocks had the engine-number stamped on the oil filter boss, the configuration of this boss changed during production. The earlier bosses were similar to those on the 3.8-liter blocks, with the five-bolt pattern to retain the aluminum filter head casting. The later blocks had, in addition, provisions for an engine mount (not used on E-types) to the front of the oil filter boss.

This block from engine 7R14012-9 has an un-stamped oil filter boss of the later type. These later blocks had the engine number stamped on the flange at the rear of the block where the bell housing attaches.

The first 4.2-liter blocks had the same style of oil filter boss as on the 3.8-liter cars. The right-most hole is one of the access ports for the oil gallery on the lower right side of the engine. These holes also give access to the oil lines to the main bearings. The hole for the main-bearing oil passageway in the middle of the block is located on the left side of the oil filter boss and is plugged with a flat-head slotted screw, as seen on the left of this picture.

An engine number stamped on the left side of the bell housing attachment flange at the rear of the block. This is engine 7R14012-9.

Later 4.2-liter blocks had an extension on the oil filter boss, towards the front of it, to accommodate an engine mount for use on other Jaguar applications of the XK engine. This is the block from engine 7R5765-9. Note the white paint on the area where the serial number is stamped (discussed on page 317).

TIMING CHAIN COVER STAMPINGS

As in the practice used with earlier XK engines, 4.2-liter engines typically had three letters stamped on the upper left of the timing chain cover and upper front of the block. These stampings are discussed in the 3.8-liter section on "Timing chain Cover Stampings."

BLOCK NUMBER STAMPINGS

As in the case of the 3.8-liter cars, an alphanumeric number was stamped on the right rear of the cylinder block. As in the case of the head-numbers, it is likely this was an inside Jaguar block numbering system assigned to all engine blocks. On some later engines, this number was stamped on the front part of the right side skirt of the block.

1 *Engine 7E4749-9 has the block number H51 stamped in the typical location at the right upper rear of the block. As with head-numbers, there are typically no leading zeros used in these numbers, such as "H051."*

2 *Another block number stamping. This one is "T519," and is found on the back of engine 7E50896-9.*

3 *The block number "AK901" (slanting 1 and not a 7 as it might be mistaken for) is stamped on the block from engine 7E53516-9, showing the later-type rear cooling water gallery cover, just to the left of the "AK901" stamping.*

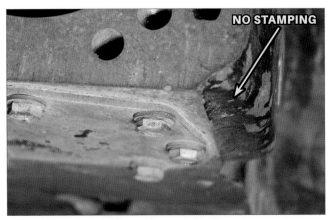

This rear view of the upper right rear of the block from Series 2 engine 7R14012-9 shows no block stamping. On at least some of these later blocks a number that appears to be the block number has been soon stamped on the skirt in front of the oil filter boss on the lower right-hand side of the block.

BB820 stamped on late 4.2-liter block 7R14012-9 on the top of the skirt of the block, just in front of the oil filter boss (outside the left of this picture).

PAINT

As with the 3.8-liter E-types, at least some of the 4.2-liter blocks had a light colored paint stripe over the engine-number stamping on the top of the boss for the oil filter. Some examples are shown here.

A reasonably well-preserved paint stripe on the top of the oil filter boss on engine 7E1310-8.

Light paint on the engine-number stamping of engine 7E15808-9.

An example of a Series 2 engine, 7R5765-9, with the light paint strip.

REAR WATER-JACKET COVER

The very early 4.2-liter blocks had a Welch plug in the casting port at the rear of the engine, in the manner of the 3.8-liter engines. The rear face of the block came further back than on the 3.8-liter cars and the Welch plug was of the cup type rather than the domed or dished type of the 3.8-liter engine blocks. Engine 7E1221-9 shows this configuration, but is the only one the authors have seen. Early in production the rear of the block was re-designed to have a bolted-on access cover on the rear of the water jacket. During 4.2-liter block production the size and shape of the cover changed. Some of the variants are illustrated here. It is not certain this is a complete list.

The early type of bolted-on rear water-jacket access cover, seen on engine 7E50086-9 (a 2+2 engine, so with engine number sequence beginning at 7E50001). Note the top central bolt hole for the bell housing on the rear of the block, just below, and central to, the bolted-on rear water-jacket access cover. This bolt hole was omitted on later engines.

View inside the rear section of the water jacket on engine 7E5316-9.

The later-type rear cover is seen here on engine 7E5316-9. Note the lack of the top central bell housing bolt hole. Contrast this picture to the lower right picture on page 315.

ENGINE BLOCK MARKINGS

Various types of cast and stamped-in markings are found on 4.2-liter blocks. A review of some of these is given here.

Several features are illustrated on this later 4.2-liter block from a Series 2 E-type: The cast date (5-3-70) at this point is located on the upper rear right-hand side rather than the lower left rear as for earlier blocks. The oil filter boss is no longer stamped with the engine number; the engine number 7R14012-9 (not seen here) is located on the outer surface of the bell housing flange on the left side of the engine. The two additional water ports (that mate to the additional holes in the later heads) are evident on the deck. They are seen located between the pair of head-stud holes between cylinders three and four.

This right side view of the Series 2 block of engine 7R14012-9 shows an impression of screws and washers left from the mold-making process. This has not been observed on earlier 4.2-liter blocks.

This view of the upper right front of engine 7R14012-9 shows an "A2" cast into the block (oriented upside-down). Similar sorts of characters are also found on various places on earlier 4.2-liter blocks.

This is a very late XK engine block. Note the pronounced scooped-out areas with vertical ridges between the cylinders. A British Leyland symbol is cast on the side of the block next to cylinder 2 (second from the rear). The authors are not aware of any such late-type block in an E-type when delivered from the factory. Note the engine mount bolted to the block just in front of the oil filter boss. This engine mount for fitting the engine in a sedan (or other Jaguars than the E-type) is the one that motivated the extension of the oil filter boss forward (including the additional forward holes) that is seen on late E-type blocks.

WATER PASSAGES ON DECK

During 4.2-liter E-type production the configuration of the cooling water channels between the head and the block changed. The mating holes on the head evolved similarly and this is discussed from in the section on 4.2-liter heads. This section examines the associated changes that took place on the deck of the block, against which the head is fastened.

E-type 4.2-liter blocks had symmetric pairs of oblong holes (cooling jacket or water jacket holes) to the right and left of each cylinder. Each side had two holes (for a total of four holes per cylinder), in contrast to the 3.8-liter blocks that had a single oblong hole on each side of the cylinder (giving a total of two holes per cylinder). This was in spite of the fact that the first of the 4.2-liter heads had a single oblong hole on each side of the cylinder (likely because early 4.2-liter heads appear to be basically the same as 3.8-liter type heads, which all had a single water jacket hole on each side). However, the new 4.2-liter XK block was introduced with dual water jacket holes on each side of every cylinder right from the start.

Later in 4.2-liter block production, however, the cooling ports on the face of the block changed. Two water-passage holes were added at the rear of the block and another two (smaller) water-passage holes were added in the region between cylinders three and four. These sets of holes were positioned laterally opposite each other from the longitudinal center line of the block face. Based on observations, it appears the two small central pair of holes was introduced before the introduction of the two larger holes at the rear. The authors have seen blocks without the rear two holes but with the two central small holes, but have never seen a block with the rear two holes but not the two central small holes.

1 View of the deck of a 3.8-liter E-type block showing the oblong single cooling port holes adjacent to the cylinders. All 3.8-liter blocks had this configuration.

2 Typical view of the dual oblong cooling water jacket ports adjacent to the cylinders of a 4.2-liter E-type block.

3 The block in engine 7E4749-9, does not have the two extra cooling water holes at the rear (as seen in the next image). The holes illustrated on the rear of the deck of the block are, from the back forward, in laterally-symmetric pairs: 1) the rear most head stud holes, 2) the oil return holes (just forward and outside of the stud holes) and, 3) directly to the left and right of the axial center line of the cylinder are the two pairs of oblong water jacket holes. In front of the cylinder is the next pair of head stud holes. From there the pattern repeats toward the front of the block (less the oil return holes which are used only at the rear of the block).

4 The block from engine 7R14012-9 shows the two additional cooling water holes at the rear of the deck. They are the two most-rearward holes just behind the last two stud holes and somewhat closer to each other. These two additional cooling water holes have significantly larger diameters than the pair of cooling water holes added between cylinders three and four. On the far left and right are the irregularly-shaped oil return holes, and between them the two rear head stud holes.

5 The central additional cooling-water holes. This is the block from Series 1 chassis 1E35732 and the engine number is possibly 7E17793-9.

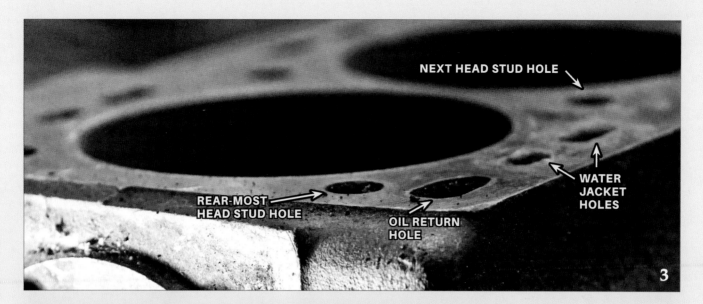

NEXT HEAD STUD HOLE

REAR-MOST
HEAD STUD HOLE

OIL RETURN
HOLE

WATER
JACKET
HOLES

3

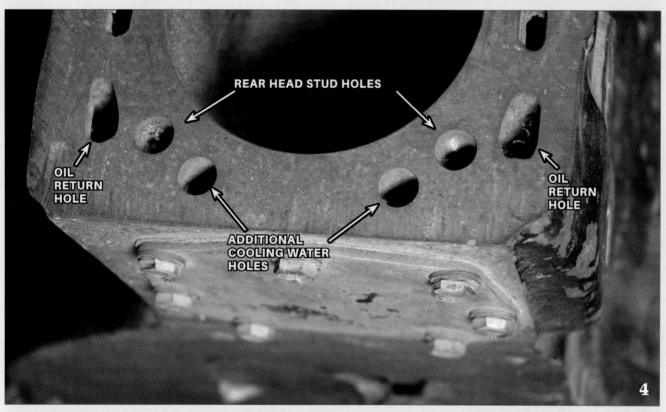

REAR HEAD STUD HOLES

OIL
RETURN
HOLE

OIL
RETURN
HOLE

ADDITIONAL
COOLING WATER
HOLES

4

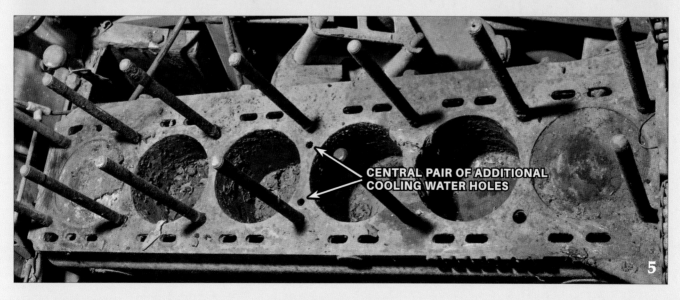

CENTRAL PAIR OF ADDITIONAL
COOLING WATER HOLES

5

In the later generation of XK blocks, as, for example, used in XJ6 sedans after the cessation of E-type production, there were five sets of the small pairs of cooling water holes, one pair between each adjacent set of cylinders. This same configuration appears to have been instituted on the cylinder heads, at or around the same time.

Two noted changes for the block in the literature are a note that the cylinder block assembly was changed (the core plugs and the block heater were changed) and the front timing cover was changed at engine numbers 7R1914/5 and 7R35388/9 and that about June 1969, the water drain spigot on the block was changed to a drain plug (the fiber washer was deleted, but the copper washer was retained) at engine numbers 7R5541/2 and 7R37654/5. Early 4.2-liter cars had a block drain spigot, as found on 3.8-liter cars.

CYLINDER HEAD AND CAMSHAFT COVERS

CYLINDER HEAD NOMENCLATURE

In this section the term "head-number" is used to refer to both the engine number stamped on the back of the timing chain gallery at the front of the head, as well as the actual head-number stamped on the raised stanchion at the rear of the head valley. It is assumed the rear number is the actual head-number, likely assigned to the head as it arrived at the factory from the foundry. The front is the engine number that appears on the head, block, flywheel and crankshaft. However, following common practice, at times "head-number" may be used to refer to the engine number stamped on the front of the head.

CYLINDER HEAD PAINT

The gold cylinder head paint used on the 4.2-liter cars up to about 1968 was close to, if not the same as, that used on the later 3.8-liter cars. Some photographs of paint from unrestored cars are shown here.

The paint on 7E3845.

The paint on 7E7256-9 appears slightly brighter than that on 7E3845-9. All these colors must appear somewhat different than when new due to aging and surface contamination.

View of the paint in the valley of head 7E7256-9.

CYLINDER HEAD PART NUMBERS

The 4.2-liter cylinder head part number system was more complicated than for the 3.8-liter cars. Shown as C14957 in the *J.30 Spare Parts Catalogue* (June 1963), the 3.8-liter cars had this head part number, (sometimes with the suffix "/1"), cast into the heads. The 4.2-liter cars had several head part numbers, including C14957/1 and there are discrepancies between the numbers found in the *J.37 Spare Parts Catalogue (November 1969)* and the *J.38 Spare Parts Catalogue (December 1966)* compared to the part numbers found cast or stamped on the heads shipped from the factory. This sort of discrepancy has been observed in other cases, for example, the 3.8-liter block part numbers.

PART NUMBER	PARTS CATALOG REFERENCE AND NOTES
C.23241	*J.37* (Nov. 1969), page 14 and *J.38* (Dec. 1966), page 15, for engines 7E50001 to 7E50021.
C.26202/1	*J.38*, (Dec. 1966) 2+2, page 15, for engines 7E50022 and subsequently.
C.26202	*Series 2 Parts List (1969)*, page 8, for engines up to 7R1914 for open and FHC and up to 7R35388 for 2+2.
C.28391	1969 Jaguar 'E' Type Interim Parts List, page 8, for engines 7R1915 and onwards for open and FHC and 7E35389 and subsequently for 2+2.

The various Parts Catalogs for the 4.2-liter cars indicated several part numbers, for example:

Some of the part numbers observed on 4.2-liter E-type heads some were cast, and some were stamped, in a manner similar to that used for the cylinder block part numbers. The following is a list of the head-numbers found on 4.2-liter cars. Here, as in other places, the parenthesis indicate that the characters contained within were stamped on (at the foundry or factory), either on a blank space or over ground-off part numbers:

    14957/1
    C(24540)
    (26200)
    C(26200/)1
    C2(62)00-2
    C26200C
    C28300
    C28300-A
    C24540
    P36677A
    P39209

The C2(62)00-2 stamping was on a poorly cast part number and perhaps the stamping was not done to change the part number, but to make it more clear. Thus it may be in fact an instance of a cast C26200-2 part number.

Data is presented below on several features found on a collection of 4.2-liter cylinder heads. These include:

- The engine numbers stamped on the back of the timing chain gallery at the front of the head (when present; engine numbers were not stamped on later 4.2-liter cars and replacement heads were issued without engine numbers stamped on)

- The part numbers

- What appears to be the foundry part number and the foundry (William Mills, WM or West Yorkshire Foundry)

- The foundry

- The head-numbers (found stamped on the cast stanchion at the rear of the head valley; all 4.2-liter E-type heads carry these)

- The letter cast into the central region of the valley

- The configuration of cooling ports on the deck of the head (single oblong cooling water ports on either side of the combustion chamber *vs.* short dual holes on either side)

- The presence or absence of two additional cooling water ports at the rear of the head (that align with companion ports on the block. The authors have seen this feature only on late long cylinder heads)

- The presence or absence of threads on the two large cooling water ports found between the three pairs of intake manifold ports

This William Mills head shows the C(24540) marking that seems to have followed the C14957/1 heads. The authors suspect the "24540" is stamped over a ground-off "14957/1." The early-type single long oblong water jacket ports on either side of the combustion chambers on the face of the head can be seen here.

ENGINE NUMBER	PART NUMBER	FOUNDRY NUMBER *	FOUNDRY	Head-number	VALLEY	SHORT OR LONG	BLOCK FACE PORTS	REAR PORTS	INTAKE PORT	NOTES
7E1221-9	14957/1	x	YWF	BF463	Z	X	X	X	Threaded	
7E3025-9	C(24540)	WM7286	WM	BE341	A	Short	Single	None	Threaded	(24540) over 14957?
7E3845-9	C(24540)	C1186	WYF	CD182	Z	Short	Single	None	No threads	(24540) over 14957
No Eng. No.	C(24540)	C1186	WYF	x	x	X	X	X	X	
7E8760-9	(26200)	C2143	WYF	CN831	Z	Short	Dual	None	No threads	
Un-stamped	C(26200/)1	C2143	WYF	DU48	Z	Long	Dual	None	No threads	
Un-stamped	C2(62)00-2	C2143	WYF	EJ462	Z	Long	Dual	None	X	
7E11567-9	C26200C	C2143	WYF	CX462	Z	Short	Dual	None	X	
7E12698-9?	C26200C	WM7286	WM	x	x	Short	Dual	None	X	
No Eng. No.	C28300	WM7286	WM	x	x	Long	Dual	None	X	
Un-stamped	C28300	WM7286	WM	CE340	A	Long	Dual	Two	X	Head No. GE340?
Un-stamped	C28300-A	WM7286	WM	IG423	None	Long	Dual	Two	X	Marks on back of head
No Eng. No.	C24540	C2143	WYF	x	x	Short	X	X	X	
Un-stamped	P36677A	WM7286	WM	M518	None	Long	Dual	None	Threaded	Plugs in intake water ports
Un-stamped	P39209	CP2626	WYF	FU829	6	Long	Dual	Two	X	Welch plugs in the valley
7D53022-9	C24540	C2143	WYF	CH499	Z	Short	Dual	None	No threads	From a MK X or 420G, but included for reference

* FOUNDRY NUMBER *refers to cast- or stamped-in markings that appear to be a labeling of the casting by the foundry, other than head or engine numbers.*

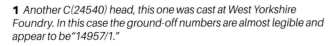

1 Another C(24540) head, this one was cast at West Yorkshire Foundry. In this case the ground-off numbers are almost legible and appear to be "14957/1."

2 A view of a West Yorkshire Foundry head showing the stamped-in 26200 part number (somewhat faint, to the right of the picture).

3 A C(26200)/1 part number. This carries the same C2143 number as the other stamped 26200 head. Possibly this is a part number used by the foundry.

1 This case of a "62" stamped on the cast in number, possibly C26200-2. This may be a clarification of the cast number, done at the foundry or factory, rather than an alteration of the part number.

2 A cast C26200C part number on a West Yorkshire Foundry head, also carrying the C2143 number.

3 A William Mills head with a cast C28300 part number. The "WM7286" number seems to appear on all 3.8 and 4.2 William Mills heads.

4 C28300-A on a William Mills head. The dual water jackets ports adjacent to the combustion chambers on the face of the head are evident here.

5 Cast C24540 on a West Yorkshire Foundry head.

6 This head with the P36677A part number is likely a factory-replacement head from the 1980s. It carries no engine number, but carries head-number M518.

7 Another later head, again likely a factory replacement head. It has no engine number, but carries head-number FU829. The meaning of the three castings shown is unknown.

ENGINE NUMBER STAMPINGS

An engine number stamped on the back of the timing chain gallery at the front of the head. In this case the dash is a "1" laid horizontally.

This engine number stamping has a dash made of a "1" laid horizontally to the right.

Later 4.2-liter heads, as well as factory-replacement heads, came with no stampings on the back of the timing chain gallery.

HEAD-NUMBER STAMPINGS

The head-number stampings at the rear of the valley of the head seem to roughly indicate the order being used for engine construction at the factory. This number continued to appear on the heads after the engine number, originally stamped on the back of the timing chain gallery at the front of the head, was discontinued. The blocks continued to get engine numbers. See additional notes under the 3.8-liter section on Head-Number Stampings.

1 A William Mills head-number stamp, this one on a 4.2-liter head from engine number 7E3025-9, showing the two screw heads or the far left and right. The orientation of the slots is not especially clear here. Again, note the width of the stanchion and the relatively rounded corners typical of a William Mills head.

2 Another William Mills rear head-number stamp, this from a 4.2-liter head without an engine-number stamp. Here the slots in the screw heads are more evident, with the left-most slot at the 10:00/4:00 position and the right-most almost vertical, close to the 12:00/6:00 position. Contrast this, for example, to the slot positions of engine R1037-9 in the chapter on 3.8-liter heads, or to head B236 below.

3 For comparison, here is a William Mills head-number stamp from a straight-port S-type head from an XK-150S. The stanchion shows clearly the two screw heads or the far left and right. Compare the orientation of the screw slots to the slot positions of engine R1037-9 (head-number B823) in the chapter on 3.8-liter heads, and to the slots on IG423 shown above.

4 This head-number is on the rear of a West Yorkshire Foundry head. The engine number stamped on the head is 7E3845-9. The stanchion here shows the shape with sharper corners. The authors have not seen the screw-head images in the stanchions on the West Yorkshire Foundry heads.

5 Another West Yorkshire Foundry head-number stanchion and stamping. In this case note the smaller font of the "U."

CYLINDER HEAD CASTING MARKS

As in the case of the 3.8-liter E-types, the casting marks varied. One set of characters seen was 330A, 380A or 368A. The authors do not know the meanings of these markings. Other marks include a stamped "V7" and a "40" or "47." Other marks are found.

1 *"Z2" cast in the water jacket area on the head from engine 7E3845-9, from the West Yorkshire Foundry. The marking is seen here through the water port between the intake ports.*

2 *This cast "M" is also located inside the cooling jacket area on another West Yorkshire Foundry 4.2-liter head and is seen through the same port.*

As in the case of the 3.8-liter heads, all the heads observed with an "A" cast in the valley were cast by William Mills and those with a "Z" were cast by West Yorkshire Foundry.

Interestingly, the authors have also observed cast marks inside the water jacket chamber of 4.2-liter heads, as shown in the figures. These marks may also be present in 3.8-liter heads, but the two brass cooling-port plugs would have to be removed to see them. This remains for future work.

OVERVIEW OF CYLINDER HEAD CONFIGURATION CHANGES

This overview section reviews the basic changes that took place during production of the 4.2-liter E-type cylinder heads. Details are given in following sections.

There were significant changes in 4.2-liter E-type heads during production. Initially, the heads were of the short type, as used on 3.8-liter cars. Later, they were increased in length, possibly in preparation for accommodating additional cooling-port holes at the rear of the head.

Initially, the long heads had only the oblong holes for water passage on either side of the combustion chambers, in the manner of the preceding short heads. During the production of the longer heads additional round cooling water holes were introduced. A pair of these holes was placed at the very rear of the head. As noted above, it is possible these holes were the reason, or one of the reasons, the long heads were introduced. Around the same point in production, or perhaps at the exact same point, two smaller holes were introduced, as a lateral pair, between combustion chambers three and four. Holes were

introduced in the block to go with these two pairs of head holes, likely around or at the same point in production. The authors do not have information on the sequence of the introduction of these holes in the head or block.

Later in production of the XK engine, still more holes were introduced. In the same manner as the two holes between combustion chambers three and four and in addition to them, eight more small-size holes were introduced. These additional holes were also configured as lateral pairs and were located between combustion chambers one and two, two and three, four and five and five and six. These additional holes have not been observed in front of combustion chamber six (the front-most chamber, just behind the timing chain gallery). Holes were introduced in late XK blocks to mate with these eight additional holes. The authors have not aware of heads or blocks known to have been supplied with E-types having these eight additional holes. It is likely that they were introduced after E-type production for use in XJ6 sedans. However, blocks and heads with these eight holes may have been produced by the factory as E-type replacement parts after the cessation of E-type production. If this is the case, these heads would be somewhat appropriate for use on 4.2-liter E-types, even though perhaps no E-types left the factory with them.

In addition, the oblong cooling water jacket passages to the right and left of the combustion chambers changed as noted below.

All 3.8-liter and 4.2-liter heads observed to date have the two rear oil return holes at the back of the head. While these holes seem to have varying shapes, the authors do not see a systematic evolution or change in these holes.

View of the face of head for engine 7E3845-9 showing the single oblong cooling ports on the right and left of each combustion chamber. This is an early short head.

A somewhat later 4.2-liter head, for engine number 7E8760-9, showing the oblong double cooling ports on the right and left of each combustion chamber. This is the short head and thus does not have the additional two cooling ports at the rear. The authors have also never seen a short head with the two small central cooling holes between combustion chambers three and four.

The next generation 4.2-liter head was the long head, with the protrusion at the head at the rear. Typically, this later head does not carry an engine number. Here, as observed on all long heads, are double oblong cooling ports on the right and left of each combustion chamber. This head lacks the additional two cooling ports at the rear and the two small central cooling holes between combustion chambers three and four.

Later in 4.2-liter head production, additional cooling water holes were introduced. Here, on the far right of this head (not carrying any engine number stamp), the two additional water holes in the head protrusion area are seen, as well as the pair of smaller extra cooling holes, centrally-located between combustion chambers three and four. These small holes are located just inside the central pair of head-stud holes. These holes have been referred to as "steam holes," but it is not known if this is factory nomenclature, or even if the terminology is an accurate description.

A yet later 4.2-liter long head, with no engine-number marking, showing the additional eight cooling ports between the remaining combustion chambers.

COOLING PORTS ADJACENT TO COMBUSTION CHAMBERS

On all XK engine heads there are oblong cooling water ports, or the water jacket ports, on the face of the head, to the right and left of the combustion chambers. On earlier 4.2-liter cylinder heads there was a single oblong port on either side of the chamber, in the manner of all previous XK engine heads. This was changed during XK engine production to a configuration with two shorter oblong ports replacing the single long port.

E-type 4.2-liter cylinder blocks have always been observed to have two pairs of oblong cooling water ports (one pair on either side of the cylinders), in the manner of the later 4.2-liter heads. However, the 4.2-liter cylinder heads were initially supplied with two single oblong ports (one port on either side of the combustion chambers, as in the manner of 3.8-liter heads) and later with two pairs of oblong ports (one pair on either side of the combustion chambers, as in the manner of the 4.2-liter blocks). Illustrations of these features of engine blocks are in the block sections.

Close-up of one of the single oblong cooling ports adjacent to the combustion chamber on a 4.2-liter head, engine number 7E3845-9.

The dual oblong cooling ports on the side of a combustion chamber on a later 4.2-liter head, engine number 7E8760-9.

CYLINDER HEAD COOLING PLUGS BETWEEN INLET PORTS

At the outset of 4.2-liter production it appears the heads had threads on the inside of the two water ports between the three pairs of intake ports. This may have been because these heads were basically 3.8-liter 14957/1 heads. Early in production these threads were omitted.

1 *A 4.2-liter cylinder head, engine number 7E3025-9, produced prior to the removal of the threads on the water ports. This design is likely a holdover from the gold-head 3.8-liter design used in the previous XK S-type engine where plugs were needed between the three separate intake manifolds. The 3.8-liter S-type XK engine was the first and only production engine to have more than one intake manifold and needed the two plugs to contain the coolant between the manifolds. The 4.2-engine reverted back to the standard Jaguar practice of using a single log-type intake manifold.*

2 *One of the two circular water ports on the intake side of the head of later 4.2-liter XK engine 7E8760-9. By this time threads were no longer included, in keeping with the more conventional single intake manifold configuration of the 4.2-liter S-type engine.*

3 *View of one of the two brass cooling plugs installed in this factory-replacement head. As a factory-replacement part, it had no engine number stamped on it (but carried head-number M518 stamped in the rear of the valley). With the plugs in place it could have been used on a 3.8-liter car with three separate intake manifolds (as apparently it was, given the outline of the paint subsequent to leaving the factory), or the plugs could be removed for use on a 4.2-liter car with the single-piece manifold. This head was from the William Mills foundry and carried the cast part number P36677A.*

CYLINDER HEAD LENGTH AND ADDITIONAL REAR COOLING PORTS

Earlier 4.2-liter cylinder heads were shorter than later 4.2-liter heads. Later in the production the 4.2-liter heads were made longer. Finally, the heads had two additional cooling ports at the rear. These ports matched up with two new water ports in the back of the block.

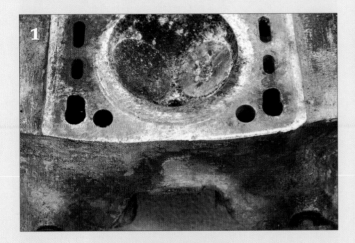

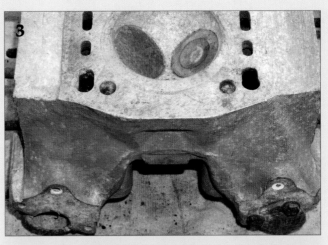

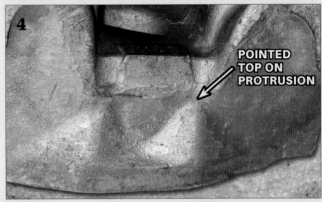

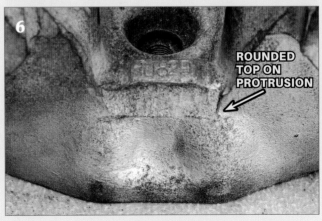

1 The rear of the face side of early-type short head, 7E11567-9.

2 The top side view of early-type short head, 7E3025-9.

3 Face side of a long head without the additional cooling ports that came later. This head carries no engine number.

4 Long head, with no engine number, top side. This head does not have the additional cooling ports. Note the pointed top on the protrusion at the rear of the head.

5 Face-side view of a long head, with no engine number, with the two additional cooling holes at the back. The various deck holes are shown here. From the top of the picture down (that is, front to back) on each side (symmetrically) there are: two oblong water ports, an oil return hole (irregularly shaped, as these often are), the hole for the rear-most cylinder head stud and the rear-most water passage port.

6 Top side view of a long head with the extra cooling holes. This head has no engine number. It appears to have a slightly different shape than the long heads without the extra cooling holes.

The two rear cooling holes added to the 4.2-liter heads were associated with two additional holes in the engine blocks. The authors have no evidence the additional two holes in the rear of the long heads and the additional two holes on the rear of the deck of the block were introduced at the same time. However, it is reasonable that they were close in the production sequence if not exactly the same.

View of the back of an early-type 4.2-liter block showing the absence of the rear-most two cooling holes.

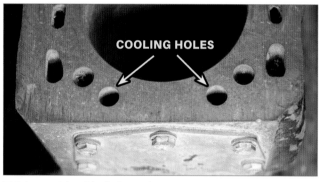

This later 4.2-liter block shows the two rear-most cooling holes that align with the associated holes in the rear of the long head.

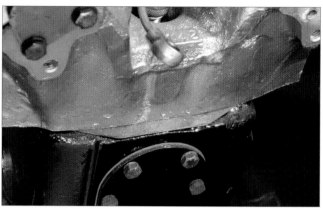

An early short 4.2-liter head in place on a 4.2-liter block. Note the block deck extends well beyond the back of the head.

A later long 4.2-liter head in place on a 4.2-liter block. Note that the center of the head extends back roughly to the rear of the block, but that the two lateral sections of the block deck are not covered by the head which does not extend as far back on its right and left.

View of a 3.8-liter engine, for reference. Note the C14957 head (nominally the length of the "short" 4.2-liter head) in the assembly extends rearward about the same amount as the standard 3.8-liter block to give a relatively flush seam. The decks of the 3.8-liter blocks were shorter than those on 4.2-liter engines.

Several changes are noted in the literature at the following engine numbers:

- ► 7E2895/6, the exhaust-side camshaft cover was changed and the fiber washer on the filler cap was changed to an O-ring.

- ► 7E6332/3, the exhaust manifold studs were changed.

- ► 7E7449/50 and 7E50021/2, in late 1966 or early 1967, the valve guides were fitted with circlips to cause a positive stop when the guides were pressed into the head the correct distance.

- ► 7R1914/5 and 7R35388/9 the cylinder head studs, the cylinder head assembly and gasket set were changed.

- ► 7R2082/3 and 7R35462/3 the camshaft covers and studs at the front of the head for fixing the camshaft covers were changed for U.S. and Canadian cars only.

- ► 7R4158/9 and 7R36599/600, about May 1969 the camshaft cover mounts at the front were changed to countersunk screws.

- ► 7R8687/8 the cylinder head assembly and the camshaft covers were changed.

- ► 7R8767/8 and 7R38894/5, about January 1970, the camshaft covers were changed so that all cars had mounting holes for the Emission control warm air duct, even if the duct was not fitted.

- ► 7E9209/10 and 7E50962/3, about December 1966, the cylinder head gasket was changed.

- ► 7E17864/5 and 7E52452/3, about December 1968, the valve seats were changed. *The Jaguar E-type: A Collector's Guide* notes that at engine numbers 7E11667/8 and 7E52686/7, about March 1967, oil seals were fitted to the inlet-valve guides.

At least some of the first type of finned camshaft covers had a separate cast-aluminum "JAGUAR" label attached. The later finned camshaft covers had this label cast into them. This is the typical configuration.

Sometime after the camshaft covers were changed from the traditional polished aluminum to the finned type, the name "JAGUAR" on the oil filler cap (on the left camshaft) was deleted. Chassis number 1E17271 (engine numbers 7E16522-9) had the Jaguar oil filler cap and 1E34580 (engine numbers 7E14113-9) and 1E35084 (engine number 7E15872-9) had the blank oil filler cap.

Interestingly, a late six-cylinder engine shown in a Series 3 E-type with "JAGUAR" on the oil filler cap is pictured in *Jaguar E-Type: The Definitive History*. This may imply that some of the late Series 2 cars had labeled oil filler caps.

However, Skilleter's *The Jaguar E-type: A Collector's Guide* featured another six-cylinder Series 3 car shown without Jaguar on the oil filler cap. Skilleter indicated that about four of these six-cylinder Series 3 cars were made, so they are likely very nonstandard and little about the production cars can be deduced from them.

Notes from the motoring press include a statement by *Autosport* magazine, October 29, 1970, that the cylinder head studs were recently increased in length and a statement was made in the May 1969 issue of *Car and Driver* that the cylinder head studs were increased in length from 4 to 12 inches. In *Modern Motor* magazine, March 1971, finned camshaft covers are shown on a late right-hand drive Series 2 engine (with three HD8 carburetors) with fins in the center to accommodate the absent center crossover pipe.

Early Series 2 cars had domed-nut retaining nuts on the front of the cam covers, in the manner of earlier Jaguars.

On the later Series 2 cars, a Phillips screw was used to retain the front of the cam covers.

The "JAGUAR" label on the finned camshaft cover of this late Series 1.5 is a separate casting from the cover.

Later cars had the "JAGUAR" label cast into the camshaft cover.

Early 4.2-liter oil filler caps had a recessed "JAGUAR" marking on them. This was discontinued sometime shortly after the introduction of the finned cam covers.

RIGHT: The authors have personally never seen this later-type oil filler cap on an E-type. It was likely only used on later cars, e.g. XJ6 sedans and possibly on E-types when owners sought a replacement. Note also the ridge spanning the cam cover retaining bolts on this later cam cover (on the right side of the picture, between the two chrome domed nuts). Contrast this to the cam covers shown elsewhere in this chapter (from E-types that lack this ridge).

A late oil filler cap without markings.

RIDGE

SUMP AND DRAIN PLUG

The sump was changed about April 1965 at engine numbers 7E2693/6.

At engine numbers 7E10008/9 and 7E52154/5, about March 1967, the front seal on the sump was changed; at engine numbers 7R5338/9 and 7R37549/50, about May 1969, the pointer for the timing marks on the crankshaft dampener was moved from the left-hand side of the engine back to the bottom of the engine (where it had been before), for cars with air conditioning or power steering; and at engine numbers 7R1345/6 and 7R35088/9, about December 1968, the pointer for the timing marks was moved from the bottom of the engine to the left-hand side.

See the "Sump" section in Chapter Six for more information.

1 The earlier 4.2-liter cars had a drain spigot to drain water from the block, on the lower left-hand side, in the manner of the 3.8-liter cars.

2 Late Series 2 cars had a block drain plug instead of the earlier spigot.

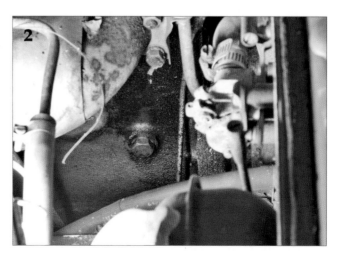

STARTER MOTOR

The authors are not aware of any changes.

ENGINE MOUNTS

The authors are not aware of any changes.

CRANKCASE BREATHER

About September 1965, the front cylinder head cover and the crankcase breather arrangement were changed from the non-U.S. type to a standard type for all cars. This occurred at chassis numbers 1E1252/3, 1E11048/9, 1E20691/2 and 1E31077/9. About May 1968, the breather pipe was changed to the type already fitted to left-hand drive cars, at chassis numbers 1E2050/1, 1E31806/7 and 1E51212/3.

OIL FILTER ASSEMBLY

At engine numbers 7E5169/70, about November 1965, the oil filter was changed from felt to paper.

The oil filter assembly was changed at engine numbers 7R2297/8 and 7R35582/3, although the nature of the change is not noted in the literature.

A late Series 2 oil filter assembly. Note the large diameter collar.

The early Series 1.5 and Series 2 oil filter assemblies were similar to those used on the earlier 3.8-liter and 4.2-liter cars.

TIMING CHAIN COVER

The bolt holding the timing chain cover to the cylinder block was changed to allow attachment of the alternator shield, at engine numbers 7E6332/3.

CRANKSHAFT DAMPENER AND PULLEY

At engine numbers 7E10956/7 and 7E52607/8, in about July 1967, the crankshaft dampener was changed.

Changes at engine numbers 7R13198/9 and 7R40325/6, in about August 1970, the crankshaft distance piece at the front of the shaft was replaced by a distance piece with an O-ring.

A bottom-mounted timing mark pointer. This one is red, but they are typically black. The damper pulley here is not an original one.

View of a side-mounted timing mark pointer with the timing marks (in degrees) marked on the crankshaft dampener pulley.

OIL DIPSTICK

The dipstick on the Series 1 and Series 1.5 cars was the same as used on the late 3.8-liter cars. With the introduction of the Series 2 cars, it was changed to a type with a red plastic disc on the top.

The Jaguar E-type: A Collector's Guide pictures two early Series 2 cars. The left-hand drive car has the plastic dipstick, while the U.S.-specification car has the early metal dipstick.

Based on observations it appears that the oil dipstick on cars prior to the introduction of the Series 2 had the traditional "STOP ENGINE, WAIT 1 MIN" warning cast in the chrome-plated brass.

The later oil dipsticks had the warning on a red plastic insert.

CRANKSHAFT, CONNECTING RODS, BEARINGS, CAPS, PISTONS AND RINGS

On page 2 of *J.37 Spare Parts Catalogue* (November 1969), it is indicated that the main bearing kit part number 10483 was "Required from Engine No. 7E.1001 to 7E.0000," and that main bearing kit part number 10766 was "Required at Engine No. 7E.0000." Perhaps the "0000" is a placeholder for an engine number transition point to be determined in the future. Placeholders are seen elsewhere in Jaguar literature. For example, on page 20 of *J.30 Spare Parts Catalogue* (August 1961) changes in the front cover and breather are said to have been "Fitted from Engine No. R.1001 to { blank }" and "Fitted to Engine No. { blank } and subs." These entries were replaced in *J.30 Spare Parts Catalogue* (June 1963) to indicate the changes occurred at 850091/2, 86004/5, 875385/6, and 885020/1. While the "0000" entries in J.37 are different in format from the blanks in J.30, it is possible they represent placeholders for information to be added later.

The Jaguar E-type: A Collector's Guide lists several changes: at engine numbers 7E1336/7, about December 1964, the connecting rods were changed (the new rods have a small hole at the small end to spray oil); at engine numbers 7E14212/3 and 7E53742/3, about July 1968, the connecting rod bearings were changed; and in January 1969, the connecting rod nuts, bolts and split pins were changed to bolts and plain nuts and the tightening torque was changed.

In July 1968 for 9:1 compression engines, the Hepworth & Grandage solid-skirt pistons replaced the Birco split-skirt pistons.

VALVES, VALVE GEAR, CAMSHAFTS, CHAINS AND SPROCKETS

Listed changes in this area: at engine numbers 7E50021/2, the shaft assembly for the intermediate timing chain sprocket was changed; at engine numbers 7R8687/8 and 7R38854/5, about November 1969, the camshafts were changed to give quieter valve operation and longer periods between valve adjustments; and at engine numbers 7R14074/5, about October 1970, the camshafts were changed so as to have no oil hole in the back. This was to reduce oil consumption.

The Jaguar E-type: A Collector's Guide notes that at engine numbers 7E50024/5, about September 1966, the intermediate sprocket was changed to cast iron.

OIL PUMP AND OIL DELIVERY SYSTEM

At engine numbers 7R7503/4 and 7R38501/2, about October 1969, the oil pump shaft was changed from one with a pinned-on inner rotor to one with a pressed-on rotor.

FUEL SYSTEM: CARBURETORS, MANIFOLDS AND ASSOCIATED EMISSION CONTROL EQUIPMENT

There were three basic styles of crossover pipes used on the Emission control cars. They occurred in the following order: the early rear-mounted crossover pipe, no crossover pipe and, last, the centrally-mounted crossover pipe.

Some Series 2 exhaust manifolds were finished with porcelain and some were not. On the last U.S.-specification Series 2 cars, with the central crossover pipe, the exhaust manifolds were not finished with porcelain and a shroud was used to direct intake air over the hot exhaust manifolds.

Sometimes the plastic damper assembly caps on the tops of the carburetors are found in a light tone instead of the standard black, but this may be the result of fading with time rather than the existence of a different type of cap. Some replacement caps had the "AUC" marking in white letters, as opposed to being molded. These caps may be replacements; it appears the caps supplied with the cars had the molded-in marks. This is illustrated in Chapter Three.

Changes noted in the literature for this area: at chassis numbers 1E1252/3, 1E11048/9, 1E20691/2 and 1E31077/8 the inlet manifold stud for the water outlet was changed and a stud and distance piece for the water outlet pipe and breather pipe were added for non-U.S. cars; at engine numbers 7E7297/8 and 7E50021/2, about September 1966, a low-lift carburetor cam was introduced to reduce engine speed when the choke was used and this included changes in the jet housing of the carburetors; at engine numbers 7R1837/8 and 7R35329/30, the inlet manifold and associated hardware, the carburetors and accelerator linkage were changed for U.S. and Canadian cars only; and at engine numbers 7R2082/3 and 7R35462/3, the rear exhaust manifold, the mixture housing on top of the rear exhaust manifold and its associated hardware, and the clip holding the dipstick were changed for U.S. and Canadian cars only.

The Jaguar E-type: A Collector's Guide notes that at engine numbers 7E1724/5, about January 1965, the inlet manifold was changed, in that the pressed-in vacuum fitting was replaced with a screwed-in one. The same source also states that at engine numbers 7E1881/2, about March 1965, the inlet manifold gasket was changed.

On the home-market Series 1.5 and Series 2 cars, the carburetors remained three S.U. HD8s.

1 *The intake-side view of an early air-intake crossover pipe on a U.S.-specification car. These early crossover pipes were polished aluminum.*

2 *The exhaust-side view of an early air-intake crossover pipe on a U.S.-specification car.*

1 This view of the crossover-pipe attachment point on the intake side of a 1968 Series 1.5 roadster chassis number 1E17271 shows domed nuts. While these do not appear to be of the style of any domed nuts used elsewhere on the E-type, the car was in one family since new and the current owner states these were the nuts it was delivered with. The authors have seen one other instance of an engine with these crossover-pipe nuts and that engine had been restored and cosmetically enhanced.

2 The exhaust-side view of the crossover-pipe retaining nuts on 1E17271.

3 The intake-side view of a later engine without an air-intake crossover pipe. Note the cover is retained by Phillips-head screws, as was typically the case not only for this cover, but for the attachment of many of the crossover pipes as well.

4 A shrouded exhaust manifold on a later Series 2 car.

5 Exhaust-side view of a late air-intake crossover pipe on a U.S.-specification car.

FUEL FILTER AND LINES

The literature notes that at chassis numbers 1E1904/5, 1E16056/7, 1E21661/2, 1E32771/2, 1E51042/3 and 1E77700/1 the fuel filter element was changed from gauze to a renewable fiber element. *Jaguar E-Type: The Definitive History*, cites a date of about July 1968 for this change, while Skilleter, in *The Jaguar E-type: Collector's Guide*, cites about February 1968. In addition, Skilleter cites chassis numbers 1E34771/2 instead of 1E32771/2 and numbers 1E50142/3 instead of 1E51042/3.

At chassis numbers 1E1895/6, 1E16009/10, 1E21628/9, 1E34633/4, 1E51016/7 and 1E77694/5, about July 1968, the fuel filter was changed to one with more filter area and at engine numbers 7E9291/2 and 7E51101/2, about December 1966, the fuel lines from the filter to the carburetors were changed.

AIR CLEANER

At chassis numbers 1E1252/3, 1E11048/9, 1E20691/2 and 1E31077/8 the base assembly for the air intake with three trumpets and the adapter for the breather pipe were changed to a standard type for all cars (U.S. cars were no different). At chassis numbers 1E1464/5, 1E12521/2, 1E21214/5 and 1E32596/7, about September 1966, the air cleaner and its support bracket were changed.

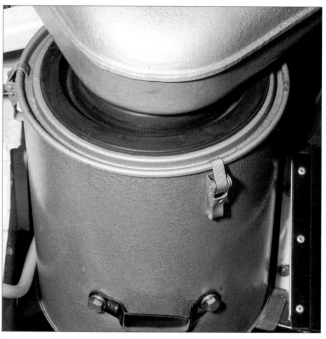

The air cleaner for Series 1.5 and early Series 2.

The late Series 2 air cleaners were more compact.

Top section of an air cleaner of the style used on the Series 1.5 and early Series 2 cars. These air cleaners were very similar to those used on 4.2-liter Series 1 cars. One obvious difference is the label pop-riveted to the top.

This charcoal canister on a 1970 Series 2 roadster was part of the fuel evaporation containment system required by U.S. regulations. It is mounted next to the brake vacuum assist on the left hand side of the car.

GAS TANK

Changes noted in the literature: at chassis numbers 1R1067/8, 1R7992/3, 1R20118/9, 1R25523/4, 1R35797/8 and 1R40667/8, about March 1969, the top part of the gas tank was changed; and at chassis numbers 1R1392/3, 1R11051/2, 1R20485/6 and 1R27050/1, the gas tank and cap were changed.

The later gas tanks had multiple, small vents on the left-hand side, as opposed to the single vent near the filter aperture.

The drain sump on the later 4.2-liter cars had a drain bolt in the bottom. This change occurred around the time of the Series 1.5.

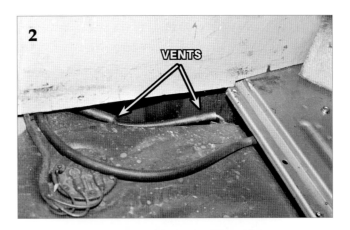

1 *The early gas tanks had a single straight vent on the top. Later 3.8 tanks, and all Series 1 4.2 tanks, had a curved vent.*

2 *Later gas tanks had multiple vents.*

3 *The early 4.2-liter gas tank sumps were similar to the later 3.8-liter sumps; they did not have a drain bolt at the bottom.*

4 *Later 4.2-liter gas tank sumps had a drain bolt on the bottom, as seen in this side view.*

5 *Bottom, view of a later sump showing the drain bolt end on.*

FUEL PUMP, MOUNT AND FUEL LINES

The fuel pump was changed from the submerged type to an outside type with the introduction of the Series 1 4.2-liter cars.

FUEL LEVEL SENDER UNIT

The authors are not aware of any design changes to the fuel-lever sender.

IGNITION SYSTEM: COIL AND BRACKET

At engine numbers 7E16754/5 and 7E54608/9, about July 1968, the coil was changed to one with a push-in high-tension coil wire and with "+" and "-" replacing SW and CB.

The coil on Series 1.5 and early Series 2 cars was found sometimes mounted on the top of the intake manifold and sometimes at the front of the cylinder head (the position it was found on in the Series 1 cars). The later Series 2 cars had the coil mounted on the right front frame cross-member.

Later replacement Lucas coils can differ markedly from those originally fitted. For example, see the section on coils in Chapter Six.

Right side view of a front-mounted coil on a Series 1.5 engine.

Left side view of a front-mounted coil on a Series 1.5 engine. This coil appears to be a later replacement; the originals were bare aluminum, not gold colored, as appears to be the case here.

A coil mounted on the intake manifold of a Series 2 engine.

The frame-mounted coil on a late Series 2.

DISTRIBUTOR

The distributor was changed at engine numbers 7R7973/4 (and 7R7506).

DISTRIBUTOR ROTOR, CAP AND WIRE RETAINERS

About April 1965, at engine numbers 7E2458/9, a water-proof cover was added to the distributor. Neither the *J.37 Spare Parts Catalogue* (*November 1969*), nor the *J.38 Spare Parts Catalogue* (*December 1966*), mentions this change, but errors and omissions have been found in Jaguar spare parts catalogs.

The spark plug wire organizing system on a Series 2 car.

A suppressor was used on the distributor cap of Series 2 cars exported to Denmark.

SPARK PLUG WIRES AND ORGANIZERS

It appears that all 4.2-liter cars, to the last Series 2s, had the vinyl conduit tube for the spark plug wires lying in the trough of the cylinder head.

SPARK PLUG CAPS

The spark plug caps came in at least two types for the Series 1 4.2-liter cars: the oval-top caps and the bowtie top caps. The bow-tie caps are more typical. These cap types are illustrated in Chapter Three.

SPARK PLUGS

Champion N.5 spark plugs were used on 4.2-liter Series 1 cars.

BALLAST RESISTOR

About January 1970, a ballast resistor was added to the ignition system. This occurred at chassis numbers 1R1392/3, 1R11051/2, 1R20485/6, 1R27050/1, 1R35642/3 and 1R42849/50.

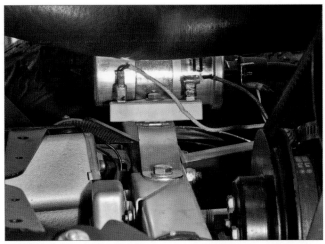

A ballast resistor on a Series 2 car. This is possibly a later replacement.

COOLING SYSTEM: RADIATOR AND FAN SHROUD

Listed radiator and shroud changes are at chassis numbers:

- ▸ 1E2050/1, 1E31806/7 and 1E51212/3, the radiator was changed to a vertical-flow type, as already fitted to left-hand drive cars (the date for this change is alternately listed as April and July of 1968);

- ▸ 1R1183/4, 1R9456/7, 1R20260/1 and 1R26319/20, the cooling fan cowl was changed;

- ▸ 1R1189/90, 1R9594/5, 1R20271/2 and 1R26401/2 the radiator was changed.

HEADER TANK

At chassis numbers 1E2050/1, 1E31806/7 and 1E51212/3, about July 1968, the header tank and cap were changed.

The Series 1 4.2-liter header tank and cap were similar to those used on the 3.8-liter cars, but they are not interchangeable. The hose attachment points were different, and there was an additional attachment point on the 4.2-liter tank.

This rear view of an NOS 4.2-liter header tank shows the two ports on the right hand side, as opposed to the single port on the 3.8-liter tanks.

This front view of a 4.2-liter header tank shows the cooling fan thermal sensor switch located on the lower front, as opposed to the top as on the 3.8-liter tanks. The switch is not installed on this NOS part, but the location of the port and the associated three holes for the retaining screws can be seen.

Later Series 1.5 and Series 2 cars had a header tank mounted on the firewall.

WATER PUMP AND PULLEY

Listed water pump and pulley changes: at engine numbers 7E1404/5 about December 1964, the pulley and water pump were changed to make removal easier (the studs and bolts for the water pump were changed to bolts); at chassis numbers 1E2050/1, 1E31806/7 and 1E51212/3, about April or July 1968, the water pump assembly was changed to the type already fitted to left-hand drive cars; and at engine numbers 7R1914/5 and 7R35388/9 the water pump assembly was changed.

The Jaguar E-type: A Collector's Guide notes that at engine numbers 7E17157/8 and 7E54836/7, about June 1968, the water pump pulley and belt were changed to increase pump speed. The same source also notes that at engine numbers 7R4488/9 and 7R36957/8 about May 1969, the water pump spindle was changed.

HOSES AND CLAMPS

The hose clamps were basically the same as those used in the 3.8-liter cars. Listed changes for hoses and clamps: at chassis numbers 1E1225/6, 1E10957/8, 1E20611/2 and 1E30981/2, about June 1965, the left-hand water-feed pipe to the heater, behind the dash panel, between the water control valve and the heater radiator, was changed; at engine numbers 7R1837/8 and 7R35329/30, the heater-hose return pipe at the right-hand side of the cylinder block was changed; and at chassis numbers 1R1195/6, 1R9642/3, 1R20277/8 and 1R26428/9, the top water hose from the radiator to the water manifold was changed.

THERMOSTAT

Production changes in the thermostat: at chassis numbers 1E2050/1, 1E31806/7 and 1E51212/3, the water outlet housing and thermostat housing were changed. The thermostat was changed to the type already fitted to left-hand drive cars. Dates of about April and July of 1968 are cited for this change; and at engine numbers 7R5263/4 and 7R37488/9, about May 1969, the thermostat was changed from 74 to 82 degrees Celsius. Some sources cite engine numbers 7R5262/3 instead of 7R5263/4 and numbers 7R37488/9 are not cited.

Changes at engine numbers 7R14048/9: The thermostat was changed about October 1970.

CHARGING SYSTEM: ALTERNATOR AND BRACKET

The alternator heat-shield arrangement went through at several configurations during the production run of 4.2-liter cars. The early 4.2-liter Series 1 cars had no alternator shield, but a metal one was added for the late Series 1 cars. Early Series 2 cars had no shield, but one was later adopted.

When air conditioning was fitted, the alternator was mounted high in front of the engine, facing towards the rear of the car.

Production changes to the alternator and bracket: at engine numbers 7E6332/3, an alternator shield was added about May 1966. The alternator shield was introduced on all E-types at the time of introduction of the 2+2. At this same point the bolt holding the timing chain cover to the cylinder block was changed to allow the attachment of the alternator shield; at chassis numbers 1R1012/3, 1R7442/3, 1R20006/7, 1R25283/4, 1R35010/1 and 1R40207/8, about January 1969, the alternator was changed to have side-entry cables, for cars not fitted with air conditioning; and at engine numbers 7R5546/7 the alternator was changed for cars without air conditioning.

The Jaguar E-type: A Collector's Guide notes that at engine numbers 7E3422/3, about June 1965, the alternator bracket was changed; and at chassis numbers 1R9456/7, 1R26319/20, 1R35332/3 and 1R42012/3, about August 1969, a composite bracket was introduced to mount the alternator, air conditioning compressor and the power steering pump.

OPPOSITE:

1 *Early cars had no shield around the alternator. This is the early alternator.*

2 *This shield was added to the alternator about the time of the introduction of the 2+2. This is again the early alternator.*

3 *At the start of Series 2 production, there was no shield on the alternator. This is the late alternator.*

4 *Later on in Series 2 production, a second type of heat shield was introduced.*

5 *When air conditioning was fitted, the alternator was relocated. Here it is seen mounted in front of the upper belt tensioner on a Series 2 2+2. This view also shows the rubber attachment point for the later crankcase breather mechanism, on the center front of the head.*

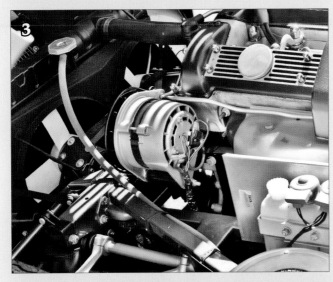

SHIELD

PULLEYS AND BELT

The alternator pulley was different on cars exported to Canada and the United States.

Listed production changes: at engine numbers 7E1404/5, about December 1964, the water pump and pulley were changed to make pump removal easier; and at engine numbers 7R5546/7 the alternator belt for cars without air conditioning was changed to a different type for cars exported to the United States and Canada.

The Jaguar E-type: A Collector's Guide notes that at engine numbers 7E17157/8 and 7E54836/7, about June 1968, the water pump pulley and belt were changed to increase pump speed.

VOLTAGE REGULATOR AND BRACKET

The authors are not aware of any production changes to the regulator or bracket.

BATTERY, CABLES, TRAY AND MOUNTS

The early batteries were of the tar-topped design (where the top of the battery is tar-covered, unlike modern batteries with injection-molded covers) similar to those supplied with the 3.8-liter cars. Later batteries had a long, red plastic single-piece cap. It is reported that this type of battery was supplied originally on 1967 2+2 chassis number 1E75930, a very original car with approximately 6,000 original miles, although this seems in conflict with evidence from the literature that indicates the early cars were supplied with the tar-topped battery.

This Lucas battery with one-piece cap was used on late E-types.

ELECTRIC: WIRING HARNESS

Wiring harness production changes from the literature at chassis numbers:

- ▸ 1E1162/3, 1E10771/2, 1E20362/3 and 1E30856/7 (except 1E20335), about June 1965, the forward wiring harness and front lamp harness were changed;

- ▸ 1E1164/5 and 1E20370/1 the forward wiring harness and the instrument panel harness were changed;

- ▸ 1E10753/4 and 1E30824/5 the instrument panel wiring harness was changed;

- ▸ 1E50165/6 and 1E75546/7 the forward wiring harness, the instrument panel harness and the alternator harness were changed;

- ▸ 1R1012/3, 1R7442/3, 1R20006/7, 1R25283/4, 1R35010/1 and 1R40207/8 the alternator harness was changed;

- ▸ 1E1412/3, 1E11740/1, 1E20999/1000 and 1E32009/10 in about March 1966, the front wiring harness was changed.

WINDSCREEN WASHER

The early 4.2-liter cars used a pump and reservoir assembly, similar to those used in the 3.8-liter cars. A glass bottle was still used, but there was no reservoir chamber around the impeller at the intake.

Changes at chassis numbers 1E1164/5, 1E10753/4, 1E20370/1 and 1E30824/5, in about June 1965, the windscreen washer bottle was changed to plastic and pre-timed operation was deleted.

All Series 1.5 and Series 2 cars had the plastic bottle.

On some late 2+2s, the bottle was located farther to the right of the engine compartment, near the end of the right-hand sill.

BRAKE LIGHT SWITCH

The authors are not aware of any production changes to the brake light switch.

The plastic pump and reservoir assembly of the later 4.2-liter cars. This is the firewall-mounted configuration.

A plastic pump and reservoir assembly on a Series 2 2+2, mounted down and to the right, at the end of the right-hand sill. The bottle is held in a black-painted sheet steel bracket attached to the region where the commission plate was affixed on earlier cars.

COOLING FAN, RELAY AND SWITCH

Changes at chassis numbers 1E1430/1, 1E12169/70, 1E21139/40, 1E32315/6, 1E50156/7 and 1E76000/1: in about September 1966, the cooling fan thermostat was changed.

The authors have seen both screws and studs with nuts used to fasten the thermostats.

Changes at chassis numbers 1E2050/1, 1E31806/7 and 1E51212/3: in about April 1968, the single cooling fan was replaced by dual cooling fans, as already fitted to left-hand drive cars. This change is listed only in *The Jaguar E-type: A Collector's Guide*.

Changes at engine numbers 7R5263/4: The cooling fan thermostatic switch was changed.

In the *Popular Imported Cars* magazine, January 1969, a five-bladed fan, with what appears to be aluminum blades, is shown mounted on the front of the air conditioner condenser on the front of the radiator of a left-hand drive Series 1.5 roadster. The associated text says that this fan was fitted on cars with air conditioning. The authors have seen no other evidence for this, however.

A discussion of a Series 2 left-hand drive roadster in *Car and Driver*, May 1969, states that two cooling fans operate thermostatically, unless air conditioning is fitted, in which case they both are kept on at all times. No mention of a third fan is made.

HORN AND RELAY

At chassis numbers 1E1062/3, 1E10771/2, 1E20362/3, 1E30856/7, but also on the earlier chassis number 1E20335, the horns were changed about June 1965. In some sources, chassis numbers 1E1162/3 are cited instead of 1E1062/3.

A horn mute was fitted to Series 2 cars exported to Holland.

TACHOMETER, PRESSURE AND TEMPERATURE SENDERS

Changes noted in the literature: at chassis numbers 1E50165/6 and 1E75546/7, the oil pressure-ignition warning light-switch adapter at the right-hand side of the cylinder block was replaced by a plug, and a control unit for the ignition warning light was added.

These production changes occurred at chassis numbers 1E1723/4, 1E13150/1, 1E21480/1 and 1E33090/1, about July 1967. There were numerous changes in the electrical equipment. An ignition warning light replaced the oil pressure switch and the old oil pressure switch in the cylinder-block oil gallery was replaced by a plug, and at chassis numbers 1Rl586/7, 1R12955/6, 1R20722/3, 1R27869/70, 1R35787/8 and 1R43772/3, about April 1970, the fan control thermostat was changed.

BRAKES AND HYDRAULICS: BRAKE AND CLUTCH FLUID RESERVOIRS AND MOUNTS

It was reported that at chassis numbers 1E1483/4, 1E12637/8, 1E21234/5, 1E32666/7, 1E50007/8 and 1E75074/5, about September 1966, a rubber cover was added to the tops of the brake fluid warning terminals.

The authors have seen no evidence that any 4.2-liter cars ever came without them.

The authors are aware of one occurrence of a small metal cap being used on the clutch reservoir of a 4.2-liter car. This occurred on chassis number 1E16928. The owner said this cap had been on the car when it was new and that another car next to it in the showroom had the same cap (this cap is illustrated in Chapter Three, as it was observed on a 3.8-liter car as well). The standard knurled clutch reservoir cap is made with white plastic. The authors have not heard nor seen any other evidence of a metal cap being fitted.

The standard knurled clutch reservoir cap was made of plastic.

BRAKE AND CLUTCH RESERVOIR HEAT SHIELD

The Jaguar E-type: A Collector's Guide states that at chassis numbers 1E1544/5, 1E12964/5, 1E21334/5 and 1E32887/8, about December 1966, a heat shield was introduced for the head pipes.

HYDRAULIC LINES, SWITCH, CYLINDERS, SERVO AND ACTIVATION MECHANISM

Changes listed in the literature at chassis numbers are:

- 1E1076/7, 1E10429/30, 1E20136/7, 1E30442/3, 1E10427 and 1E20132, the hydraulic pipe from the front flexible hose to the front brake calipers was changed;

- 1E1412/3, 1E11740/1, 1E20999/1000 and 1E32009/10, about March 1966, new brake and clutch master cylinders and pedal housings were fitted to standardize the two-seater cars with the 2+2 cars and the brake light switch was re-positioned;

- 1E1560/1, 1E13010/1, 1E21341/2 and 1E32941/2, about November 1966, the clutch and brake master cylinders were modified to have shorter pushrods to change pedal angles and to improve the accelerator pedal angle. There was also a change in the accelerator pedal assembly.

The Jaguar E-type: A Collector's Guide reports that at chassis numbers 1R1060/1, 1R7829/30, 1R20101/2, 1R25438/9, 1R35098/9 and 1R40507/8, in about March 1969, the master cylinder spacer (for the clutch?) was changed.

BRAKE VACUUM SYSTEM

At chassis numbers 1E1019 /20, 1E10323/4, 1E20081/2 and 1E30268/9 the vacuum reservoir was changed.

The 4.2-liter reservoirs may have been supplied new with "TRICO" markings, as illustrated in the 3.8-liter section in Chapter Three.

MISCELLANEOUS: STEERING

At chassis numbers 1E1412/3, 1E11534/5, 1E20992/3 and 1E31764/5, about March 1966, the steering assembly was changed (a seven-tooth pinion replaced the eight-tooth one) to improve steering when radial-ply tires were fitted.

The Jaguar E-type: A Collector's Guide states that at chassis numbers 1E1234/5, 1E11165/6, 1E20632/3 and 1E31243/4, about November 1965, the rack and pinion assembly was changed.

HEATER

The Jaguar E-type: A Collector's Guide states that at chassis numbers 1E2038/9 and 1E21783/4, about April 1968, the dashboard was revised. The heater controls, choke and switches were changed and the heater box was changed. This may also be the introduction of the rocker switches, which was possibly simultaneous with the addition of the glovebox lid (except for the 2+2 cars, which had it earlier).

DRIVETRAIN:
BELL HOUSING, FLYWHEEL, CLUTCH, SLAVE CYLINDER AND TORQUE CONVERTER

Some early 4.2-liter cars may have had a flywheel inspection hole in the bell housing, as on the 3.8-liter cars. Most 4.2-liter cars do not have this inspection hole.

It is interesting to note that there is evidence of black paint being sprayed near the edges of the front of the bell housing (as well as sometimes on the top bolts of the gearbox and the front of the cylinder head), with much over spray. This is seen, for example, on pages 163 (a 3.8-liter) and 369 (a 4.2-liter) of *Jaguar E-Type: The Definitive History*.

The later bell housings did not have inspection holes.

LEFT: *The early 4.2-liter bell housings had an inspection hole on the upper left side. This housing is likely from an early 4.2-liter car, but may be from a later 3.8-liter car.*

Changes listed in the literature at engine numbers:

▸ R2587/8 and 7R35730/1, about March 1969, the clutch cover assembly was changed to a new one with stronger springs (in some sources, an exception is given for engine numbers 7R2784 to 7R2791);

▸ 7E4606/7 the clutch slave cylinder, return spring and operating rod were changed;

▸ 7R9709/10 and 7R39111/2, about March 1970, the clutch operating rod was altered to allow greater adjustment tolerances;

▸ 7R10747/8 the release bearing and cup assembly were changed;

▸ 7E52275/6 the torque converter housing was changed (for cars fitted with automatic transmissions).

▸ 7E7810/1 and 7E50046/7, about September 1966, the clutch disc was made a little convex (the new disc is marked with light blue and purple paint near the center);

▸ 7E13500/1 and 7E53581/2, about July 1968, the clutch was changed from a Laycock to a Borg & Beck diaphragm type;

▸ 7E12159/60 and 7E53209/10, about January 1968, the adjuster and pivot pin for the clutch operating rod was changed;

▸ 7E11818/9 and 7E52716/7, about January 1968, the number of bolts holding the bell housing to the cylinder block was reduced from nine to eight, with the top one being omitted.

1 The early 4.2-liter bell housings had a center top attachment bolt.

2 Later 4.2-liter bell housings did not have the center top attachment bolt. Notice that the raised area in the casting was still present, even though no hole was drilled for a bolt.

3 This bell housing with the top central hole and side hole (seen on the left of the picture) has recessed regions around the bolt bosses on the top. This is seen below the bent steel rear engine mount that is bolted to the top of the bell housing. This is either an early 4.2-liter bell housing, or from a 3.8-liter car. In any case, this sort of design was probably used on early 4.2-liter cars.

RECESSES AROUND BOLT BOSSES

LARGE BOLT BOSSES

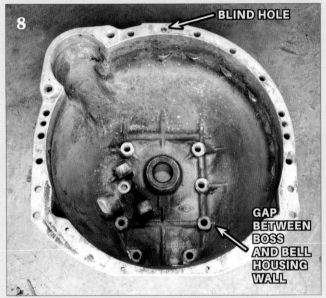

BLIND HOLE

GAP BETWEEN BOSS AND BELL HOUSING WALL

SMALL BOLT BOSSES

4 It appears the earlier bell housings were cast at West Yorkshire Foundry.

5 Later bell housings generally show a legend that appears to be "DIALOY" in a lozenge-shaped frame.

6 Inside view of an early-type West Yorkshire Foundry bell housing showing the bosses around the bolt holes where the transmission-attachment bolts pass through. The bosses are smaller than typically found on later bell housings.

7 The bosses on this later Dialoy housing are among the larger type the authors have observed.

8 Here a Dialoy housing has very small bosses. Note the bosses on second horizontal pair of holes from the bottom do not reach to the outer wall of the bell housing. It is likely there are even more boss designs than the ones shown here. Note also here that the top central bell housing-to-engine bolt hole is partially drilled out. This blind hole comes in from the side of the bell housing facing the viewer.

TRANSMISSION AND MOUNTS

In November 1964, a chamfered idler gear was introduced to reduce gearbox noise.

Listed changes for the transmission:

- EJ245/6, about January 1965, the housing for the rear oil seal and its gasket, were changed;

- EJ944/5, about March 1965, the roller bearing on the gearbox constant pinion shaft was changed;

- EJ3169/70 the constant pinion shaft was changed to include an oil thrower and the spacer under the roller bearing was no longer required (this change is listed as occurring both about September 1965 and February 1966).

At engine numbers 7E51451/2, about September 1966, the automatic transmission kickdown control rod and cable and the automatic transmission itself, were changed.

Additional changes at transmission numbers:

- EJ7919/20 and EJS7919/20, about November 1966, a retaining washer was added to the shift lever.

- EJ11776/7 and EJS11776/7, about July 1967, the synchromesh spring was changed

- KE11768/9 and KJS2858/9, about March 1970, the clutch release bearing was changed (the new one was stated to be identified by a ridge in the bore of the thrust pad;

Changes at engine numbers 7R6572/3 and 7R38135/6, about August 1969, the oil seal in the speedometer drive gear was changed; and at chassis numbers 1R35656/7 and 1R43164/5, about January 1970, the automatic-transmission selector lever was changed.

In *Motor Sport* magazine, April 1966, the transmission is said to be a ZF unit, but the authors have seen no other evidence for this. In fact, in the May 1969 issue of *Car and Driver*, while discussing a left-hand drive Series 2 roadster, it is stated that the box is not a ZF. In *Car* magazine, June 1970, the gearbox is referred to as a Jaguar unit and no mention is made of ZF.

FLYWHEEL AND CLUTCH

Both 10-inch diameter and 9.5-inch diameter clutches were used on 4.2-liter cars.

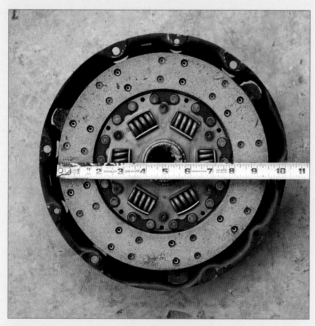

While some 4.2-liter clutches were 10-inches in diameter, for a while 9.5-inch diameter clutches were used.

Pressure plate from a 4.2-liter car. This is one variant; the earlier pressure plates were 10-inches in diameter, but this changed to the 9.5-inch size shown here. There is a diaphragm spring in this pressure plate, as opposed to the coil springs used on some 3.8-liter cars.

DRIVESHAFT

The authors are not aware of any production changes to the driveshaft.

DIFFERENTIAL

Production changes for the differential at chassis numbers:

- 1E1151/2, 1E10702/3, 1E20328/9 and 1E30771/2, about May 1965, the axle ratio was changed from 3.31:1 to 3.07:1 for all cars except those exported to the United States, Canada and Newfoundland, which were 3.54:1. Some sources cite chassis numbers 1E1072/3 instead of 1E10702/3;

- 1E10739/40 and 1E30806/7 the 3.54 rear end assembly was changed for cars exported to the United States, Canada and Newfoundland;

- 1E1177/8, 1E10783/4, 1E20396/7, 1E30861/2 (for 3.07:1 rear ends), 1E10739/40 and 1E30806/7 (for 3.54:1 rear ends), in about June 1965, the rear end changed to a type with driveshaft flanges as part of the driveshafts.

The Jaguar E-type: A Collector's Guide notes that at chassis numbers 1E1886/7, 1E15981/2, 1E21619/20 and 1E34602/3, in about September 1967, the Powr-Lok differential was discontinued as standard, except for the U.S. 3.54:1 ratio axle.

The Series 2 final drive unit was changed at chassis numbers 1R1243/4, 1R9939/40, 1R20334/5 and 1R26575/6 (except numbers 1R9929/30 were cited instead of 1R9939/40, possibly in error).

CHASSIS: FRONT WHEEL HUBS

The authors are not aware of any production changes to the front wheel hubs.

A-ARMS AND PIVOTS

As with the 3.8-liter car, the A-arms of the 4.2-liter cars came in both dark and light finishes. The dark finishes were likely black paint, while the light-finished ones were plated. From the evidence it appears the dark A-arms were found only on some early 4.2-liter Series 1 cars and subsequently all A-arms were bright.

Production changes in the A-arms at chassis numbers:

- 1E1038/9, 1E10337/8, 1E20097/8 and 1E30291/2, about March 1965, the sealing at the front ball joints was improved;

- 1E1046/7, 1E10337/8, 1E20099/100 and 1E30301/2 (and 1E1021, 1E20083 and 1E30271) the left-hand tie rod lever was changed;

- 1E1076/7, 1E10429/30, 1E20136/7 and 1E30442/3 (and 1E10427 and 1E20132) the front suspension was changed.

FRONT TORSION BARS

About August 1970, larger diameter torsion bars were fitted to right-hand drive cars at chassis numbers 1R1775/6 and 1R20954/5. At chassis numbers 1E50874/5 and 1E77406/7, in about July 1968, the diameter of the torsion bars was increased.

FRONT SHOCK ABSORBERS

The authors are not aware of any production design changes to the front shock absorbers.

FRONT ANTI-ROLL BAR

The authors are not aware of any production design changes to the front anti-roll bar.

REAR ANTI-ROLL BAR

The authors are not aware of any design changes.

REAR WHEEL HUBS AND CARRIERS

While the early 4.2-liter rear hub carriers have the same appearance as the 3.8-liter ones, later on in 4.2-liter production the shape of the casting was changed. The early-type casting has smooth side walls, while the later type has the side walls dipped in near the lower pivot mounting points.

The rear hub carrier and its oil seal were changed at chassis numbers 1E1236/7, 1E10978/9, 1E20638/9 and 1E31002/3. At chassis numbers 1E1762/3, 1E15109/10, 1E21488/9 and 1E34302/3, about July 1967, the rear hub carriers were changed.

Initially, 4.2-liter cars had rear hub carriers with smooth side walls, in the manner of this later 3.8-liter type hub.

Later rear hub carriers had a dipped-in region on the side.

RADIUS ARMS, TRAILING ARMS AND HALFSHAFTS

At chassis numbers 1E1925/6, 1E16720/1, 1E21668/9, 1E34850/1, 1E51066/7 and 1E77704/5, in the first part of 1968, grease nipples were reintroduced on the halfshaft universal joints. In some references, chassis numbers 1E16126/7 are cited instead of 1E16720/1 and numbers 1E50166/7 are cited instead of 1E51066/7.

REAR SPRINGS, SEATS AND SPACERS

At chassis numbers 1E1376/7, 1E11363/4, 1E20899/900 and 1E31526/7, about November 1965, the rear coil springs were changed and at chassis numbers 1E1489/90, 1E12692/3, 1E21253/4 and 1E32684/5, about September 1966, a rubber seat was added to the top of the spring in the rear transmission mount and the spring retainer was changed.

As in the 3.8-liter cars, the authors are not aware of any deviations from a black-painted finish on the rear springs.

REAR SHOCK ABSORBERS

At chassis numbers 1E1292/3, 1E11120/1, 1E20762/3 and 1E31176/7, about November 1965, the rear shock absorbers were changed.

BRAKES

Listed changes in the brakes at chassis numbers:

▸ 1E1046/7, 1E10337/8, 1E20099/100 and 1E30301/2 (and 1E1021, 1E20083 and 1E30271), about February 1965, shields were added to the front brake discs;

▸ 1E1046/7, 1E10337/8, 1E20099/100 and 1E30301/2 (and 1E1021, 1E20083 and 1E30271) the bolt and washer mounting for the front caliper to the stub axle carriers was changed;

▸ 1E1076/7, 1E10429/30, 1E20136/7 and 1E30442/3 (and 1E10427 and 1E20132), about March 1965, the front calipers were altered to move the bleed screw to the inner side of the assembly.

With the introduction of the Series 2 cars, the brakes were changed to Girling.

Series 2 listed changes in the brakes at chassis numbers:

▸ 1R1243/4, 1R9939/40, 1R20334/5 and 1R26575/6, the mounting of the rear brake calipers to the final drive unit changed and the adapter plate was discontinued;

▸ 1R1410/1, 1R11302/3, 1R20509/10, 1R27173/4, 1R35647/8 and 1R42993/4, about November 1969, the front flexible brake hose was changed.

PARKING BRAKE

At chassis numbers 1R35421/2 and 1R42400/1, about March 1970, the handbrake lever was changed to one with a different material in the pivot pin and lever.

FRONT WHEEL WELLS AND ENGINE COMPARTMENT UNDERSHIELDS

At chassis numbers 1E1386/7, 1E11546/7, 1E20936/7 and 1E31778/9, in about March 1966, a mud shield was fitted to the front frame.

WHEELS, WEIGHTS AND HUBCAPS

With the onset of the U.S. regulations came the change from the eared to the earless knock-off hubcaps. As in the case of the 3.8-liter cars, earlier Series 1 4.2-liter cars shipped to Germany had the early version of the earless knock-off hubcaps (as mentioned in Chapter Three). The U.S.-regulation earless knock-off hubcaps had three rounded lobes instead of the two square lobes of the early earless variety.

The newer three-lobed version was introduced for the U.S. market at or very close to the introduction of the Series 1.5 cars. Standardization of earless knock-off hubcaps for all cars came in sometime after the introduction of the Series 2. Therefore, some non-U.S. Series 2 cars have eared hubcaps.

The literature notes that at chassis numbers 1E1813/4, 1E11534/5, 1E21517/8, 1E34338/9, 1E50911/2 and 1E77474/5, a forged center hub and straight spokes were introduced for chrome wire wheels only. Some sources cite chassis numbers 1E15486/7 instead of 1E11534/5. Dates of May 1967 and July 1968 are cited for this change. Note that these are not the same numbers as the introduction of the Series 1.5 cars, but are close (see Chapter One). This is the introduction of the "easy-clean" wheels.

At chassis numbers 1E1852/3, 1E15752/3, 1E21578/9, 1E34457/8, 1E50971/2 and 1E77601/2, about July 1968, a forged hub was introduced for the painted wire wheels.

Series 2 changes occurred at chassis numbers 1R1053/4, 1R20072/3 and 1R35098/9 with earless knock-off hubcaps introduced on right-hand drive cars (as on the left-hand drive cars) about February 1969.

Right-hand drive Series 2 cars are seen with and without eared knock-off hubcaps.

While most 4.2-liter cars seem to have had chrome wheels, painted wheels were also available.

The disc wheel option came in after the introduction of the Series 2 and therefore was not available on early Series 2 cars. The disc wheel option cost more than the standard wire wheels.

The original wheel weights found on the Series 1 4.2-liter cars were marked with the weight and clipped to the rim of the wheel in the usual way.

The Series 1 4.2-liter E-types were initially fitted with the same style of wheel used on 3.8-liter cars. It is possible a few late Series 1 cars may have been fitted with the new easy-clean hub Series 1.5 and Series 2 wheels, and some early Series 1.5 cars may have been fitted with the early wheels. Note the early-type eared knock-off hubcaps.

The flat hub, sometimes called the "easy-clean" hub, wheel was introduced approximately with the Series 1.5 cars. Note the earless knock-off hubcaps that were a result of the U.S. Federal regulations commencing in 1968.

1 *Turbo Disk pressed steel wheels were an option on Series 2 E-types. This type of wheel was continued to be offered on the Series 3 V-12 cars. It is likely the six-cylinder cars had this escutcheon in the center, similar to the horn button. However, it appears some Series 3 V-12 cars and possibly some six-cylinder Series 2 cars, may have had the Jaguar head in the middle with a black background.*

2 *This hubcap from a Turbo Disk wheel from a Series 2 car shows a feature like the horn press in the center of the steering wheel.*

3 *This hubcap shows an unlabeled Jaguar-head image surrounded by black. These were used on sedans and possibly some E-types. This hubcap is interchangeable in fit with the one with the horn press image in the center.*

4 *This Turbo Disk wheel is from a Series 3 V-12. The hubcap came fitted with a Jaguar head and black background, as used on sedans.*

5 *At some point during E-type production, spoke nipples with the three-slot configuration shown at the left were used. The earlier wheels had the single slot. The authors are not sure when this came in, but the three-slot spokes are often found on Series 2 type wire wheels.*

6 *The earliest type of 4.2-liter E-type wheel was the early dished-in center hub (now often referred to as "curly hub").*

7 *Rear view of the early curly hub.*

8 *This is a modern reproduction wheel, in the general type of the early curly-hub Series 1 E-type wheel design. Note the thicker section of the central hub.*

1 *Close-up of an original curly hub. Note the ends of the spokes are not sunk into the hub, as is seen on some later reproductions.*

2 *Close-up of the outer part of the hub on a modern reproduction early curly-hub Series 1 type wire wheel. Here the thicker section of the reproduction hub is evident. Also, the spoke heads can be seen to be sunken into the thicker hub. These hubs may have been machined or cast, but do not appear to be stamped or swaged, in the manner of the original curly-hub wheels.*

3 *Inner view of the hub of an original curly-hub wheel. Note the spoke heads are not sunken into the hub.*

4 *Inner view of a hub from a modern reproduction wheel. Note the spoke heads appear to be sunken into the hub, as in the view from the outer side.*

5 *Modern reproduction wire wheels are often seen with this RTV-like (Room Temperature Vulcanization) material covering the spoke nipples. The authors have never seen any such material on original wheels. However, a rubber rim band or rim strip was used to cover the spoke nipples in the central valley of an original wheel. This was to protect the inner tube from the spoke nipples and spoke-ends, although this rim band does not seem to appear in the Spare Parts Catalogue. The coating on these modern wheels is likely to permit fitting of tubeless tires by preventing air leakage around the spoke nipples.*

TIRES AND TUBES

Initially, the 4.2-liter cars were supplied with Dunlop RS.5 tires, but Dunlop radials were used later. The later-type 3.8-liter RS.5s are similar, or possibly, in some cases, identical to those used on early 4.2-liter cars. The first radials were SP.4ls and they were first fitted as standard in England in October 1965. As with the later 3.8-liter cars, when whitewalls were fitted, they were the narrow type.

At chassis numbers 1E1408/9, 1E11714/5, 1E20977/8 and 1E32008/9, about March 1966, the standard tires were changed to Dunlop SP.41 HR tires, except for cars exported to Australia, Canada, Newfoundland, New Zealand, or the United States and at chassis numbers 1E1919/20, 1E16098/9, 1E21668/9, 1E34846/7, 1E51058/9 and 1E77704/5, about July 1968, the tires were changed to Dunlop SP Sport and whitewalls were used for cars exported to the United States.

In *Motor* magazine, January 13, 1968, it is stated that radial tires came in with the Series 1.5 cars, but it is likely they were standard earlier.

Motor magazine, September 7, 1968, pictures a Series 1.5 roadster with tires that are stated to be Dunlop SP Sport. The Dunlop SP Sport radials were adopted on the Series 1.5, but had been an option on the home-market cars since 1965. *Car and Driver*, May 1969, in discussing a left-hand drive Series 2 roadster, stated that the tires are 185VR15 Dunlop SPs. A right-hand drive Series 2 2+2 is stated to have come with Dunlop SP Sport tires in *Car* magazine, June 1970.

At least some loading and tire specification plates from late Series 2 cars indicate "185.VR15, SP.SPORT" tires.

The early 4.2-liter cars were fitted with Dunlop RS.5s, in the same style as the late 3.8-liter cars. When whitewalls were included on these tires, they were narrow, as seen here.

According to *Modern Motor*, March 1971, Dunlop Aquajet tires were standard on a late right-hand drive Series 2 coupe (an Australian car).

The tires on the 4.2-liter cars were either blackwalls or narrow whitewalls. In *Jaguar E-Type: The Definitive History*, it is stated that for the Series 2 cars, the U.S.-delivery cars were fitted with whitewalls and that for other markets a different whitewall was available as an option.

Close-up of a late RS.5 with italic letters and narrow whitewall. As with the 3.8-liter cars, both whitewall and blackwall tires were fitted.

Dunlop SP41 radial tires replaced the cross-ply RS.5s. Here is a blackwall example on a Series 1 wheel.

An SP41 with lettering in outline. This lettering has been observed on early Dunlop radial tires.

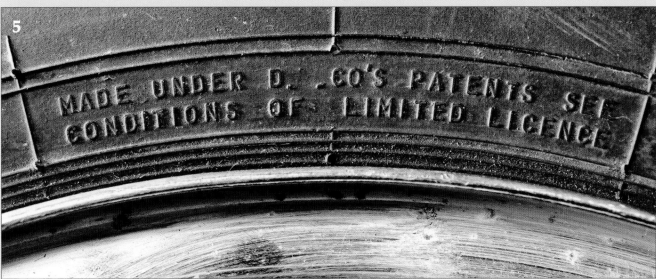

1 Some markings on the front of the SP41.

2 The size designation is given as "185-15 (185-380)." In this section on the front of the SP41 it is referred to as an "SP RADIAL."

3 The rear carries a "MADE IN GREAT BRITAIN" legend.

4 Also on the rear is a mold insert, but without any markings.

5 Another legend on the rear of the same SP41.

6 The SP41s were superseded by Dunlop SP Sports. This a narrow whitewall version, with outline lettering. This tire is mounted on what is likely its original later flat, or "easy-clean," hub.

1 The outline lettering that the authors suspect was the initial form of the lettering style on Dunlop radial tires.

2 The size designation on the same SP Sport as shown in Figure 1 showing the outline lettering style.

3 The SP Sport is referred to as a "DUNLOP RADIAL." It carries the words "TUBED TYPE."

4 Legend denoting number of plys and loading limits. The tire is labeled as "RAYON," and it carries a DOT designation.

5 On the reverse of the same SP Sport is the licensing information and the modern "D" in a chevron Dunlop trademark.

6 Mold insert markings on the rear of the Dunlop SP Sport. This may be an indicator of which plant produced the tire.

7 This Dunlop SP Sport differs in many ways from the tire shown earlier. The lettering is no longer in outline and many of the markings are different. This may be a later tire from a Series 3 V12 car; it is shown here for comparison purposes.

8 "DUNLOP SP SPORT" lettering on this second example. Here, as in the previous example, the newer Dunlop trademark is to the left of the main legend.

9 As in the case of the earlier SP Sport illustrated here, this tire is also referred to as an "SP RADIAL" on the front. The size designation is now given as ER70VR15.

10 The mold insert states "TUBELESS."

11 Loads and pressure legend on a mold insert on the front of the SP Sport.

12 The "MADE IN GREAT BRITAIN" and "RAYON" legends, as well as the ply ratings.

The back of the tire gives the license information and again states "TUBELESS" in a mold insert.

REAR SUBFRAME, MOUNTS AND STOPS

At chassis numbers 1E1408/9, 1E11714/5, 1E20977/8 and 1E32008/9, about March 1966, special rear suspension bump-stops were used to avoid fouling the new Dunlop tires.

TUBING AND CABLES

The authors are not aware of any production changes.

FRONT SUBFRAME

The front subframe assembly changed at chassis numbers 1R1187/8, 1R9569/70, 1R20269/70, 1R26386/7, 1R35352/3 and 1R42117/8 (but 1R3532/3 and 1R42117/8 were not included).

On some late Series 2 cars, the frame grounding strip is fitted between the upper-right front subframe mount and the firewall. This strip has been observed affixed both with a bottom mounting and with a top mounting.

A bottom-mounted grounding strip from the front subframe to the firewall on a late Series 2 roadster.

The grounding strips on the late Series 2 cars were also mounted on the top of the subframe bolt.

EXHAUST SYSTEM

The exhaust manifold changed in the U.S.-specification cars as the crossover-pipe arrangements changed. This is discussed earlier in this chapter.

EXHAUST HEAT SHIELDS

The authors are not aware of any production changes to the exhaust heat shields.

LEFT: *The typical orientation of a fuel filter bracket on an early 4.2-liter car (seen from above looking straight down) with the firewall on the left. The fuel outlet pipe leading to the carburetors (in the upper right quadrant of the picture) is made of rigid metal, as opposed to the flexible polymeric lines used on the 3.8-liter cars. Only one of the two holes on the mounting flange is being used for attachment to the frame (the unused hole is seen on the flange). Using only one mounting bolt helps the filter mate to the rigid fuel outlet pipe. Use of the polymeric lines on 3.8-liter cars did not require this arrangement.*

REAR PIPES AND RESONATORS

The Series 1 4.2-liter cars had the usual short, large-diameter section and long small-diameter section resonators used with the later 3.8-liter cars. Resonators with slightly turned-down tips are shown on a coupe in the July 1966 issue of *Road & Track*. These may be after-market units, but the car in question appears from the text to be new.

At chassis numbers 1E1598/9, 1E13181/2, 1E21379/80, 1E33119/20, 1E50155/6 and 1E75991/2, about December 1966, the mufflers changed from being welded to the tailpipes to being clipped to them. A similar change occurred earlier during 3.8-liter production at chassis numbers 850178/9, 860011/2, 875607/8 and 885058/9.

At chassis numbers 1E1689/90, 1E13846/7, 1E21450/1, 1E33708/9, 1E50640/1 and E76933/4, about July 1967, the linkage between the tailpipes was changed from bolted to welded. This change would bring the inter-tailpipe mounting configuration back to the welded type of the 3.8-liter cars of 1961.

With the restyling of the Series 2 rear end, the resonators had to splay around the license plate.

The circular-type muffler clamps, as used on the 3.8-liter cars (as seen on the bottom of page 260), were used on the 4.2-liter cars, at least into Series 1.5 production.

The splayed-out resonators of the Series 2 cars. The bumper guard across the tops of the overriders is an after-market part.

CHAPTER 6

10
20
30
40
50
60
70
80
90
100
110
150
160
SMITHS
MPH
IGNITION
FUEL
HEADLAMPS

FEATURES RELATING TO BOTH 3.8-LITER AND 4.2-LITER CARS

This chapter covers features of the E-type that do not appropriately fit in the basic model categories: 3.8-liter or 4.2-liter (spanning Series 1, Series 1.5, and Series 2). In addition, while it is not the goal of this book to describe the difference between the different basic models, in a few cases where there might otherwise be confusion, the differences between 3.8- and 4.2-liter cars are discussed.

CRANKSHAFT GRUB PLUGS

The grub plugs found on the drilled-out oil channels on the XK-engine crankshafts appear to have been changed at the transition from the 3.8-liter to the 4.2-liter engine design. It appears the threaded plugs on the 3.8-liter crankshafts are always smaller than those on the 4.2-liter crankshafts.

A threaded plug from a 4.2-liter crankshaft, these are larger than those typically seen on 3.8-liter crankshafts.

A small-diameter 3.8-liter threaded plug.

VALVE CLEARANCE ADJUSTMENT SHIMS

The valve clearance of E-types was adjusted by selecting appropriately-sized shims to go between the top of the valve stem and the inside top of the tappet. A system of letters was used to indicate the size of the shim (this is given in the Jaguar Service manuals and the parts catalogs).

Various sizes and shapes of characters were used to mark the shims. Some shims had the prefix to the part number, C2243, stamped or etched into them, with the remainder of the part number (the letter denoting size) opposite the part number. For example, part number C.2243/K, an adjusting shim (referred to as a "Pad" in the *J.30 Spare Parts Catalogue (June 1963)* might have C2243 along one side of one face, with the K opposite it. Typically shims so marked have the markings etched or stamped into the surface, rather than being a shallow surface marking.

Some shims were marked by what appears to be an etching process, which principally discolors the surface, but does not noticeably cut down into it. These letters come in different sizes and are sometimes surrounded by a circle. In both types of shim marking systems a "+" or "-" was sometimes used as a suffix to the letter marking. The temporal sequence of these different types of markings is not known, nor is it known if there was a progression of marking types or if they were used at the same time.

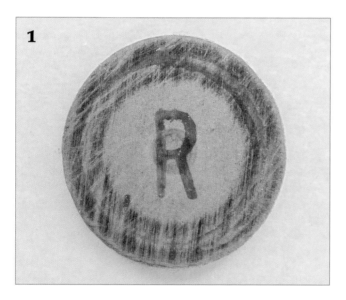

1 An "R" marked shim. This character is large, and does not have a circle around it.

2 An "R" marked shim. This character is large and has a circle around it.

3 A "P+" marked shim, this one carrying the first part of the part number opposite the size marking. Markings are by inset stamps or etching. This shim surface shows pronounced machining marks and some others are quite smooth.

4 A shim with a "Q" size marking. This shim has been used and shows the central circular wear mark where the top of the valve stem made contact. The depth of the "Q" marking is evident in that it is still present in the region where the wear occurred (the very top of the "Q").

5 Another "Q" marked shim, this one with the light etching. This is one of the "smooth" types of shims; other show clear machining marks.

6 Several lightly-marked shims showing some of the various lettering styles and surface marks.

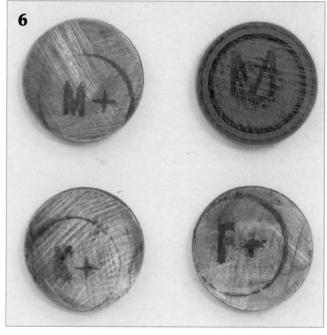

7 At least two types of shims exist. On the left is a used shim with tapered shoulders and from the worn surface finish it can be seen to have not made contact around the edge. The shim on the right was also used, but the wear on the surface indicates contact essentially right to the edge. It appears most of the shims are of the type on the right. Perhaps the one on the left is an after-market shim.

SUMP

This section discusses some differences between the late 3.8-liter finned sumps and the 4.2-liter sumps. The rear of the 3.8-liter sumps had a 180-degree raised ridge at the rear to mate with the rear main seal mount, while the 4.2-liter sumps had a recessed channel in this same section, as illustrated here.

BELOW: On the left is an early non-finned 3.8-liter sump, a later finned 3.8-liter sump is in the middle and a 4.2-liter sump is on the right. Note the thin flanges on the lower half of the circumference of the opening at the rear of the first two sumps. Note also that the rear of the 4.2-liter sump on the right has a wide flange around the lower half of the circumference. This lower 180-degree half-circle mates against the outside surface of the rear main seal housing. Note the four ribbed supports on the flange.

This is a 3.8-liter sump, showing the 180-degree circumferential flange with no groove. The rear main seal housing (that on its inner surface seals against the rear of the crankshaft) is the part that mates up with this flange on the rear of the sump. There is a gasket strip between the lower part of the rear main seal and the curve in the sump. Note the inner circumference is raised.

The relieved groove in the rear of a 4.2-liter sump.

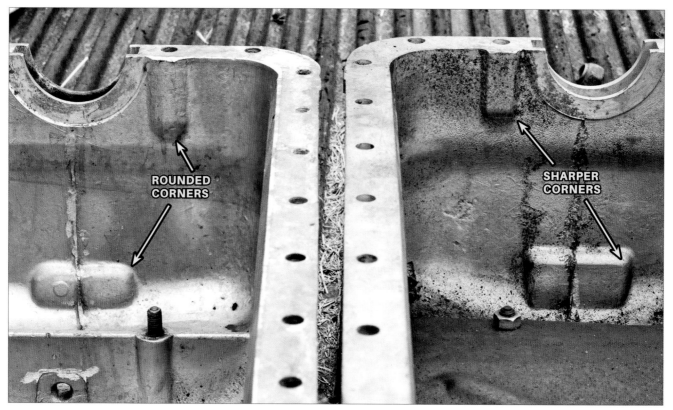

View of the inside of the front of a 3.8-liter sump, on the left, and a Series 1 4.2-liter sump, on the right. The 3.8-liter sump has rounded corners on the bosses for the bolt hole nearest the front main seal, and on the boss for the timing marker bolt holes cast in the bottom front of the sump. Note the sharper corners on the edges of the same bosses on the 4.2-liter sump.

HOSES AND CLAMPS

There were several different manufacturers of the cooling-system hose clamps used on E-types. Some of the ones observed by the authors are discussed here.

CHENEY DOUBLE GRIP HOSE CLAMPS

One of the most common types of cooling system hose clamps is the Cheney Double Grip.

The "DOUBLE GRIP BS3628" clamp.

The "DOUBLE GRIP BS3628" clamp.

The "DOUBLE GRIP" with clamp, showing the size.

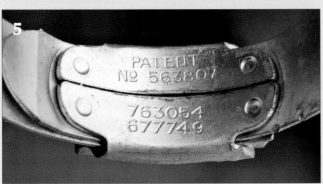

1 The "DOUBLE GRIP" lamp, showing the size.

2 The "DOUBLE GRIP" AGS.605 clamp. This seems to be one of the most common types.

3 The "DOUBLE GRIP" AGS.605 clamp.

4 A "1A" marking on a Cheney Double Grip clamp.

5 Patent markings on a Cheney Double Grip clamp.

6 Round symbol on a Cheney Double Grip clamp.

7 BS mark on a Cheney Double Grip Clamp. If the Cheney clamp has a BS number, or the British Standard kite mark, the clamp was made in 1963 or later.

8 "HE" markings on a Cheney Double Grip clamp.

CHENEY CONNECT HOSE CLAMPS

Another common cooling system hose clamp is the Cheney Connect.

The "CONNECT" AGS.605 clamp.

The "CONNECT" AGS.605 clamp.

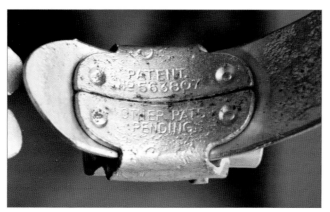

Patent markings on the inside of a Cheney Connect clamp.

OTHER CHENEY HOSE CLAMPS

A Cheney AGS.605 clamp with size denoted.

The AGS.605 clamp with size denoted. In this case, "00."

Patent markings on the inside of a Cheney AGS.605 clamp.

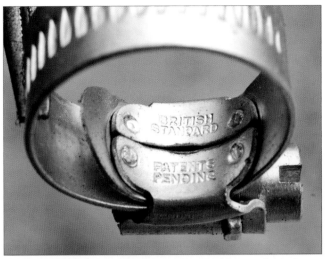

A different type of patent marking, no actual patent numbers given, on the inside of a Cheney AGS.605 clamp.

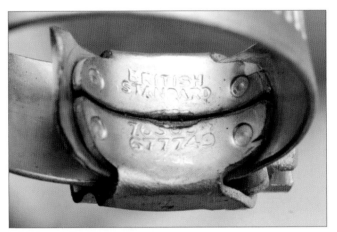

"BRITISH STANDARD" and patent marking on a Cheney AGS.605 clamp.

JUBILEE HOSE CLAMPS

Jubilee was another type of clamp found on E-types.

Top part of markings on Jubilee clamp.

Lower part of markings on Jubilee clamp.

BS and other markings on the side of a Jubilee clamp.

Inside view of a Jubilee clamp.

TERRY'S HOSE CLAMPS

Top view of a "TERRY'S SECURITY" clamp.

Bottom view of a "TERRY'S SECURITY" clamp.

Inside view of a "TERRY'S SECURITY" clamp.

Oetiker Hose Clamps was another type the authors have seen on E-types.

CARBURETORS: FLOAT CHAMBER TAGS

See information on this topic in the 3.8-liter section. This section contains some 4.2-liter car comments, but principally relates to 3.8-liter cars, so is retained in Chapter Three, beginning on page 180.

IGNITION COIL

Data was collected on many coils during the research for this book. The coils examined included those dated somewhat before E-type production commenced, to those made years after E-type production ended. Many, but not all, of the coils were known to be from E-types. Thus caution is advised in examining the data.

The following table shows data collected from coils. The "CB/SW" or "+/-" markings are those molded into the plastic top of the coil, as is the "MADE IN ENGLAND" marking. All coils had "LUCAS" molded in. The other markings (the date, model and what is referred to here as "type" markings) are stamped into the bottom of the aluminum can housing of the coil. The exception is the very late coils that have the bottom markings on a sticker.

The "SA12" marked coils are the special equipment coils. These have corrugated brown molded tops. Otherwise, all the tops listed in the table are molded in black plastic, unless "white" is noted in the "notes" column. The authors have never seen other colors than these three and are not aware of any E-type leaving the factory with a white molded coil top.

Some coils from cars earlier than the E-type are included in the table (to show the sequence of numbers), and at the end of the table some coils after E-type production are included. These late coils may have been made as NOS units that may have been fitted to E-types by dealers as replacements.

Spade connectors came in several variations, as illustrated here. However, as noted above, it is not certain all the combinations shown here were fitted to E-types at the factory. Early E-type coils generally had screw-on spade connectors, while later ones were fitted with rivets.

The information in the following table is from a collection of Lucas coils, mostly or all from Jaguars and many from E-types. *J.30 Spare Parts Catalogue (June 1963)*, cites, on page 277, under coil part number C.8749, the additional numbers "45067/D-HA.12." However, from observations of unrestored cars it is probable that coils carrying part number 45104 were fitted by the factory as well. As with 4.2-liter engine blocks and numerous other examples, the parts catalog is often not correct.

CONTACT MARKING	CONTACT ATTACHMENT	"MADE IN ENG" MARKING	DATE (LEFT)	DATE (RIGHT)	MODEL	TYPE	12V STAMP	NOTES
CB/SW	Screw	None	5	55	HA12	45054D	No	CB/SW raised
CB/SW	Screw	None	10	55	HA12	45067B	No	CB/SW raised
CB/SW	Screw	None	1	56	HA12	45067B	No	CB/SW raised
CB/SW	Screw	None	5	58	HA12	45067E	No	
CB/SW	Screw	None	8	58	HA12	45067E	No	
CB/SW	Screw	None	8	58	HA12	45067E	No	
CB/SW	Screw	None	8	58	HA12	45067E	No	
CB/SW	Screw	None	8	58	HA12	45067E	No	
CB/SW	Screw	None	10	58	HA12	45075D	No	
CB/SW	Screw	None	11	58	HA12	45067E	No	
CB/SW	Screw	None	1	59	HA12	45104B	No	Unrestored car 875026
CB/SW	Screw	None	1	59	HA12	45067?	No	
CB/SW	Screw	None	5	59	HA12	45067F	No	
CB/SW	Screw	Large	3	60	HA12	45067H	No	
CB/SW	Screw	Medium	3	60	HA12	45067H	No	
CB/SW	Screw	None	5	61	HA12	45104F	No	Unrestored car 876163
CB/SW	Screw	Medium	2	62	HA12	45067J	Yes	
CB/SW	Rivet	Medium	7	62	HA12	45401K	Yes	
CB/SW	Screw	None	5	63	SA12	45058J	Yes	
CB/SW	Rivet	Medium	6	63	HA12	45104K	Yes	
CB/SW	Rivet	Medium	6	63	HA12	45104K	Yes	
CB/SW	Rivet	Medium	6	63	HA12	45104K	Yes	
CB/SW	Rivet	Medium	6	63	HA12	45104K	Yes	
CB/SW	Rivet	Medium	3	64	HA12	45169A	Yes	
CB/SW	Rivet	Small	4	64	HA12	45104K	Yes	
CB/SW	Rivet	Medium	9	64	HA12	45102H	Yes	

CONTACT MARKING	CONTACT ATTACHMENT	"MADE IN ENG" MARKING	DATE (LEFT)	DATE (RIGHT)	MODEL	TYPE	12V STAMP	NOTES
CB/SW	Rivet	Medium	10	64	HA12	45104K	Yes	
CB/SW	Rivet	Large	1	65	HA12	45102H	Yes	
CB/SW	Rivet	Medium	1	66	HA12	45169B	Yes	
CB/SW	Screw	None	7	66	SA12	45058J	Yes	
CB/SW	Rivet	Medium	10	66	HA12	45169B	Yes	
CB/SW	Rivet	Small	3	67	HA12	45102H	Yes	
CB/SW	Rivet	Small	5	67	HA12	45102H	Yes	
+/-	Screw	None	10	67	SA12	45058J	Yes	
CB/SW	Rivet	Medium	11	67	HA12	45169B	Yes	
CB/SW	Rivet	Small	11	67	HA12	45169B	Yes	
CB/SW	Rivet	Small	11	67	HA12	45169B	Yes	
+/-	Rivet	None	6	68	SA12	45058K	Yes	
+/-	Rivet	None	47	69	SA12	45058L	Yes	
+/-	Rivet	Small	24	69	HA12	45208A	No	
+/-	Rivet	Small	46	69	HP12	45212A	No	
+/-	Rivet	Small	09	70	16C6	45225D	No	
+/-	Rivet	None	08	71	SA12	45058L	Yes	
+/-	Rivet	None	51	72	SA12	45058L	Yes	
+/-	Rivet	Small	43	72	13G12	45234B	Yes	
+/-	Rivet	None	05	73	SA12	45058L	Yes	
+/-	Rivet	Small	8	73	13C12	45224B	Yes	
+/-	Rivet	?	13	73	13C12	45234B	No	
+/-	Rivet	Small	38	73	13C12	45256A	No	
+/-	Rivet	Small	38	73	13C12	45256A	No	
+/-	Screw	?	38	73	13C12	45256A	No	
+/-	Screw	Small	47	73	22C12	45264A	No	
+/-	Rivet	Small	37	74	16C6	45232E	No	White
+/-	Rivet	Small	22	75	16C6	45232E	No	
+/-	Rivet	Small	50	75	16C6	45232E	No	
+/-	Screw	?	47	77	15C6	45263B	No	White
+/-	Screw	Small	6	78	16C6	45351A?	No	
+/-	Screw	?	12	78	16C6	45251A	No	
+/-	Screw	Small	38	79	22C12	45264E	No	
+/-	Screw	Small	13	85	23C12	43293C	No	
+/-	Screw	?	48	85	35C6	45315J	No	
+/-	Screw	None	6	92	15P6	45350A	No	BYS, white
+/-	Screw	None	6	94	11P12	45334A	No	BYS, white
+/-	Screw	None	04-03	02	DLB198		No	Sticker, date is "TESTED", white
+/-	Screw	None	17-09	03	DLB198		No	Sticker, date is "TESTED", white
+/-	Screw	None	None	None	G3		No	BFU, 21949601
+/-	Screw	None	None	None	K1		No	21949601
CB/SW	Screw	None	X	X	X	X	X	Unrestored car 885056

"CB/SW" MARKS

The Lucas coils from at least sometime in the 1950s and up to around 1967, had the terminals marked "CB" (for "Contact Breaker") and "SW" (for "Switch"). These markings were molded into the plastic cap, next to the terminals. On older coils, generally those before E-type production, these markings were on raised round stanchions. Later the markings were flush, or close to flush, with the surface of the plastic molding, but still often had circles showing around the characters (from the mold inserts containing the letters). These markings were later changed to a "+" and a "-," around 1967 (see below).

An early HA12 coil, type 45067, dated "1 56," showing the raised stanchions generally seen on some coils dated before the introduction of the E-type.

"SW" and "CB" marks in mold-insert circles on a 45067E coil dated "8 58."

"+/-" MARKS

The "CB/SW" markings were replaced by "+" and "-" marks, also molded in. Typically, these marks seem to have been stamped into the mold and were not placed on mold-inserts, so there is no circle around them.

"-" and "+" markings next to the contacts. In this case the "MADE IN ENGLAND" is in the small font and the terminals are riveted on instead of screwed on. While not seen here, the "+" and "-" marks are typically molded in on both sides of each terminal.

"SW" and "CB" marks on a later coil, marked 45102H and dated "9 64."

"LUCAS" MARKS

While some small variances have been seen in the "LUCAS" letters, it appears that all Lucas coils found on English cars from around the E-type's era carried this molded-in logo.

"LUCAS" lettering of the standard type on a 16C6 coil dated "06 78."

This later 23C12 coil dated "13 85" has smaller characters in the "LUCAS" logo.

"MADE IN ENGLAND" MARKS

The legend "MADE IN ENGLAND" came in various sizes of font, once it was introduced. The earlier coils do not have this legend.

This HA12 coil dated "1 59" does not have the "MADE IN ENGLAND" legend.

This 16C6 coil dated "50 75" has the small legend.

This 13C12 coil dated "38 73" has the small legend, but with an "A" above it. This is the only example that the authors have seen.

BOTTOM STAMPINGS

The coil type, date and other information was typically stamped on the bottom of the aluminum-can body of the coil. This data is tabulated in the table on pages 381 and 382, and some examples are illustrated here.

This HA12 coil dated "3 60" has the large logo.

An early (dated "5 61") HA12 coil. This earlier type did not have the "12V" marking found on later coils. This coil is still in situ on 876163. The date stamp "5 61" is interpreted, as in other Lucas components found on E-types, as May 1961. This straightforward dating system changed on later coils.

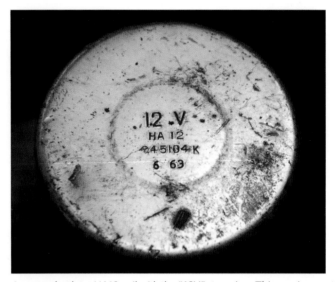

A somewhat later HA12 coil with the "12V" stamping. This one is dated "6 63."

This HA12 coil dated "9 64" has the medium legend. Note the riveted terminals of the single spade connector.

RIGHT: This much later (date "24 69") HA12 coil has much larger lettering for the "HA12," and interestingly is not marked with "12V." The authors are not sure how to interpret such date codes where the first two digits create a number with a value outside the range 1 to 12 (the numbers 1 to 12 typically suggest the month in the date, with the following two digits representing the year). The marking "50 75" seems likely to indicate 1975, but the meaning of the 50 is not evident. When interpreting these sorts of marks, the last two digits have been interpreted as the year, and the first two have been ignored (for the time being).

1 *An HA12 coil from well before E-type production. This one is dated "5 55," and has no "12V" marking.*

2 *A "Special Equipment" coil, marked SA12 dated "10 67," and stamped with "12V."*

3 *An HP12 coil dated "46 69."*

4 *A 13C12 coil dated "13 73."*

5 *A late coil (after E-type production) of the 16C6 type, dated "12 78."*

6 *Another very late coil, this one dated "6 92."*

7 *A very late coil without a date.*

8 *A very late coil, labeled with a sticker instead of stampings. This one is dated "17/09/03."*

SPADE CONNECTORS

Various types of spade connectors for the low-tension terminals were used on the Lucas coils.

This coil is configured with screw connectors and double spade connectors.

Another configuration was rivet connections with single spade connectors.

OVERLEAF: *The earliest coil connector arrangement observed on E-types is shown here. The coil had screw connectors with single spade connectors on each one. This is the configuration shown in Plate 51 of the J.30 Spare Parts Catalogue (June 1963.)*

A coil with rivet connections and one double and one single spade connector. Another spade configuration (riveted double spade connectors) is seen in the picture on the bottom right.

A coil with double connectors on one side and triple on the other.

SPECIAL EQUIPMENT COIL

The Lucas coil as fitted to the E-type was offered in a "Special Equipment" version, identified by a red painted top with a corrugated neck. The coils were marked SA12, instead of HA12 as for the early standard coils. The Special Equipment coil does not appear in the parts catalogs.

The top of a Lucas Special Equipment coil. This one has screw-on terminals with "SW/CB" markings. It is an SA12, 45053 dated "5 63."

A Special Equipment coil, marked SA12 45058L, dated "05 73," and showing riveted double-spade connectors with "+/-" markings. The red paint is evident here; it appears all Special Equipment coils were colored in this way.

REPLACEMENT COILS OF LATER MANUFACTURE

The Lucas coils continued in production after E-type production ended. These later coils are occasionally found on E-types, fitted as later replacements for lost or defective originals. Among these are white-top coils, as seen in this section. These white coils have only been observed with screw-on connectors.

This white-top coil is marked 15C6 45263B and dated "47 77." As seems to be typical of these white coils, the connectors are of the screw-on type.

This white-top coil is marked B.Y.S. 11P12 45334A and dated "06 94."

COOLING FAN MOTOR

The cooling fan motors have several types of alphanumeric stampings on them, and possibly two different helicities, or rotation directions. In this discussion CW designates clockwise rotation when looking in the direction of forward motion of the car (right-handed rotation) and CCW designates counter-clockwise rotation (left-handed rotation).

While later motors seem to have their direction of rotation indicated by an arrow stamped on the front casing, early ones do not have an arrow. Based on observations, the marking of the rotation direction seems to have come in by March of 1968 and remained through production of the rectangular-shaped fan motors (those preceding the later change to round motors much later in production).

If it is assumed CCW rotation is the standard, then blades would need to be designed to push the air in the usual direction (away from the radiator and back toward the engine) when rotating in a CCW direction. A CW rotating fan would require a fan blade with a reversed pitch; motors and fans would need to be matched. The Series

Stampings on a cooling fan dated "261" (February 1961), from left-hand drive roadster 875026. Here the stamping reads "78378B 3GM 261 12V GC." A mirror was used to photograph these marks and the picture was subsequently reversed.

POSSIBLE CAR	PART NO	GM STAMP	M/YR	VOLTAGE	ROTATION DIRECTION
3.8	78378B	3GM	2 61	12V GC	Not indicated
3.8	78378D	3GM	6 62	12V GC	Not indicated
3.8	78378D	3GM	1 63	12V GC	Not indicated
4.2 S1	78378D	GM	5 66	12V GC	Not indicated
4.2 S1	78378D	GM	11 66	12V GC	Not indicated
S1.5 or 2	78462A	GM	3 68	12VGC	CW
S2	78462A	3GM	5 70	12VGC	CW
S2	78462A	3GM	6 70	12VGC	CW
S2	78378D	3GM	14 70	12VGC	CCW
S2	78378D	3GM	53 70	12VGC	CCW
S2	78378D	3GM	17 71	12VGC	CCW
S2	78378D	3GM	48 71	12VGC	CCW
S2	78378D	3GM	52 71	12VGC	CCW

Spare Parts Catalogues, J.30, J.37 and *J.38,* all list C.16452 as the motor number and C.16687 as the fan blade number. No changes during production are shown. Unrestored roadster 875026, roadster 875109 (has had extensive repairs), and restored coupe 885620 all have CCW fans and blades. This subject bears further research.

On a related topic, it does not appear that the change in polarity from positive ground in the 3.8-liter cars to the more conventional negative ground comes to bear on the situation of motor rotation direction. Testing of some motors suggests they turn the same way, regardless of the polarity of their driving power.

LEFT: *Data on some cooling fan motors.*

1 *This fan motor dated "6 62" (June 1962) has no arrow indicating direction of motion. The stamping reads "78378D 3GM6 62 12V GC." The fan blade indicates CCW rotation for this motor that has no direction of rotation marked on it. Assuming the blade is original, as it appears, this offers some information on rotation direction.*

2 *This motor with stamping "78462A 3GM 6 70 12VGC" has a CW direction of motion marked with an arrow stamp, located directly below the alphanumeric stamp. The "6 70" indicates June of 1970.*

3 *Here the stamping reads "78378D 4871 3GM 12VGC," and under it, the arrow indicates a CCW direction of motion. What is apparently the date stamp, "4871," may refer to April or August 1971.*

4 A selection of fan blades. The helicity of each blade needs to be matched to that of the motor rotation to pull the air through the radiator and direct it toward the back of the car. The orientation of the twist of the fan blades out of the plane of rotation determines the helicity, and this, along with the motor rotation direction, determines air flow direction. Notice also, that some of the blades have domed rivets holding the shaft mount, while others have flattened heads.

5 This close-up of the fan selection in the above Figure 4 shows details of the riveted hubs. The fan on the left rotates CW and its hub has two holes drilled in it, while the CCW fans seen on the right

have no such holes. It is not clear if this is how all fans are, or just this selection.

6 This NOS fan carries a label with part number "C016687;" the J.30 Spare Parts Catalogue (June 1963) cites C.16687.

7 Side view of the NOS fan of Figure 6 above. The notch for coupling with the motor output shaft is pointed up in this picture. The fan blade can be seen to be of the CCW type.

FRONT SUBFRAME NUTS AND BOLTS

Numerous assembly line pictures of cars show the nuts and bolts holding the front subframe together and onto the car as unpainted. Engine compartment pictures of many cars also show unpainted bolts and the authors have found no instances of original pictures of 3.8-liter cars with painted subframe bolts, and it seems the painting occurred later on, at least for some of the bolts, during Series 1.5 production (see that section).

Jaguar E-Type The Definitive History, on page 163, indicates the front subframes were painted as individual components and bolted together into a unit before installation on the body tub (for at least sometime, with the engine and transmission installed). Likely this procedure changed in 1966, during 4.2-liter car production.

1 *Unpainted rear bolts on a front subframe as was typical throughout 3.8-liter production and into 4.2-liter production.*

2 *It appears later in 4.2-liter production the rear bolts on the front subframe were painted, possibly with the frame on the car. This may be an example here, as this one-family-owned Series 1.5 car, 1E17271, is generally very original. Note the lower bolt, holding on the fuel filter bracket, is unpainted. It may have been added later in the production of this car, when the fuel filter was installed.*

3 *Typical unpainted front subframe bolts on a Series 1.5 car, chassis 1E17271. It appears subframe bolts on 3.8-liter and early 4.2-liter were black plated, with later 4.2-liter painted in body color.*

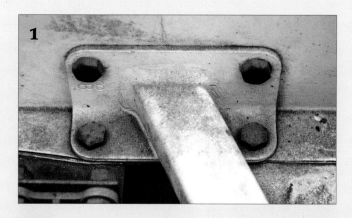

STEERING WHEEL AND COLUMN

The finish of the steering wheel changed from polished to brushed at approximately the introduction of the Series 1.5 cars.

SPEEDOMETER

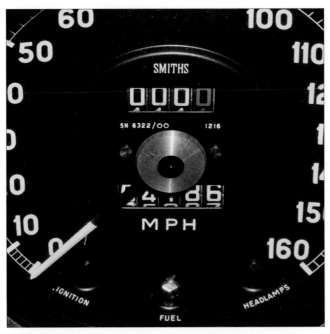

The numerals in the tripometer on the 3.8-liter cars were tightly-spaced in a single rectangular aperture. This is in contrast to the speedometers used for the 4.2-liter cars where each digit had its own aperture and the digits were widely spaced. It is likely the transition between these two types occurred at the transition from 3.8-liter cars to 4.2-liter Series 1 cars, but this is not certain.

NOS speedometer for a 4.2-liter car showing the widely-spaced tripometer digits, each in its own aperture.

DEFROSTER VENT GRILLS

The stamped sheet steel grills over the outlet of the defroster vents on the top of the dash top were painted a semi-gloss black. These grills evolved over E-type production, but it is likely the evolution occurred at the model transitions between 3.8-liter, 4.2-liter and 5.3-liter. These changes are not technically "production changes," and lie outside the scope of this book, whose topic is evolution within the four six-cylinder model groups rather than between them. Nonetheless, these variations are little-known, and in fact may not have occurred exactly at the 3.8/4.2/5.3 transition points. Thus they are presented here.

All defroster vent grilles observed to date have been made from stamped sheet metal, painted low-gloss black. The first type grille, as used nominally on all 3.8-liter cars and seen here on 879032, had sharp edges that bore down on the dash covering material. This often cut through the cover material. This problem has not occurred in the example shown here.

It appears that all 4.2-liter cars had this modified grille design, with a small skirt protruding out around the periphery, presumably to reduce the tendency of the grille to cut the dash top trim material. This example is from 1E10706.

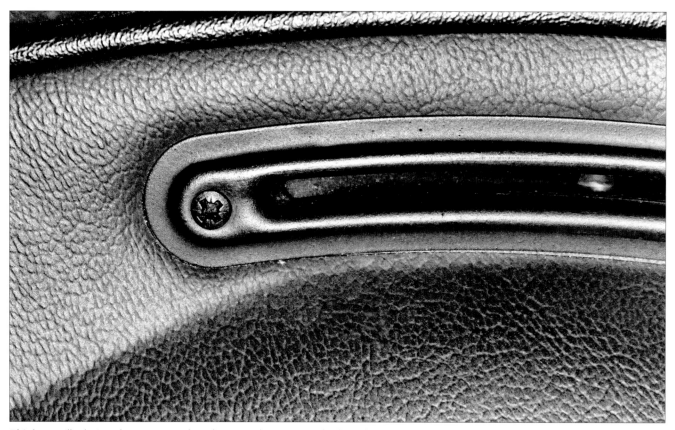

This later grille design, that appears to have been used on V12 cars, had a wider skirt. This is the grille from 1S20001. While V-12 Series 3 cars are not the subject of this book, this feature is included here to complete the evolutionary series.

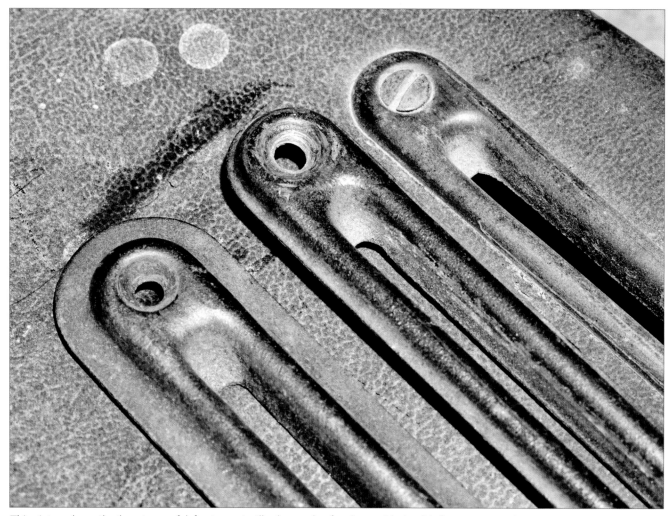

This picture shows the three types of defroster vent grills observed so far, shown side-by-side for easy comparison.

GLASS MARKING SYSTEMS

In addition to the relatively straightforward process used to date castings and electrical equipment, a somewhat cryptic system was apparently used to inscribe the manufacture date on laminated glass components. While the process of dating glass on British cars is well-known and goes back well before the E-type, the exact details of the system are not completely clear. While the authors are not aware of a period document from any glass manufacturer describing the system, such a document has been discussed in various sources: "On The Road Again," perhaps by B. Barlow, "The MGA With An Attitude, DATE CODES on Windscreen Glass – WT-103A," perhaps by Barney Gaylord, but stated to be "based on the original work by Neil Cairns," "From the Frame Up, LLC, Tech Tips: CR302: Triplex Glass. Originality for MG-T Cars," and UK Autotalk Forum posting by Colin Hedger, September 13, 2007. In addition, the authors have been examining marked pieces of laminated glass on English cars for decades. However, as with assessing any aspect of a car for which there is not a completely detailed history, there is always the risk a given piece of glass could have been replaced at some point.

Research suggests the system(s) used during E-type production to indicate date of glass manufacture was to place dots over and below various letters in the etched glass markings, as well as within features of the markings themselves. The system apparently works thus: a dot located under the letters of the word "TOUGHENED" indicates the ending digit of the year of manufacture, and a dot over one of the letters of the word "TRIPLEX" indicates the quarter in which the glass was made. Two systems have been proposed: one where dots over the first four letters "T," "R," "I" and "P," indicate the four quarters, and another where dots over the first and last letters, "T," "R," "E" and "X" indicate the four quarters of the year.

It has been suggested that no dot above one of the letters of "TOUGHENED" indicates a year ending in the digit "0," and it has also been suggested that a dot to the right of the letter "D" indicates a "0" ending digit. For example, if a dot is under the T in "TOUGHENED" it would indicate manufacture in a year ending in "1," and a dot over the "R" in "TRIPLEX" would indicate manufacture in the second quarter of the year.

In addition, a dot is often found in the middle of the circle between the "X" markings (this has been speculated to indicate the decade. The authors do not think that this is the case). Other than this suggestion, the authors are not aware of any decade markings used during the period of manufacture of the E-type.

This is what the authors understand to be the basic system, although, as noted below, there may be variants.

A few 1961 and 1962 roadster windscreens have been noticed to be marked on the lower right-hand side with the script letters "Shat-R-Proof," with "SAFETY PLATE" on two lines below, and below that "R" in a circle followed

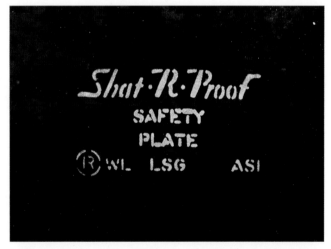

A "Shat-R-Proof" marking at the lower right side of a 1962 roadster windscreen. It is possible the dot in the region above the "t" and "R" could be a date mark. On a somewhat earlier E-type there appeared to be a similar dot just above the right side of the "R," perhaps indicating a different date of manufacture. Too few of the "Shat-R-Proof" markings have been observed by the authors to yet draw conclusions, and no mention of the "Shat-R-Proof" markings was found in a literature search.

This typical marking from an early car has "AS2" above a circle of letters spelling out TRIPLEX TOUGHENED with an S below. Below that is the British standard Kite Mark with the B facing up, the V on the bottom and the S inside the V, meaning British Standard Verification. Inside the TRIPLEX TOUGHENED circle are three "X" marks, two adjacent to each other on the bottom and one more centered above these two on the top. Typical dot marks are shown.

by "WO LSG AS1." One of these windscreens appeared to be very old when observed in 1973.

For SUNDYM tinted glass other dating systems have been proposed. At least in some of the SUNDYM glass cases the "SUNDYM" name replaces the word "TOUGHENED," and often there are two dots (instead of one as seems to be the case with the "TOUGHENED" marking) under the letters of "SUNDYM." It has been speculated that the ordinal values from the two dots should be added to give the last digit of the year. For example, a dot under "U" and a dot under "D" (both in the word "SUNDYM") would indicate 2 + 4 = 6, so a year ending in the digit 6. The authors have not seen any documents from Jaguar or any other manufacturer concerning this. The main support for this theory is the apparent correlation between the marking on original cars and the car's approximate assembly dates when these are known.

This headlight cover has the "X" (in "TRIPLEX") marked and a dot above and between the "X" (in "TRIPLEX") and the "D" (in "TOUGHENED"). This might indicate the last quarter of 1960, consistent with the mark coming from an early 1961 car. Note the orientation of the mark is roughly parallel to the leading curved edge of the glass and trim. On later cars, the mark was oriented perpendicular to the leading edge.

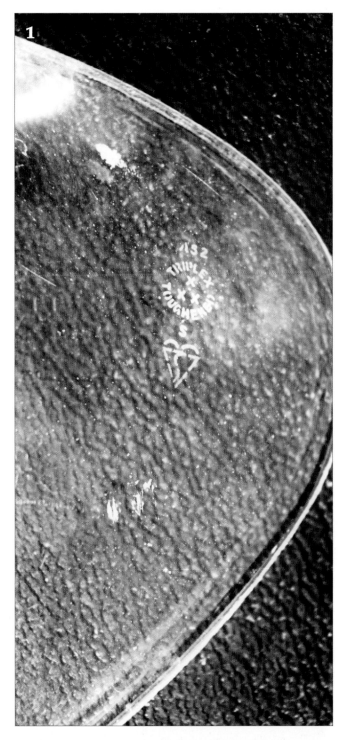

1 This mark from the rear glass of a 3.8 coupe has the "O" in "TOUGHENED" and the "T" in "TRIPLEX" marked, which would be first quarter of 1962, a result reasonable for a 3.8-liter car.

2 This etched mark shows the "SUNDYM" two-dot markings. Assuming the summing system for a dating process described in the text, this indicates a year ending in 2 + 6 = 8, which could be 1968, a plausible date for this window from an E-type coupe.

3 On this early 1961 upper-center windscreen etching there is a dot above the "R" in "TRIPLEX" and dots above each of the "Es" in "AGREE." It has been speculated that this may indicate the second quarter (the dot above the "R" in "TRIPLEX") and a year ending in the digit 9 (4 + 5 = 9) for the dots above the last two letters of "AGREE".

CHAPTER 7

OPTIONS AND VARIATIONS

This chapter describes some of the factory- or dealer-available options that could be specified for the six-cylinder E-type cars.

3.8-LITER CARS

CRANKSHAFTS

The authors have seen crankshafts apparently polished at the factory for competition. One example of this is in right-hand drive roadster chassis number 850008, part of the "ZP 525 Project" that had a polished crankshaft and rods.

TRANSMISSION (OR GEARBOX)

The configuration of the optional close-ratio gearbox was noticeably different from the standard gearbox in the use of an input-shaft oil seal mounted directly on the cast-iron gearbox housing itself (instead of the seal being contained in the aluminum bell housing, as with standard gearboxes). In addition, it had a built-up layshaft (instead of the standard single-piece layshaft of the standard gearbox).

Side view of the two layshafts: The built-up layshaft of the optional close-ratio gearbox is at the top, and the standard single-piece layshaft is at the bottom. The splines of the built-up layshaft are clearly evident here. The gears are assembled on the close-ratio layshaft from the left side.

GEAR	STANDARD EB - JS GEARBOX RATIO	CLOSE-RATIO EB - CR GEARBOX RATIO
First	3.37	2.98
Second	1.86	1.75
Third	1.283	1.21
Fourth	1	1

LEFT: *Two layshaft gears. On the left is the single-piece unit of the standard gearbox, and on the right is the built-up layshaft of the optional close-ratio gearbox. The central shaft is visible as a separate unit inserted in the inside splines of the topmost gear.*

LEFT: *View from the first-gear end of the two types of layshafts discussed in this section. The single-piece standard layshaft is on the left, and the optional built-up close-ratio layshaft is on the right. The splines are clearly evident on the shaft where they insert into helical gears on the lower part of the shaft.*

BELOW: *Front end views of the standard gearbox (left) and close-ratio gearbox (right). The input shafts of both gearboxes are seen protruding out of the front face of the gearboxes. The oil seal on the input shaft of the standard gearbox (left) is in the bell housing, not shown in this picture. What is seen on the standard gearbox is the outer face of the large input-shaft bearing, located at the front surface of the gearbox, with no oil seal over it. In contrast, the optional close-ratio gearbox on the right has the input-shaft oil seal housing (with seal inside) bolted to the front of the gearbox; no additional seal in the bell housing is required. This seal has a cast iron cover, held with four bolts (seen on the front of the right-hand gearbox, held by two lock wires) bolted to the front of the gearbox. The oil seal is contained within this cover. A special bell housing, without its own oil seal, and with room to accommodate the seal housing on the gearbox, is used with the optional close-ratio gearbox.*

AXLE RATIOS

In the *J.30 Spare Parts Catalogue (August 1961)*, the standard axle ratio is referred to as 3.31:1, and alternate ratios are given. This is in contrast to the June 1963 version, where the standard ratio is referred to as 3.07:1, again with alternates listed.

In *Jaguar Sports Cars*, Skilleter stated that the early standard axle ratio was 3.31:1, and that 2.9:1, 3.07:1, and 3.54:1 were options.

About October 1962, 3.07:1 became the standard rear-axle ratio for all cars except those going to the United States or Canada, for which the standard ratio was 3.31:1, with 3.54:1 being the alternate ratio.

Listed changes at chassis numbers:

▶ 879758/9 and 888966/7, about September 1963, the 3.07:1 rear end ratio was made standard for Italy, France, Germany, Belgium and the Netherlands.

▶ 850736/7, 861225/6, 879820/1, and 889002/3, about September 1963, the 3.31:1 rear end ratio was made standard for all countries except Italy, France, Germany, Belgium, the Netherlands, the United States, Canada and Newfoundland.

▶ 879751 to 879808, 880025/6, 888952 to 888994, and 889123/4, about September 1963, the 3.54:1 rear end ratio was made standard for the United States, Canada and Newfoundland.

WHEELS

A racing rear wheel, painted in stoved aluminum, was offered. More information is given in the Chapter Three and Five.

TIRES AND TUBES

Dunlop R5 6.00x15-inch racing tires and tubes were offered for the front wheels, and Dunlop R5 6.50x15-inch tubes for the rear wheels. More information is given in the "Tires and Tubes" sections of Chapter Three and Chapter Five.

STEERING WHEEL

This Nardi was a relatively-common after-market steering wheel. The E-type wheel, sometimes referred to as a "Duncan Hamilton" wheel, is so attractive, though, that it seems there were fewer instances of steering wheel modifications in the E-type than in other contemporary sports cars.

Close-up of a Nardi wheel, with the signature "E. Nardi" (Enrico Nardi) on the right hand spoke.

MIRRORS

Wing mirror part number C.19909 was available as an option for front fender mounting from 1961 on.

SEATBELTS

Changes at chassis numbers 850300/1, 860112/3, 876358/9, and 885317/8: seatbelts were introduced as an option, and seatbelt attachment points were introduced about January 1962. *The Jaguar E-type: A Collector's Guide* quotes chassis numbers 875358/9 instead of 876358/9. *Jaguar International Magazine*, March 1986, cites chassis numbers 850200/1 instead of 850300/1.

The authors have seen a Service Bulletin from mid- to late 1962 stating that within a short period of time Jaguar will issue Jaguar-specific seatbelts. They suspect that the initial "Jaguar-specific" seatbelts are the ones produced by Hickok with the Jaguar wing crest stamped on a chrome surface, as seen in Figure 1 on page 414, as these U.S.-made seatbelts have been observed in a Jaguar NOS box. If this is so, it would suggest that prior to about 1963 seatbelts were supplied by dealers (possibly from stock they chose), or perhaps not supplied at all, and that subsequently the Hickok winged seatbelts were available as a Jaguar option.

By 1964, the coupes were fitted with shoulder-harness fixing points on the lower frame of the rear vent windows.

One version of Hickok seatbelts on an early U.S.-specification car. It is likely that these were fitted in the United States.

Back view of the Hickok seatbelts.

1 *Side view of the Hickok seatbelt buckle.*

2 *The label stitched on the Hickok seatbelt strap. The label has been temporally held down with tape for the photograph.*

3 *A shoulder-harness mount on the lower edge of the vent-window frame of a 1964 coupe.*

RADIO, SUPPRESSOR CAPACITOR AND BLANKING PLATE

A variety of radios was used. Motorola and Radiomobile radios were used, but also radios marked World Radio, Ltd., Made in England. The same radio may carry various names on the front. Some of these are: "JAGUAR," "Signature Custom Line" (in script), and "PLAYMATE."

The radio is described as "H.M.V. Radiomobile (optional extra)" in the specifications section of the road test in *The Motor* magazine, May 22, 1961. Three radios of different bands are discussed as optional in the June 1963 version of the *Spare Parts Catalogue*. A Playmate radio is shown on the cover of *The E-Jag News* magazine, August 1976, and in *The E-Jag News* magazine, March 1982. A Radiomobile radio and two speakers were described as the standard option in *Jaguar Sports Cars. The Autocar*, March 17, 1961, also stated that twin speakers were used. However, it is likely one speaker was standard. There are two grilles,

and this may have led to the two-speaker idea. On chassis number 875026 there is only one speaker, and it is on the left side. It could be that there was always one speaker, and it was put on the driver's side. The two grilles would accommodate right-hand drive and left-hand drive cars. At chassis numbers 850786/7, 861388/9, 880630/1, and 889525/6, about March 1964, the radio was changed to one with only one speaker, suggesting there were two before. The authors have generally observed only one speaker on cars appearing to retain their original configuration.

While the front appearance of these radios is often the same, some have small trim plates on the right and left, sitting over the large front plate. Some do not. The trim plates come in flat black and frosted silver with horizontal lines. Sometimes only the large trim plate is fitted.

ABOVE: *The "Signature Custom Line" type of radio is often found on 3.8-liter cars. Note here the "Davis Custom" lettering in similar characters to "Signature Custom Line," and the number "76858" in the background. These two features are generally not apparent, but are brought out here by the lighting. This radio has similar componentry and housing to the Motorola radios, and may be a Motorola variant.*

RIGHT: *The bottom of the "Signature Custom Line" radio, with "WORLD RADIO LTD." markings.*

1 The top of this "Signature Custom Line" radio has no markings.

2 The bottom view of the Motorola radio from 876577 showing both Motorola, Chicago, and World Radio, London, markings. The top did not carry any markings.

3 This Motorola radio was another common type fitted to 3.8-liter cars. This one was fitted to left-hand drive roadster chassis number 876577. It carried a "Motorola" marking on the front, while many other Motorola radios carried other labels (as seen here, e.g. "PLAYMATE," "SIGNATURE CUSTOM LINE"), and one labeled "JAGUAR" (not shown here).

4 A Motorola radio with "PLAYMATE" markings. This one has the "WORLD RADIO LTD." label on the case.

5 Another type of Motorola radio, this one unmarked, except for the frequency units of MC/S. This radio was observed several decades ago in a very original 3.8-liter left-hand drive coupe.

6 This "INLAND ALL TRANSISTOR" radio is representative of AM radios fitted to 3.8-liter E-types, perhaps by dealers or perhaps as an after-market radio.

7 An AM Blaupunkt radio in a car shipped to the United States.

8 A Blaupunkt AM radio. Typically, the Blaupunkt units found in E-types are somewhat later models, and receive both AM and FM, and often SW signals. The style of this radio is of an earlier type than usually seen, with the patterned aluminum back plate with rounded corners.

1 This sort of radio marked only "ALL TRANSISTOR" was often seen in 3.8-liter E-types.

2 This "PYE" radio is another type seen in 3.8-liter cars. This one is from left-hand drive coupe chassis number 885056.

3 A "MOTOROLA SOLID STATE" radio of roughly the period of E-types.

4 Another type of "MOTOROLA SOLID STATE" radio.

5 This is the blanking plate supplied by the factory when no radio was to be fitted. It was trimmed in the same color as the interior.

6 A suppressor capacitor mounted on the left-hand side of the firewall of an early E-type, below the heater.

4

5

6

A suppressor capacitor mounted on the front of the head, behind the coil. Sometimes more than one of these capacitors are fitted, in the different locations seen here.

Another common location for a suppressor capacitor is on the top left front frame member, just to the left of the generator.

LOCKING GAS CAP

A locking gas cap is listed in the *J.30 Spare Parts Catalogue* *(June 1963)* as part number C.12816, WB.7/8653.

Top view of the optional Wilmot-Breeden locking gas cap, with keyhole cover closed.

View of the locking gas cap with the WILMOT BREEDEN key in place.

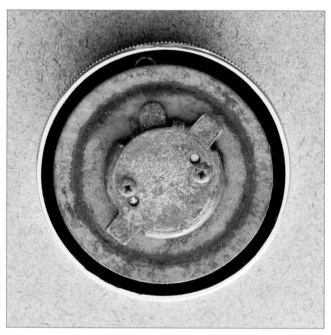

Inside view of the locking gas cap, showing the locking tang extended in the locked position (facing upward in the picture).

Inside markings of the optional locking gas cap: "MADE IN ENGLAND BY WILMOT BREEDEN Ltd," with an "088" stamp.

KEY FOB

A key fob was an option, either number 5194, fob (part number 11/721) with Jaguar wings, or number 9036, fob (part number 11/723) with Jaguar badge. Both are listed in the June 1963 version of the *J.30 Spare Parts Catalogue (June 1963)*. What appears to be the reverse of the exact same type of fob has been shown online on a Mike Hawthorne website. The fob shown was marked in apparently the same type of characters as shown in the fob here. It read: "MIKE HAWTHORNE, The Tourist Trophy Garage, Ltd., FARNHAM, SURREY, Tel: (number not clear)." The fob was shown possibly in connection with what may be one of Mike Hawthorne's 3.4-sedans, VDU 881. If this is so, it would date the fob likely before Hawthorne's death in 1959. Jon Pollock (www.jonpollockrestorations.com) shows a photograph of the back of another fob, similar in appearance to the Hansgen and Hawthorne fobs,

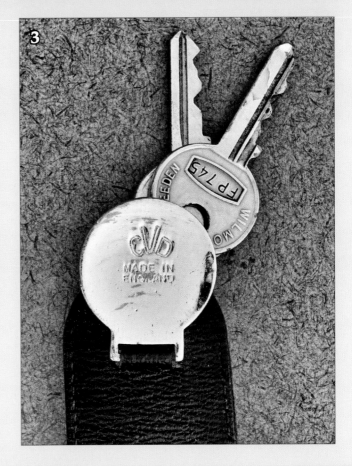

1 *The key fob and keys supplied new with an early U.S.-specification car. This is likely key fob number 11/723.*

2 *Back view of the key fob and key. Notice the name of the dealership embossed on the leather.*

3 *Back view of the Jaguar medallion on the fob. The CUD lettering is in a different style from the block-type letters used in the early 1970s.*

with information on the Hornberg dealership, stating "C.H. HORNBERG JR, JAGUAR CARS, (the address and telephone number are not still legible). The lettering was similar to the Hansgen and Hawthorne fobs. The authors have also heard reports of another such fob, perhaps from the Hoffman dealership. The similarity of these fobs and their markings suggests this may be the type of fob mentioned in the *J.30 Spare Parts Catalogue (June 1963)* and maybe is the standard type issued with Jaguar cars during the period leading up to the E-type. More data is needed to better understand this.

TINTED GLASS

The tinted Sundym glass became an option for the rear window on the coupe at chassis numbers 860478/9 and 886013/4.

ANTI-MIST ELEMENT: COUPE

The anti-mist element for the rear window of the coupe was offered as an option soon after the introduction of the car, in late 1961 or early 1962. The authors have observed the tightly-spaced heater wires on 3.8-liter cars, as well as on some 4.2-liter cars.

The early-type coupe rear window heater wires were tightly-spaced. Here they are shown, running vertically, behind an etched glass marking for scale.

The tightly-spaced early-type heater wires were actual wires embedded between layers of glass, and made contact with two metallic strips, one on the top and one on the bottom of the window. This view is of one end.

FLYWHEEL

A lightened flywheel was available for 4.2-liter cars. Apparently the factory also made a lightened 3.8 flywheel, but the authors have never observed one of these. 3.8-liter flywheels have 104 gear teeth, while 4.2-liter flywheels have 133 teeth, as shown in the illustrations (earlier XK-series 3.4-liter flywheels have 132 teeth).

1 *Two 4.2-liter flywheels, the standard production type on the left, and the optional lightened wheel on the right. The lightened 4.2-liter flywheel is basically the same at the standard 3.8-liter flywheel, but has a different number of teeth.*

2 *A lightened 4.2-liter flywheel on the left, and a standard 3.8-liter flywheel on the right. Note the 3.8-liter type wheel has fewer starter-gear teeth.*

3 *A standard 3.8-liter type flywheel on the left, and what is likely a flywheel from a 3.8-liter sedan on the right. Note that the sedan wheel is heavier, much like the standard 4.2-liter E-type flywheel.*

AIR CONDITIONING

In *The Jaguar E-type: A Collector's Guide*, Skilleter stated that air conditioning was offered on later left-hand drive 3.8-liter cars: "Later offered (at a cost of £100), but few 3.8 E-types seem to have had this extra fitted." However, no mention is made of this in the *J.30 Spare Parts Catalogue (June 1963)*, and the authors have never seen a 3.8-liter E-type with factory-installed air conditioning.

HARDTOP

According to the *Spare Parts Catalogue*, the first type of detachable hardtop mounting assembly became available on production cars at chassis numbers 850023/4 and 875026/7. However, even though this was the listing of the start of the hardtop mounts being available on the car itself, there are instances of cars, likely with chassis numbers earlier than 850024 and 875027, that were fitted with a removable hardtop. For example, on page 221

of *Jaguar E-Type: The Definitive History*, a period picture of a roadster on display at the New York Auto Show, likely 875003, is seen with a removable hardtop. The mounts between the hardtop and the car do not show in the picture, but it is likely there was some mounting provision on the car itself, predating the mounts referred to as becoming available at chassis numbers 850023/4 and 875026/7. In any case, many 3.8-liter E-types with chassis numbers after 850023/4 and 875026/7 were not fitted with hardtop mounts as delivered, so perhaps in at least some cases the mounts were an option for those ordering a hardtop. In *Car and Driver*, May 1961, an unusual hardtop is shown on an early car, and the caption says it's aluminum. While some aluminum hardtops may have been fitted to some or all of the twelve lightweight cars, the authors are not aware of any production hardtops that were not constructed from fiberglass. *In The Jaguar E-type: A Collector's Guide*, Skilleter stated that a light alloy hardtop was used on competitions Es instead of the fiberglass hardtop of the standard road cars.

An outside view of the optional fiberglass removable hardtop.

An inside view of the optional fiberglass removable hardtop.

CLUTCH

A competition clutch was available.

BUMPER GUARDS

Both front and rear bumper guards are often found on E-types. When they were in general use in the 1960s and 1970s, it seems more cars were fitted with these guards, especially on the front, which was most vulnerable. While it is very likely these guards were strictly after-market items (or fitted by dealers), there is some evidence some might have been fitted by the factory. *Road Test* magazine, May 1965, suggests the 4.2-liter cars were delivered with the guards, although this may be referring to how some dealers delivered the cars.

An unusual lower-section-only front bumper guard was fitted to an early right-hand drive coupe. A similar guard is seen on a French-delivery car in *European Automobiles of the 50s and 60s*.

A typical front bumper guard. This illustration is from a Series 1 4.2-liter car, but these guards were available throughout Series 1 production.

A typical rear bumper guard. This is a Series 1.5 4.2-liter car, but the guard is the same as used on Series 1 cars.

This unusual lower-section-only front bumper guard was fitted to a right-hand drive coupe manufactured in 1961 or 2.

LUGGAGE

According to Porter in *Original Jaguar E-Type*, fitted luggage is said to have been available for the E-Type, and a case is shown. The authors have seen no other evidence of this, and perhaps Porter is referring to after-market luggage.

4.2-LITER CARS

OPTIONS AND VARIATIONS: AXLE RATIOS

A limited-slip differential was standard on Series 1 4.2-liter cars. A 3.54:1 differential was used for Series 2 cars exported to the United States and Canada without limited-slip; a 3.07:1 differential was used for cars exported to these countries with limited-slip; and all other countries had a 3.07:1 differential as standard.

WHEELS

The May 1965 issue of *Road Test* stated that chrome wheels are an option, but most of the cars sold in the United States have chrome wheels, and painted wheels are available by special order only.

Wire or pressed steel wheels (Turbo Disks) were available for the Series 2 cars.

TIRES AND TUBES

In *Jaguar E-Type: The Definitive History*, states Dunlop SP Sport radials were adopted on the Series 1.5, but had been an option on the home-market cars since 1965.

MIRRORS

With the introduction of the Series 1.5, the U.S.-specification cars came fitted with a driver's side sideview mirror. This curved-stem exterior mirror, seen mounted on an early Series 1.5 coupe in *Motor*, January 13, 1968, is stated to be an item specified by the U.S. safety regulations. However, no exterior mirror is shown on a

The side-view mirror on a U.S.-specification car.

right-hand drive Series 2 2+2 in the June 1970 issue of *Car* magazine, so it was not supplied on cars for all markets.

The left-hand sun visor for right-hand drive, FHC cars came with a mirror at special order only.

SEATBELTS

Seatbelts are said to be an option on an early left-hand drive coupe pictured in *Road Test* magazine, May 1965. In *Motor*, April 30, 1966, in one illustration, seatbelts are mentioned as if standard, but on another page they are cited as optional.

For the early 2+2 cars, seatbelt anchorages were standard. Seatbelts became available for the rear seats at chassis numbers 1E50573/4 and 1E76888/9 (and certain other individual earlier cars).

Pictures of 2+2 interiors in the general literature during the

period of E-type production show two common seatbelt configurations: seatbelts with shoulder harnesses, and seatbelt mounts with no seatbelts fitted. In one case, in *The Jaguar Story*, a 2+2 is shown with front lap seatbelts but no shoulder harnesses. *Autocar* magazine, October 12, 1967, in discussing a Series 1 right-hand drive roadster, stated that seatbelt anchorages were built in, but that seatbelts were an option.

In the *Series 2 Parts Catalogue (1979)*, an escutcheon and screw for the safety harness fastening points of the FHC models are listed as not required when a safety harness is fitted.

There were different sorts of seatbelts fitted to the 4.2-liter cars. Hickok seatbelts with the Jaguar wing stamping were supplied with some U.S.-specification Series 1 4.2-liter cars, perhaps fitted at the dealership. Later on, the Kangol magnetically actuated three-point seatbelts were supplied. The upper attachment point on the three-point seatbelts was originally a bolt, but later this was changed to a reel.

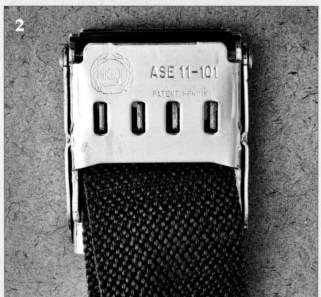

1 *Top view of a Hickok buckle as seen on Series 1 cars. These were likely used on later 3.8-liter cars as well.*

2 *Bottom view of a Hickok buckle.*

3 *Side view of the Hickok buckle.*

4 *This view of the NOS Hickok seatbelts shows the label stitched on the seatbelt.*

5 *These seatbelts were often seen on 4.2-liter Series 1 cars. The side-view of the Jaguar cat, in relief, is very similar to that used on the front of the ashtrays on 3.8-liter cars up to about 1964.*

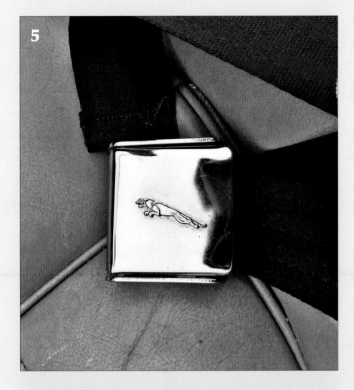

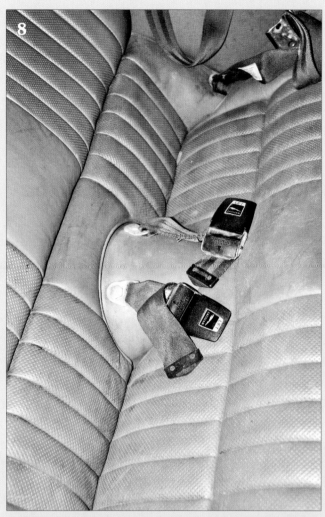

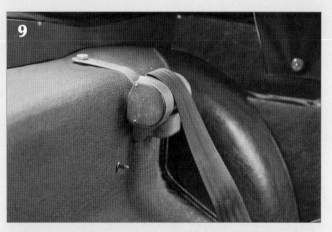

6 A magnetic Kangol buckle as used on Series 2 cars.

7 An early bolt-mounted shoulder harness mount from a Series 2 car.

8 Kangol seatbelts in the back seat of an early Series 2 2+2.

9 View of a left-hand side reel for a Kangol seatbelt in a late Series 2 roadster.

10 View of a right-hand side reel for a Kangol seatbelt in a late Series 2 roadster.

View of a left-hand side reel for a Kangol belt in a late Series 2 coupe.

View of a right-hand side reel for a Kangol belt in a late Series 2 coupe.

RADIO, SUPPRESSOR CAPACITOR, ANTENNA AND BLANKING PLATE

Radios generally fitted to 4.2-liter Series 1 cars were the Motorola, Radiomobile and Blaupunkt. A common radio for the Series 2 cars was the Philips AM/FM/SW.

An interesting Smith Radiomobile radio was fitted to a French-market 1967 model Series 1 coupe. It had nine separate bands that were accessed by turning the back knob on the right side. As this knob turned, a cylinder with nine different frequency-label strips on it rotated behind the frequency display window. The frequencies ranged from 600 KHz to 17.9 MHz.

The radio antennas were typically fitted to the cowl, on the same side as the steering wheel.

When no radio was fitted, a blanking plate was fitted by the factory. See illustration in the "Console Frame, Trim, and Components" section of Chapter Two.

A suppressor capacitor is shown bolted to the front subframe, next to the alternator, on an early left-hand drive coupe in *Cars Illustrated*, March 1965.

An AM/FM/SW Blaupunkt radio of the sort often fitted to Series 1 cars.

Another variant of the common AM/FM/SW Blaupunkt radio. Contrast the layout of the screen and buttons here to the other similar radio shown. Note the short-wave band here is denoted as "M" instead of "SW" on both the selection button and on the screen. Also, this button is located on the left here, as opposed to the center. In addition, the design of the screen is different, and there are not metallic centers on the knobs. Both types have been observed on E-types.

This unusual ten-band Smith Radiomobile radio is from a 1967 French-specification left-hand drive coupe.

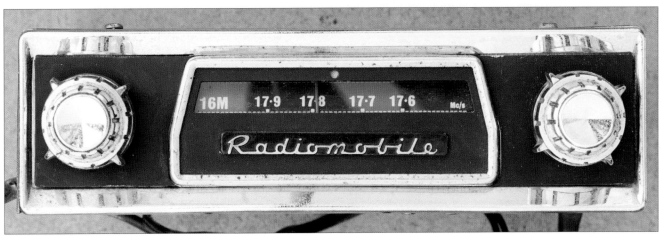

The same radio, with a different band selected to illustrate how it changes bands. Note that the frequency band is different and the right rear knob has been turned.

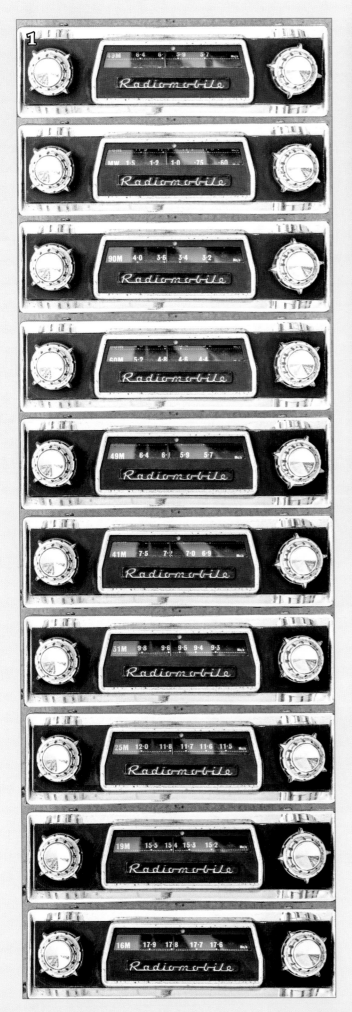

1 A sequence stepping through the ten bands of the Smith Radiomobile showing the rotating right-hand side knob and the frequencies of the ten bands.

2 A radio marked "JAGUAR" in a Series 2 2+2.

3 This Philips AM/FM/SW radio fitted to a U.S.-specification Series 2 car was often fitted to later 4.2-liter E-types. The center button, marked S, is for short-wave operations.

4 Another Blaupunkt radio but with the face plate rotated 180-degrees. It is not clear which, if either, orientation was considered to be "correct."

5 This type of Blaupunkt radio was often seen in 4.2-liter cars.

6 Two component radios such as this Becker were found in Series 1 4.2-liter E-types.

LOCKING GAS CAP

The locking gas cap (WB.7/8653, Jaguar part number C.12816) is listed as an option in the *J.37 Spare Parts Catalogue (November 1969)* and *J.38 Spare Parts Catalogue (December 1966)*. It is listed merely as part number C.12816 in the *Series 2 Parts List (1969)*. This is the same Jaguar part number as used for the 3.8-liter cap.

KEY FOB

The Series 1 fobs are listed in the *J.37 Spare Parts Catalogue (November 1969)* and *J.38 Spare Parts Catalogue (December 1966)*, where two key fobs are listed: part number 11/721 with the Jaguar wings, and part number 11/723 with the Jaguar badge. This appears to be the same key fob that was an option on the 3.8-liter cars. A key fob that was supplied new with a Series 1 2+2 is almost identical to the fob that came with an early 3.8-liter roadster, with the only prominent difference being the size of the Made in England lettering on the back of the escutcheon. The complete history is known on the cars from which these two fobs came, and in both cases the fobs were supplied by the dealers when the cars were delivered to their first owners.

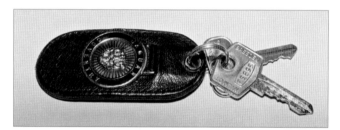

The key fob and keys supplied new with a Series 1 2+2. This is basically the same fob seen earlier (although there are minor differences), and is likely the one listed in the J.37 Spare Parts Catalogue (November 1969).

The back view of the Jaguar medallion on the fob. Contrast the lettering here to the fob shown earlier, supplied new with an early 3.8-liter car.

HARDTOP

The removable hardtop was available throughout the production run of 4.2-liter cars. The three clasps to retain the hardtop to the top of the windscreen were altered in the same manner as those for the roadster convertible top clasps during the transitions from Series 1 to Series 1.5 and to Series 2. Other than this the authors are not aware of any changes to the hardtop during 4.2-liter production.

TINTED GLASS

Tinted glass in the rear coupe window is listed as an option for the Series 1 cars in the *J.37 Spare Parts Catalogue (November 1969)* and *J.38 Spare Parts Catalogue (December 1966)*. While it does not seem to be listed in the Series 2 parts catalogs, this does not ensure it was not available as a factory option, as Jaguar spare parts catalogs sometimes have errors and omissions.

ANTI-MIST ELEMENT

In *Jaguar E-Type 3.8 & 4.2 6-cylinder; 5.3 V12*, Jenkinson stated that the coupe rear-window heater element came in with 4.2-liter cars. However, it is discussed as an option for the 3.8-liter cars in Chapter Four, so there is some ambiguity here. It is listed as a Series 1 option in the *J.37 Spare Parts Catalogue (November 1969)* and *J.38 Spare Parts Catalogue (December 1966)*. In both cases there is no mention of starting serial numbers, implying it was available from the beginning of the 4.2-liter production.

A de-mister switch with integral light is shown on a Series 1 car in the line drawing in Jaguar handbook E/131/6.

On late Series 1.5 and Series 2 cars, the rear-window defroster system was different than on prior cars. The spacing and size of the wires were larger, and the switch

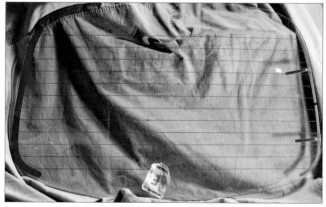

The later heated windows were of a one-piece laminated pattern. The spacing between the parallel elements was much greater than that of the earlier individual wires. Some early 4.2-liter coupes may have been supplied with the high-density wires (as shown in the 3.8-liter section).

was moved to the center switch row. The indicator light remained above the brake warning light.

Later on in Series 2 production, all cars were produced with a hole for the light. The hole was plugged if there was not a defroster fitted. This applies even to roadsters.

At chassis numbers 1E21222/3, 1E32608/9, 1E50001, and 1E75001 the rear defroster switch was changed and a warning light was added. The warning lamp dims when the side lamps are on. Dates of April 1966 and July 1967 were given in various sources for this change.

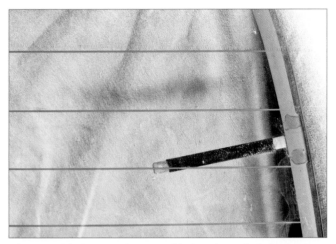

Close-up of the laminated pattern of the later heated window system.

A rear-window defroster switch with warning light from a Series 1 4.2-liter coupe. Similar types of switches and warning lights were used on 3.8-liter coupes with heated rear windows.

The indicator light for the rear-window defroster on the Series 2 cars was located in approximately the same location as the control switch had been on earlier cars.

The late Series 2 cars all came with a hole in the dash for the rear-window defroster indicator light. When no rear defroster was fitted, the hole was plugged. This plug is on the dash of a 1971 Series 2 roadster.

The rear-window defroster switch on the Series 2 cars was located on the central switch row.

AIR CONDITIONING

Air conditioning became a standard option on the Series 1.5 cars, but some late Series 1 cars may have been supplied with it. Mention is made of air conditioning being fitted to an early 4.2-liter coupe in *Autosport* magazine, March 11, 1966, but it is not stated whether or not it was a factory installation.

An air-conditioner dipstick was available for servicing the air conditioning, according to the open and fixed-head coupe parts catalog.

The air conditioning was changed from the early type (which did not permit the fitting of power steering) to the later type at chassis numbers 1R1183/4, 1R9456/7, 1R20260/1, and 1R26319/20. The fixed-head coupe catalog states that the late-type installation was also fitted to chassis numbers 1R1152, 1R9207, 1R9451, 1R9453, 1R20223, and 1R20245.

The Jaguar E-type: A Collector's Guide states that Series 1 cars with air conditioning have an expansion tank mounted on the firewall with a 13lb. cap (in addition to the header tank), as of June 1967.

In the January 1969 issue of *Popular Imported Cars*, a five-bladed fan, with what appears to be aluminum blades, is shown mounted on the front of the radiator air conditioner condenser on a left-hand drive Series 1.5 roadster. The associated text says that this fan was fitted on cars with air conditioning. The authors have seen no other evidence for such a fan.

In a feature on a Series 2 left-hand drive roadster, *Car and Driver*, May 1969, stated that two cooling fans are operated thermostatically, unless air conditioning is fitted, in which case they are both kept on at all times.

In *Jaguar E-Type: The Definitive History*, Porter states that Series 2 air conditioning was not available on right-hand drive cars.

The air conditioning receiver had several different mounting positions, as seen in the illustrations.

1 *Some air conditioning receivers were mounted on the left-hand side of the engine compartment.*

2 *An air conditioning receiver mounted on the right-hand side of the engine compartment on a Series 2 car.*

3 *The air conditioning compressor on a Series 2 car.*

4 *This interior view shows an air conditioning installation on a Series 2 car. Note the console differs from the one used when an automatic transmission was fitted.*

5 *Lower view of a Series 2 air conditioning installation showing the blower input in the top of the right-hand side footwell.*

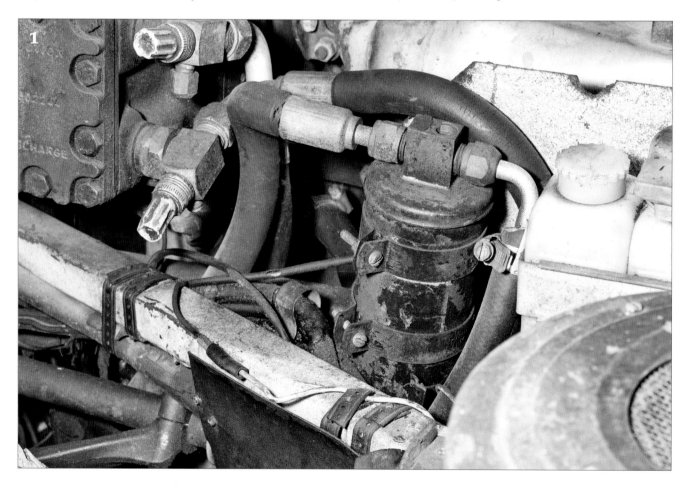

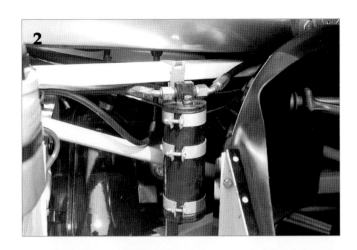

An alternate air conditioning console for a 2+2 car with automatic transmission. Note the absence of a cigar lighter.

TRANSMISSIONS

The Borg-Warner Model B automatic transmission was an option on the 2+2 only.

FLYWHEEL

An optional racing flywheel was available (see the 3.8-liter section on page 410).

BLOCK HEATER

A block heater is listed as an option in the *Series 2 Parts List (1969)*.

At engine numbers 7E16335/6 and 7E54361/2, about July 1968, cylinder block heaters were made standard for Canada.

A 240-volt block heater was available, but not for use in Canada.

BUMPER GUARDS

In *Road Test* magazine, May 1965, the bumper guards are said to be a $60 option, but one that the cars typically come with. The front guards are shown, and it is suggested that they may have been fitted to the cars at the dock. The test car shown in *Car and Driver*, February 1965, has a front bumper guard fitted, but none on the rear.

POWER STEERING

There is some ambiguity in the literature about the fitting of power steering. *Road & Track*, January 1969, stated that power steering was a new option that came in with the 2+2. *Motor* magazine, March 21, 1970, stated that power steering came in as an option after the introduction of the Series 2 cars, and therefore was not available on very early Series 2 cars.

Power steering was available on cars with manual transmissions, and one such car, a right-hand drive Series 2 2+2, is cited in the November 18, 1970, issue of *Autocar*.

OIL COOLER

The Jaguar E-type: A Collector's Guide states that an oil cooler kit was available as an option for all Series 1 cars from April 1969.

The optional power-assisted steering rack available on later 4.2-liter cars.

Front view of a power steering pump on a Series 2 car. The drive pulley is on the left, and the high-pressure line to the steering rack is on the right.

View across the left-hand side upper wishbone fulcrum shaft showing the input point of the high-pressure line into the steering rack.

Rear view of a power steering pump. The feed line from the reservoir is on the right. The high-pressure line exits the pump in the middle (at a point facing away from the engine block) and leads toward the front of the car and down to the steering rack.

A power steering fluid reservoir on a Series 2 car.

CHAPTER 8

LABELS AND MARKS

INTRODUCTION

This section discusses some of the labels and markings found on E-types. It does not treat the casting and part-number markings that are discussed in the respective sections for the components carrying those markings. For example, block, head, transmission and bell housing casting marks, including part numbers (cast or stamped) are discussed in those sections. Variations in the commission plate and part serial numbers are treated in this section, as are writing, labels, stickers, *etc.* placed in various locations on the cars. Date markings are also covered in this section.

COMMISSION PLATE

The Series 1 cars had the large plate commission plate used in earlier Jaguars. This plate had the chassis number, engine number, body number and transmission number stamped in the top section, with the list of lubricants in a matrix below. The plates were made of aluminum; the transition from brass (or possibly copper) to aluminum commission plates having occurred during the XK series in the 1950s. These plates were located on the firewall of very early prototype-cars, then subsequently on the top of the right-hand sill, then later (during 4.2-liter production) on the top of the left-hand sill, and finally ending up back on the firewall on the V-12 cars. The size of the commission plate changed as well, going to a smaller footprint sometime after it moved to the top of the left-hand sill.

There were many variations in the commission plates. For example, the matrix of lubricants came with various numbers of rows and columns: 6x6, 7x6 and 7x7. Later on, during Series 2 production, the commission plate was simplified and reduced in size with the lubricants no longer being listed. Evolution of the commission plate has been discussed in the literature, including work by Ian Howe.

While the authors have seen only a few 7x6 E-type commission plates, no two have been identical. Taking the commission plate from 885005 as a reference point for the 7x6 plates, these variations were observed:

▸ On an early plate, in row 5, column 6, "POID 90" was seen instead of "HYPOID 90," and in row 6, column 6 the box was seen to be empty instead of having the "140" denotation.

▸ On the only 7x6 plate the authors have seen on a somewhat later car, 875109, row 5, column 1 contained "MOBILUBE G X 90" instead of "MOBILUBE G X," and row 6, column 3 had "SPIRAX 140 E P" instead of "SPIRAX C."

▸ In a photograph of the 7x6 commission plate from 850003 the authors were not able to see any variations from the 885005 plate. However, the reprint of the photograph was not clear, so perhaps little can be deduced from it.

It is interesting to note that even in the few 7x6 E-type plates the authors have seen, both the "CHASSIS No." marking preceding the stamped chassis number (the same as the notation typically found, for example, before the chassis number stamping box in the 6x6 plates) was found, as well as the "CAR No." marking (as typically found in the later 7x7 plates). 885005 has "CHASSIS No." while 850003 and 875109 have "CAR No." The information from 850003 is derived from pages 176 and 179 of *All About the Jaguar E-Type*; this plate was not seen.

No significant variations were seen in the 6x6 commission plates that appear to have been used on the majority of outside latch cars. As noted above, the "CHASSIS No." marking was always seen on the 6x6 plates, and never "CAR No."

The 7x7 plates that were used for the majority of E-type production came in many varieties, shown and in the

1 The 7x6 commission plate on prototype coupe 885005. This early plate shows "HYPOID 90" and "140" in rows 5 and 6 of column 6. It is likely some other early versions of the 7x6 plate have "POID 90" in row 5, column 6, and an empty row 6 column 6.

2 This later 7x6 plate has "MOBILUBE G X 90" in row 5, column 1, instead of the earlier "MOBILUBE G X." In row 6, column 3 it has "SPIRAX 140 E.P.," instead of the "SPIRAX C" of the earlier 7x6 E-type plates. Note also the "STEERING BOX" marking instead of the earlier "STEERING GEAR"

3 A typical 6x6 commission plate from an outside latch car. The authors have always seen these with the "CHASSIS No." marking, and not "CAR No."

JAGUAR CARS LTD COVENTRY, ENGLAND

CAR No. 875109   ENGINE No. R 1138–9
BODY No. R 1129   GEARBOX No. EB 239 JS

RECOMMENDED LUBRICANTS

		MOBIL	WAKEFIELD	SHELL	ESSO	B.P.	S.A.E
ENGINE	SUMMER	MOBILOIL A	CASTROL XL	X-100 30	ESSO EXTRA 20W/30	ENERGOL 30	30
	WINTER	MOBILOIL ARCTIC	CASTROLITE	X-100 20/20W	ESSO EXTRA 20W/30	ENERGOL 20	20
	TROPICAL	MOBILOIL A.F.	CASTROL XXL	X-100 40	ESSO EXTRA 40/50	ENERGOL 40	40
GEARBOX		MOBILOIL A	CASTROL XL	X-100 30	ESSOLUBE 30	ENERGOL 30	30
REAR AXLE		MOBILUBE GX90	CASTROL HYPOY	SPIRAX 90.E.P.	EXPEE COMPOUND 90	ENERGOL E.P. 90	HYPOID 90
STEERING BOX		MOBILUBE C.140	CASTROL D	SPIRAX 140 E.P.	GEAR OIL 140	ENERGOL 140	140
WHEEL HUBS		MOBILGREASE No 5	CASTROLEASE W.B.	RETINAX A	ESSO HIGH TEMP. GREASE	ENERGREASE N.3.	H.M.P. GREASE

VALVE CLEARANCE (COLD)—INLET 0.04 INS. EXHAUST 0.06 INS.

JAGUAR CARS LTD. COVENTRY, ENGLAND

CHASSIS No. 875026   ENGINE No. R 1037–9
BODY No. R1044   GEARBOX No. EB 137 JS

RECOMMENDED LUBRICANTS

		MOBIL	WAKEFIELD	SHELL	ESSO	B.P.	S.A.E
ENGINE	SUMMER	MOBILOIL A	CASTROL XL	X-100 30	ESSO EXTRA 20W/30	ENERGOL 30	30
	WINTER	MOBILOIL ARCTIC	CASTROLITE	X-100 20/20W	ESSO EXTRA 20W/30	ENERGOL 20	20
	TROPICAL	MOBILOIL A.F.	CASTROL XXL	X-100 40	ESSO EXTRA 40/50	ENERGOL 40	40
GEARBOX		MOBILOIL A	CASTROL XL	X-100 30	ESSOLUBE 30	ENERGOL 30	30
REAR AXLE		MOBILUBE GX	CASTROL HYPOY	SPIRAX 90.E.P.	EXPEE COMPOUND 90	ENERGOL E.P. 90	HYPOID 90
STEERING GEAR / WHEEL HUBS		MOBILGREASE No 5	CASTROLEASE W.B.	RETINAX A	ESSO HIGH TEMP. GREASE	ENERGREASE N.3	H.M.P. GREASE

VALVE CLEARANCE (COLD)—INLET 0.04 INS. EXHAUST 0.06

		MOBIL	CASTROL	SHELL	ESSO	B.P.	DUCKHAM	REGENT CALTEX/TEX ACO
ENGINE	SUMMER	MOBILOIL A	CASTROL XL	X-100 30	ESSO EXTRA 20W/30	ENERGOL 30	NOL 30	ADVANCED HAVOLINE 30
	WINTER	MOBILOIL ARCTIC	CASTROLITE	X-100 20/20W	ESSO EXTRA 20W/30	ENERGOL 20	NOL 20	ADVANCED HAVOLINE 20/20
	TROPICAL	MOBILOIL AF	CASTROL XXL	X-100 40	ESSO EXTRA 40	ENERGOL 40	NOL 40	ADVANCED HAVOLINE 40
GEAR BOX		MOBILOIL A	CASTROL XL	X-100 30	ESSO EXTRA 20W/30	ENERGOL 30	NOL 30	ADVANCED HAVOLINE 30
REAR AXLE		MOBILUBE GX 90	CASTROL HYPOY	SPIRAX 90 E.P.	GEAR OIL GP 90	ENERGOL EP 90	HYPOID 90	UNIVERSAL THUBAN 90
STEERING BOX		MOBILGREASE MP	CASTROLEASE LM	RETINAX A	ESSO MULTI-GREASE H	ENERGREASE L.2.	LB 10.	MARFAK MULTI PURPOSE 2
WHEEL HUBS		MOBILGREASE MP	CASTROLEASE LM	RETINAX A	ESSO MULTI-GREASE H	ENERGREASE L.2.	LB 10.	MARFAK MULTI PURPOSE 2

VALVE CLEARANCE (COLD) INLET 004 INS. EXHAUST 006 INS.

		MOBIL	CASTROL	SHELL	ESSO	B.P.	DUCKHAM	REGENT CALTEX/TEX ACO
ENGINE	SUMMER	MOBILOIL A	CASTROL XL	X-100 30	ESSO EXTRA 20W/30	ENERGOL 30	NOL 30	ADVANCED HAVOLINE 30
	WINTER	MOBILOIL ARCTIC	CASTROLITE	X-100 20/20W	ESSO EXTRA 20W/30	ENERGOL 20	NOL 20	ADVANCED HAVOLINE 20/20
	TROPICAL	MOBILOIL AF	CASTROL XXL	X-100 40	ESSO EXTRA 40	ENERGOL 40	NOL 40	ADVANCED HAVOLINE 40
GEAR BOX		MOBILOIL A	CASTROL XL	X-100 30	ESSO EXTRA 20W/30	ENERGOL 30	NOL 30	ADVANCED HAVOLINE 30
REAR AXLE		MOBILUBE GX 90	CASTROL HYPOY	SPIRAX 90 E.P.	GEAR OIL GP 90	ENERGOL EP 90	HYPOID 90	UNIVERSAL THUBAN 90
STEERING BOX		MOBILUBE C 140	CASTROL D	SPIRAX 140 E.P.	GEAR OIL ST 140	ENERGOL 140	NOL EP 140	UNIVERSAL THUBAN 140
WHEEL HUBS		MOBILGREASE MP	CASTROLEASE LM	RETINAX A	ESSO MULTI-GREASE H	ENERGREASE L.2.	LB 10.	MARFAK MULTI PURPOSE 2

VALVE CLEARANCE (COLD) INLET 004 INS. EXHAUST 006 INS.

4 A 7x7 commission plate. This plate from the early coupe, 885009, is taken as a reference point from which to describe variations. The "CAR No." marking has been observed on all E-type 7x7 plates examined, and "CHASSIS No." has not been seen. These 7x7 plates have the two-word marking "GEAR BOX" instead of the earlier single-word "GEARBOX" typically seen on 7x6 and 6x6 E-type plates. "STEERING BOX" is again used instead of "STEERING GEAR."

5 This plate from inside latch roadster 875837 has different lubricants in row 6, "STEERING BOX," than found on the 885009 plate.

Plate 1:

JAGUAR CARS LTD. COVENTRY, ENGLAND.

CAR No. 876577   ENGINE No. R3653-9

BODY No. R2925   GEAR BOX No. EB2760JS

RECOMMENDED LUBRICANTS

		MOBIL	CASTROL	SHELL	ESSO	B.P.	DUCKHAM	REGENT CALTEX/TEX ACO
ENGINE	SUMMER	MOBILOIL A	CASTROL XL	X-100 30	ESSO EXTRA 20W/30	ENERGOL 30	NOL 30	ADVANCED HAVOLINE
	WINTER	MOBILOIL ARCTIC	CASTROLITE	X-100 20/20W	ESSO EXTRA 20W/30	ENERGOL 20	NOL 20	ADVANCED HAVOLINE 20/20
	TROPICAL	MOBILOIL AF	CASTROL XXL	X-100 40	ESSO EXTRA 40	ENERGOL 40	NOL 40	ADVANCED HAVOLINE 40
GEAR BOX		MOBILOIL A	CASTROL XL	X-100 30	ESSO EXTRA 20W/30	ENERGOL 30	NOL 30	ADVANCED HAVOLINE
REAR AXLE		MOBILUBE GX 90	CASTROL HYPOY	SPIRAX 90 E.P.	GEAR OIL GP 90	ENERGOL EP 90	HYPOID 90	UNIV THUBAN
POWER STEERING SYSTEM		MOBILFLUID 200	CASTROL TO AUTO TRANS FLUID GRADE A	SHELL DONAX	ESSO AUTO TRANS FLUID GRADE SS	ENERGOL AUTO TRANS FLUID TYPE A	NOLUMATIC	AUTOMATIC
WHEEL HUBS		MOBILGREASE MP	CASTROLEASE	RETINAX A	ESSO MULTI-GREASE H	ENERGREASE L.2.	LB 10	MARFAK MULTI PURPOSE 2

VALVE CLEARANCE (COLD) INLET .004 INS. EXHAUST .006 INS.

Plate 2:

JAGUAR CARS LTD. COVENTRY, ENGLAND.

CAR No. 1E35736   ENGINE No. 7E18057-9

BODY No. 4E27657   GEAR BOX No. KE1959

RECOMMENDED LUBRICANTS

		MOBIL	CASTROL	SHELL	ESSO	B.P.	DUCKHAM	REGENT CALTEX/TEX ACO
ENGINE	SUMMER	MOBILOIL A	CASTROL XL	X-100 30	ESSO EXTRA 20W/30	ENERGOL 30	NOL 30	ADVANCED HAVOLINE 30
	WINTER	MOBILOIL ARCTIC	CASTROLITE	X-100 20/20W	ESSO EXTRA 20W/30	ENERGOL 20	NOL 20	ADVANCED HAVOLINE 20/20
	TROPICAL	MOBILOIL AF	CASTROL XXL	X-100 40	ESSO EXTRA 40	ENERGOL 40	NOL 40	ADVANCED HAVOLINE 40
GEAR BOX		MOBILUBE GX90	CASTROL HYPOY	SPIRAX 90 EP	GEAR OIL GP 90	ENERGOL EP 90	HYPOID 90	UNIVERSAL THUBAN 90
STEERING BOX		MOBILUBE GX 90	CASTROL HYPOY	SPIRAX 90 E.P.	GEAR OIL GP 90	ENERGOL EP 90	HYPOID 90	UNIVERSAL THUBAN 90
REAR AXLE		MOBILGREASE MP	CASTRCLEASE LM	RETINAX A	ESSO MULT-GREASE H	ENERGREASE L.2.	LB 10.	MARFAK MULTI PURPOSE 2
WHEEL HUBS		MOBILGREASE MP	CASTROLEASE LM	RETINAX A	ESSO MULT-GREASE H	ENERGREASE L.2.	LB 10.	MARFAK MULTI PURPOSE 2

VALVE CLEARANCE (COLD) INLET .004 INS. EXHAUST .006 INS.

1 Roadster 876577's plate shows another set of different lubricants in the steering box row, marked here "POWER STEERING SYSTEM." The authors are aware of no power steering systems being factory installed on 3.8-liter E-types, so it seems likely this plate was fitted to 876577 in error, and it was intended for a sedan.

2 This commission plate for 4.2-liter roadster 1E35736 shows different lubricants in row 4, "GEAR BOX," possibly the result of the change from the Moss box to the all-synchro box of the 4.2-liter cars. The row 6 "STEERING BOX" lubricants are those of the plate used for 885009.

Plate 3

		MOBIL	CASTROL	SHELL	ESSO	B.P.	DUCKHAM	REGENT CALTEX/TEXACO
ENGINE	SUMMER	MOBILOIL A	CASTROL XL	X-100 30	ESSO EXTRA 20W/30	ENERGOL 30	NOL 30	ADVANCED HAVOLINE 30
	WINTER	MOBILOIL ARCTIC	CASTROLITE	X-100 20/20W	ESSO EXTRA 20W/30	ENERGOL 20	NOL 20	ADVANCE HAVOLINE 20
	TROPICAL	MOBILOIL AF	CASTROL XXL	X-100 40	ESSO EXTRA 40	ENERGOL 40	NOL 40	ADVANCED HAVOLINE
GEAR BOX		MOBILOIL GX90	CASTROL HYPOY	SPIRAX 90 EP	GEAR OIL GP 90	ENERGOL EP 90	HYPOID	UNIVERSAL THURAN
REAR AXLE		MOBILUBE GX 90	CASTROL HYPOY	SPIRAX 90 E.P.	GEAR OIL GP 90	ENERGOL EP 90	HYPOID	UNIVERSAL THURAN
POWER STEERING SYSTEM		MOBILFLUID 200	CASTROL AUTO TRANS FLUID	SHELL DONAX T.6	ESSO AUTOTRANS FLUID GRADE 56		NOLUMATIC	
WHEEL BEARINGS		MOBILGREASE MP	CASTROLEASE LM	RETINAX A	ESSO MULTI-GREASE	ENERGREASE L.2	LB 10	MARFAK MULTI PURPOSE 2

Plate 4

		MOBIL	CASTROL	SHELL	ESSO	B.P.	DUCKHAM	REGENT TEX/TEXACO
ENGINE	SUMMER	MOBILOIL A	CASTROL XL	X-100 30	ESSO EXTRA 20W/30	ENERGOL 30	NOL 30	ADVANCED HAVOLINE 30
	WINTER	MOBILOIL ARCTIC	CASTROLITE	X-100 20/20W	ESSO EXTRA 20W/30	ENERGOL 20	NOL 20	ADVANCED HAVOLINE
	TROPICAL	MOBILOIL AF	CASTROL XXL	X-100 40	ESSO EXTRA 40	ENERGOL 40	NOL 40	ADVANCED HAVOLINE 40
AUTOMATIC TRANSMISSION		MOBILFLUID 200	CASTROL TQ AUTO TRANS FLUID GRADE A	SHELL DONAX T.6.	ESSO AUTOTRANS FLUID GRADE 56	ENERGOL AUTO TRANS FLUID TYPE A	NOLUMATIC	352 EXAMATIC FLUID
		MOBILUBE GX 90	CASTROL HYPOY	SPIRAX 90 E.P.	GEAR OIL GP 90	ENERGOL EP 90	HYPOID 90	UNIVERSAL THURAN 90
		MOBILGREASE MP	CASTROLEASE LM	RETINAX A	ESSO MULTI-GREASE H	ENERGREASE L.2	LB 10.	MARFAK MULTI PURPOSE 2
		MOBILGREASE MP	CASTROLEASE LM	RETINAX	ESSO MULTI-GREASE H	ENERGREASE L.2	LB 10.	MARFAK MULTI PURPOSE 2

3 This plate from P1R42679 shows the new gear box lubricants in row 4. Being fitted with power steering, it has the "POWER STEERING SYSTEM" lubricants as shown in row 6 for 876577 above (only here this is not an error, as it is on the 876577 plate).

4 This is the plate for 1E75631BW, a car fitted with an automatic transmission. This is denoted by the "BW" suffix on the serial number, indicating a Borg-Warner automatic transmission is fitted. The commission plate reflects this as well, with "AUTOMATIC TRANSMISSION No." replacing the "GEAR BOX No." of the manual-transmission 7x7 plates. Automatic transmission lubricants are given in row 4.

1 *Another automatic transmission plate, this one for P1R43622BW. This automatic-transmission car is also fitted with power steering, as noted by the "P" prefix on the serial number. The authors have no evidence for a car ever leaving the factory with screws affixing the commission plate, and suspect these are replacements for the original pop-rivets. Row 6, "POWER STEERING SYSTEM," gives the lubricants for power steering.*

2 *This commission plate from P1R43892BW, a later Series 2 car, shows the omission of the lubricant table.*

3 *This interesting later commission plate from a Series 2 car states "DAIMLER CO. LTD. COVENTRY ENGLAND," instead of the usual "JAGUAR CO. LTD. COVENTRY ENGLAND." Likely a mix-up at the factory.*

illustrations. In all cases, they were seen to be marked "CHASSIS No." and not "CAR No."

Data on the configuration of commission plates from various cars is shown here. Care has been taken to exclude data from plates that clearly were, or appeared to be, reproductions. The starred entries are from photographs printed in published literature or XKEdata.com (on February 4, 2015). The rest are from direct observation. This list covers only the first basic style of commission plate with the lubricant list. Subsequently the lubricants were not listed.

Interestingly, the four serial numbers given on the commission plate (chassis, engine, transmission and body), and those on the components themselves, occasionally differed. This is discussed in the Serial Number Anomalies section following.

3.8-LITER E-TYPES	
Chassis No.	Rows X Columns
RHD roadsters	
*850003	7x6
LHD roadsters	
875026	6x6
875045	6x6
*875039	6x6
*875048	6x6
*875088	6x6
*875103	6x6
875109	7x6
*875119	6x6
875122	6x6
*875139	6x6
*875160	6x6
*875169	6x6
875206	6x6
875837	7x7
875954	7x7
876577	7x7
877841	7x7
879032	7x7
879152	7x7
879406	7x7
879725	7x7
879997	7x7
LHD coupes	
885005	7x6
885009	7x7
885013	7x7
885018	7x7
885056	7x7
885066	7x7
885130	7x7
888325	7x7
889403	7x7
889560	7x7
889644	7x7
890061	7x7
890132	7x7

4.2-LITER Series 1 and Series 1.5 E-TYPES	
Chassis No.	Rows X Columns
LHD roadsters	
1E10577	7x7
1E11439	7x7
1E11770	7x7
LHD coupes	
1E35057	7x7
1E35732	7x7
1E35736	7x7
LHD 2+2s	
1E75631BW	7x7
1E76093?	7x7

4.2-LITER S2 E-TYPES	
Chassis No.	Rows X Columns
LHD roadsters	
1R11654	6x6
RHD coupes	
1R26606	7x7
1R40453	7x7
LHD 2+2s	
P181037BW	7x7
P1F26238BW	7x7
P1R42679	7x7
P1R43622BW	7x7
P219270BW	7x6

SERIAL NUMBER MARKINGS

One of the characters found in the serial number stamping is the dash between the engine number and the digit denoting the compression ratio (typically a "9"). This dash has been made with different stamps; sometimes a long dash, sometimes short, and also made with a stamp for the digit "1" laid on its side, pointing either to the right or the left. In the table presented here, PS indicates a short normal dash, PL indicates a long normal dash,

ENDING No.	TYPE	MARK ON HEAD OR BLOCK
3.8-LITER E-TYPE ENGINES		
R1004-9	R	Head
R1030-9	R	Block
R1030-9	PL	Head
R1037-9	R	Head
R1037-9	R	Block
*R1073-9	L	Head
*R1074-9	R	Head
R1078-9	R	Head
R1157-9	L	Head
*R1091-9	PL	Block
*R1248-9	R	Head
*R1251-9	R	Block
R1301-9	PS	Head
R1393-9	PS	Head
R1395-9	R	Head
R1423-9	L	Head
R1423-9	R	Block
R1447-9	PS	Head
R1464-9	R	Block
R1464-9	PS	Head
R1816-9	L	Head
R1956-9	R	Head
R1986-9	R	Block
R1986-9	R	Head
*R2131-9	R	Head
*R2131-9	R	Block
R3081-9	L	Head
R3653-9	R	Head
R4143-9	R	Block
R4143-9	PS	Head
R4432-9	R	Block
R8305-9	R	Block
R8305-9	PS	Head

ENDING No.	TYPE	MARK ON HEAD OR BLOCK
R8627-9	PL	Block
R8878-9	R	Block
RA1100-9	R	Head
RA1249-9	PL	Head
RA1381-9	PS	Head
RA1894-9	L	Head
RA1908-9	PL	Block
RA2017-9	L	Head
RA3074-9	PL	Block
RA5259-9	PL	Block
RA6464-9	L	Head
RA7315-9	R	Head
4.2-LITER S1 and S1.5 E-TYPE ENGINES		
7E3845-9	R	Head
7E4122-9	R	Head
7E6466-9	PL	Block
7E8263-9	PL	Block
7E17321-9	PL	Block
7E50086-9	R	Head
7E50086-9	PL	Block
7E50896-9	PL	Block
7E53417-9	PL	Block
7E53516-9	PL	Block
7E56466-9	PL	Block
4.2-LITER S2 E-TYPE ENGINES		
7R35669-9	PL	Block
XK150S 3.4-LITER ENGINES		
VS2090-9	PS	Head
MK X ENGINES		
ZA7367-9	PL	Block
ZB1804-8	PL	Block
ZB2006-8	PL	Block

3.8-liter E-type head R1078-9 shows a right-pointing "1" used as a dash.

R indicates the dash is a numeral "1" lying on its side pointing to the right, and L indicates the dash is a numeral "1" lying on its side pointing to the left. The right-most column indicates the location of the serial number marking, on a cylinder head or engine block. This list is for E-types, XK-150S and MK X cars (all fitted with the XK S-type engine). The starred entries are from photographs printed on XKEdata.com (on February 4, 2015). The rest are from direct observation.

A right-pointing "1" is used as the dash on 3.8-liter E-type block R4432-9.

3.8-liter E-type head RA2017-9 has a left-pointing "1" for a dash.

3.8-liter E-type block RA3074-9 has the long dash.

3.8-liter E-type head R1464-9 has the short dash.

This pre-E-type engine shows a dash made from a right-pointing "1" digit stamp, in the manner seen on E-type engines. Note that the "1" stamp is of a different style from those used on E-types, with a flat base and a single top serif facing directly leftward. The E-type font has no base serif, and the top serif points down and to the left. Nonetheless, the same procedure was used here.

SERIAL NUMBER ANOMALIES

The authors have long observed anomalies in the co-ordination of serial numbers between the commission plate stampings, and the stampings on the components themselves. However, they have never seen an instance of a factory-supplied engine or transmission where the sub-assemblies themselves do not carry the correct serial number of the overall unit. That is, no evidence has been observed of an engine being shipped from the factory with the engine numbers stamped on the block, head, crankshaft, or flywheel differing from one another. Likewise, no evidence has been seen for a transmission shipping with differing serial numbers on the case and cover.

The serial numbering of prototype production car engines may have been somewhat erratic. Even excluding the experimental engines (prefixed with an "E"), the engine numbering in the standard "R" sequence apparently showed irregularities. On page 73 of *The Most Famous Car in the World*, it is stated that from "recently discovered period paperwork" (no further description given) engine R1001-9, the one apparently first fitted to 885002, was "re-numbered" R1019-9, presumably by the factory. This paperwork apparently also states a second engine, R1001-9, known as "No. 2 R1001-9," was also re-stamped, in this case to E5019-9.

However, on page 80 of the article "77 RW," (apparently authored by Paul Skilleter, *Classic Jaguar World* V. 13, n. 4, May 2001 pp. 80-85), a photograph shows the engine from a car stated to be 850003, and the associated text notes: "R1001-9 after being lifted from the car." On page 84 of the same reference there is a photograph of the

block stamping which looks like "R1001-9." Incidentally, as expected for a very early E-type engine, the two-piece intermediate sprocket shows clearly in the picture on page 81. Thus, if Porter is correct that there were at least two R1001-9s, and perhaps one or both were re-stamped to different numbers, it appears there were possibly up to three R1001-9s (if the engine from 850003 were a different one from the two associated with 885002).

The authors have seen several examples of the numbers stamped on the commission plate not matching those of the individual components. For example, on page 179 of the Porter's "*Most Famous...*", Porter states, referring to coupe 885002, the subject of his book, "the chassis number was stamped as 875002 D/N." He points out the "D/N" stands for De Normanville, thus indicating an overdrive, which could not be fitted to E-types. Also, if the "875" prefix is not a misprint, this is another mis-stamping on the same commission plate. Other examples that have been reported or observed are: left-hand drive roadster chassis number 875014 has engine R1023-9 (reportedly in agreement with the archives in England) but apparently the number plate shows R1033-9; left-hand drive roadster chassis number 875331 has body number R1442 on the commission plate but R1443 on the firewall body plate and what appears to be 1443 on the right rear of the bonnet; and left-hand drive roadster chassis number 875954 has body number R2202 on the commission plate but body number plate R2210 in the boot. Another such anomaly was reported by the owner of left-hand drive coupe 885620, that has V1836 on the commission plate and Heritage Certificate, but V1839 on the body tag. Especially interesting is chassis number 875738, that carries body number R1988 on the bonnet and body tag,

Commission plate and body tag removed from body shell of 875954. Note the plate is stamped with body number R2202, but the plate from the left side wall of the boot reads R2210. Mismatches such as this, between the number on the body plate and that on commission plate, appear to be the most common. Note that there are what appear to be crayon marks on the R2210 body number tag from the boot, perhaps a mark made at the factory to indicate the number does not match the commission plate. Perhaps the body number on the commission plate, R2202, was written in the same crayon on the left boot bulkhead after the R2210 was scribbled out but this is speculation.

The commission plate from 1E10320, with the car number stamped only as "10320." This is discussed further on page 24.

but R1821 on the commission plate, a difference of 167, and not a one or two digit shift.

While these particular data do not support this statement, it seems from experience over many years that there are more cases of discrepancies between body numbers on the tags and the commission plate than there are discrepancies between engine numbers on the engines and the commission plate.

The literature shows an anomaly in the serial number stamping on the front cross member where the chassis number is typically stamped (on the top of the right-most end). On at least one car produced by the Experimental Department, chassis 850003, it appears (from page 209 of *All About the Jaguar E-type*, by Paul Skilleter Books, a reprint from a June 2001 *Jaguar World* article) that the body number, "1004" (representing body "R1004") is stamped on the right top of the front cross member in place of the expected "850003." In the illustration the characters are stamped toward the middle of the frame member rather than toward the front, as is typical for early production cars. However, the caption states the frame member is new and that "this part transferred from the original frame," so perhaps a section of metal with the number was excised from the original front cross member and welded into the new one. If this was done, the location of the stamping could have changed. On page 163 of *All About the Jaguar E-type* the commission plate of 850003 is shown, and there, too, the chassis number 885003 and the body number R1004 are reversed in the locations where they are stamped on the plate.

Lastly, a recent report was made (in JCNA's *Jaguar Journal*, Vol. 62, no. 4, July-August 2016) of a chassis number mismatch between the frame markings and the commission plate, comprised of two reversed digits, on a XK-150. This illustrates other Jaguar models have the same errors.

CALIFORNIA TAGS

As noted in Chapter One, cars sold in California had small aluminum tags denoting the year of the car screwed or pop-riveted near the commission plate or body tag. The

screws used appear similar to those used to hold the heater box together, although, since these were installed in California rather than at the factory, it is unlikely they are completely identical. A few California tags observed by the authors are shown here. While some of the cars are restored, it is likely the locations and attachment mechanisms (pop-rivets or screws) are representative of the original configuration. Note also the different marking on the tags, using dashes, slashes and periods. More research is needed to better understand this topic.

MISCELLANEOUS LABELS AND MARKINGS

This "J/62"California tag is attached next to a firewall-mounted body number tag with pop-rivets on early left-hand drive roadster 875045. Note that the car has a tag with a 1962 model year, even though it is a quite early 1961 car. This is not unusual in U.S.-market cars.

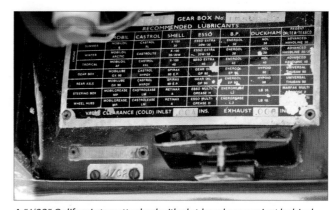

A "J/62" California tag attached with slot-head screws just behind the sill-side part of the outside bonnet latch.

The "J/62"tag is attached with pop-rivets between the two unused outside latch bracket mounting screws on an early inside latch car.

Another example of an early inside latch car with the California tag mounted between the two outside latch mount screws, attached with pop-rivets. This tag is labeled "J-62" instead of "J/62."

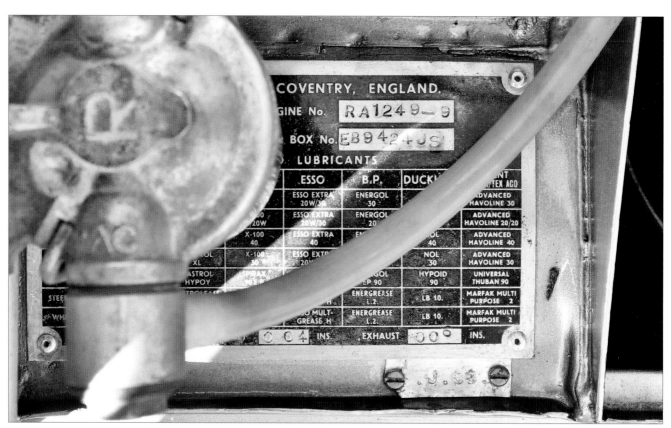

A ".J.63." tag, attached with slot-head screws, on a later 3.8-liter car.

JAGUAR CARS LTD. COVENTRY, ENGLAND.

CAR No. 1E 30670 ENGINE No. 7E 2726-9
BODY No. 4E 2096 GEAR BOX No. EJ1739

RECOMMENDED LUBRICANTS

		MOBIL	CASTROL	SHELL	ESSO	B.P.	DUCKHAM	REGENT GALTEX/TEX AGO
ENGINE	SUMMER	MOBILOIL A	CASTROL XL	X-100 30	ESSO EXTRA 20W/30	ENERGOL 30	NOL 30	ADVANCED HAVOLINE 30
	WINTER	MOBILOIL ARCTIC	CASTROLITE	X-100 20/20W	ESSO EXTRA 20W/30	ENERGOL 20	NOL 20	ADVANCED HAVOLINE 20/20
	TROPICAL	MOBILOIL AF	CASTROL XXL	X-100 40	ESSO EXTRA 40	ENERGOL 40	NOL 40	ADVANCED HAVOLINE 40
GEAR-BOX		MOBILUBE GX90	CASTROL HYPOY	SPIRAX 90 EP	GEAR OIL GP 90	ENERGOL EP 90	HYPOID 90	UNIVERSAL THUBAN 90
REAR AXLE		MOBILUBE GX 90	CASTROL HYPOY	SPIRAX 90 E.P.	GEAR OIL GP 90	ENERGOL EP 90	HYPOID 90	UNIVERSAL THUBAN 90
STEERING BOX		MOBILGREASE MP	CASTROLEASE LM	RETINAX A	ESSO MULT- GREASE H	ENERGREASE L.2.	LB 10.	MARFAK MULTI PURPOSE 2
WHEEL HUBS		MOBILGREASE MP	CASTROLEASE LM	RETINAX A	ESSO MULT- GREASE H	ENERGREASE L.2.	LB 10.	MARFAK MULTI PURPOSE 2

VALVE CLEARANCE (COLD) INLET 004 INS. EXHAUST 006 INS.

This later "J65." tag, attached with slot-head screws, is located inboard from the front part of the commission plate on a 4.2-liter car, chassis number 1E30670.

A 1966 4.2-liter car with a label apparently marked "FAJ66" with the "A" stamped in. The "F" is not too clear, but appears to be here. This one is held on by slot-headed screws.

Some of the labels on 3.8-liter E-types include: a run-in sticker applied to the inside of the driver's side windscreen; metal tabs bolted down under some of the cover retaining bolts of at least some differentials (indicating ratio), aluminum straps inscribed with dates wrapped around the brake and clutch master cylinders; and a Lucas Screenjet sticker on some of the windscreen-washer bottles.

In the spare-tire well of the boot of 3.8-liter cars, next to where the spark-arrester DC connections are made for the fuel pump, an aluminum warning label is pop-riveted to the sheet metal. It appears this label is present on all 3.8-liter cars. In addition to the warning label pop-riveted to the sheet metal, the plastic lid of the spark arrester itself has a warning message on it: "IMPORTANT, DISCONNECT BATTERY BEFORE REMOVING COVER"

Howe notes (E-Type Forum website on October 5, 2014) that the cover for the terminal block came in two varieties, one with three lines, the second and third lines reading: "DISCONNECT BATTERY" "BEFORE REMOVING COVER," and another type with four lines, "DISCONNECT" on the second line followed by "BATTERY BEFORE" on a third line, and then "REMOVING COVER" on a fourth line. The authors have also observed that this terminal block cover was initially formed from a dark textured material, and subsequently replaced with a dark smooth plastic material. The authors are not aware of any correlation between the textured and smooth cover types and the two different types of lettering. This is the subject of future work

On some cars, a small label is affixed to the windscreen-washer-fluid motor, under the spade connectors.

Some very early cars had a rectangular decal on the rear of the right cam cover. This is seen, for example, in an assembly line picture on page 163 of Jaguar E-Type: The Definitive History, as well as in other early photographs.

Due to U.S. regulations, cars exported to the United States beginning about April 1, 1968, had a tire recommendation plate in the inside of the glovebox lid, telling the capacity weight of the car, seating capacity and distribution, tire pressure, and tire size. A variety of these plates were used, listing different specifications based on what type of car they were affixed to (e.g. two-seater vs. 2+2, and different tire types).

An information panel was molded in the wall of the tires, but some early tires had a label glued to them. See also the TIRES AND TUBES sections (pages 250 forward and pages 363 forward).

A negative earth warning label was affixed to the heater in the Series 1 4.2-liter cars. Based on observations, it appears this label did not appear on Series 2 cars, although it has been observed on Series 1.5 cars.

The run-in sticker was affixed to the inside of the driver's side of the windscreen. A Jaguar head was printed on the side facing outward, and the run-in instructions were printed on the inside, facing the driver.

On some cars, a seatbelt-anchorage compliance plaque was used. This was sometimes mounted in the area above the right-hand side number plate, both facing to the right on the side of the footwell, and on the firewall above the right-hand side number plate. It is also found on the firewall above the left-hand side number plate. There are 1965, 1968 and 1969 versions of this plate.

At least three types of tuning-specification labels were applied to the air cleaners of the cars fitted with emission controls. While the early triangular-shaped air cleaner plenum was still fitted, this label was made of aluminum and was pop-riveted to the top of the air cleaner.

The tuning-specification plaque is shown on the rear, carburetor side of the air cleaner triangle plenum on a very early Series 1.5 car in Motor, January 13, 1968, and on a U.S. model Series 2 air cleaner in Skilleter's book, but is absent from an English-specification car on the same page.

With the introduction of the later-type air cleaner, this label took the form of a sticker. There were at least two types of these tuning-specification stickers that were fitted to the late-type Series 2 air cleaner. They have also been seen mounted farther back on the air cleaner.

Small, red plastic stickers were used on at least some of the Stromberg carburetors fitted to the Emission control cars. These say "FOR EMISSION CONTROL SYSTEM, PATENTS APPLIED FOR."

When the serial number plate was changed to the small, doorjamb-mounted version late in Series 2 production (see page 39), the tappet adjustment specification was removed. However, sometime before the number-plate change took place, this tappet information was supplied on a Tappet Clearance sticker affixed to the inner edge of the exhaust camshaft cover.

On the convertible top of 4.2-liter cars, there was an aluminum label warning to put the seats forward before lowering or raising the top.

On some Series 1 cars, a round inset emission control certification was on top of the crankcase breather pipe on the front of the cylinder head.

As with the 3.8-liter cars, the early 4.2-liter cars had a Lucas sticker on the coil. This differed from the 3.8-liter coil label in that Negative Earth was printed on it.

A brake fluid specification sticker is found on some cars. This was sometimes affixed to the back of the heat shield, or on the firewall, just above the heater. On some right-hand drive cars, this sticker was fitted on the right-hand side of the firewall, just above the mounting for the brake fluid reservoirs.

Replacement brake fluid reservoir caps sometimes carried metallic testing labels; see "Dated Components" section of Chapter Two.

On some late U.S.-specification Series 2 cars, an emission control sticker was affixed to the inside of the right wheel well wall, inside the bonnet.

As in the case of the 3.8-liter cars, the brake master cylinder often carried a strap with information on it.

At engine numbers 14268/9, about December 1970, the designation of the compression ratio of the engine was changed from a number to a letter, thus H was for high compression, S for standard compression, and L for low compression.

The "JAGUAR" badge on the camshaft covers of Series 1.5 and Series 2 cars came in two types, as discussed previously.

Various other labels appeared on some cars. For example, small rectangular labels were sometimes found on the side of the alternator and on the windscreen squirter bottle and motor.

In recent restorations the authors have observed two decals, a rectangular one on the air cleaner drums in blue with white outline stating "MADE IN ENGLAND, COOPERS (in a curved white border), PATENTS PENDING, FOR SERVICE...," and a round one on the windscreen wiper motor in red and black stating "REPLACE YOUR WIPER BLADES ONCE A YEAR" Based on period literature research and observations of cars the authors suspect no such decals were ever applied to E-types at the factory or dealerships.

A selection of some of the labels found on E-types is shown in this section.

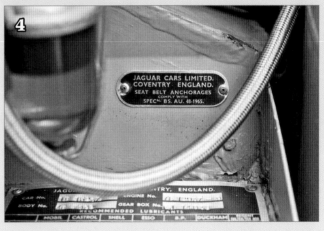

1 The 43/13 tab on this differential cover denotes a 3.31:1 axle ratio.

2 A fuel pump connection warning plaque was mounted in the spare-tire well. Note above it the label on the lid of the spark arrester for the fuel pump DC power connection. Variations in the label on this lid are discussed in the text.

3 A Lucas Screenjet sticker on the frame holding the glass windscreen washer bottle. This sort of bottle was used on 3.8-liter and early 4.2-liter cars. This sticker has been seen, in restored cars, applied to the bottle itself. The authors doubt this was an original configuration from the factory.

4 A 1965 seatbelt anchorage compliance plaque on a Series 1 car. This appears to be the earliest type of these pop-riveted plates with rounded edges. This type is usually seen on the lower left-hand side of the firewall, behind the voltage regulator.

1 The first style of cover for the spark arrestor for the fuel-pump connection.

2 The second style of spark-arrestor cover. This picture gives a larger overview of the cover in situ. The pop-riveted on label below the black rubber spark-arrestor box carries a similar message in red letters.

3 This plate attesting to compliance with U.S. Federal safety standards as of January 1, 1968 was typically affixed to the outer left-hand side of the firewall, just to the left of the mounting point of the top right arm of the right side member assembly of the space frame. The authors have seen an instance of a January 1, 1968 tag mounted on the outer side of the horizontal sheet metal surface below the fuel sediment bowl filter (the area where the 3.8-liter commission plates were located). The observation was of a restored car, so additional skepticism should be applied to this information.

4 A January 1, 1968 certification plate in another location. This one is on the lower left of the firewall behind the voltage regulator. This is the same place the January 1, 1969 plates have been seen.

5 A January 1, 1969 certification plate on the lower left of the firewall behind the voltage regulator.

6 An unusual French brake fluid sticker on the back of a brake and clutch reservoir heat shield. The authors have only seen one instance of this sticker.

7 A brake fluid sticker on the top left of the firewall on a late 4.2-liter car.

8 An example of the many crayon markings found in various places on the car. This is a typical body number marking on the upper left front of the firewall.

7

8

DATED COMPONENTS

The Lucas electrical components used on the car were, for the most part, dated with a month and year designation, such as "6 60" to indicate June of 1960. A slightly different system used for later-dated components, beginning around the late 1960s, is discussed on page 385.

Another component that carries a date is the engine block. On its lower left-hand side, in front of and below the dipstick location, is a designation, such as "27-2-61" indicating February 27, 1961, cast into the block (discussed in another section). Likely this is the casting date. Similarly, later 3.8-liter transmission housings have what appears to be a casting date on them. These casting dates are discussed further in the sections for engine blocks and transmissions.

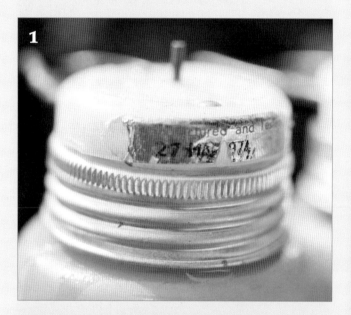

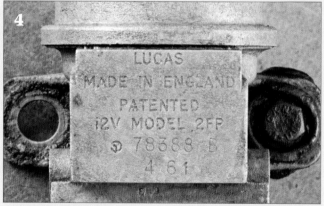

1 This metallic label was affixed to a later-type metal-topped reservoir cap that was fitted as a replacement part sometime after six-cylinder E-type production ceased. It is marked "Manufactured and Tested 27 MAR 1974." The authors have seen no evidence of such labels being fitted to caps supplied new with the cars.

2 Dated aluminum straps were found on the brake master cylinders. On the early left-hand drive roadster, chassis 875026, the date "22-4-61" is hand-written rather than stamped.

3 Another, later master cylinder strap, this one, with the more typical stamped characters, showing the date "9-5-62."

4 A "4 61" date stamped on an early-type submerged fuel pump.

5 A "4 61" date stamped on a distributor body.

6 A "5 61" date stamped on the bottom of a coil.

7 A "6 61" date mark on the windscreen washer from early left-hand drive coupe 885056. This motor has the short "A B C" sticker typically seen on 1961 and 1962 cars.

8 A date of "2 61" (or possibly "12 61") on a windscreen wiper motor.

9 This label on a windscreen washer pump motor contains more information than the earlier labels that only had "A B C" on the sticker. This type seems to have come in about 1963, and it contains filling information. The authors have seen other additional stickers on these pumps with similar instructions, but with a different appearance.

CHAPTER 9

JAGUAR

4·2 "E" TYPE & 2+2

OPERATING, MAINTENANCE
AND SERVICE HANDBOOK

LITERATURE

This section discusses various items of literature issued by the factory or by factory dealers. It is broken into five subcategories: driver's handbooks and dust jackets; pouches and service vouchers; service manuals; *Spare Parts Catalogs*; and service bulletin books. This is a brief overview of a large topic.

DRIVER'S HANDBOOKS

The 3.8-liter E-type driver's handbook comes in several varieties. The version is denoted on the first page of the handbook, where E/122/X is printed, with X being a number from 1 to at least 6. In the E/122/1 handbook, the earliest version, the only way listed to open the bonnet is with a T-key. Thus E/122/1 seems correct for the very early cars. From research of surviving cars: Chassis number 875026 came with handbook E/122/1.

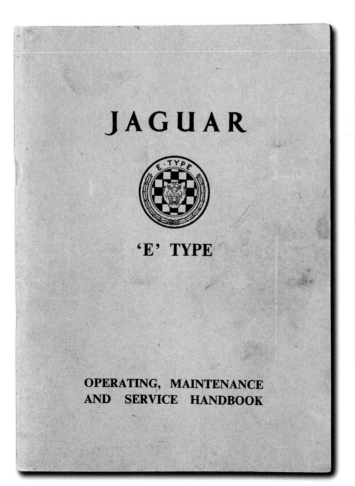

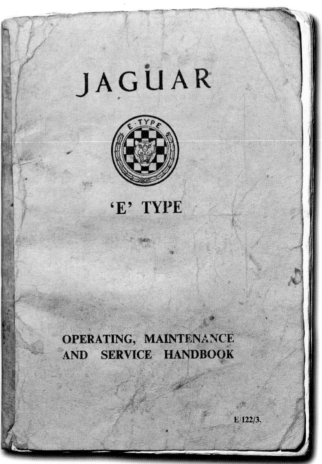

LEFT: *The cover of an early handbook. It does not denote the 3.8-liter displacement of the car (as all E-types at that point were 3.8-liter cars), nor does it denote the revision number that later showed up on the cover. It appears to have been always denoted inside the book.*

ABOVE: *This later 3.8-liter handbook has the revision number "E/122/3." appearing on the cover.*

CAR IDENTIFICATION

It is imperative that the Car and Engine numbers, together with any prefix or suffix letters, are quoted in any correspondence concerning this vehicle. If the unit in question is the Gearbox the Gearbox number and any prefix or suffix letters must also be quoted. This also applies when ordering spare parts.

Car Number .. ..

Stamped on the right-hand frame rear mounting bracket above fuel line filter.

Engine Number .. ..

Stamped on the right-hand side of the cylinder block above the oil filter and at the front of the cylinder head casting.

/8 or /9 following the engine number denotes the compression ratio.

Gearbox Number .. ..

Stamped on a shoulder at the left-hand rear corner of the gearbox casing and on the top cover.

Body Number .. ..

Stamped on a plate attached to the right-hand side of the scuttle.

Key Numbers .. ..

(a) The keys provided operate the ignition switch and door locks.

v

The early "E/122/1" handbooks appear to all have a missing picture of the commission plate on page v.

CAR IDENTIFICATION

It is imperative that the Car and Engine numbers, together with any prefix or suffix letters, are quoted in any correspondence concerning this vehicle. If the unit in question is the Gearbox the Gearbox number and any prefix or suffix letters must also be quoted. This also applies when ordering spare parts.

Car Number

Stamped on the right-hand frame cross member above the hydraulic damper mounting.

Engine Number

Stamped on the right-hand side of the cylinder block above the oil filter and at the front of the cylinder head casting.

/8 or /9 following the engine number denotes the compression ratio.

Fig. 1. *The identification numbers are also stamped on the plate shown here.*

Gearbox Number

Stamped on a shoulder at the left-hand rear corner of the gearbox casing and on the top cover.

Body Number

Stamped on a plate attached to the right-hand side of the scuttle.

Key Numbers

The keys provided operate the ignition switch and door locks.

v

By the later "E/122/3" revision handbooks the line drawing of the commission plate was included on page v, as intended. There are many other similar variations in factory literature, but this one in particular is noted as it is somewhat dramatic.

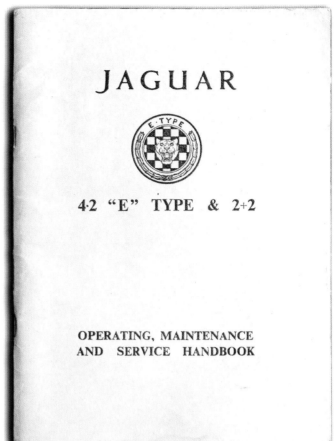

ABOVE: *This later revision of the handbook also covers the 2+2 models.*

TOP LEFT: *This red vinyl cover was used on some drivers' handbooks. It seems it was found most often on the earlier 3.8-liter cars. The authors have observed some early cars with the Jaguar winged logo printed in blue rather than gold.*

This early version of a 4.2-liter E-type handbook does not mention the 2+2, a model that was not introduced until later in 4.2-liter production.

Handbook E/122/1 sometimes came with an insert, "Amendments and Additions to the Jaguar 'E' Type Operating, Maintenance and Service Handbook." This publication is only a few pages long and carries no publication number. It gives revised information on serial numbers, timing, capacities, bonnet latch, lowering the convertible top and so on.

In handbook E/122/5, the bonnet opening is indicated as inside only, although the cars are illustrated with outside bonnet latches. E/122/6 shows only the inside bonnet opening and the illustrations show 4.2-liter Series 1 cars in the coupe and roadster models.

The handbook is reproduced in E/122/5 form. The reproductions are not marked as such, but the photographic reproductions in the front are of lower quality than the original publications.

A dark-red vinyl dust jacket with a gold Jaguar wings crest was sometimes supplied with the handbook.

A red and black lubrication chart was folded and put in the driver's handbook. An early one was marked SM.3/61 in the right lower corner.

There are yet many more variations in these handbooks.

POUCHES AND OTHER MATERIAL

In addition to the driver's handbook, the purchaser of a new E-type received other papers and pouches. Included were a service voucher book, a warranty booklet, a listing of Jaguar dealers and a pouch.

Service voucher books came with the car. These have dark burgundy covers with a yellow Jaguar wings crest, the name "JAGUAR," and "PERIODIC MAINTENANCE VOUCHERS" in white letters and "Issued by THE SERVICE DEPARTMENT, JAGUAR CARS LIMITED, COVENTRY, ENGLAND" in yellow at the bottom. One version of the book is marked E/119/2 in the lower right of the inside cover, and likely the 2 is a postscript that changed.

Another book contained listings of Jaguar dealers. The cover on one example is white with a globe, the Jaguar wings crest, "JAGUAR OVERSEAS DISTRIBUTORS AND DEALERS" printed in blue and "20th EDITION, SEPTEMBER 1960." The date is on the lower left outside cover and there is no apparent printing number. The dates appear to vary.

A break-in windscreen sticker was stuck to the inside corner of the windscreen, on the steering wheel side. It had the Jaguar head and "JAGUAR" in silver letters on black on the front and break-in instructions on the back. A warranty booklet was also included.

A Series 2 handbook in its pouch. There were other variations.

Some typical material supplied with the handbook in the pouch. There were many variations of this material.

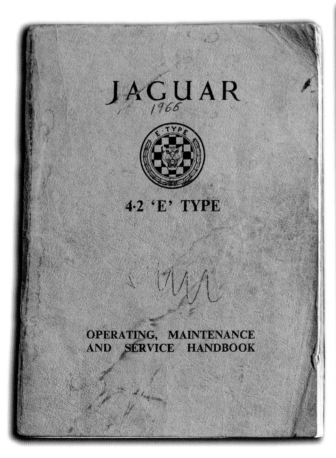

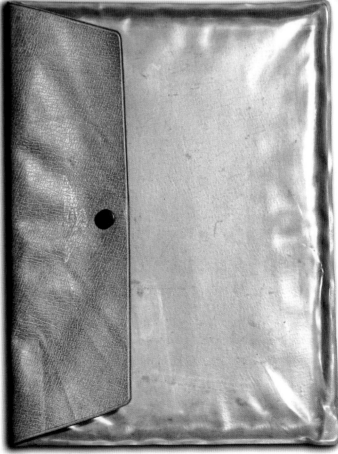

A 4.2-liter handbook and its plastic pouch. This pouch is typical for the 3.8-liter and early 4.2-liter cars.

SERVICE MANUALS

The service manual was an option; it did not automatically come with a new car.

The 3.8-liter E-type service manual comes in several varieties. The version is denoted on the title page, where E/123/X is printed, with X being a number from 1to at least 5.

The early printing series of the service manuals were bound in signatures held in place by two brass screws, while later versions were bound in a four-ring loose leaf notebook that allowed pages to be added at any place.

On the earliest printing of the manual, the numbers 3.8 do not proceed the name E-type on the spine, cover, title page, or introductory pages to the various sections. In addition, there is no designation of printing series at all in this book; the lower left-hand corner of the front page is blank.

The authors have seen a printing series of the manual as late as E/123/3 that was bound with brass screws. This manual was with a 1965 4.2-liter roadster, but it is not clear it was supplied or ordered near or at the same time as the car.

The authors are not aware of any reproductions of the service manual that try to duplicate the original in overall appearance. It appears that the reprints seen (so far) of the manual are easily distinguishable from the original. In particular, there is the perfect-bound reprint by Robert Bentley, Inc., Cambridge, Massachusetts, that consists of the 4.2-liter E-type driver's handbook, the 3.8-liter service manual with the 4.2-liter supplement and the special tuning handbook. This book has two pages (of the original manual) reduced and printed side-by-side on a single page and is easily distinguishable from an original. There are likely other reproductions as well and their description and identification remain as future work.

Similar to the service manual, there was a special tuning manual that gave recommended modifications to prepare the cars for racing.

The service manuals for the Series 1 4.2-liter cars consisted of a 3.8-liter service manual with a 4.2-liter supplement. The suffixes of the printing numbers of the supplements involved letters as well as numbers.

While the service manual available with most Series 1 4.2-liter cars seems to have been the ring-bound type, at least one instance is known where an early, bolt-bound unnumbered 3.8-liter manual was supplied with a 4.2-liter supplement for a 1967 car. The supplement was much like the usual ones found in the ring-binder type manuals, but it had an introduction section with ghost-views of the entire car. The supplement was publication number E/123A/l.

The more common 4.2-liter supplements were the ring-bound type. Their printing numbers went at least as high as E/123B/2.

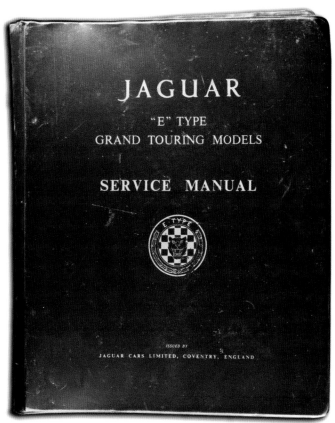

This cover of an early manual does not indicate 3.8. It is bound in signatures held together by two brass bolts.

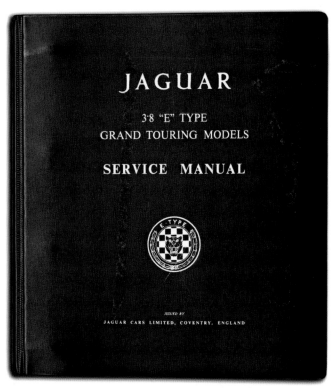

The cover of this later manual has 3.8 markings. It is held together with four chromed-steel rings.

SPARE PARTS CATALOGS

Like the service manual, no Jaguar *Spare Parts Catalogue* came automatically with an E-type. The 3.8-liter E-type *Spare Parts Catalogue* came in at least two versions, both designated as publication *J.30 Spare Parts Catalogue (June 1963)*. The first was published in August 1961, and the second was an updated reprint published in June 1963. This reprint was designated as AL1. These two books are similar in appearance, but with quite different content inside. The June 1963 reprint contains many more notes on production changes than does the original printing of *J.30 Spare Parts Catalogue (June 1963)*. Consequently, the June 1963 book is longer, at 322 pages, than the *J.30 Spare Parts Catalogue (August 1961)*, at 307 pages.

Both versions have a similar cover, depicting the August 1961 date. The reprint designation is found on page ii where the June 1963 reprint note is shown in the lower right-hand corner. Another difference between the two versions of the books is seen on the title page, where the August 1961 version reads: "ENGINE NUMBERS R1001 Onwards." The June 1963 version reads "ENGINE NUMBERS R1001 Onwards, RA1001 Onwards," reflecting the RA continuation of the engine numbering system.

There are many other differences between the two catalogs. The cover on the August 1961 version has the Jaguar wings and crest, as well as the words "SPARES DIVISION" AND "JAGUAR 'E' TYPE" embossed into the vinyl cover. Some early June 1963 versions have embossed, while some later ones have the words flat-printed on the vinyl. On the August 1961 version, the name "A.E. WALKER, LTD., LONDON, N.l." is embossed on the inside of the back cover in the lower left. Later versions had the words "PRODUCT OF ENGLAND A.E. WALKER LTD. LONDON. N.1 (1968)" embossed under the lip of the chromed-steel bracket that the rings are mounted in. The chromed-steel mount for the four

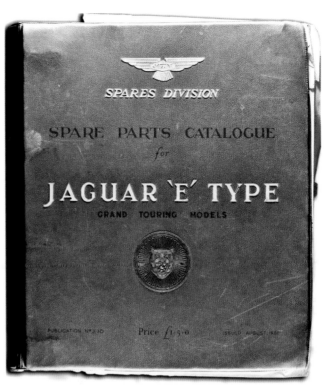

The cover of early parts catalog. Many features are in relief. Later on, the features were printed on a flat plastic surface.

This close-up of the cover of an early parts catalog shows the Jaguar wings and the lettering in relief.

binding rings in the August 1961 version is embossed with a pattern of small, parallel lines and "Combi" in script. The June 1963 version has no lines and "Combi" is in block letters.

There are instances where tentative indications of changes were put in the August 1961 version. For example, space was left on page 40 of the August 1961 version to accommodate changes that were upcoming. After part number C.17540, the base assembly for the air intake box, it says "Fitted From Engine No. R1001 to R," with the ending engine number omitted. In fact, when the information was later included in the June 1963 version, it was done by chassis number, not by engine number.

The authors are not aware of any reproductions of the *Spare Parts Catalogue* that try to duplicate the original in overall appearance.

Unlike the 3.8-liter cars, where there was only one *J.30 Spare Parts Catalogue (June 1963)*, there were at least four types of 4.2-liter *Spare Parts Catalogue*s. *J.37 Spare Parts*

The cover of a later 3.8-liter parts catalog with a flat printed surface as opposed to the early embossed cover.

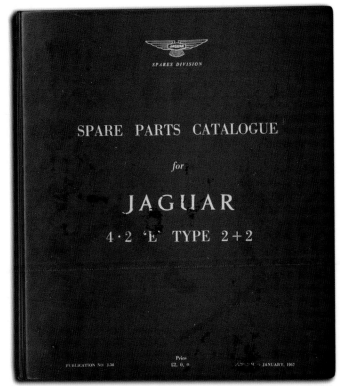

ABOVE: J.38 Spare Parts Catalogue *(December 1966)*.

Catalogue (November 1969) covers the Series 1 4.2-liter cars (but does not go quite to the end of the Series 1 production). It came in its initial version of November 1965, and in a reprint version of November 1969. The *J.38 Spare Parts Catalogue* covers the Series 1 2+2 cars and appears to have come only in the December 1966 version. The authors are not aware of any *Spare Parts Catalogue* specifically covering the Series 1.5 cars.

The Series 2 cars are covered by at least two catalogs. The first of these is the *Series 2 Parts List (1969)*, which covers the early Series 2 cars. More complete coverage is given in the microfiche parts listings, *Series 2 Parts Catalogue (1979)*.

BELOW: *A Jaguar Parts Master Price List book. Bound with two screws, it listed the prices of individual spare parts for a range of Jaguars, and was issued around the time of production of the E-type.*

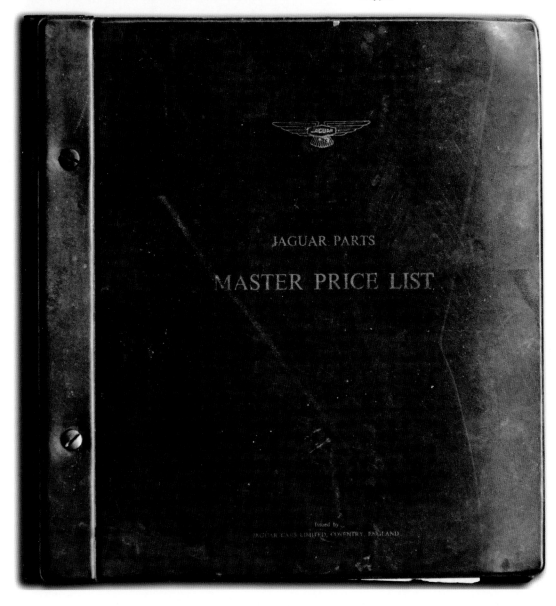

CHAPTER 10

JAGUAR/DAIMLER
SEAT BELTS

FITTING INSTRUCTIONS

Applicable to "E" Type, Mark 2 and Mark 10 models and Daimler V8 Saloon which incorporate seat belt anchorage points.

NOS PARTS
AND
PACKAGING

The term NOS as used here includes parts originally made by the factory (or delivered to the factory from their standard suppliers) specifically to act as repair or replacement parts for cars in the field. These parts were made when the cars were still in production or sometime thereafter, but not decades later. NOS parts also include standard production parts, made or purchased by the factory for use on the assembly line, but subsequently held in reserve by the factory for repair or replacement use. NOS parts are in a different category than parts made by third-party suppliers (those other than the factory or its original suppliers) for repair. Modern and specially-made reproduction parts for repair or restoration of cars are also not NOS parts, in spite of the fact that some of these modern parts may have been produced by the same manufacturers who originally made parts for the cars when they were still in normal production.

NOS parts in themselves are considered collectibles. As such the packaging, labels, tags and markings are of interest, and are considered here as part of this analysis of the original state of E-types. The subject is large and this treatment is a beginning only and not comprehensive.

It is important to note that an NOS part is not necessarily the fully correct part for a given car. It may have been made at a different point in time than the car receiving it. For example, a later "LUCAS L.705" license plate light could have been used to replace an originally-fitted early "BUTLERS" light, since each are "correct" in the sense of their Jaguar part numbers and function. However, only the "BUTLERS" light would be historically correct for an early 3.8-liter car. The same is true of other NOS parts, including dated parts, such as electrical or glass parts that could carry date markings too early or too late for the manufacture date of a given car. Parts with casting numbers, such as T-key covers, could have incorrect casting marks for the period of a given car.

An example in this latter category are 3.8-liter blocks with the casting number C.17212/1. These blocks appear to have been supplied only as a replacement part (see page 1 of *J.30 Spare Parts Catalogue (June 1963)*, and may have never been installed in a car leaving the factory (the C.17212/1 block is discussed in more detail on page 153 of this book). If this assumption is correct, while the C.17212/1 block is a factory-supplied NOS part, its casting number would not have been found on any cars as they left the factory (although its fitment to a 3.8-liter car missing its factory-fitted engine block, while not resulting in an "original" configuration, might be considered appropriate in the sense of the block being supplied by the factory as a replacement part).

In addition, NOS replacement for most parts originally carrying serial numbers, such as blocks, cylinder heads, transmissions, and frame members, appear to not have serial numbers stamped on them, as would be expected. It is not clear what the situation is for differentials and radiator NOS replacements. Serially-numbered parts fitted to a car at the factory are unique, and once lost can not be accurately replaced with NOS or other replacement parts. This effect is manifested clearly in the value placed on "matching number" cars.

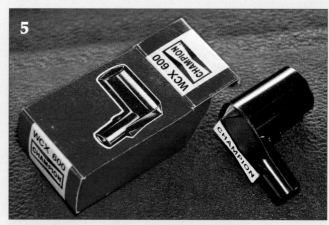

1 NOS Smiths fuel gauge with original box. This is an earlier type box with the black background and red Jaguar name and winged symbol. Note the black plastic cover placed over the port where the gauge-illumination light fixture is inserted during installation, presumably to prevent debris from entering the gauge chamber during shipping and storage.

2 These early NOS mufflers are marked with crayon.

3 This NOS later-type 3.8-liter E-type ashtray was supplied in the black and red box with "JAGUAR," "DAIMLER" markings and Jaguar wings.

4 NOS early round-top Champion spark plug cap wrapped in wax paper and in the black and red Champion box. There is a bow-tie shaped "CHAMPION" logo on the bottom of the box.

5 NOS later-type, bow tie-shaped spark plug cap and red Champion box.

6 NOS bulk box that dispensed later-type Champion plug caps in their individual packaging.

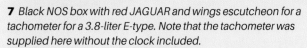

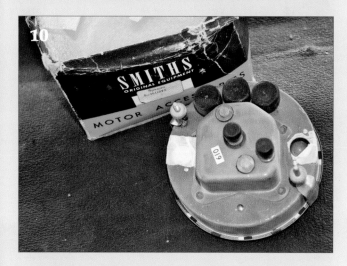

7 Black NOS box with red JAGUAR and wings escutcheon for a tachometer for a 3.8-liter E-type. Note that the tachometer was supplied here without the clock included.

8 Stickers showing on the end of the tachometer box, showing its use for both Jaguar and Daimler cars, and noting the glass lens included in the box. Only Jaguar is shown on the box pattern.

9 NOS speedometer in "SMITHS" cardboard box. This one has two warning lights instead of three, so it is from a sedan. The illustration shows Smiths packaging with a vertical black stripe.

10 NOS E-type speedometer with "SMITHS" box. This speedometer has green filters for the dash illumination lights, so the packaging is likely a later, post 1966 or 1967, style.

11 NOS Smiths voltage regulator with red, white and black Lucas box. The label is dated "6 71," so package style is 1971 or earlier.

1 *Lucas box for the early-type RB310 aluminum-case voltage regulator.*

2 *Lucas packaging for a turn signal/headlight-flasher switch mechanism.*

3 *Inside view of Lucas packaging with NOS turn signal/headlight-flasher switch mechanism and wax paper packing.*

4 *NOS corrugated radiator hose with a cloth pattern and with Jaguar label on the end. Likely a John Bull type NOS hose.*

5 *This corrugated hose has a smooth surface and is likely to be an after-market unit.*

6 *NOS seatbelt, packaging and insert. The package graphics are black and red with JAGUAR and the winged symbol, and no Daimler markings.*

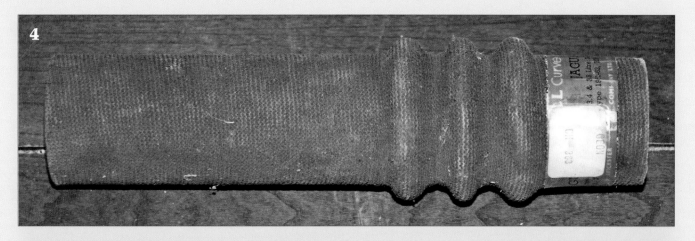

C12424/R
UPPER COOLING HOSE
MULTI APPL.

JAGUAR/DAIMLER
SEAT BELTS

FITTING INSTRUCTIONS

Applicable to "E" Type, Mark 2 and Mark 10 models and Daimler V8 Saloon which incorporate seat belt anchorage points.

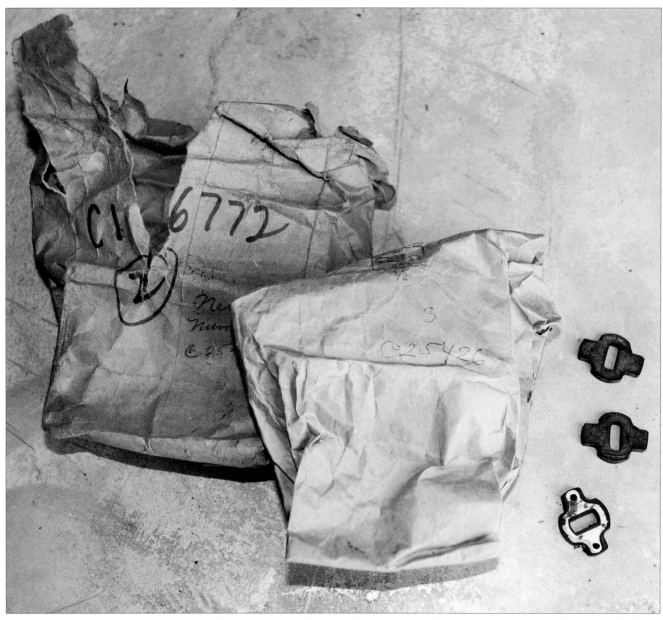

These coupling adapters (attaching the rear of the intake cam to the input of the electronic tachometer-readout generator) were supplied in multiples in brown paper bags with the part number "C16772" written with a marker on the bag. This sort of NOS part packaging was used for many small parts supplied loose.

Two types of labels on NOS side/flasher lamp lenses on "LUCAS" boxes. The wrapping paper seen at the bottom of the picture was used in some cases to protect the side/flasher lamp lenses. Note on the top box the last digit of part number 54572374 was changed to a 5, changing the part number from that of a white/amber side/flasher lamp lens (for non-U.S. cars) to that of a white/white flasher lens (for U.S.) cars. Perhaps this was to correct an error.

NOS automatic transmission shift lever in plastic "JAGUAR - Daimler" marked packaging.

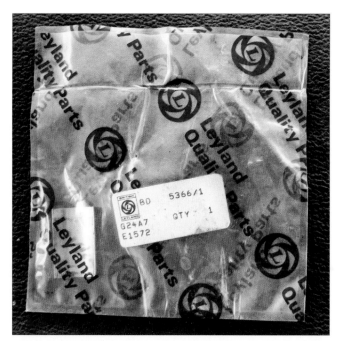

A later-type plastic bag. This is Leyland NOS packaging for a chrome finisher join piece for the trim on the rear window. It carries the BD5366 part number markings.

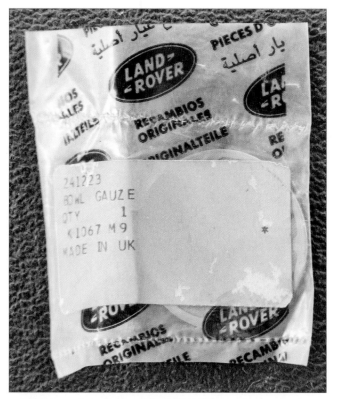

Another type of plastic bag with LAND ROVER marked packaging for a 7299 gauze fuel filter. This, again, is packaging produced much later than the end of E-type production.

RIGHT - 1: *This NOS budget lock mechanism (T-key lock clasp or bonnet clasp), used to retain the bonnet of the first 500 E-types, is marked with a tag carrying the part number BD16015. It appears that some additional writing was perhaps added later, "28-12-3" and "XKE." Since the E-type was not generally referred to as an XKE in England, these later marks may have been added while the part was in inventory in the U.S.*

RIGHT - 2: *Reverse of the tag shown above. The markings appear similar to the apparently-added marks on the reverse of the tag, and seem to specify the price of the part, $1.28.*

An NOS "BUTLERS" marked license plate light in a Lucas box with red and black graphics. Note, as an aside, that the chrome hood preventing the light from shining to the rear of the car has no markings. The denotation of England as the country of origin is marked opposite "BUTLERS" on the chromed frame.

Another license plate light, this one is the later type marked "LUCAS," and "L.705." It is in a still later-type box, all red with diagonal markings. Here the country of origin, England, is denoted on the hood and not on the frame.

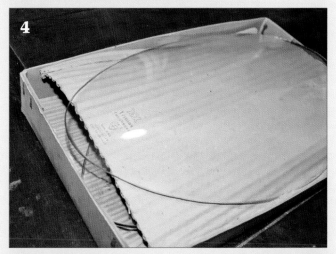

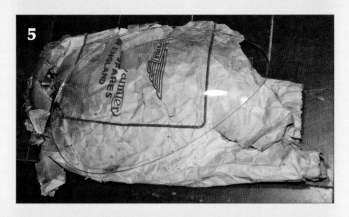

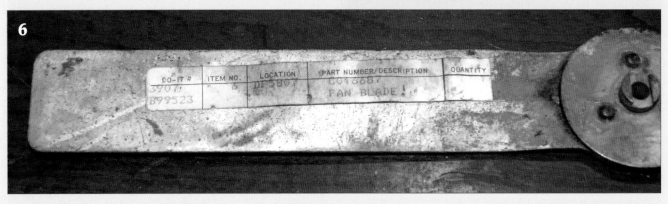

1 Markings on an NOS outside latch bracket assembly. Due to the marker pen writing it is possible this is a part produced somewhat later than the production time of outside latch cars, or a label added at a later date. The meaning of the red dot is not known.

2 Markings on the bottom of an NOS outside bonnet latch bracket assembly. This type of masking-tape part labeling, with hand-written part number in pen or pencil was common.

3 NOS headlamp glass packaging and label.

4 Inside view of NOS headlight packaging with the glass inside. Note the large "XXX" marking on the glass that was used from around the late 1960s.

5 Another style of packaging for the NOS headlight glass. Again, a later type of glass marking is seen here.

6 Label affixed to an NOS cooling fan blade. Given that the label indicates the location on it, this may be a label affixed as part of an inventory system at a dealer or parts distributor, rather than a factory-applied sticker. From the computer-generated appearance of the tag it was likely applied in the 1970s or 80s.

7 Red protective coating is apparent on this intermediate sprocket.

8 NOS Lucas map lamp in red box with the Lucas lion symbol, an earlier-type marking for Lucas E-type parts.

9 NOS Beck packaging of a termination to a speedometer drive cable, along with crimping tool to install it. This component is not shown as a separately-supplied piece in J.30 Spare Parts Catalogue (June 1963), but, since this NOS part was recently obtained from a closed Jaguar dealership inventory, it may have been available through dealers.

10 NOS parking brake lever assembly with part number information written on tape on the handle.

11 Two NOS chrome finishers for an E-type coupe, wrapped in protective adhesive covering marked "JAGUAR CARS LTD. COVENTRY."

A link to couple the output shaft of the windscreen washer motor to the driveshaft leading down to the pump impeller, along with its NOS packaging, a small envelope marked as "LUCAS GENUINE SPARE PARTS."

NOS windscreen washer motor in red Lucas box.

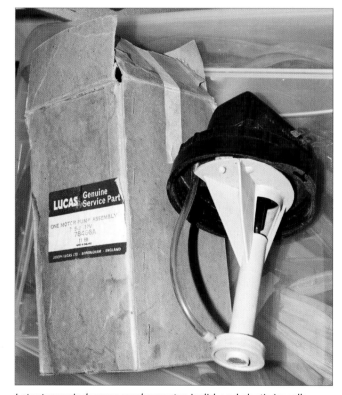

Later-type windscreen washer motor, jar lid, and plastic impeller, with its NOS packaging. This was sometimes used as a replacement for 3.8-liter windscreen washer assemblies.

LEFT - **1:** *NOS replacement gearbox top cover for a 4.2-liter all-synchromesh type gearbox. In this case the NOS part carries the part number written directly on it with a marker.*

LEFT - **2:** *Inside view of the same NOS 4.2-liter gearbox cover, showing it also carries the part number on the inside surface.*

NOS flywheel and packaging from the British Leyland era.

Another example of a part number being written directly on a replacement part. In this case these are upper steering column mounting brackets. Part number C29140 indicates this is a Series 2 part.

NOS upper steering column mounting bracket with the C part number on a sticker.

NOS 4.2-liter competition flywheel with part numbers painted on, as well as having what appears to be a label.

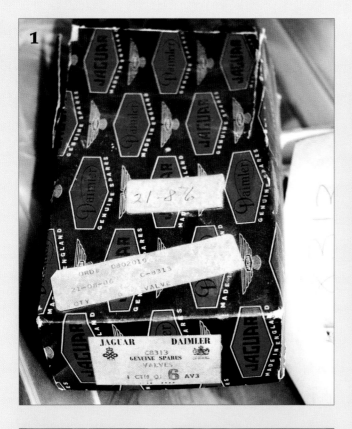

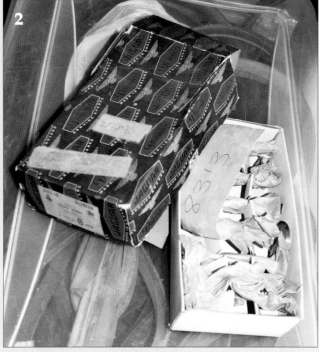

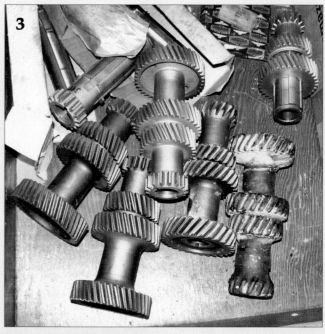

1 Red and black box for NOS valves with "JAGUAR," "Daimler" and the Jaguar wings symbol. A "JAGUAR," "DAIMLER" part number sticker is affixed on it.

2 Inside view of the NOS valves in their packaging. Note each valve is individually wrapped and is held in place by a slotted cardboard baffle in the bottom of the box.

3 Various sorts of NOS transmission layshafts. These include the single-piece Moss-type shafts with straight-cut gear teeth for the non-synchromesh first gear, later 4.2-liter type all synchromesh shafts with helical first gear, and some multi-piece layshafts. The multi-piece shafts may be from XK-120s, Mk Vs or early E-types with close-ratio gearboxes. The all-synchromesh layshaft on the lower right of the picture is still coated with a protective coating, likely a Cosmoline-type material or similar.

4 Early-type 3.8-liter NOS distributor. Note the wax-paper wrapping for the wire nuts and the Lucas red and black box with the part number and description printed on the top.

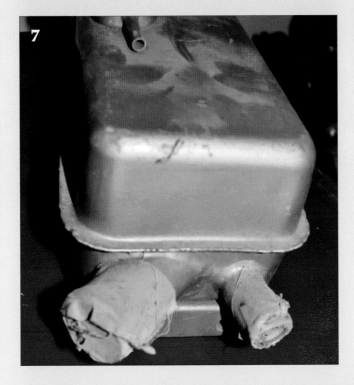

5 This NOS late 4.2-liter type distributor with the corrugated cardboard cover over the base to protect it during storage and shipping.

6 NOS 4.2-liter type header tank. For shipping and storage the inlet and outlet tubes are closed with cloth tape.

7 A close-up view of the cloth tape sealing the ports on the NOS header tank.

8 NOS packaging for cylinder sleeves of various sizes. These packages are from Nylen Products and Ramsco, and could have been one of the NOS liners used on E-types for rebuilds at dealers in the U.S., even though they may or may not be official Jaguar suppliers.

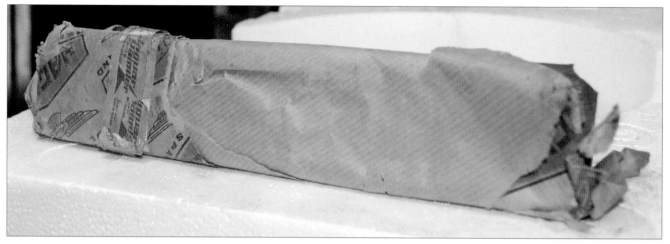

NOS ashtray panel assembly packaging with "JAGUAR ENGLAND" marking on the paper and sealed with "JAGUAR" Daimler tape.

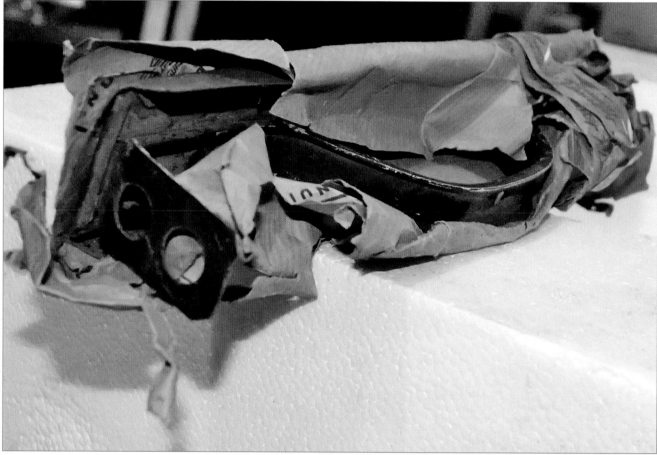

Rear view of ashtray panel assembly packaging showing the part inside.

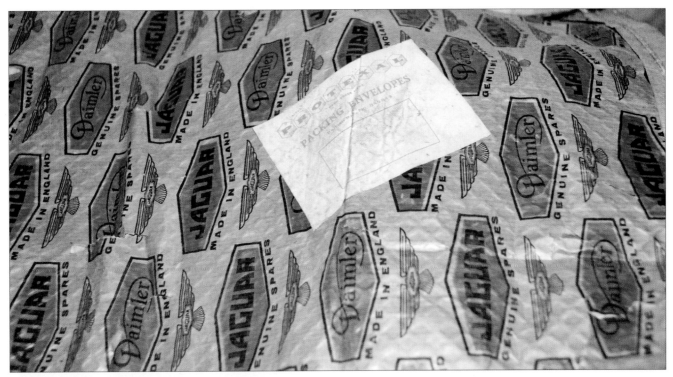

"PROTEXAL" label on a "JAGUAR" and "Daimler" marked flexible packaging container for a windscreen.

British Leyland label on a boot lid lock mounting bracket. This later-type labeling likely dates from the 1970s or 1980s.

3.8-LITER CHANGES
BY SERIAL NUMBER

This appendix lists the changes given in various published sources, including the relevant Jaguar parts catalogs. The listing is in order of chassis number, with right-hand drive roadster number (chassis number 850001, forward) determining position in the list. For every entry the chassis number (or engine or transmission number, as appropriate) is given for the transition point, and a description of the change (if known).

For this appendix, two references were used for 3.8-liter changes: *J.30 Spare Parts Catalogue (June 1961)* and *J.30 Spare Parts Catalogue (August 1963)*. The former is very early, and does not contain much information for this book in its text. It does, however, contain many illustrations that are similar, but not identical to, those in the AL1 reprint of June 1963. These differences often contain production change information. Since the June 1963 reprint does not go to the end of 3.8-liter E-type production in 1964, it will not list some of the later changes. At least some of these can be found in the other references used here.

It should be noted that no single source lists all the changes chronicled here, reflecting the somewhat confused state of the "official" production change lists. This does not mean, however, that all the entries here are complete, or that some of them are not in error (even though they may be from reputable sources). It will be many years before the full correct list is known, if it ever is.

The dates cited for the changes are approximate, and often different sources cite different dates. As Philip Porter noted in *Jaguar E-Type: The Definitive History*, the dates are when dealers were informed, so the changes occurred earlier.

While extensive effort has been spent compiling this list, there is often confusion as to what happened, when it happened, and sometimes even if it happened.

CHANGES IN ORDER OF CHASSIS NUMBER

850023/4
875026/7
▸ First type of detachable hardtop mounting assembly begins.

850047/8
860001
875132/3
885001
▸ About August 1961, a water deflector was fitted to the front stub axle carrier.

850078/9
▸ About October 1961, a new plastic license plate holder was introduced.

850087/8
875299/300
▸ About October 1961, the chrome finisher at the top of the doors was changed.

850087/8
875309/10
▸ About September 1961, the chrome finisher on the windscreen glass was changed.

850089/90
860003/4
875331/2
885014/5
▸ About October 1961, the handbrake assembly was changed to the auto-adjust type.

850091/2
875373/4
▶ About October 1961, the sealing rubber around the windows was changed.

850091/2
860004/5
875385/6
885020/1
▶ First 500 production ends at these chassis numbers. About September 1961, the bonnet latch, escutcheon, and so on were changed to inside lock. The rubber buffer cushioning the bonnet sides in the closed position was discontinued; this change was due to the new inside latch.

Numerous other changes were made:

▶ The front cover and breather assembly, and the flexible breather pipe to the open vent, were changed to a vent into the air-intake box.

▶ The base assembly for the air-intake box was changed to accept the vent.

▶ The gas tank was changed with the fitting of a one-piece sump.

▶ The fuel pump, bracket, pipe, and filter bracket were changed.

▶ The bracket for mounting the fuel filter to the frame was changed.

▶ The bonnet and front fender assemblies were changed with the bonnet latch moved inside.

▶ An extension assembly for the coil bracket was added.

▶ The generator was changed (part number 22531/A-C45.PV5/6 changed to 22902/A-C42).

▶ The voltage regulator and bracket were changed (part number 37304A/RB.310 changed to 37331A/RB.340).

▶ Earth cables were added for the cigar lighter.

▶ The outer rear hub bearings were enlarged.

▶ It was claimed in *Jaguar International Magazine*, March 1986, that the pressed-in louvers began in October 1961, but this actually occurred later.

850091/2
875385/6
▶ The hardtop fitting kit was changed.

850103/4
860005/6
875495/6
885025/6

▶ About October 1961, the driveshaft was changed and the driveshaft universal joints were enlarged.

850117/8
860006/7
875520/1
885032/3
▶ About October 1961, the single center drain tube for the boot lid aperture was changed to two tubes on the right and the left.

850136/7
860007/8
875541/2
885038/9
▶ About October 1961, the rear-suspension coil springs were enlarged, the seats for the springs were changed, and the aluminum packing piece at the top was dropped.

850168/9
860009/10
875589/90
885050/1
▶ About November 1961, the cigar lighter was changed.

850168/9
860009/10
875590/1
885050/1
▶ About November 1961, the support bracket for the rear engine mount was changed.

850178/9
860011/2
875607/8
885058/9
▶ About December 1961, the welded-together exhaust tailpipe assembly was changed to a two-piece assembly.

850209/10
860012/3
875760/1
885085/6
▶ About November 1961, two more rubber corner pads were added to the battery clamp.

850232/3
860020/1
875858/9
885104/5
▶ About December 1961, the clutch pedal, the bushing in the boss of the clutch pedal, and the housing for the clutch pedal and brake pedal were changed. The brass bush in the brake and clutch pedal housing was changed to impregnated plastic.

875910/1
885124/5
  ▶ The washers and collars on the connecting lever between the drop arm and the control rod of the throttle linkage were changed.

876014/5
885155/6
  ▶ The brake master cylinder assembly was changed.

850238/9
860138/9
876457/8
885384/5
  ▶ The front subframe assembly and hinge were changed.

860138/9
885384/5
  ▶ The front subframe assembly was changed on the coupes. In the *J.30 Spare Parts Catalogue (June 1963)*, a different front subframe assembly is listed as used on all roadsters, and no changes are listed.

  ▶ The bonnet hinge was changed on the coupe only. In the *J.30 Spare Parts Catalogue (June 1963)*, the later-type coupe bonnet hinge is listed for use on all roadsters.

850248/9
860020/1
875910/1
885124/5
  ▶ About January 1962, the spacing collar and washer on the accelerator pedal assembly were changed, and the accelerator-pedal lever assembly was changed.

850253/4
860022/3
875963/4
885142/3
  ▶ About January 1962, the front suspension assembly was changed. The front and rear brake caliper assemblies were changed from malleable iron to cast iron, and the pistons were changed to have an integral backing plate.

850254/5
860026/7
876014/5
885155/6
  ▶ About February 1962, the front and rear brake master cylinder assemblies were changed. The modification gave a more positive location of the rear spring support to the piston.

850254/5
860026/7
876030/1
885160/1
  ▶ About January 1962, the fuel pipe from the pump and its bracket were changed. The attachment of the line to the pump was now through a banjo fitting.

850273/4
861186/7
878020/1
886748/9
  ▶ About November 1962, the relay for the fan motor was changed and the forward wiring harness was changed.

850288/9
860028/9
876116/7
885205/6
  ▶ About February 1962, the tachometer was changed.

850290/1
860032/3
876129/30
885209/10
  ▶ About February 1962, the front suspension assembly was changed. The brake pad material was also changed.

850300/1
860112/3
876358/9
885317/8
  ▶ About January 1962, seatbelts were introduced as an option, and seatbelt attachment points were introduced. In *The Jaguar E-type: A Collector's Guide*, Skilleter quotes chassis number 875358/9 instead of 876358/9; *Jaguar International Magazine*, March 1986, quotes chassis numbers 850200/1 instead of 850300/1.

850321/2
860121/2
876394/5
885334/5
  ▶ About February 1962, the front and rear shock absorbers were changed.

850327/8
860138/9
876470/1
885398/9
  ▶ Calendar year 1961 production ended and 1962 production began.

850356/7
877430/1

> ▶ About July 1962, the hardtop mounting brackets were changed.

850357/8
860175/6
876581/2
885503/4

> ▶ In late winter of 1962, the floor assembly was changed to include footwells. Note that the *J.30 Spare Parts Catalogue (June 1963)* lists chassis numbers 876381/2 instead of 876581/2, the numbers given in other sources. *The Jaguar Service Bulletin* lists the body numbers for the change as OTS: 2879/2889, FHC:1635/1647.

> ▶ At the same time, Flintkote was added to the front floor. The front carpets were also changed.

860175/6
885503/4

> ▶ The bracket for the muffler was discontinued.

850376/7
860192/3
876638/9
885571/2

> ▶ About March 1962, the balance link for operation of the master cylinders was changed.

876664/5
885566/7

> ▶ About March 1962, a cable for the steering column lock connector to the instrument panel wiring was introduced along with the combined ignition switch-steering column lock for cars going to Germany.

860194/5
885584/5

> ▶ About March 1962, the glass and clasps for the rear quarter lights were changed. The mounting for the attachment block for the catch arm to the quarter-light frame was changed from brazed to screwed.

850403/4
860231/2
876846/7
885735/6

> ▶ About March 1962, the spring, covers, plunger, and so forth on the rack and pinion housing and the rack friction damper were changed.

850455/6
876974/5

> ▶ The hardtop fitting kit was changed.

850474/5
860374/5, including 860365

> ▶ About May 1962, the accelerator pedal assembly was changed to facilitate heel-and-toe operation.

850474/5
860374/5, including 860365
876998/9
885870/1

> ▶ About May 1962, the brake pedals were changed. The brake connecting lever was also changed to increase the mechanical advantage; an eccentric barrel nut was installed to adjust the servo arm.

850479/80
860386/7
877044/5
885887/8

> ▶ About May 1962, the driveshaft was changed, and "sealed for life" universal joints were introduced. A gaiter was fitted to the sliding joint, and the grease nipples on the universal joints and sliding joint were deleted.

850499/500
860435/6
877154/5
885970/1

> ▶ About May 1962, the horns were changed. The cable to the front lamp connector was changed.

850499/500
860425/6
877275/6
886045/6

> ▶ About May 1962, the hardware for the rack and pinion assembly was changed; a two-stud mount was introduced for the rack thrust plate, and the studs with locknuts replaced the two hexagon-headed setscrews.

850503/4
860450/1
877182/3
885984/5

> ▶ About June 1962, the oil seals in the hub carriers, for the fulcrum shafts, were changed.

860478/9
886013/4

> ▶ About May 1962, the frame for the door window and the rubber seal and the seal retainer for the cantrail were changed. The headlining on the cantrail and rear trim panels, the headlining, the panel assembly for trimming the windscreen header rail, and the trim panel assembly for the windscreen header rail were all changed. The chrome finishers on the roof gutters were changed.

- The casing assembly on the boot lid and the boot lid hinge assembly were changed. The prop supporting the boot lid in the open position, the pivot bracket on the boot lid for the prop, and the bracket on the body receiving the prop were all changed. The striker and safety catch for the boot lid lock and the screw for the interior light were changed. The glass, the hinge, and the catch for the quarter light were changed.

- The door shells and hinges were changed. In *The Jaguar E-type: A Collector's Guide*, Skilleter cites this change with chassis numbers 860475/6 instead of 860478/9. The fuel filler box and its lid were changed. Skilleter cites chassis numbers 860475/6 instead of 860478/9.

- The rear fender assembly, the tail panel below the boot lid, the boot gutters, the casing assembly at the rear side of the luggage compartment floor, the roof panel assembly, the windscreen header panel assembly, scuttle top panel and windscreen pillars, the cantrail panel assembly, the drip bead on the cantrail panel assembly, the windscreen pillar assembly, the underframe, the closing panels under the screen pillars, the outer skills, the roof panel, the rear fenders, and the boot lid were changed. The support panel for the boot lid aperture was also changed.

- About June 1962, the glass in the boot lid (clear or Sundym), and the chrome finisher at the top of the rubber seal for the boot window were changed. In *The Jaguar E-type: A Collector's Guide*, Skilleter cites this change with chassis numbers 860475/6 given instead of 860478/9. This was part of the extensive rework of the coupes that took place at these chassis numbers.

- Several other changes occurred about June 1962 as well: The front subframe assembly and bonnet hinge were changed. The sealing rubber around the boot lid aperture was changed from one piece to two pieces. The stop/tail/flasher lamps were changed because of the altered body panels.

850506/7
877201/2
- About May 1962, the door shell assembly was changed, and some cars before these chassis numbers were also modified. The chrome finisher at the top of the doors was changed, and some cars before these chassis numbers may have also been modified.

860580/1
886088/9
- About July 1962, the strikers for the luggage-floor hinged extension latches, and the rubber buffers for the extension in its raised position were changed.

850526/7
860580/1
877355/6
886092/3
- About June 1962, the body underframe assembly, floor assembly, and rear end body shell were changed. This included modifying the rear bulkhead of the body shell to include recesses to allow the seats 1-1/2 inches more rearward travel.

- In *The Jaguar E-type: A Collector's Guide*, Skilleter stated that a temporary modification had been carried out on the driver's side shortly after the introduction of the car.

- The seat slides were also changed, as were the mat assembly on the floor behind the seats, the mat assembly on the rear bulkhead panel, and the moquette face piece for the lower bulkhead panel, the casing assembly below the quarter light, the hinged extension for the luggage compartment floor, and the support rail assembly for the hinged extension in its lowered position.

850526/7
860583/4
877354/5
886094/5
- In summer or early fall of 1962, the fuel line from the pump to the gas tank outlet connection was changed from the Vulkollan material to Nylon.

850547/8
860646/7
877487/8
886213/4
- About June 1962, the lower tubular-shaft steering column was changed to a one-piece forging, and the seal where the shaft passes through the dash was changed.

850547/8
860646/7
877488/9
886218/9
- About June 1962, the clutch master cylinder was changed to give more positive location for the main spring support to the piston.

850548/9
860660/1
877518/9
886246/7
▸ About June 1962, the screw jack was changed to the cantilever type with integral handle, and the container for the jack was introduced.

850549/50
▸ Was the first transition point from tubular to solid forgings, then the original tubular type was again used for 850553 and 850554, and finally the solid forgings were adapted again at 850554/5.

860657/8
▸ 877534/5 was the first transition point from tubular to solid forgings, then the original tubular type was again used for 877545 to 877549, and the final transition to solid forgings came at 877549/50.

886246/7
▸ About July 1962, the rear end halfshafts were changed from a tubular construction to solid forgings. NOTE: Based on observations, it appears this sort of interleaving of the adaptation of a change in production occurred at other times, but few examples such as this one are recorded in the *Spare Parts Catalogue* [this example is from p.98, 1963 *J.30 Spare Parts Catalogue (June 1963)*].

▸ 850550/1 was a transition point of the handbrake assembly, then it transitioned back for 850553 and 850554, then back again at 850554/5.

860663/4
▸ 877534/5 was a transition point of the handbrake assembly, then it transitioned back for 877540 to 877566, then back again at 877566/7.

886262/3
▸ About July 1962, the handbrake assembly on the rear brakes was changed [this example is from p.111, 1963 *J.30 Spare Parts Catalogue (June 1963)*].

850554/5
860663/4
877566/7
886262/3
▸ The handbrake cable assembly was changed.

850555/6
860677/8
877556/7
886282/3
▸ About July 1962, the brake and clutch reservoir assemblies, including their mounting brackets, were changed. There is a slightly different listing for the bracket change in the *J.30 Spare Parts Catalogue (June 1963)*.

877556/7
886282/3
▸ The shield for the reservoirs was changed. The brake reservoir assembly and its bracket were also changed.

850558/9
860691/2
877578/9
886305/6
▸ About July 1962, the three studs on the thrust plate and the mounting rubber for the rack and pinion were changed.

850565/6
860677/8
▸ About July 1962, the mounting bracket for the fluid reservoirs changed. This is listed only in *Jaguar International Magazine*, March 1986.

850572/3
860722/3
877660/1
886381/2
▸ About August 1962, the rubber pads under the corners and end of the battery clamp were changed to a single pad.

850577/8
860740/1
877735/6
886455/6
▸ About September 1962, the mounting screws for rear calipers to the final drive unit were changed.

850583/4
860832/3
877963/4
886685/6
▸ About September 1962, the rear hubs and hub carriers were changed, and water throwers were added.

850587/8
860862/3
878036/7, including 876665-878036 for cars shipped to Germany.
886753/4, including 885567-886753 for cars shipped to Germany.
▸ About October 1962, the upper steering column assembly was changed, and felt bearings were replaced with Vulkollan bearings. The lock and ignition switch assembly on the steering column was changed from Neiman to Waso Werken, and a cable was introduced to connect the steering column lock connector to the instrument panel wiring.

850609/10
860912/3
878301/2
887131/2

▶ About October 1962, the patterns on the aluminum trim panels on the assembly above the gearbox and on the assembly over the gearbox and drive-shaft cover were changed. This is likely the change from the etched dot pattern aluminum trim to the embossed cross pattern aluminum trim.

861013/4
887316/7

▶ About December 1962, the boot lid prop and its bracket were changed.

861056/7
888066/7

▶ About February 1963, the interior mirror assembly was changed.

850647/8
861070/1
878936/7
888138/9

▶ A combination screwdriver (Phillips head or conventional) was introduced.

850648/9
861061/2
878888/9
888081/2

▶ About January 1963, the rubber mounts at the rear of the gearbox were changed to a spring mount, except for the following cars: chassis numbers 850653, 850654, 861087, 878895, 878900, 878907, 878908, 878913, 878914, 878915, 878926, 878936,878937, 878939, 878958, 878986, 879005, 879024, 879049, 888086, 888096, 888101, 888103, 888109, 888113, 888117, 888118, 888120, 888134, 888157, 888178, and 888238. In *The Jaguar E-type: A Collector's Guide,* and *Jaguar International Magazine,* March 1986, chassis numbers 850646/7 were given instead of 850648/9, and slightly different omission lists are given in some sources.

▶ The heat shield assembly was changed, probably to accommodate the new gearbox mount. *J.30 Spare Parts Catalogue (June 1963)* states that these chassis numbers were fitted with the early shield: 850653, 850654, 861087, 878895, 878900, 878907, 878908, 878913, 878914, 878915, 878926, 878936, 878937, 878938, 878958, 878986, 879005, 879024, 879049, 888086, 888096, 888101, 888103, 888109, 888113, 888117, 888118, 888120, 888134, 888157, 888178, and 888238.

850649/50
861079/80, including 860365
878963/4
888168/9

▶ The brake connecting lever between the pedal shaft and the plate of servo bellows was changed.

850653, 850654
861087
878895, 878900, 878907, 878908, 878913, 878914, 878915, 878926, 878936, 878937, 878939, 878958, 878986, 879005, 879024, 879049
888086, 888096, 888101, 888103, 888109, 888113, 888117, 888118, 888120, 888134, 888157, 888178, 888238

▶ These cars were fitted with the transmission rear end covers that were fitted to transmissions just prior to EB8858JS.

850654/5
861085/6
878979/80
888184/5

▶ About March 1963, the brake fluid reservoir caps were changed, and a level indicator was adopted. This change, as stated, is not correct. Level indicators had been fitted from the beginning of E-type production. Perhaps this is referring to one other of the several changes that took place in the reservoir caps that have been observed to have taken place.

850655/6
879023/4

▶ About March 1963, the seal assemblies at the rear of the wheel arches were changed.

850656/7
861090/1
879043/4
888240/1

▶ About March 1963, the radiator header-tank assembly was changed; the 4lb. pressure cap was changed to a 9lb. one.

▶ The water hose between the engine water outlet and the header tank was also changed.

861092/3
888256/7

▶ About August 1963, the mat assembly on the luggage compartment floor changed from a two-piece to a one-piece unit.

861098/9
888301/2

▶ About August 1963, the trim panel for the shut pillar, the casing assembly at the side of the luggage compartment floor, and the hinged extension assembly for the luggage compartment floor were changed.

- The shut pillar was changed. This is listed only in *Jaguar International Magazine*, March 1986.

- The catch operating the quarter lights was changed. The casing assembly below the quarter lights and the quarter-light catches were changed. The casing assembly at the side of the luggage compartment floor and the hinged extension assembly for the luggage compartment floor were changed.

850656/7
861426/7
888759/60
889696/7

- About January 1964, a cover was introduced for the brake fluid reservoir cap. Due to the date, right-hand drive coupe and left-hand drive chassis numbers, and the nature of the change, it is likely the chassis numbers 850656/7 here should be 850806/7. This is listed only in *The Jaguar E-type: A Collector's Guide*.

850678/9
861105/6
879131/2
888326/7

- About April 1963, various parts in the rear suspension, such as wishbones, mountings at inner fulcrum shafts, and the bracing plate, were changed.

850680/1
861120/1
879159/60
888352/3

- About April 1963, a canvas and rubber seal for the left-hand front frame undershield was introduced.

850695/6
861149/50
879291/2
888512/3

- About May 1963, the ashtray was changed.

850701/2
861168/9
879323/4
888542/3

- About November 1963, the clock in the tachometer was changed to one fitted with a rectifier. The clock dial is marked CE.1111/01 (except for a few early ones that were marked CE.1111/00 in error). A black sleeve indicates that the clock is fitted with a rectifier.

850707/8
861171/2
879331/2
888559/60

- About May 1963, a keeper plate was added to the anti-roll bar bushes. It is not clear if this reference is to the front or the rear anti-roll bar.

850708/9
861174/5
879342/3
888566/7

- About May 1963, the grab handle and its fixings were changed, and its position was slightly changed.

850712/3
861177/8
879372/3
888611/2

- About June 1963, the engine compartment undershields were increased in size and a cover was placed over the hole in the right-hand side shield, under the oil filter.

850713/4
861178/9
879422/3
888657/8

- About June 1963, a trim panel was fitted to the hinge face of the door and was retained by the door light-switch striker.

861178/9
888658/9

- About June 1963, "various new items" of boot lid trim were added. These "various new items" may include the "E-TYPE" badge, and perhaps a "3.8" plate that may have appeared on some late 3.8-liter cars, although since only coupe chassis numbers are listed the change is likely related only to trim around the rear window. A 1963 E-type roadster (chassis number 879325) was observed in the 1960s to be fitted with an "E-TYPE" trim piece (apparently the same as those subsequently used on 4.2-liter cars) on the boot lid in addition to the "JAGUAR" trim piece. There was no "3.8" or "4.2" trim. Of course, the "E-TYPE" trim could have been added after delivery of the car, but this would have had to occur when the car was relatively new; generally during this period E-types were not seen to be modified in such small details. The car appeared in other ways quite original and unmodified. Outside of this observation, the authors have seen no evidence that any 3.8-liter cars left the factory with other than just a "JAGUAR" plate on the boot lid.

879440/1
888672/3

- About June 1963, for cars with 3.54:1 rear ends, the rear end was changed. For cars with 3.54:1

rear ends, the rear brake discs were increased in thickness to 1/2-inch, the brake pad material was changed to Mintex M.59, and the rear calipers were mounted on adapter plates, as opposed to bolted direct.

879460/1
888694/5

▶ About June 1963, for cars with 3.31:1 rear ends, the rear end was changed. For cars with 3.31:1 rear ends, the rear brake discs were increased in thickness to 1/2 inch, the brake pad material was changed to Mintex M.59, and the rear calipers were mounted on adapter plates, as opposed to bolted direct.

850721/2
861184/5
879493/4
888705/6

▶ About June 1963, for cars with 3.07:1 rear ends, the rear end was changed. For cars with 3.07:1 rear ends, the rear brake discs were increased in thickness to 1/2 inch, the brake pad material was changed to Mintex M.59, and the rear calipers were mounted on adapter plates, as opposed to bolted direct.

850722/3
861202/3
879550/1
888759/60

▶ About August 1963, two fork ends replaced the compensator inner-lever link in the handbrake. Some sources cite chassis numbers 850727/8 rather than 850722/3.

850723/4
861186/7

▶ About June 1963, the fan motor relay was discontinued and the front wiring harness was changed.

850723/4
861188/9
879495/6
888697/8

▶ About June 1963, armrests were added to the doors.

850725/6
861197/8
879550/1
888766/7

▶ About August 1963, the turn signal/headlight-flasher switch was changed. The striker plate (likely the one in the turn signal/headlight-flasher switch) was changed.

850729/30
861203/4
879576/7
888790/1

▶ About June 1963, the filter in the clutch fluid reservoir was changed.

850734/5
861218/9
879680/1
888885/6

▶ About August 1963, two more windscreen-pillar outside chrome trim pieces were added.

879758/9
888966/7

▶ About September 1963, the 3.07:1 rear end ratio was made standard for Italy, France, Germany, Belgium, and the Netherlands.

850736/7
861215/6
879760/1
888858/9

▶ About August 1963, the console was changed. The new one had an armrest with storage space.

▶ This change was not made on chassis numbers 850725, 850727, 879531, 879543, 879545, 879546, 879553, 879556, 879562; these cars come before the listed change, so likely this means the new consoles were fitted to these earlier cars before it was made standard.

850736/7
861225/6
879820/1
889002/3

▶ About September 1963, the 3.31:1 rear end ratio was made standard for all countries except Italy, France, Germany, Belgium, the Netherlands, the United States, Canada, and Newfoundland.

850751/2
861253/4
879802/3
889029/30

▶ About September 1963, the front finisher trim panel was changed from embossed aluminum to leather. Since the change is from aluminum to leather, it is likely this is the front finisher panel to the console, not the dash (which was trimmed in vinyl on the later 3.8-liter cars).

850751/2
861255/6
879892/3
889053/4
(and some prior cars)

   ▶ About September 1963, the front carpets were changed to a type with a plastic heel pad.

850754/5
861270/1
879989/90
889095/6

   ▶ About September 1963, the mufflers and their mounts were changed.

880025/6
889123/4
(including 879751 to 879808 and 888952 to 888994)

   ▶ About September 1963, the 3.54:1 rear end ratio was made standard for the United States, Canada, and Newfoundland.

861274/5
880165/6
889134/5

   ▶ About November 1963, the wiper arms were changed to carry longer blades.

850766/7
861294/5
880212/3
889235/6

   ▶ About November 1963, the A-post rubber seals were changed. On the roadsters, the two-piece seal was replaced by a one-piece seal, and on the coupes, the separate cantrail seal and A-post seals were replaced by a single seal. The seal retainer on the cantrails on the coupes was no longer required after this change.

850767/8
880290/1

   ▶ About January 1964, a hole was added to the number-plate panel at the rear to allow access to the boot lid latch in case the release cable should break. Access was by using a right-angle 3/16-inch-diameter rod. A rubber seal was inserted in this hole.

850771/2
861324/5
880411/2
889346/7

   ▶ About November 1963, the carpet fasteners were changed.

850778/9
861341/2
880458/9
889374/5

   ▶ About November 1963, the sealing rubber on the door shut pillar was changed.

850784/5
861363/4
880561/2
889451/2

   ▶ About December 1963, the differential breather was changed to one with an extension tube on the differential cover.

850785/6
861383/4
880614/5
889503/4

   ▶ About January 1964, the ashtray was changed. The new one is not interchangeable with the old. This is likely the institution of the large, rectangular ashtray.

850785/6
861385/6
880618/9
889509/10

   ▶ About January 1964, the fuel pump was changed. The operating pressure went up.

850786/7
861388/9
880630/1
889525/6

   ▶ About March 1964, the radio was changed to use only one speaker. Based on observations of many cars, however, is appears that at least some earlier cars were delivered with only one speaker. The radio panel part of the console was also changed.

880631/2
889526/7

   ▶ About April 1964, sealed-beam headlights were adopted for cars going to Brazil, Canada, Chile, Colombia, Cuba, Dominican Republic, Egypt, El Salvador, Greece, Guatemala, Haiti, Hawaii, Jordan, Lebanon, Madeira, Mexico, Newfoundland, Nicaragua, Panama, Persian Gulf, Peru, Philippines, Puerto Rico, Saudi Arabia, Syria, the United States, Uruguay, Venezuela, and South Vietnam.

850805/6
861423/4
880754/5
889688/9

   ▶ In late winter or early spring of 1964, the roller bearing seals in the halfshaft universal joints were changed, and covers for the journal assemblies were added. *The Jaguar E-type: A Collector's Guide* gives chassis numbers 889697/8 as the left-hand drive coupe chassis for the change, not 889688/9.

850806/7
861426/7
880759/60
889696/7
▶ About March 1964, the protective caps for the brake fluid level indicators were changed.

850807/8
861445/6
880834/5
889779/80
▶ About March 1964, the brake pedals were changed to improve attachment to the pedal shaft, and a tab-washer was added to the pinch bolt.

850808/9
861445/6
880839/40
889786/7
▶ About March 1964, the interior door trim was changed.

850810/1
861460/1
880870/1
889819/20
▶ About March 1964, the turn signal/headlight-flasher switch clamp bracket was changed from being a part of the switch to being part of the steering column.

850818/9
861480/1
880982/3
889966/7
▶ About April 1964, the upper steering column bearings were changed from Vulkollan to another polymer, Elastollan.

850824/5
861520/1
881152/3
890170/1
▶ About April 1964, the front bush in the rear-suspension radius arms was changed.

850839/40
861549/50
881202/3
890234/5
▶ About April 1964, the starter solenoid was changed to reduce water leakage.

850842/3
861556/7
881260/1
890250/1
(and a few earlier cars)
▶ About April 1964, the rubber seals were improved. It is not clear what seals this is referring to.

850856/7
881249/50
▶ About April 1964, the chrome finishers on the top of the doors were changed.

850858/9
861604/5
881281/2
890317/8
▶ About May 1964, the striker for the turn signal/headlight-flasher switch was changed.

861615/6
890339/40
▶ About May 1964, the rear casings at the side of the luggage compartment floor were changed.

850882/3
861661/2
881437/8
890487/8
▶ About May 1964, the grille bar mounts were changed to incorporate a rubber mount.

850888/9
881590/1
▶ About August 1964, the chrome finishers at the sides of the windscreen were changed.

850907/8
861719/20
881696/7
890714/5
▶ About October 1964, packing rings were added to the top of the rear springs.

850907/8
861722/3
881705/6
890721/2
▶ About October 1964, the gas cap was changed. This may be the end of the reeded-edge chrome steel fabricated cap and the beginning of the cast fluted cap.

850934/5
861780/1
881863/4
890847/8
▶ About October 1964, the feed pipe filter to the fuel pump was changed.

850934/5
881864/5
▶ About October 1964, the convertible top cover was changed.

850942
861798
881885
890871
▶ End of 3.8-liter E-type production.

CHANGES IN ORDER OF ENGINE NUMBER

R1008/9
▶ In June 1961, the size of the oil pump was increased for right-hand drive cars.

R1075/6
▶ About October 1961, the separate intermediate timing chain sprockets were replaced by a single-piece unit.

R1216/7
▶ About August 1961, the inlet camshaft was changed to have a hole in the base.

R1458/9
▶ In October 1961, the crankshaft pulley was changed. The new crankshaft pulley was cast iron instead of alloy.

R1509/10
▶ The dynamo mounting bracket, pulley, and fan for dynamo pulley were changed. The generator adjusting link and the bolts securing the timing cover to the cylinder block were changed.

R1844/5
▶ About October 1961, the generator adjusting link was changed and a jockey pulley assembly was added.

R1845/6
▶ The bolts securing the timing cover to the cylinder block were changed.

R2563/4
▶ About December 1961, the rear end crankshaft cover was changed, an asbestos oil seal was added, and the crankshaft was codified accordingly. The cover assembly for the rear of the cylinder block, and the associated hardware, changed.

R2599/600
▶ About December 1961, the oil thrower at the rear of the exhaust camshaft, the sealing port at the left rear of the cylinder head, and the cover for the left-hand (exhaust) camshaft were changed.

R2933/4
▶ About January 1962, the air-balance pipe was changed to accommodate the simplified throttle linkage; the air-balance pipe changed from three bosses to two. The slave shaft assembly for throttle operation was changed to two slave shafts from the previous arrangement with three slave shafts using a flexible coupling.

R3161/2
▶ About February 1962, the big end connecting rod bearing clearances were reduced.

R3690/1
▶ About March 1962, the head stud holes in the cylinder head gasket were enlarged.

R3854/5
▶ About March 1962, the spark plug cables were increased in length and rerouted. The spacers for the spark plug leads were changed.

R5000/1
▶ About May 1962, the inlet camshaft was drilled to reduce cold-starting noise.

R5249/50
▶ About June 1962, the pulley for the water pump was changed to accept the new duplex belt, and the material of the pulley was changed from aluminum to cast iron. The crankshaft pulley for the fan belt, and the dynamo and jockey pulley assemblies were changed to accept the new duplex belt. The early fan belts were of the single-grooved type, and the later belts were of the wide, double-grooved type.

R5399/400
▶ About June 1962, the sump filter basket was changed to have four semi-circular cutouts.

R5532/3
▶ About June 1962, the intermediate damper assembly for the upper timing chain was changed.

R6417/8
▶ About September 1962, the sump drain plug was changed to steel.

R6723/4
▶ About September 1962, the inlet valve guides were lengthened.

R7103/4
▶ About September 1962, the connecting rods and pistons were changed. The upper pressure ring was chamfered on its inner edge, and a two-part scraper ring introduced. The connecting rods had an oil spray hole added near the small end, and were marked with yellow paint near the rib.

R7194/5
- About October 1962, the dowels between the bearing caps and the cylinder block were enlarged.

R7307/8
- About October 1962, the crankshaft was changed.

R8138/9
- About November 1962, the vibration damper for the lower timing chain was changed.

R8299/300
- About November 1962, a quick-lift thermostat with a higher opening temperature was fitted.

R9520/1
- About February 1963, a quick-lift thermostat with a higher opening temperature was fitted.

R9527/8
- About December 1962, the spark plugs were changed to Champion UN.12Y.

R9699/700
- About February 1963, the dipstick was changed.

RA1099/100
- About March 1963, the automatic fan belt tensioning system was changed.

RA1100/1
- The carrier for the jockey pulley was changed.

RA1381/2
- About April 1963, the distributor and vacuum suction pipe were changed.

RA2077/8
- About June 1963, the oil pump was changed, and the oil suction pipe was changed to 3/4 inch instead of 11/16 inch.

RA2289/90
- About August 1963, rubber sleeves were fitted to the spark plug wires where they enter the distributor cap.

RA2463/4
- The needle valve and seat in the carburetor float chamber was changed to Delrin acetal resin, and changes were made in the lid and hinged lever. In *The Jaguar E-type: A Collector's Guide*, Skilleter cites a date of about June 1963 for this change, and in *Jaguar E-Type: The Definitive History*, Porter cites about April 1964. This is another example of extremely different dates being cited for a given change.

RA2971/2
- About September 1963, the exhaust valves were changed to be made of a different material.

RA3289/90
- About September 1963, the water pump impeller was changed.

RA4115/6
- About January 1964, the throttle spring bearings in the carburetors were changed to an impregnated plastic material.

RA4573/4
- About March 1964, the sump drain plug was changed.

RA4974/5
- About March 1964, the oil filter was changed.

RA5633/4
- About April 1964, the spark plug cables were changed.

RA5648/9
- About March 1964, the pistons were changed to have chamfer and oil drain holes below the control ring (to reduce oil use). This is listed only in *The Jaguar E-type: A Collector's Guide*.

RA5736/7
- About April 1964, the cylinder heads on E-types and Mk X cars were made the same. It is not clear from this if the E-type head or the Mk X head, or both, were changed.

RA5800/1
- About April 1964, the clutch was changed to the Laycock diaphragm type and the flywheel was changed to accept either Borg & Beck or the diaphragm clutch.

RA5885/6
- About April 1964, the jockey pulley bracket was changed to have impregnated plastic bushes instead of the brass bushes used earlier.

RA6024/5
- About May 1964, the lower timing chain intermediate damper was changed. The new damper was positioned differently and was attached to two tapped bosses on the cylinder block.

RA6419/20
- About August 1964, the front timing cover was changed so that the oil seal could be changed without removing the cover.

RA6453/4
- About May 1964, the crankshaft dampener was changed.

RA6603/4

▸ About May 1964, a support was added to the first intermediate bearing cap to support the oil delivery pipe, and this support replaced a lock washer that was on the cap before.

RA6745/6

▸ About August 1964, the scraper rings on the pistons were changed for 8.0:1 and 9.0:1 compression ratio engines. The new rings were Maxiflex 50.

RA6833/4

▸ About July 1964, the distributor was changed on the 9.0:1 compression ratio engines, and a plastic ring impregnated with magnetized metal particles replaced the metal magnetic ring in the oil filter assembly.

RA7175/6

▸ About October 1964, the intake manifold gasket was changed from cupronickel to a tin-plate material.

RA7201/2

▸ About October 1964, the distributor was changed on 8.0:1 compression ratio engines.

RA7323/4

▸ About August 1964, engine-lifting brackets were added to the cylinder head. Some head studs had to be made longer. The spark plug cables had to be lengthened to accommodate the new engine-lifting brackets.

CHANGES IN ORDER OF TRANSMISSION NUMBER

EB245/6JS

▸ The rear end transmission cover and the speedometer driver gear were changed.

EB1653/4JS

▸ The dowel screws in the transmission gear-selection mechanism were changed.

EB8858/9JS

▸ About February 1963, the rear end cover of transmission was changed. This change was related to the change in the rear engine mounting.

4.2-Liter Changes by Serial Number

This appendix lists the changes given in various published sources, including the relevant Jaguar parts catalogs. The listing is in order of chassis number, with right-hand drive roadster number (chassis number 1E1001 forward for Series 1, and 1R1001 forward for Series 2) determining position in the list. For every entry the chassis number (or engine or transmission number, as appropriate) transition point is given, and a description of the change, if known. In cases where a change is listed only by a single reference other than the factory literature, that reference is cited.

For this appendix the sources used were: *J.37 Spare Parts Catalogue (November 1969)*; *J.38 Spare Parts Catalogue (December 1966)*; *Series 2 Parts List (1969)*; *Series 2 Parts Catalogue (1979)*; and the same published sources as used in the 3.8-liter section above (the notes appearing at the beginning of that section apply here as well). In particular, note that the dates cited for the changes from *The Jaguar E-type: A Collector's Guide*, *Jaguar E-Type: The Definitive History*, and *Jaguar International Magazine*, March 1986, are approximate.

CHANGES IN ORDER OF CHASSIS NUMBER

1E1011/2
1E10312/3
1E20079/80
1E30251/2
- About January 1965, spacers were introduced at the front mounts of the seat slides where they attach to the floor.

1E1019/20
1E10323/4
1E20081/2
1E30268/9
- The vacuum reservoir was changed.

1E1038/9
1E10337/8
1E20097/8
1E30291/2
- About March 1965, the sealing at the front ball joints was improved.

1E1039/40
1E10337/8
1E20097/8
1E30292/3
- About January 1965, the seat slide fittings were changed. Contrast the cited date of January 1965 to the March 1965 date given in the change listed just above, noting that two of the four chassis number transition points of the above change are the same. This is one of many examples of the unreliability of reported dates for production changes, and the value, instead, of tying production changes to the more reliable chassis numbers.

1E1046/7, including 1E1021
1E10337/8
1E20099/100, including 1E20083
1E30301/2, including 1E30271
- About February 1965, shields were added to the front brake discs. The left-hand tie rod lever was changed. The bolt and washer mounting for the front caliper to the stub axle carriers was changed.

1E1060/1
1E10359/60
1E20102/3
1E30349/50
- The cockpit panel assembly at the side of the gearbox was changed. About November 1964, the leather shift boot was changed to a rubber boot.

1E1062/3
1E10771/2
1E20362/3, including 1E20335
1E30856/7
- ▶ The horns were changed.

1E1069/70
1E10425/6
1E20116/7
1E30401/2
- ▶ The body shell underframe and rear end assembly were changed.

1E20116/7
1E30401/2
- ▶ About February 1965, the casing assembly below the quarter lights was changed and the pocket assembly in the casing below the quarter lights was deleted. The cover assembly over the spare wheel and gas tank and forward luggage floor area were trimmed, and the old luggage floor mat was done away with. The rear-wheel arch covers were changed from moquette trimmed to PVC trimmed. The hinged extension board and its support rail assembly were changed. Some carpets and Hardura mats and insulating felts and interior trim were changed.

- ▶ About March 1965, body shell changes took place.

1E1076/7
1E10429/30, including 1E10427
1E20136/7, including 1E20132
1E30442/3
- ▶ About March 1965, the front suspension was changed. The front brake caliper was changed. The front calipers were altered to move the bleed screw to the inner side of the assembly. The hydraulic pipe from the front flexible hose to the front brake calipers was changed.

1E1103/4
1E10045/6
1E20207/8
1E30033/4
- ▶ About June 1965, the speedometer cable was changed.

1E1151/2
1E10702/3
1E20328/9
1E30771/2
- ▶ About May 1965, the axle ratio was changed from 3.31:1 to 3.07:1 for all cars except those exported to the United States, Canada, and Newfoundland, which were 3.54:1. Some sources cite chassis numbers 1E1072/3 instead of 1E10702/3; likely the 1E1072/3 citation is an error.

1E10739/40
1E30806/7
- ▶ The 3.54:1 rear end assembly was changed for cars exported to the United States, Canada, and Newfoundland.

1E1162/3
1E10771/2
1E20362/3, including 1E20335
1E30856/7
- ▶ About June 1965, the forward wiring harness and front lamp harness were changed.

- ▶ The horns were changed.

1E1164/5
1E20370/1
- ▶ The forward wiring harness and the instrument panel wiring harness were changed.

1E1164/5
1E10753/4
1E20370/1
1E30824/5
- ▶ About June 1965, the windscreen washer bottle was changed to plastic, and pre-timed operation was deleted.

1E10753/4
1E30824/5
- ▶ The instrument panel wiring harness was changed.

1E1177/8
1E10783/4
1E20396/7
1E30861/2
- ▶ For 3.07:1 rear ends

1E10739/40
1E30806/7
- ▶ For 3.54:1 rear ends

- ▶ About June 1965, the rear end assembly was changed for cars exported to the United States, Canada, and Newfoundland. About June 1965, the rear end changed to a type with driveshaft flanges as part of the driveshafts. The 3.07:1 rear end assembly was changed for all countries except the United States, Canada, and Newfoundland.

1E1201/2
1E10847/8
1E20501/2
1E30889/90
- ▶ About June 1965, the console was changed. This may be the point at which the vinyl shift boot was introduced.

- ▶ The driveshaft tunnel changed.

1E1225/6
1E10957/8
1E20611/2
1E30911/2
(and some previous chassis)

- ▶ About June 1965, a speedometer-drive access aperture, with cover, was added to the right-hand side gearbox side panel.

1E1225/6
1E10957/8
1E20611/2
1E30981/2

- ▶ About June 1965, a rubber sealing plug was added to seal the gearbox apertures. The left-hand water-feed pipe to the heater, behind the dash panel, between the water control valve and the heater radiator, was changed.

1E1234/5
1E11165/6
1E20632/3
1E31243/4

- ▶ About November 1965, the rack and pinion assembly was changed.

1E1236/7
1E10978/9
1E20638/9
1E31002/3

- ▶ The rear hub carrier and its oil seal were changed.

1E1252/3
1E11048/9
1E20691/2
1E31077/8

- ▶ About September 1965, the front cylinder head cover and the crankcase breather arrangement were changed from the non-U.S. type to a standard type for all cars. The inlet manifold stud for the water outlet was changed, and a stud and distance piece for the water outlet pipe and breather pipe were added for non-U.S. cars. The base assembly for the air-intake with three trumpets and the adapter for the breather pipe were changed to a standard type for all cars (U.S. cars were no different).

1E1285/6
1E11117/8
1E20752/3
1E31170/1

- ▶ About September 1965, the front closing panel assemblies for the cockpit and sills were changed.

1E1292/3
1E11120/1
1E20762/3
1E31176/7

- ▶ About November 1965, the rear shock absorbers were changed.

1E20851/2
1E31412/3

- ▶ About November 1965, the coupe rear-door support went from post-type prop (where a single post was swung out from a single pivot point to be seated in a socket) to the hinged type (where the prop was made of two pieces hinged in the middle and permanently attached on both ends)

1E1333/4
1E11157/8

- ▶ About November 1965, sealing panels were added between the rear bulkhead panel and wheel-arch valances.

1E1376/7
1E11363/4
1E20899/900
1E31526/7

- ▶ About November 1965, the rear coil springs were changed.

1E1386/7
1E11546/7
1E20936/7
1E31778/9

- ▶ About March 1966, more mud shielding was fitted to the front frame.

1E20938/9
1E31787/8

- ▶ About March 1966, a vanity mirror was added to the passenger's sun visor.

1E20952/3
1E31919/20

- ▶ About February 1966, the coupe window frame seals were changed from felt to a flocked runner.

1E1408/9
1E11714/5
1E20977/8
1E32008/9

- ▶ About March 1966, the standard tires were changed to Dunlop SP.41 HR tires, except for cars exported to Australia, Canada, Newfoundland, New Zealand, and the United States. The speedometers were changed to reflect the Dunlop tire change. Special rear-suspension bump stops were used to avoid fouling the new Dunlop tires.

1E1411/2
1E11727/8
1E20995/6
1E32008/9

▶ The bracket assembly for the rear bumpers was changed. An attachment bracket assembly for the rear bumpers was introduced.

1E1412/3
1E11534/5
1E20992/3
1E31764/5

▶ About March 1966, the steering assembly was changed (a seven-tooth pinion replaced the eight-tooth pinion) to improve steering when radial-ply tires were fitted.

1E1412/3
1E11740/1
1E20999/1000
1E32009/10

▶ About March 1966, the brake light switch was repositioned. The front wiring harness was changed. The rear bumper fittings were changed so that the bumpers could be removed from outside the car. New brake and clutch master cylinders and pedal housings were fitted to standardize the two-seater cars with the 2+2 cars, and the brake light switch was repositioned.

1E1418/9
1E11802/3
1E21037/8
1E32039/40

▶ The trimmed base assembly of the seats, and the screws and washers mounting them to the slides, were changed.

1E1423/4
1E11885/6
1E21075/6
1E32089/90

▶ An O-ring was placed on the bonnet latch operating rod to prevent vibration of the rod.

1E12024/5
1E32193/4

▶ About December 1965, a hazard warning light (or four-way flasher) was fitted as standard. Porter's *Jaguar E-Type: The Definitive History* cites this change as occurring for U.S. cars in about July 1967.

1E21133/4
1E32267/8

▶ About September 1966, the hinged extension board in the luggage area was changed.

1E1430/1
1E12169/70
1E21139/40
1E32315/6
1E50156/7
1E76000/1

▶ About September 1966, the cooling fan thermostat was changed.

1E1457/8
1E12033/4
1E21206/7
1E32200/1

▶ About March 1966, the upper steering column was changed. About September 1966, the turn signal/headlight-flasher switch was changed.

1E1464/5
1E12521/2
1E21214/5
1E32596/7

▶ About September 1966, the air cleaner and its support bracket were changed.

1E21222/3
1E32608/9
1E50001
1E75001

▶ The rear defroster switch was changed and a warning light was added. The warning lamp dims when the side lamps are on. Dates of April 1966 and July 1967 were given in various sources for this change.

1E1478/9
1E12579/80
1E21227/8
1E32631/2

▶ About September 1966, the bonnet, including front fenders, front bumpers, and heater air-intake plenum, were changed to the type as used on the 2+2s.

1E1483/4
1E12637/8
1E21234/5
1E32666/7
1E50007/8
1E75074/5

▶ About September 1966, a rubber cover was added to the tops of the brake fluid warning terminals. This entry may be an error; reported 3.8-liter changes list such rubber covers being added at chassis numbers 850656/7, 861426/7, 888759/60, and 889696/7 at about January 1964. The authors have generally observed these covers being used on the later 3.8-liter cars and on 4.2-liter cars. It is also possible that this entry may be referring to a change in the covers, rather than the introduction of the covers on 4.2-liter cars. This point needs further research.

1E1489/90
1E12687/8

▶ About September 1966, sun visors were added.

1E1489/90
1E12692/3
1E21253/4
1E32684/5

▶ About September 1966, a rubber seat was added to the top of the spring in the rear transmission mount, and the spring retainer was changed.

1E1497/8
1E12716/7
1E21265/6
1E32691/2

▶ About September 1966, the illumination color of the instruments and switch label strip was changed from blue to green.

1E21311/2
1E32765/6

▶ About September 1966, the regulator channel for the wind-up windows was changed.

1E1544/5
1E12964/5
1E21334/5
1E32887/8

▶ About December 1966, a heat shield was introduced for the head pipes. This may be referring to the alternator heat shield.

1E1560/1
1E13010/1
1E21341/2
1E32941/2

▶ About November 1966, the clutch and brake master cylinders were modified to have shorter pushrods, to change pedal angles, and to improve the accelerator pedal angle, and a change was made in the accelerator pedal assembly.

1E50121/2
1E75862/3

▶ About December 1966, the screws retaining the chrome beads at the top of the doors were changed to retainers and rivets.

1E1598/9
1E13181/2
1E21379/80
1E33119/20
1E50155/6
1E75991/2

▶ About December 1966, the mufflers changed from being welded to the tailpipes to being clipped to them. This is an unusual entry, since a similar change occurred earlier during 3.8-liter production at chassis numbers 850178/9, 860011/2,875607/8, and 885058/9. The authors are not aware of early 4.2-liter cars having mufflers welded to the tailpipes.

1E1606/7
1E13205/6
1E21387/8
1E33149/50

▶ About March 1967, the right-hand side scuttle top casing (under dash panel) was changed from Rexine-trimmed aluminum to fiberboard.

1E50422/3
1E76663/4

▶ The trim panels above the rear door aperture, as well as the headlining, was changed.

1E50573/4
1E76888/9
(and certain individual earlier cars)

▶ Seatbelts were available for the rear seats.

1E1657/8
1E13386/7
1E21388/9
1E33139/40

▶ About March 1967, the windscreen glass was changed.

1E1685/6
1E13588/9
1E21441/2
1E33548/9
1E50585/6
1E76910/1

▶ About March 1967, the shift lever boot was changed to Ambla (a vinyl material) from the grommet that was used previously. This is likely the introduction of the third type of shift lever boot as found on late Series 1 and early Series 2 cars.

1E1685/6
1E13724/5
1E21442/3
1E33643/4

▶ About March 1967, the center scuttle top casing was changed from Rexine-covered aluminum to fiber-board.

1E1689/90
1E13846/7
1E21450/1
1E33708/9
1E50640/1
1E76933/4

▶ About July 1967, the linkage between the tailpipes was changed from bolted to welded.

1E50660/1
1E76949/50

▶ About July 1967, the upper squab of the back seat was changed.

1E50680/1
1E77376/7

▶ About July 1968, the package trays were changed.

1E1692/3
1E13951/2
1E21450/1
1E33774/5

▶ About July 1967, the drain tray on the doors was changed.

1E1711/2
1E14582/3
1E21472/3
1E34146/7
1E50709/10
1E77046/7

▶ About January 1968, the motif bar and its rubber mountings were changed.

1E1723/4
1E13150/1
1E21480/1
1E33090/1
1E50165/6
1E75546/7

▶ About July 1967, there were numerous changes in the electrical equipment, an ignition warning light replaced the oil pressure switch, and the old oil pressure switch in the cylinder block oil gallery was replaced by a plug. For the 2+2s, at least, the forward wiring harness, the instrument panel wiring harness, and the alternator harness were changed.

1E13804/5
1E33688/9
1E76921/2

▶ About July 1967, a cover was added to the four-way flasher switch panel (for those cars with four-way flashers).

1E1762/3
1E15109/10
1E21488/9
1E34302/3

▶ About July 1967, the rear hub carriers were changed.

1E50874/5
1E77406/7

▶ About July 1968, the diameter of the torsion bars was increased.

1E1813/4
1E11534/5
1E21517/8
1E34338/9
1E50911/2
1E77474/5

▶ New wheels with the forged center hub and straight spokes were introduced for the chrome wire wheels only. Some sources cite chassis number 1E15486/7 instead of 1E11534/5. Dates of May 1967 and July 1968 are cited for this change.

1E15179/80
1E34582/3

▶ About January 1968, U.S. Federal specification cars were introduced. This is listed only in *The Jaguar E-type: A Collector's Guide*. It is possible that 1E15179/80 should be 1E15979/80.

1E1852/3
1E15752/3
1E21578/9
1E34457/8
1E50971/2
1E77601/2

▶ About July 1968, a forged hub was introduced for the painted wire wheels. This is very likely the "easy-clean" hub.

1E1863/4
1E15888/9
1E21583/4
1E34249/50
1E50974/5
1E77644/5

▶ About July 1967, the headlight covers were discontinued. This may be the introduction of the open headlights without the other modifications attributed to Series 1.5 cars, *i.e.* the Series 1.25 cars. In *Jaguar E-Type: The Definitive History*, Porter stated that about January 1968 the bonnet was changed to give direct access to the headlights, but he listed chassis numbers 1E34549/50 instead of 1E34249/50.

1E1886/7
1E15981/2
1E21619/20
1E34602/3

▸ About September 1967, the Powr-Lok differential was discontinued as standard, except for the U.S. 3.54:1 ratio axle. This is listed only in *The Jaguar E-type: A Collector's Guide.*

1E1895/6
1E16009/10
1E21628/9
1E34633/4
1E51016/7
1E77694/5

▸ About July 1968, the fuel filter was changed to one with more filter area.

1E1904/5
1E16056/7
1E21661/2
1E32771/2
1E51042/3
1E77700/1

▸ The fuel filter element was changed from gauze to a renewable fiber element. *Jaguar E-Type: The Definitive History* cites a date of about July 1968 for this change, while *The Jaguar E-type: A Collector's Guide* cites about February 1968. In addition, the latter cites chassis numbers 1E34771/2 instead of 1E32771/2, and numbers 1E50142/3 instead of 1E51042/3.

1E1919/20
1E16098/9
1E21668/9
1E34846/7
1E51058/9
1E77704/5

▸ About July 1968, the tires were changed to Dunlop SP Sport, and whitewalls were used for cars exported to the United States.

1E1925/6
1E16720/1
1E21668/9
1E34850/1
1E51066/7
1E77704/5

▸ In early 1968, grease nipples were reintroduced on the halfshaft universal joints. In some references, chassis numbers 1E16126/7 are cited instead of 1E16720/1, and numbers 1E50166/7 are cited instead of 1E51066/7.

1E2038/9
1E21783/4

▸ About April 1968, the dashboard was revised. Heater controls, choke, and switches were changed, a lid was added to the glovebox, and the heater box was changed. This is likely also the point of introduction of the rocker switches, which was probably simultaneous with the addition of the glovebox lid (except for the 2+2 cars, which had it earlier).

1E2050/1
1E31806/7
1E51212/3

▸ The radiator was changed to a vertical-flow type, as already fitted to left-hand drive cars. The date for this change is alternately listed as April and July of 1968.

▸ About July 1968, the header tank and cap were changed.

▸ About April or July 1968, the water pump assembly, the thermostat, and the breather pipe were changed to the type already fitted to left-hand drive cars. The water outlet housing and thermostat housing were changed.

▸ About April 1968, the single cooling fan was replaced by dual cooling fans, as already fitted to left-hand drive cars. This is listed only in *The Jaguar E-type: A Collector's Guide.*

1E16537/8
1E34944/5
1E77837/8

▸ About July 1968, the water temperature gauge was changed to one with zones only marked, as opposed to the earlier calibrated gauge. This is listed only in *The Jaguar E-type: A Collector's Guide.*

SERIES 2 CHASSIS
(Note that the prefix is now "R")

1R1012/3
1R7442/3
1R20006/7
1R25283/4
1R35010/1
1R40207/8

▸ About January 1969, the alternator was changed to have side-entry cables, for cars not fitted with air conditioning. The alternator harness was changed.

1R35018/9
1R40238/9

▸ The handbrake lever assembly was changed.

1R1053/4
1R20072/3
1R35098/9
- ▶ About February 1969, earless knock-off hubcaps were introduced on right-hand drive cars (as on the left-hand drive cars).

1R7747/8
1R25430/1
- ▶ The choke assembly was changed.

1R1057/8
1R7795/6
1R20087/8
1R25430/1
- ▶ The screen rail fascia and the defrosting equipment were changed.

1R1057/8
1R20094/5
1R35098/9
- ▶ About December 1968, a steering column lock was fitted to right-hand drive cars.

1R1060/1
1R7829/30
1R20101/2
1R25438/9
1R35098/9
1R40507/8
- ▶ About March 1969, the master cylinder spacer was changed.

1R1067/8
1R7992/3
1R20118/9
1R25523/4
1R35797/8
1R40667/8
- ▶ About March 1969, the top part of the gas tank was changed.

1R1084/5
1R20094/5
1R35098/9
- ▶ About December 1968, a steering column lock was fitted to right-hand drive cars.

1R1137/8
1R8868/9
1R20211/2
1R26004/5
- ▶ About May 1969, the perforated leather trim was ▶ introduced for the seats, and the headrests were changed. The following cars were also fitted with the early seats: chassis numbers 1R8870, 1R8871, 1R8873, 1R8874, 1R8875, 1R8876, 1R8877, 1R8878, 1R8879, 1R8880, 1R8881, 1R8882, 1R8883, 1R9029, 1R9042, 1R9069, 1R9070, 1R9077, 1R9147, 1R9169,

1R9172, 1R9174, 1R9185, 1R9195, 1R9255, 1R9328, 1R9244 (perhaps 9244 is an error, 9344 seems more likely to be correct), 1R9350, 1R9396, 1R9419, 1R26002, 1R26007, 1R26010, 1R26022, 1R26023, 1R26025, 1R26028, 1R26033, 1R26051, 1R26053, 1R26057,1R26069, and 1R26078.

1R9456/7
1R26319/20
1R35332/3
1R42012/3
- ▶ About August 1969, a composite bracket was introduced to mount the alternator, air-conditioning compressor, and the power steering pump.

1R1183/4
1R9456/7
1R20260/1
1R26319/20
- ▶ The cooling fan cowl was changed. The air conditioning was changed from the early type (which did not permit the fitting of power steering) to the later type which probably did permit it. As a special note, the *Series 2 Parts List (1969)* states that the later-type installation was also fitted to chassis numbers 1R1152, 1R9207, 1R9451, 1R9453, 1R20223, and 1R20245.

1R1184/5
1R20263/4
- ▶ The upper steering column assembly was changed.

1R1187/8
1R9569/70
1R20269/70
1R26386/7
1R35352/3
1R42117/8
- ▶ About June 1969, the bonnet-lifting springs were replaced by a gas-filled cylinder.

- ▶ The front subframe assembly changed; chassis numbers 1R3532/3 and 1R42117/8 were not included in this change.

1R1189/90
1R9594/5
1R20271/2
1R26401/2
- ▶ The radiator was changed.

1R1195/6
1R9642/3
1R20277/8
1R26428/9
- ▶ The top water hose from the radiator to the water manifold was changed.

1R9859/60
1R26532/3
1R42381/2

▶ About April 1969, the starter switch was changed to one that isolated some auxiliaries while the starter was cranking.

1R1243/4
1R9939/40
1R20334/5
1R26575/6

▶ The mounting of the rear brake calipers to the final drive unit changed, and the adapter plate was discontinued.

▶ The final drive unit was changed (chassis numbers 1R9929/30 were cited in the *Series 2 Parts List (1969)* instead of 1R9939/40, possibly in error).

1R35421/2
1R42400/1

▶ About March 1970, the handbrake lever was changed to one with a different material in the pivot pin and lever.

1R1301/2, and some cars after 1R1277
1R10151/2, and some cars after 1R10114
1R20365/6, and some cars after 1R20354
1R26683/4, and some cars after 1R26649
1R35457/8, and some cars after 1R35440
1R42559/60, and some cars after 1R42539

▶ About August 1969, the seat assemblies were adapted to take headrests as an optional extra, but chassis numbers 1R35457/8 and 1R42559/60 were mentioned in the *Series 2 Parts List (1969)*.

1R1325/6
1R10334/5
1R20390/1
1R26755/6

▶ Armrests were added to the doors.

1R1348/9
1R10522/3

▶ The sun visor mechanism was changed.

1R1351/2
1R10536/7
1R20424/5
1R26834/5
1R35563/4
1R42676/7

▶ About October 1969, the type of battery in the clock was changed. Some references cite chassis numbers 1R1350/1 instead of 1R1351/2, and numbers 1R24424/5 instead of 1R20425/6.

1R1392/3
1R11051/2
1R20485/6
1R27050/1
1R35642/3
1R42849/50

▶ About January 1970, a ballast resistor was added to the ignition system.

▶ The side lamps were changed, but their colors remained the same. The gas tank and cap, as well as the fascia panel assemblies, were changed. Chassis numbers 1R35642/3 and 1R42849/50 were not included in these three changes.

1R1410/1
1R11302/3
1R20509/10
1R27173/4
1R35647/8
1R42993/4

▶ About November 1969, the front flexible brake hose was changed.

1R35649/50
1R42551/2

▶ About October 1969, a defroster-tube extension was fitted.

1R35656/7
1R43164/5

▶ About January 1970, the automatic transmission selector lever was changed.

1R11973/4
1R27480/1

▶ The stop/tail/flasher lamps were changed for cars exported to Canada, Greece, Portugal, and the United States only, but the color of the lens remained red.

1R1586/7
1R12955/6
1R20722/3
1R27869/70
1R35787/8
1R43772/3

▶ About April 1970, the fan control thermostat was changed.

1R13427/8
1R28054/5

▶ The side lamps changed, for cars exported to Canada and the United States only.

1R14065/6
1R28294/5

▶ The headlights were changed for cars exported to Belgium, Czechoslovakia, Holland, Germany, Poland, Rumania, and Switzerland.

1R1775/6
1R14120/1
1R20952/3
1R28319/20
▸ The headlight dip switch was changed.

1R1755/6
1R20954/5
▸ About August 1970, larger-diameter torsion bars were fitted to right-hand drive cars.

1R35815/6
1R43923/4
▸ About May 1970, the handbrake lever assembly was changed. The new one was longer and angled upward.

CHANGES IN ORDER OF ENGINE NUMBER

"7E1001 to 7E0000" and then "7E0000 and subs."
An unusual entry is found on page 2 of the *J.37 Spare Parts Catalogue (November 1969)*: it is stated that there was a change in the standard size main bearing kits, with the earlier kit (part number 10483) "Required from Engine No. 7E1001 to 7E0000," and the later kit (part number 10766) "Required at Engine No. 7E0000 and subs." The authors are not certain what engine number transition point is actually being referred to here, but suspect the zeros may be place holders for numbers that will be decided upon later. There is a similar situation where blank spaces were used as placeholders for numbers to be added later. See the discussion on page 340.
▸ The main bearings were changed. This is cited on page 2 of the *J.37 Spare Parts Catalogue (November 1969)*.

7E1336/7
▸ About December 1964, the connecting rods were changed. The new rods have a small hole at the small end to spray oil.

7E1404/5
▸ About December 1964, the water pump and pulley were changed to make removal easier. The studs and bolts for the water pump were changed to bolts.

7E1724/5
▸ About January 1965, the inlet manifold was changed. The pressed-in vacuum fitting was replaced with a screwed-in one.

7E1881/2
▸ About March 1965, the inlet manifold gasket was changed.

7E2458/9
▸ About April 1965, a waterproof cover was added to the distributor.

7E2693/4
▸ About April 1965, the sump was changed.

7E2895/6
▸ The exhaust-side cam cover was changed, and the fiber washer on filler cap was changed to an O-ring.

7E3422/3
▸ About June 1965, the alternator bracket was changed.

7E4606/7
▸ The clutch slave cylinder, return spring, and operating rod were changed.

7E5169/70
▸ About November 1965, the oil filter changed from felt to paper.

7E6332/3
▸ The exhaust manifold studs were changed. The bolt holding the timing chain cover to the cylinder block was changed to allow attachment of the alternator shield.

▸ About May 1966, an alternator shield was added.

7E7297/8
7E50021/2
▸ About September 1966, a low-lift carburetor cam was introduced to reduce engine speed when the choke was put on. This included changes in the jet housing of the carburetors.

7E7449/50
7E50021/2
▸ In late 1966 or early 1967, the valve guides were fitted with circlips to ensure their location in the head.

7E50021/2
▸ The shaft assembly for the intermediate timing chain sprocket was changed.

7E50024/5
▸ About September 1966, the intermediate sprocket was changed to cast iron.

7E7810/1
7E50046/7
▸ About September 1966, the clutch disc was made a little convex. The new disc is marked with light blue and purple paint near the center.

7E9209/10
7E50962/3
- ▶ About December 1966, the cylinder head gasket was changed.

7E9291/2
7E51101/2
- ▶ About December 1966, the fuel lines from the filter to the carburetors were changed.

7E51451/2
- ▶ About September 1966, the automatic transmission kick-down control rod and cable were changed.

7E51451/2
- ▶ The automatic transmission was changed.

7E10008/9
7E52154/5
- ▶ About March 1967, the front seal on the sump was changed.

7E52275/6
- ▶ The torque-converter housing was changed.

7E10956/7
7E52607/8
- ▶ About July 1967, the crankshaft dampener was changed.

7E11667/8
7E52686/7
- ▶ About March 1967, oil seals were fitted to the inlet valve guides. This is listed only in *The Jaguar E-type: A Collector's Guide*.

7E11818/9
7E52716/7
- ▶ About January 1968, the number of bolts holding the bell housing to the cylinder block was reduced from nine to eight, with the top one being omitted.

7E12159/60
7E53209/10
- ▶ About January 1968, the adjuster and pivot pin for the clutch operating rod was changed.

7E13500/1
7E53581/2
- ▶ About July 1968, the clutch was changed from a Laycock to a Borg & Beck diaphragm type.

7E14212/3
7E53742/3
- ▶ About July 1968, the connecting rod bearings were changed.

7E16335/6
7E54361/2
- ▶ About July 1968, cylinder block heaters were made standard for Canada.

7E16754/5
7E54608/9
- ▶ About July 1968, the coil was changed to one with a push-in high-tension coil wire, and with "+" and replacing "SW" and "CB."

7E17157/8
7E54836/7
- ▶ About June 1968, the water pump pulley and belt were changed to increase pump speed. This is listed only in *The Jaguar E-type: A Collector's Guide*.

7E17864/5
7E52452/3
- ▶ About December 1968, the valve seats were changed.

SERIES 2 ENGINES
(Note that the prefix is now "R")

7R1345/6
7R35088/9
- ▶ About December 1968, the pointer for the timing marks was moved from the bottom of the engine to the left-hand side.

7R1837/8
7R35329/30
- ▶ The inlet manifold and associated hardware, the carburetors, and accelerator linkage were changed for U.S. and Canada cars only. The heater-hose return pipe at the right-hand side of the cylinder block was changed.

7R1914/5
7R35388/9
- ▶ The cylinder head studs, the cylinder head assembly, and gasket set were changed. The cylinder block assembly was changed (the core plugs and the block heater were changed), and the front timing cover was changed. The water pump assembly was changed.

7R2082/3
7R35462/3
- ▶ The camshaft covers and studs at the front of the head for fixing the camshaft covers were changed for U.S. and Canada cars only. The rear exhaust manifold, the mixture housing on top of the rear exhaust manifold and its associated hardware, and the clip holding the dipstick were changed for U.S. and Canada cars only.

7R2297/8
7R35582/3
- ▶ The oil filter assembly was changed.

7R2587/8
7R35730/1
> About March 1969, the clutch cover assembly was changed to a new one with stronger springs. In some sources an exception is given for engine numbers 7R2784 to 7R2791.

7R4158/9
7R36599/600
> About May 1969, the camshaft cover mounts at the front were changed to countersunk screws.

7R4488/9
7R36957/8
> About May 1969, the water pump spindle was changed.

7R5263/4
7R37488/9
> About May 1969, the thermostat was changed from 74 to 82 degrees Celsius. Some sources cite chassis numbers 7R5262/3 instead of 7R5263/4, and do not cite the 7R37488/9 transition point.

7R5263/4
> The cooling fan thermostatic switch was changed.

7R5338/9
7R37549/50
> About May 1969, the pointer for the timing marks on the crankshaft dampener was moved from the left-hand side of the engine back to the bottom of the engine (where it had been before), for cars with air conditioning or power steering.

7R5541/2
7R37654/5
About June 1969, the water drain spigot on the block was changed to a drain plug, and the fiber washer was deleted, but the copper washer was retained.

7R5546/7
> The alternator was changed for cars without air conditioning. The alternator belt for cars without air conditioning was changed to a different type for cars exported to the United States and Canada.

7R6305/6
7R38105/6
> About August 1969, the engine number stamping was moved from the area above the oil filter to the leftside bell housing flange, near to the dipstick.

7R6572/3
7R38135/6
> About August 1969, the oil seal in the speedometer drive gear was changed.

7R7503/4
7R38501/2
> About October 1969, the oil pump shaft was changed to one with a pressed-on inner rotor from one with a pinned-on inner rotor.

7R7973/4 and 7R7506
> The distributor was changed.

7R8687/8
7R38854/5
> About November 1969, the camshafts were changed to give quieter valve operation and longer periods between valve adjustments.

7R8687/8
> The cylinder head assembly was changed (possibly related to the camshaft change above). The camshaft covers were changed.

7R8767/8
7R38894/5
> About January 1970, the camshaft covers were changed so that all cars had mounting holes for the Emission control warm air duct, even if the duct was not fitted.

7R9709/10
7R39111/2
> About March 1970, the clutch operating rod was altered to allow greater adjustment tolerances.

7R10747/8
> The release bearing and cup assembly was changed.

7R13198/9
7R40325/6
> About August 1970, the crankshaft distance piece at the front of the shaft was replaced by a distance piece with an O-ring.

7R14048/9
> About October 1970, the thermostat was changed.

7R14074/5
> About October 1970, the cams were changed so as to have no oil hole in the back. This was to reduce oil consumption.

7R14268/9
> About December 1970, the designation of the compression ratio of the engine was changed from a number to a letter, thus H=high compression, S=standard compression, and L=low compression.

CHANGES IN ORDER OF TRANSMISSION NUMBER

EJ245/6

 ▸ The housing for the rear oil seal and its gasket were changed.

 ▸ About January 1965, the housing for the rear transmission oil seal was changed.

EJ944/5

 ▸ About March 1965, the roller bearing on the gearbox constant pinion shaft was changed.

EJ3169/70

 ▸ About September 1965 or February 1966, the constant pinion shaft was changed to include an oil thrower, and the spacer under the roller bearing was no longer required.

EJ7919/20
EJS7919/20

 ▸ About November 1966, a retaining washer was added to the shift lever.

EJ11776/7
EJS11776/7

 ▸ About July 1967, the spring for the synchromesh thrust members was changed.

KE11768/9
KJS2858/9

 ▸ About March 1970, the clutch release bearing was changed. The new one can be identified by a ridge in the bore of the thrust pad.

DR. THOMAS F. HADDOCK

Dr. Thomas F. Haddock is the author of several books, including *Jaguar E-Type 6 & 12 Cylinder Restoration Guide*, and its precursor, *Jaguar E-Type Six-Cylinder Restoration & Originality Guide*. The first was the *Classic Motorbooks* number two best seller when introduced, and each has gone into several reprints. Dr. Haddock has lectured on E-type originality at JCNA meetings, and has acted as a consultant in the production of the JNCA judging guide for E-types. He has experience in archaeology and the conservation of technical and artistic artifacts.

DR. MICHAEL C. MUELLER

Dr. Michael C. Mueller is an internationally recognized expert on Jaguar sports cars. He is on the JCNA Concours Committee, and is an active JCNA concours judge. His collection includes approximately 50 E-types, including many early-production examples, as well as truckloads of NOS and rare parts. The majority of the cars are un-restored and are still in their original state. This collection is a significant source of information on the detailed evolution of the E-type.

BIBLIOGRAPHY ////

Some of the references reviewed in the compilation of this book are listed here. While an effort was made in this book to cite all production changes to the six-cylinder Jaguar E-type, it is likely some such information contained in the following references was missed. This is due, in part, to the fact that most of the new information in this book was derived from observations of many individual cars, rather than on a literature review. A more complete examination of all these references, as well as others, remains for future work.

OFFICIAL JAGUAR PUBLICATIONS

In the following list, the abbreviated version of the Parts and Spares Catalogue publication names that are used in the text are shown first and are then followed after the colon by the full reference.

Jaguar "E" Type Operating, Maintenance and Service Handbook, Jaguar Cars Ltd., Coventry England, Jaguar Publication E/122/1

Jaguar "E" Type Operating, Maintenance and Service Handbook, Jaguar Cars Ltd., Coventry England, Jaguar Publication E/122/3

3.8 Interim Spares List (April 1961): Jaguar "E" Type Service Technical Notes and Interim Spares List, issued by Jaguar Cars Inc. Parts and Technical Service Departments, 42-50 Twenty-first Street, Long Island City 1, N.Y., April 1961

J.30 Spare Parts Catalogue (August 1961): Spare Parts Catalogue for Jaguar 'E' Type Grand Touring Models, Jaguar Cars Ltd., Coventry, England, Jaguar Publication J.30, August 1961

J.30 Spare Parts Catalogue (June 1963): Spare Parts Catalogue for Jaguar 'E' Type Grand Touring Models, Jaguar Cars Ltd., Coventry, England, Jaguar Publication J.30, June 1963 Reprint (A.L.1.)

J.37 Spare Parts Catalogue (November 1969): Spare Parts Catalogue for Jaguar 4.2 'E' Type Grand Touring Models, Jaguar Cars Ltd., Coventry, England, Jaguar Publication J.37, November 1969 Reprint

J.38 Spare Parts Catalogue (December 1966): Jaguar 4.2 'E' Type '2+2' Spare Parts Catalogue, Jaguar Cars Ltd., Coventry, England, Jaguar Publication J.38, December 1966

Series 2 Parts List (1969): Jaguar/Daimler Interim Parts List, 1969 Jaguar 'E' Type, Open, Fixed Head Coupe, 2+2 models, no Jaguar Publication number apparent

Series 2 Parts Catalogue (1979): Series 2 E-Type Open & Fixed Head Coupe Parts Catalogue, Part number RTC9873FA, Jaguar Cars Ltd., Coventry, England, January 1979, in microfiche format

Jaguar 'E' Type Operating Maintenance and Service Handbook, Jaguar Cars Ltd., Coventry, England, Jaguar Publication E/122/1

Amendments and Additions to the Jaguar 'E' Type Operating, Maintenance and Service Handbook, a small pamphlet included with some E/122 maintenance and service handbooks

Jaguar 'E' Type Operating, Maintenance and Service Handbook, Jaguar Cars Ltd., Coventry, England, Jaguar Publication E/122/6

Jaguar 'E' Type Grand Touring Models Service Manual, Jaguar Cars Ltd., Coventry, England, no Jaguar Publication number (an early version)

Jaguar 3.8 'E' Type Grand Touring Models Service Manual, Jaguar Cars Ltd., Coventry, England, Jaguar Publication No. E/123/5

Supplementary Information for 4.2 Liter 'E' Type and 2+2 Cars, Jaguar Cars Ltd., Coventry, England, Jaguar Publication No. E123B/2

Jaguar 4.2 'E' Type & 2+2 Operating, Maintenance and Service Handbook, Jaguar Cars Ltd., Coventry, England, Jaguar Publication E/131/6

Jaguar Service Bulletins, various

JAGUAR CLUB OF NORTH AMERICA PUBLICATIONS

Jaguar "E" Type, 3.8 L. & 4.2 L., no author cited, JCNA, 36th Annual General Meeting, Charlotte, North Carolina, March 3-6, 1994

JCNA Series 1 E-type Judge's Guide, Bob Stevenson, JCNA, Accepted at the 45th Annual AGM, March, 2003, 7th ed., June 2013, www.jcna.com/library/tech/e-type1.pdf

JCNA Model Year '68 E-type Judges' Guide, Stew Cleave, JCNA, Accepted at the 48th Annual AGM, Seattle, Washington, March 2006

JCNA Series 2 E-Type Judge's Guide, Stew Cleave, JCNA, Accepted at the 46th Annual AGM, Long Beach, California, March 11-14, 2004

MAGAZINES

(The) Autocar, March 17, 1961; April 26, 1963; May 14,1965; February 18, 1966; June 10, 1966; October 12, 1967; April 25, 1968; April 25, 1968; November 18, 1970

Autosport, December 14, 1962; August 21, 1964; October 23, 1964; March 11, 1966; August 5, 1966; October 29, 1970

Canada Track and Traffic, May 1961

Car, November 1965; June 1970

Car and Car Conversions, October 1966

Car and Driver, May 1961; December 1961; July 1963; February 1965; April 1966; May 1969; April 1982

The Car Collector, December 1978

Cars Illustrated, November 1963; March 1965

Classic and Sportscar, April 1986

The E-Jag News Magazine, August 1976; March 1982

The E-type, March 2011; May, 2011; July 2011; August 2011 (a series of articles on early E-types by Ian Howe)

Jaguar International Magazine, March 1986

Jaguar Quarterly, April 1991

The Milestone Car, Winter 1974

Modern Motor, November 1961; March 1971

The Motor, March 22, 1961; May 22, 1961; February 21, 1962; October 31, 1964; March 12, 1966; April 30, 1966; January 13, 1968; September 7, 1968; September 14, 1968; December 20, 1969; March 21, 1970

Motor Magazine, March 15, 1961

Motor Racing, April 1961; May 1961; April 1966

Motor Sport, April 1961; July 1962; January 1965; April 1966; April 1967

Motor Trend, July 1961

Motoring Life, 1961; 1963

Newsletter of the Jaguar Club of Northwest Ohio, July 1984

Popular Imported Cars, January 1969

Road & Track, May 1961; April 1964; April 1966; July 1966; October 1966; June 1969; August 1969; January 1969; September 1974

Road Test, May 1965

Popular Mechanics, June 1961

Science & Mechanics, December 1968[V. 39, N. 12]

Special Interest Autos, December 1979

Sports Car World, October 1963

Sporting Motorist, 1966

Worlds Fastest Sports Cars, 1966

BOOKS

All About the Jaguar E-Type. Paul Skilleter Books, PJ Publishing, Ltd., 2010

Cunningham. Richard Harman, Dalton Watson Fine Books, Deerfield, Illinois

E-Type: End of an Era. Chris Harvey, St. Martin's Press, New York, 1977

European Automobiles of the 50s and 60s. Alberto Martinez, and Jean-Loup Nory, Vilo, Inc., New York, 1982

Factory-Original Jaguar E-Type. Anders Ditlev Clausager, Herridge & Sons, Ltd., 2011

Jaguar. Lord Montagu of Beaulieu, A. S. Barnes & Co., Inc., Cranbury, New Jersey, 1967

Jaguar: Britain's Fastest Export. Lord Montagu of Beaulieu, Ballantine Books Inc., New York, 1971

Jaguar E-Type: The Definitive History. Philip Porter, Foulis, Haynes, Yeovil, Somerset, England, 1989

Jaguar E-Type 3.8 & 4.2 6-cylinder; 5.3 V12. Denis Jenkinson, Osprey Publishing Limited, London, 1982

The Jaguar E-type: A Collector's Guide. Paul Skilleter, Motor Racing Publications, London, 1979

Jaguar E-Type Six-Cylinder Restoration and Originality Guide. Thomas F. Haddock, Classic Motorbooks, Osceola, WI, 1991

Jaguar E-Type 6 & 12 Cylinder Restoration Guide. Thomas F. Haddock, Classic Motorbooks, Osceola, WI, 1997

Jaguar Sports Cars. Paul Skilleter, Haynes, GT Foulis & Co. Ltd, Sparkford, Yeovil, Somerset, 1975

The Jaguar Tradition. Michael Frostick, Dalton Watson, Ltd., London, 1973

Original Jaguar E-Type. Philip Porter, Bay View Books, Ltd., Bideford, Devon, England, 1990

The Jaguar Story. Joseph H. Wherry, Chilton Book Co., Philadelphia, 1967

The Most Famous Car in the World. Philip Porter, Orion

The New Jaguar Guide. Herb W. Williamson, Sports Car Press, New York, 1964

Tuning S.U. Carburetors, Third Edition. SpeedSport MotoBooks, Middlesex, England, 1975 (no author cited)

Walt Hansgen. Michael Argetsinger, David Bull Publishing, Phoenix, Arizona, 2006

INTERNET

Howe, Ian, posting on etypeuk.com forum, Jun 21, 2014, 9:02 pm, http://forum.etypeuk.com/viewtopic.php?t=2006&start=70.

http://www.xkedata.com/catalog/numbers/

SERIES 1, 3.8-LITER

COMPANIES AND MEDIA

Design:	Jodi Ellis Graphics
Printer:	Interpress Co. Ltd., Hungary
Printing Equipment:	Komori LS 440 PH
Page Size:	219 mm x 304 mm
Text paper:	130 gsm Multiart Silk
End paper:	140 gsm Woodfree Offset
Dust jacket:	150 gsm Glossy Artpaper
Casing:	Foil stamping on front and spine, on black Geltex, over 3 mm board
Chapter Heads:	Marion Regular
Sub Heads:	Marion Bold
Body Text:	10 pt. Palatino Regular
Captions:	8.5 pt. Aileron Italic